NOLLYWOOD STARS

NEW DIRECTIONS IN NATIONAL CINEMAS

Jacqueline Reich, editor

NOLLYWOOD STARS

MEDIA AND MIGRATION IN WEST AFRICA
AND THE DIASPORA

Noah A. Tsika

INDIANA UNIVERSITY PRESS
Bloomington & Indianapolis

This book is a publication of

INDIANA UNIVERSITY PRESS
Office of Scholarly Publishing
Herman B Wells Library 350
1320 East 10th Street
Bloomington, Indiana 47405 USA

iupress.indiana.edu

© 2015 by Noah A. Tsika
All rights reserved

No part of this book may be reproduced or utilized in any form or by any means, electronic or mechanical, including photocopying and recording, or by any information storage and retrieval system, without permission in writing from the publisher. The Association of American University Presses' Resolution on Permissions constitutes the only exception to this prohibition.

∞ The paper used in this publication meets the minimum requirements of the American National Standard for Information Sciences—Permanence of Paper for Printed Library Materials, ANSI Z39.48–1992.

Manufactured in the
United States of America

*Library of Congress
Cataloging-in-Publication Data*

Tsika, Noah, 1983-
 Nollywood stars : media and migration in West Africa and the diaspora / Noah A. Tsika.
  pages cm — (New directions in national cinemas)
 Includes bibliographical references and index.
 ISBN 978-0-253-01571-6 (cl : alk. paper) — ISBN 978-0-253-01575-4 (pb : alk. paper) — ISBN 978-0-253-01580-8 (eb) 1. Motion pictures—Nigeria—History and criticism. 2. Motion picture actors and actresses—Nigeria. I. Title.
 PN1993.5.N55T85 2015
 791.4309669—dc23

2014049507

1 2 3 4 5 20 19 18 17 16 15

For the women of Nollywood.
And for the late Christy Essien-Igbokwe.

A fantasy reel spooled through my mind, my meter-long face emoting on a cinema screen. Hollywood meant nothing. Why be a plankton in the ocean when I could be a big fish in an emerging pond? Nollywood now seemed a more dignified enterprise, something I could take seriously.

—NOO SARO-WIWA,
Looking for Transwonderland: Travels in Nigeria.

CONTENTS

- *Preface and Acknowledgments* xi
- *A Note on Orthography and Taxonomy* xxv

- Introduction: Global Stars in Nigeria's Postindependence Firmament—From Ossie Davis to *Doctor Bello* 1

1. From Yorùbá to YouTube: Studying Nollywood's Star System 29

2. Glittering Video: Format, Fashion, and the Materiality of Nollywood Stardom 68

3. A Mobile Glow: Nollywood Stardom and Corporate Globalism 116

4. When Stars Collide: *Lady Gaga* and the Pirating of a Globalized Persona 164

5. Nollywood's Progeny: Stardom and the Politics of Youth Empowerment 212

6 Professionalizing Childhood: Nollywood and the New Youth Transnationalism 250

- Afterword: Honoring Nollywood Stars 294

- *Notes* 301
- *Bibliography* 313
- *Filmography* 331
- *Index* 337

PREFACE AND ACKNOWLEDGMENTS

Before embarking on a detailed investigation of Nollywood stardom, it is necessary to acknowledge some of the historical, political, and cultural reasons for the absence of conventionally defined film stars from the firmament of classical African cinema. If one of Nollywood's outstanding contributions to African screen media has been the industry's cultivation of a range of globally recognizable African movie stars, then it is important to point to the longstanding difficulty of entering African films, and African film studies, into dialogue with diverse conceptions of stardom. Nollywood did not arrive at its star system overnight; with more than a little help from the Nigerian television industry, it developed it against the backdrop of an African cinematic practice that, since independence, had proscribed movie stars—even as it was forced, perhaps paradoxically, to canonize directors as auteurs in an effort to raise capital and awareness. Such contradictions are rooted in Western ethnographic filmmaking, but even the celebrated Frenchman Jean Rouch, who dubbed so many of his onscreen subjects with his own histrionic voice, could not possibly overshadow a series of remarkable African performers. When Rouch made *Moi, un noir* in 1958, employing the controversial practice of shared anthropology, he helped turn actor Oumarou Ganda—playing a character nicknamed "Edward G. Robinson" and patterned partly after Robinson's Hollywood persona—into a cinematic icon whose ambivalence about working with Rouch would reach expression in his own films, especially *Cabascabo* (1968). Roughly a decade after making

Moi, un noir, Rouch relied upon rising star Safi Faye to confer considerable glamour upon his film *Petit à petit* (1968)—a reliance that Faye would later criticize, although not because she was averse to screen acting, as her own films (particularly 1972's *La passante*) would prove. Apart from Rouch's controversial works, there was Lionel Rogosin's antiapartheid docudrama *Come Back, Africa* (1959), which opens with a title card assuring the spectator that no professional performer appears in the film, but which later lingers on the dazzling musical star (and future Grammy winner) Miriam Makeba, who sings two rousing songs to rapt diegetic audiences. Rouch's divisive works seem at times to reflect the dominance of his Western perspective, and Rogosin's *Come Back, Africa*—an antiapartheid film by a wealthy, well-connected white New Yorker—credits allegedly amateur participants with their first names only, thus rendering them semi-anonymous and compelling the curious spectator to do some digging. Nevertheless, neither Rouch nor Rogosin could apparently resist the allure of charismatic stars, and the contributions to their films of Ganda, Faye, and Makeba (among many others) suggest an exciting and understudied subject.

As is well documented, social realist techniques—often derived from but never reducible to Soviet traditions—comprised the mode in which many of the first postindependence African films were forged. African cinema's earliest interpretations of social realism entailed a narrative and thematic interest in collective experiences at the expense of a glamorizing individuation of actors; a reliance on static long shots and uninterrupted long takes; and a tendency to telegraph (through music, lighting, costuming, and set design) the shared, abstracted, class-specific identities of visible human figures. Simply put, social realism did not exactly lend itself to the consolidation of movie stardom in postcolonial sub-Saharan Africa; neither did Fernando Solanas and Octavio Getino's theory of Third Cinema, with its focus on an imperfect, communitarian aesthetic practice as a means of resisting multiple forms of oppression. An equally discursive as well as practical obstacle to African movie stardom was the impact of Italian neorealism, which, as Télesphore Mba Bizo, Melissa Thackway, and Rachel Gabara (among others) have demonstrated, followed a circuitous route to influence African filmmakers in the adoption of nonprofessional performers. If such Italian neorealist classics as *Bicycle Thieves* (Vittorio De Sica, 1948) and *La Terra Trema* (Luchino Visconti, 1948) are almost unimaginable with bona fide, prominently billed, conventionally skilled film stars in their central roles, then so are such postindependence African features as Ousmane Sembène's *Mandabi* (1968), made without a traditional script at a time when Wolof was not a written language, and Djibril Diop Mambéty's *Touki Bouki* (1973), with its focus on inexperienced, alienated Senegalese youths not yet sure of their own social identities. Finally, it would be difficult to overestimate the legacy of the 1975 Algiers Charter of the Pan-African Federation of Filmmakers, which, in outlining a political project for African cinema, explicitly renounced the sort of Western individualist ethos on which movie stardom would seem to rest. If, according to the charter, African filmmakers were to extend the terms and conditions of Third Cinema to shape a truly liberationist artistic practice, then they would need to free themselves of the Western fetish for famous faces.

That does not mean that great acting was anathema to classical African cinema; it does, however, suggest why the names of individual performers are so little known. Who, exactly, provides the human face of Sembène's "black girl"—who (literally) embodies his eponymous *La Noire de . . .*? What was this woman doing in Dakar in the mid-1960s, and what was her offscreen experience, around the same time, in the south of France? Who plays Sembène's Faat Kiné, and does she share her character's special, unapologetically sexual, and altogether irreverent brand of Senegalese feminism? Does she endorse it in her daily life, and does the character linger in her consciousness, at least as she expresses it publicly? The difficulty of answering these and related questions speaks to the lack of documentation surrounding acting as individuated labor in West Africa. Millions of moviegoers worldwide have seen Sembène's iconic *La Noire de . . .*; how many of them can name the woman (Mbissine Thérèse Diop) who portrayed the title role? Of those who have seen *Faat Kiné* (2001), how many remember—or ever took note of—the name Venus Seye? How many are aware that Joseph Gaï Ramaka, in casting his *Karmen Geï* (2001), deliberately turned to one of the stars of *Touki Bouki*, the marvelously talented Magaye Niang, to portray a key role while also providing a platform for the Senegalese pop star El Hadj N'Diaye? Such questions, whose answers can hardly be heartening, remind us that, in analyses of African cinema, auteurism has tended to eclipse even the simplest considerations of acting (let alone of stardom).

Efforts to rectify this problem have emerged in the blogosphere, as several pioneering writers (many of them operating well beyond the boundaries of academia or salaried journalism) have turned their attentions to the performers whose contributions to African cinema are as astonishing as they are egregiously understudied. Exemplary in this respect is the writing, teaching, and activism of Beti Ellerson, whose *African Women in Cinema Blog* is a remarkable archive of information about several key figures. Admirably, Ellerson does not limit the scope of her ongoing analysis to such prominent African auteurs as Safi Faye, Cheryl Dunye, and Fanta Régina Nacro, but extends her celebrations to include those African performers who, for far too long, have gone without recognition. In April 2010, she blogged about Mbissine Thérèse Diop, calling her "a pioneer in African cinema," providing her biography (complete with a filmography far longer than the one that appears on IMDb, for example), and detailing her specific acting choices and their impact on the authorship of *La Noire de . . .* Since beginning this book, I have looked to Ellerson for inspiration, confirmation, and a series of insights about African film acting that simply can't be found in many places, scholarly or otherwise.

Given the realities and contingencies of filmmaking in Africa—the harsh economic limitations; the constant, diffuse threats of neocolonialism; and the potential for explosive local cultural controversies—African cinema stardom has tended to suggest a contradiction in terms, but only for those who assume that such stardom must rest upon a stable set of shared popular meanings. Since the publication in 1979 of Richard Dyer's *Stars*, film scholars have attempted to demonstrate that stardom, as a discursive construction but also as a professional-industrial system unto itself, is dependent upon a dizzying diversity of meanings, many of them contradictory. Stardom may, as Dyer has suggested, attempt to manage a wide range of contradictions, but it cannot eradicate them, and the process of management itself proves the importance of the contradictions; a star image, almost by definition, holds the power to straddle various dividing lines. As a discipline, the study of stardom has not yet infiltrated analyses of African cinema, except through the not entirely unrelated discourse of auteurism. Ousmane Sembène was, of course, a major star in his own right (and, like Hitchcock, a director who made amusing cameo appearances in his films). But Sembène was specifically an auteur—a "behind-the-scenes" star whose renown had much to do with the ongoing relationship between his directorial style and the politics that he publicly espoused. Like that of several other celluloid filmmakers,

Sembène's work has inspired extensive scholarly coverage of African auteurism—coverage that has largely proscribed the study of African stardom even as it has sought to uncover the creative contributions of individual Africans to a vast collection of cinematic productions.

In spite of Nollywood's obvious deviations from classical African cinema, the academic study of the industry has, in several conspicuous instances, been similarly enmeshed in auteurism, even when rooted in an anthropological focus on broad, sociocultural patterns. It is by now commonplace to view Nollywood as offering the technological and even ideological opposite of African art films: with a couple of low-grade, analog camcorders in tow, the Nigerian videographers Reginald Ebere and John Ikem set out in the mid-1990s to make a melodrama about female genital mutilation, titled *Scars of Womanhood*; they could hardly have anticipated that, nearly ten years later, Sembène would tackle the very same topic using not only pricey celluloid film stock but also his own repertoire of "respectable" social realist devices. Jonathan Haynes, a pioneer in Nollywood studies, has turned to auteurist analyses—the sort that might, for instance, help us to make sense of the aesthetic as well as political differences between Ebere's *Scars of Womanhood* (1997) and Sembène's *Moolaadé* (2004)—but he has also acknowledged their inescapable limitations and their obvious (perhaps even pretentious) partiality toward the figure of the director.

If dispensing with an all-encompassing auteurism helps shed light upon the contributions of stars to Nollywood cinema, then it is perhaps equally necessary to downplay the importance of Nigerian distributors, whose roles tend, in academic accounts, to take on an exaggerated significance vis-à-vis stardom. While I do not deny that distributors have exerted a considerable collective influence on Nollywood films and on Nollywood stars, I believe that a scholarly focus on distributors' aspirations for Nollywood stardom threatens to efface the actual artistic autonomy of individual performers and to eclipse their increasingly global import by suggesting that they are beholden to the local "mafia" of marketers, whose authority has steadily been diminishing with the turn toward online platforms and outside agents. Nollywood producers may deplore what satellite television and internet distribution have done to their profit margins, but no one can deny that a star's visibility on Africa Magic or her popularity on YouTube and Twitter has enriched her iconicity, and no Onitsha marketer is going to deactivate her online accounts or revoke her visas. I thus break free, in this book, of another discursive construction that has conspired to obscure stars' agency and artistry—that of the local video distributor who decides, like Don Corleone, who gets to become famous. In the groundbreaking *African Film: New Forms of Aesthetics and Politics,* Manthia Diawara relates a rumor that gained considerable traction around 2008, about the Nollywood star Genevieve Nnaji having been temporarily banned from the industry, as a consequence of what is commonly called "the Idumota factor," in reference to the legendary marketplace on Lagos Island, with its historically domineering distributors. Alternately dubious and indignant, Diawara asks director Zeb Ejiro to elucidate the rumor. Ejiro, in Diawara's telling, alleges that Nnaji had become too big for her britches, what with her "selfish" interest in expanding her star persona across multiple platforms—in pushing it beyond mere moviedom. Nnaji wanted—sin of sins!—to become a singer, model, activist, and fashion designer, in addition to an actress. That she was, in reality, able to succeed in these and other pursuits gives the lie to Ejiro's tale of talent tamed, and to his confidence in the capacity of Nigerian distributors to chasten and circumscribe Nollywood's stars—to keep them in subservient, even infantilized positions. In this book, I look less at subjection and servitude than at liberation and possibility, not out of crackpot optimism but because Nollywood stars (especially women) have managed to confront obstacles—masculinist, nationalist, ageist, and otherwise—in order to transcend imposed limitations. This is not, in other words, a simple story of star versus distributor.

If Nollywood, with its inescapable commercialism, intersects with the allegedly more politically engaged, art-conscious African celluloid cinema at the level of auteurism, with world-famous filmmakers like Kenneth Nnebue, Tunde Kelani, Lancelot Oduwa Imasuen, and Kunle Afolayan, it differs dramatically in its relationship to thespianism. While I am disposed to believe that screen acting is potentially always generative of stardom, regardless of national, industrial, or sociocultural context, and while, like Beti Ellerson, I rue the lack of attention to, say, Sembène's masterly performers, I know that Nollywood's specific conditions have always been conducive to the creation and promotion of what iROKOtv.com refers to as "true movie stars." As a result, I find the scholarly neglect of the industry's star system to be thoroughly surprising, to say the least. This book seeks to remedy that neglect, and it reflects my longstanding commitment to tracking Nollywood's individual stars, their highly skilled performance techniques, and the complex personae that they have cultivated across countless borders, both literal and figurative. A former actor, I am constitutionally incapable of ignoring the multidirectional significance of screen performance, and my inner thespian responds to Nollywood's leading lights with lingering awe.

Several Nollywood stars, directors, producers, screenwriters, cinematographers, and costume designers generously agreed to address my many questions in person (including at bustling film festivals and award ceremonies in Africa, Europe, and the United States), by phone, by e-mail, via Skype, or via Twitter. They are Funke Akindele, Niyi Akinmolayan, Eniola Badmus, Rita Dominic, Yinka Edward, Dakore Egbuson, Sharon Ezeamaka, Omotola Jalade-Ekeinde, Ramsey Nouah, and Rita C. Onwurah. This book is not a compendium of biographies, but I hope that it benefits from what I have learned of the lives of numerous stars over the past several years. Nollywood's icons never cease to surprise me, and I hope, as well, that I have done some justice to their manifold accomplishments.

This book addresses ethnicity in a way that may seem unfashionable to some (including a few stars), but while I am well aware of the extent to which many young Nigerians actively resist the prejudiced proscriptions of their parents and grandparents—the familiar injunctions against crossing cultural boundaries and blurring ethnic lines—I am also interested in taking seriously the social persistence of the taboos that they transgress and the expectations that they subvert. That is not only because so many Nollywood films derive much melodramatic mileage from clashes between, say, Igbo and Yorùbá sensibilities, but also because so many Nollywood stars have expressed the difficulties that they have faced in navigating the industry's various informal divides between Igbo/English and Yorùbá production sectors—to say nothing of the complicated dynamics of a rare Kannywood-to-Nollywood crossover success like Ali Nuhu.

There are, to be sure, more than a few extremely conservative stars, who routinely disseminate to the press their essentialist, reactionary conceptions of class, gender, and especially ethnicity, but this book focuses on the both systematized and informal methods through which Nollywood's star system enables bold, innovative, transcultural and transnational choices in performance and promotion, marking stars as potential vessels for progressive developments in the arts as well as in politics. I am interested less in the survival of the old than in the emergence of the new, less in the endurance of an orthodox binarism than in the appearance of dialectical and hybridized approaches to public life and popular culture in West Africa and the diaspora.

That I take these matters so seriously has, I am sure, more than a bit to do with my family background. I thank my parents, Mary and Ronald Tsika, for promoting mobility within and beyond their own diverse family, for refusing to privilege any one religion (or even religiosity at all), any fixed professional identity, or any one mode of cultural expression. Our surname, in Shona, connotes cultural citizenship; it refers to the knowledge of a variety of social formations that a child, in balancing life at school and life at home, must acquire in order to become a moral adult, a cultural constituent, and a cultural producer. My parents seemed never to lose sight of the concept of *tsika* as they reared me amid multiple obstacles. My artist mother produces work that is syncretic—thrillingly so. In attempting to honor the syncretism of an African popular art like Nollywood, I also, in my own way, attempt to honor her. Together, my parents made college and graduate school possible, but they also instilled in me a passion for the arts that is immeasurable, because it is a reflection of their own. They were—and they remain—mavens in my life.

In 2010, entrenched in documentary studies, I became interested in the practical, pedagogical value of the more "observational," documentary-style Nollywood films that were then making their way to Senegal (where, as I experienced firsthand, they were being used as teaching tools at various NGOs and youth organizations). With these experiences in mind, I presented a paper at the Society for Cinema and Media Studies annual conference. Not yet prepared to move beyond my scholarly attachment to African art films in order to better perceive the realities of Nollywood production, and using Nollywood films strictly as reflections of a cultural imperialism that could only be painful in places where Sembène had shot his classics, I made a few errors in characterizing Nigerian filmmaking conditions. Jonathan Haynes, who was in the audience for my presentation, firmly yet supportively corrected my errors during the question-and-answer session. Speaking with him afterward, I discovered that I knew more about Nollywood than I realized—and certainly more than the academic traditions that then enveloped me would seemingly appreciate. Like the ever-encouraging Manthia Diawara, a mensch and a mentor, Jonathan convinced me to "let go"—to honor what I loved, the legendary stars of Nollywood, who had been engaging and inspiring me since childhood, and who could, I suddenly saw, offer a compelling entrée into an intimidatingly complex industry.

At annual meetings of the African Studies Association, I have had the pleasure and the privilege of conversing and collaborating with a number of Nollywood scholars, including Kenneth Harrow, Carmela Garritano, Moradewun Adejunmobi, Connor Ryan, Lindsey Green-Simms, and Jane Bryce. Carmela was an early champion of this project and one of its first readers; I thank her for providing astute assessments of an early version of chapter 1, and I thank *Black Camera* for publishing it. Even when she had multiple deadlines of her own, Carmen McCain read and commented on my introduction, as well as excerpts from all of my chapters, providing incisive criticism at key moments. My thanks and gratitude go as well to Christina Lane, who read and offered encouraging, helpfully critical comments on the entire manuscript. Daniel Fox managed to reignite my passion for acting by sharing his extensive expertise as a performer.

Colgate University provided early support for this project, including a Faculty Development Grant, and I thank my colleagues in Film & Media Studies and Africana & Latin American Studies, especially Lynn Schwarzer, Mary Moran, Carol Ann Lorenz, Raymond Watkins, and Elizabeth Marlowe. I would also like to thank the students in my Colgate classes on the cinemas of West Africa, especially Togbor Wentum and Chelsea Faryke, for their insights into Nollywood stardom.

The City University of New York, Queens College, was crucial to the researching and writing of this book, and I thank my colleagues in Media Studies, especially Karen Mandoukos, Richard Maxwell, Ellen C. Scott, Roopali Mukherjee, Amy Herzog, Anupama Kapse, and Jonathan Buchsbaum. I am extremely grateful to my Queens College students for contributing to this project in diverse and often unexpected ways. Among them, Ochuko Ojakovo helped me plan a prolonged research trip to West Africa; and Georgina Pierre-Louis and her mother, Rosemay Thompson, fed my Nollywood obsession by sharing several dozen VHS cassettes, VCDs, and DVDs with me.

I would like to thank everyone at Indiana University Press for supporting this project. Given my longstanding commitment to studying unpopular, critically reviled forms of film and television, I wrote my PhD dissertation on the US military's WWII-era production of educational documentaries—

those screened for soldiers only and that tackled subjects from the lofty (gender and racial integration, interethnic "cooperation") to the lowly (latrine graffiti, the cheap thrills of stabbing a dummy done up to look like Hitler). My NYU committee members guided me with considerable discernment, supporting my project while providing insightful criticism. Academic publishers were not nearly so encouraging, however; nor were the anonymous readers some of them solicited, who routinely condemned my manuscript for its focus on "bad" critical objects—on "basic nuts-and-bolts films" that "no one wants to see." In an indication, perhaps, of my perversely stubborn ways, I moved immediately from these art-conscious objections to a book project on the popular Nigerian "home videos" that have an even worse global critical reputation than American World War II training films. Nearing completion on my first draft, I e-mailed Raina Polivka, whom I had not yet met, and asked if Indiana University Press, which I had always understood to be the premiere publisher of works in African film studies, would be interested in a book on Nollywood stardom. If Nollywood films are reviled critically, then so, for the most part, is a focus on stars, smacking as it does of mere fandom, of something obsequious and trite; my manuscript was thus doubly apt to elicit the kind of snobbish condemnation that had been leveled against my previous projects. Raina and Jacqueline Reich were enormously supportive, however, shepherding the project through various stages; I cannot thank them enough. My grateful thanks also go to Dee Mortensen, Jenna Whittaker, Peter Froehlich, Rhonda Vander Dussen, Darja Malcolm-Clarke, June Silay, Michelle Sybert, and, for her expert and educative copyediting, Jane Kupersmith.

Support for this project was provided by a PSC-CUNY Award, jointly funded by The Professional Staff Congress and The City University of New York. Additional support for this book was provided by a series of grants from the Queens College Division of Arts and Humanities, by the Queens College Office of Research and Sponsored Programs, and by the Research Foundation of CUNY. Funds from these sources enabled me to travel, acquire materials, obtain permissions, and finish the manuscript. I would like to thank Dean of Faculty William McClure, Paul DuBois, and Myra Berman.

Thanks to Brendan Carroll of California Newsreel for permission to use images from the films *Thunderbolt* (Tunde Kelani, 2000), *Ezra* (Newton I. Aduaka, 2007), and *This is Nollywood* (Franco Sacchi, 2007), all of which are available for purchase through the company. Bic Leu, a creator of the excellent blog *Finding Nollywood*, kindly agreed to let me use an image of Funke Akindele.

Eric Grimm, my partner and best friend, has been an unwavering source of love and encouragement. He provided considerable practical support, helping me get the hang of Twitter so that I could stay in touch with many of my sources (including Nollywood stars), brainstorming titles, sorting images, and sharing my enthusiasm for the likes of Omotola, Oge, and Funke (not to mention Mercy, Tonto, and Eniola). After I described the remarkable, mind-bending plot of the Nollywood film *Girls on Fire*, Eric hastened to set up an iROKOtv-PLUS account that I could use in my research and in my teaching. With his humbling critical acumen, sheer good sense, and extraordinary courage and patience, Eric has been by my side as I have put this book together. Whether imitating Eddie Vedder or engaging in more serious pursuits, we have managed to construct, piece by piece, a shared and dynamic life of which I am deeply proud.

In researching this book, I heard from a number of Nollywood stars who shrugged off my suggestion that their on-screen shape-shifting—their mastery of a wide range of accents, their capacity to traverse linguistic, cultural, and even gendered borders, their openness as performers to enacting a diversity of African and diasporic nationalities—holds considerable symbolic and practical value, that it matters politically, even (perhaps especially) in the twenty-first century, and amid Nollywood's globalizing tendencies. For these particular stars, ethnic prejudice is simply part of the past, a mortifying product of bygone times. These stars would apparently like to seem modern and cosmopolitan—untethered to anything that might limit their global commercial appeal and circumscribe them as "ethnic" or "specialized"—and so it is perhaps obvious why they would want to publicly reject any "confining" self-definitions. But for every Karen Igho who claims an apolitical alliance with "acting for acting's sake," there is an Eniola Badmus who describes a sobering experience of ethnic prejudice. For Badmus, who self-identifies as Yorùbá, the professional pressure to act in English, adopt an Igbo stage name, and expunge even the littlest hint of Yorùbáland from her emergent star persona was so extreme—and so seemingly constant—that it drove her to develop a proudly resistant image, that of the "Gbogbo Big Girl" (a Yorùbá-inflected designation that draws attention to Badmus' status as a plus-sized star who delights, often boastfully and loquaciously, in her own physical dimensions). I thank Eniola, in particular, for enlightening me, for helpfully articulating an experience that may not resonate with a hip "postethnic" or "metaethnic" perspective but that is nevertheless tangible to her, part of her own professional, empirical reality. I also thank her for bearing with my broken Yorùbá and for being, like Funke Akindele, Sharon Ezeamaka, and Omotola Jalade-Ekeinde, such a generous supporter via Twitter.

In an essay on Nollywood's relationship to Yorùbá theatrical traditions, Wole Ogundele suggests that one of the "losses" associated with a Yorùbá performer's transition from stage to screen is that of a participatory audience—the type of audience tasked with shaping an in-progress performance through audible and visible feedback. With the advent of Twitter, Facebook, Instagram, and other social networking sites, these circumstances have shifted considerably, as screen stars update their fans from far-flung sets, live-tweeting about production methods and performance choices, and as the fans themselves write back, offering praise, fashion tips, and even links to other stars and their specific personae. I myself often participate in this process, furnishing the feedback that Nollywood stars so often solicit. I can't resist.

I thank Funke Akindele for offering insight into the development of Jénífà, arguably her most popular character to date—and a character that she herself created from scratch, as a screenwriter. Of particular interest to me has long been Jénífà's iconic combination of pantaloons (or, in some scenes, equally baggy "sorority-girl" sweatpants), high-heeled brown leather boots, and a beret; using social media to share various images—including of a special Jénífà birthday cake baked by her fans—Funke helped me to think about the cultural, aesthetic, and economic significance of fashion, but also about fashion's sheer materiality. I have been an unrestrained Funke fan since first watching her, in 1997, on TV's *I Need to Know*, a Nigerian program produced by the United Nations Population Fund on which her character navigated the complexities of adolescent reproductive and sexual health education. If, as I often tell my friends and family members, Nollywood's *Lady Gaga* remains one of my favorite films, then that is largely because of Funke's stunning work in a small but pivotal role. She's an acting original, and her face, appearing on various commodity tie-ins—from posters to postcards, T-shirts, and even my artist mother's own original portrait in oil—brightens my daily life.

I thank Omotola Jalade-Ekeinde first and foremost for her artistry and activism, but also for understanding why I was so interested in her groundbreaking cameo role on the American television series *Hit the Floor* and for using Twitter to guide that interest away from a wide-eyed fandom toward a more committed investigation of industrial contexts and political implications. I will never forget receiving a message of encouragement from Omotola at a time when she was even busier than usual—preparing, in the fall of 2013, to speak at the World Innovation Summit for Education in Qatar. I know that I join many millions of voices worldwide in thanking Omotola for her inspiration.

That this book is dedicated to the women of Nollywood should not come as a surprise to those who know anything at all about the industry, which, as Wole Ogundele pointed out some twenty years ago, works to recognize and satisfy the female consumer in ways that are often generative of female star images. Perhaps the actress Toyin Alausa puts it best in the documentary *This is Nollywood*. "What I love the most is the act of being somebody else—playing someone else, something different from your real self," she says. "You could be asked to play a prostitute, a doctor... you could be asked to play anything that you are not. In Nollywood, a woman can do virtually anything." Indeed, as I hope the following pages confirm.

A NOTE ON ORTHOGRAPHY AND TAXONOMY

In this book, which traces the development of Nollywood stardom across a variety of platforms, I employ full diacritics in order to identify Yorùbá words and phrases according to standard Yorùbá orthography. That these diacritics rarely appear in Nollywood promotional materials—or even onscreen during credit sequences—does not mean that they are unimportant to the identities of individual Yorùbá stars, many of whom strive to create their own avenues of publicity amid certain homogenizing linguistic and orthographic pressures. My adherence to Yorùbá orthography is therefore more than just a scholarly matter; it also, as the following pages detail, resonates with the efforts of Yorùbá stars to use diacritics for their own, self-produced commodity tie-ins (such as Jénífà T-shirts in the case of Funke Akindele, or cosmetics in the case of "Gbogbo Big Girl" Eniola Badmus). As Nollywood stars so often suggest, style is a multidirectional matter.

When it comes to the titles of individual Nollywood films, there are numerous complications to consider—none more exasperating for the style-conscious (and also space-conscious) scholar than the fact that Nollywood, for a whole host of reasons that this text periodically seeks to elucidate, routinely produces lengthy films that need to be divided into component parts for the purposes of distribution (whether via VHS, VCD, DVD, satellite, or broadband). Take, for instance, one of the star-centered filmic subjects of this text: Ubong Bassey Nya's 2012 melodrama *Lady Gaga*. Standard scholarly practice would divide the film into four parts, according to the inescapable conventions of Nollywood marketing. But the titles "Lady Gaga: Part 1" and "Lady Gaga: Part 2" aren't simply unwieldy; they are also absent from the film's onscreen credit sequences (as are the stylized titles "Lady GagaA" and "Queen GagaA" that iROKOtv.com, one of the internet's prime, licensed sources for streaming Nollywood films, has adopted as a somewhat misleading means of product differentiation). In this book, Ubong Bassey Nya's over-four-hour film goes by only one title: *Lady Gaga*. My intention is not merely to save space (by rejecting the burdensome phrases "part 1," "part 2," "part 3," and "part 4") but also to respect the narrative continuity that characterizes those films that become divided during distribution, whether due to material storage limitations, interrupted postproduction schedules, or idiosyncratic market imperatives. Likewise, when I refer to Ubong Bassey Nya's *BlackBerry Babes* films (2011–2012) as "the BlackBerry Babes trilogy," my intention is to identify three separate melodramas, each of whose credits identify it as a self-contained affair, in contrast to the multiplying tactics of marketing. When necessary, I distinguish between, say, the second and third films in the trilogy—*Return of BlackBerry Babes* and *BlackBerry Babes Reloaded*—but not among the many, hour-long "parts" that, say, Sanga Entertainment, iROKOtv, and Africa Magic have identified and upheld.

Any attempt to pinpoint Nollywood's industrial parameters is bound to elicit criticism, particularly considering certain technological developments and associated changes in the production, distribution, and exhibition of Nollywood films. According to the broadest of popular definitions, Nollywood is in many ways a hybrid affair, combining multiple languages, specializing in a whole host of genres, and habitually poaching talents from the realm of television production (a realm that is still, amid the horizontal integration of American multinational corporations like Viacom, held in extremely high esteem in Nigeria, which in 1959 became the first African country to develop a national television station). Famously, the industry now known as Nollywood turned to English-language productions in 1994, when Kenneth Nnebue made the galvanizing *Glamour Girls*, about a young woman's efforts to acclimate to modern city life, with its rampant unemployment and attendant pressures to enter an informal economy through prostitution. Since its inception, Nollywood has mainly been restricted to spheres of production in urban Lagos, the media hub of southwestern Nigeria, but Ghanaian and diasporic shooting locations have occasionally been crucial, and the industry has come to embrace an array of African languages. In this book, Nollywood remains emphatically separate from Kannywood (Nigeria's Hausa-language, Kano-based film industry, with its rootedness in the Islamicate cultures of the north), but it includes more than simply English-, Yorùbá-, and Igbo-language productions: films in Bini, Ibibio, Esan, Idoma, Igala, Nupe, Twi, and Tiv count, too.

Finally, this text rejects an inelegant but well-entrenched phrase: "video film." While many Nigerians continue to refer to Nollywood products as "home videos" (even amid growing access to online platforms, satellite television, and mobile playback devices), the word "film" enjoys, in Lagos and beyond, both a vernacular popularity as well as a broad practical and explanatory utility. In this text, Nollywood movies—whether shot on a cheap analog camcorder in 1994, on a more sophisticated digital device in 2005, or on 35 mm in 2014—are all, and equally, "films." My intention is not to dismiss or subsume format specificity. In fact, in chapter 2, I closely examine the significance of VHS and VCD to the formation of Nollywood's star system, and I suggest some of the ways that individual stars have used specific storage formats (as well as those formats' unmistakable aesthetic components and undeniable affective dimensions) in order to define or augment their own star personae. This book takes Nollywood seriously—deeply so. If the industry's audiovisual products deserve to be called films, then its famous faces are most assuredly movie stars—as glamorous, as talented, and as tenacious as any the globe has ever known.

NOLLYWOOD STARS

Introduction

Global Stars in Nigeria's Postindependence Firmament
From Ossie Davis to *Doctor Bello*

Shot in Nigeria and New York, and featuring African and American performers, the Nollywood-Hollywood coproduction *Doctor Bello* (Tony Abulu, 2012) had its world premiere at the Kennedy Center in Washington, where the question of stardom's transnational reach inspired a series of lively discussions. Like such notable international coproductions as Bernardo Bertolucci's *1900* (1976), which united Italian, French, and American performers, and *Cloud Atlas* (Tom Tykwer and Andy and Lana Wachowski, 2012), whose far-flung financing sources required the participation of talents as varied as Tom Hanks, Hugo Weaving (a Nigerian-born Australian), and Doona Bae (from South Korea), *Doctor Bello* brought together a wide range of global participants, from the Nollywood icons Genevieve Nnaji, Stephanie Okereke, and Ebbe Bassey, to the Hollywood stars Isaiah Washington and Vivica A. Fox (who appeared in another Nigerian-American coproduction, Jeta Amata's *Black Gold*, in 2011). Financed by over two dozen corporations and state agencies in West Africa and the United States, *Doctor Bello* acquired its cast members according not to some unquestioning, purely commercially driven capitulation to transnationalism, but instead to some rather nuanced, thematically relevant strategies. A film about the human links between New York and Nigeria—between Africa and its diaspora—*Doctor Bello* tells the story of an American cancer specialist (Washington) whose Nigerian nurse convinces him to meet with the mysterious titular physician, leading him to Lagos and a possible cancer cure. The film evokes what its characters call "the Brooklyn-African underground"—the complex circuits of knowledge that link Nigerians and Americans through a shared awareness of art, culture, and physical and mental health. With its transnational cast and a story that details some of the legacies of *Négritude* (a cultural movement that Aimé Césaire succinctly described in terms of "the simple recognition of the fact of being black and the acceptance of this fact"), *Doctor Bello* belongs to a long Nollywood tradition that both relies upon and thematizes the mobility of stardom.[1]

That *Doctor Bello* is, in part, a product of the Nigerian government's emergent efforts to support film production—that the project was hardly a "private" affair—complicates its relationship to Nollywood history, more so than does its use of Hollywood stars. When, in 2010, Nigerian President Goodluck Jonathan established a 200-million-dollar initiative to support filmmaking, producer-director Tony Abulu became its first benefactor, receiving a $250,000 loan toward the production of *Doctor Bello*.[2] By contrast, the Nollywood model, as it developed during the 1990s, involved an emphatic, effective rejection of the typical terms and conditions of Western-style filmmaking. In the first few decades following independence (ca. 1960), West Africa remained enmeshed in neocolonialist circuits, which tended to compel filmmakers to ply their trade according to European models of cinematic art—and with, in a vast majority of cases, French government financing. If, as Robert Stam and Ella Shohat suggest, colonialism was characterized by "direct political and military control," then neocolonialism can be seen as "abstract, semi-indirect, largely economic forms of control whose linchpin is a close alliance between foreign capital and the indigenous elite."[3] What Manthia Diawara describes as "the French government's paternalistic attitude and neocolonial practices toward African filmmakers" placed severe restrictions upon cinematic expression in postindependence francophone countries, while former British colonies like Ghana and Nigeria remained dominated by monopolistic U.S., European, and Lebanese film-distribution companies that, primarily through the practice of block booking, saturated local markets with films produced outside of Africa.[4]

While Ousmane Sembène, Safi Faye, and Souleymane Cissé, among other West African auteurs, were developing their own cinematic visions in a constant, often contentious negotiation with global financiers (with Sembène himself declaring that foreign aid was "tainted with paternalism and neocolonialism"), Nigeria was experiencing an even rockier state of affairs: the development, following a devastating civil war, of various, contested indigenization measures; and the factious creation of the Nigerian Film Corporation and the National Film Distribution Company, both of which would destabilize considerably—amid charges of corruption and profligacy—following the petro-naira boom. When, in 1981, the Motion Picture Association of America (MPAA) responded to these circumstances by ceasing to distribute Hollywood films in Nigeria, it helped create what Brian Larkin has called a "pirate infrastructure"; penalizing the Nigerian government for misappropriating copyrighted media, and creating a vast cinematic gap that demanded filling, the MPAA ushered in an era of rampant bootlegging that radically reduced the prospects for a coherent national film industry, sowing the seeds of distaste for traditional, licit modes of consumption.[5] Further complications included the confusions engendered by successive military governments, which tended to swing precipitously between rejecting the significance of cinema and embracing documentary as the filmic mode most apt to glorify their regimes, à la Leni Riefenstahl's plainly partisan *Triumph of the Will* (1935). Finally, a steep rise in urban crime discouraged millions of Nigerians from visiting cinema houses, especially during evening hours; more than simply expensive and imperialist, celluloid films required darkened public spaces that proved physically dangerous to spectators.

Despite these inauspicious conditions, certain ideals of global cinema stardom began to take root among Nigerian artists and intellectuals between the late 1960s and the early 1990s. By the mid-1970s, with the independent production of the first Yorùbá-language film—Ola Balogun's *Ajani Ogun* (1976), starring Adeyemi "Ade Love" Afolayan (father of top Nollywood director Kunle Afolayan)—micronationalism at the level of ethnolinguistics was coexisting with expansive conceptions of stardom, accelerating the development of such charismatic screen personalities as Moses "Baba Sala" Adejumo, with his diverse props (including giant, thick-rimmed, glassless glasses) and ever-present smoking pipe, and Hubert "Osetura" Ogunde, with his contrastingly sober, priestly demeanor. Though remarkably fraught, the pre-Nollywood history of Nigerian cinema reveals that *Doctor Bello* is not the first star-centered project to attempt to bridge ethnic, cultural, and economic gaps between Lagos and Los Angeles. In the 1970s, iconic Hollywood actor Ossie Davis directed a pair of important films in Nigeria, bringing his considerable star power—as well as his own conception of Négritude—to bear upon Nigerian narrative subjects. Shooting his first Nigerian feature, an adaptation of Wole Soyinka's 1964 play *Kongi's Harvest*, on location in Ibadan, Oyo, and Abeokuta, Davis described the film as being focused on "the struggle for power between a dictator who represents the distortion of all that is new, and an old decrepit king, who represents the corruption of all that is old. Caught in between are average people, old people, students and farmers, who try to find their way out between two violent struggles."[6] Davis' "artist's statement" aptly synthesizes so many salient Nigerian subjects: the ongoing struggle between traditionalism and modernity; the corruption that can come in a multiplicity of forms; the sheer ethnic, cultural, religious, and linguistic diversity of a nation-state whose boundaries were created by colonialism and enforced through a variety of postindependence modes of governance; and the quotidian strategies of resistance—what Michel de Certeau famously consolidates as "the practice of everyday life"— of the individuals who are so often caught in between polarizing political developments.

In terms of local support for *Kongi's Harvest*, Davis' star magnetism was abetted by the Nigerian artist-intellectual Soyinka, who wrote the film's script and who portrayed the eponymous president.[7] The promise of a shared transnational stardom, inflected through postindependence conceptions of Négritude, quickly disintegrated, however, as Soyinka denounced and disowned the final cut of *Kongi's Harvest*, describing in a 1979 lecture the persistent challenges of cultural translation.[8] Davis did not give up, however. After directing his remarkable but little-seen American films *Black Girl* (1972) and *Gordon's War* (1973), Davis returned to Nigeria in 1976 to shoot *Countdown at Kusini* (retitled *Cool Red* for distribution in American markets). The story of an independence struggle in a fictitious African colony, *Countdown at Kusini* represented Davis's final attempt to create what is conventionally defined as an international coproduction—a film combining funds from at least two national sources. Sponsored by a series of Nigerian investors (who were plentiful and, as Karin Barber points out, increasingly committed to cultural endeavors during the oil boom of the 1970s) but also by a transnational women's organization, the black sorority Delta Sigma Theta, *Countdown at Kusini* encountered several obstacles during production in Lagos, from inclement weather to an unyielding Nigerian Department of Information, which strongly objected to the script's uncritical references to American exceptionalism. (In the original draft, a black American jazz musician travels to Africa in order to "inspire" colonized populations to start a revolution; successful in this task, he becomes an icon of African independence, superseding even the most politically committed "locals.") In terms of casting, *Countdown at Kusini* had what *Kongi's Harvest* did not: Davis and his wife, Ruby Dee, as stars. But the couple's combined iconic power only complicated the project, further inspiring local criticism of the film's reliance on "the American perspective." With postproduction limited to venues in the United States, and with Davis maintaining final cut, the question of whether *Countdown at Kusini* could preserve any truly Nigerian credentials seemed moot. While *Ebony* magazine, borrowing the basic vocabulary of Négritude, praised the finished film as a victory for "blacks everywhere"—a powerful indication of "what black love and perseverance can produce"—*Countdown at Kusini* was poorly distributed in Nigeria, much to the chagrin of investors who had hoped for a truly transnational success.[9]

When, nearly two decades later, the development of inexpensive, user-friendly video technologies enabled Nigerians to sidestep typical funding sources and production protocols, what is now known as Nollywood was born. As Jonathan Haynes has pointed out, the central irony of the industry is that its astonishing success has been a function of the extreme economic hardships engendered in Nigeria by structural adjustment programs (World Bank and International Monetary Fund policies to "develop" the global South by making privatization a prerequisite for economic aid, which often arrives in the form of debilitating, high-interest loans, accompanied by devaluation). Driving the final nail into the coffin of state support for cinema, structural adjustment programs have effectively divested Nigeria of traditional cinematic practices in the realms of production, distribution, and exhibition. Since the early 1980s, movie theaters have disappeared from the country at an astonishing, indeed devastating rate, while even the most compromised sources of public funding for film production have similarly evaporated—even in the Islamicate cultures of the north, where Adamu Halilu's Hausa-language adaptation of Tafawa Balewa's *Shehu Umar* received federal sponsorship in 1976. Attempts to revive theatrical exhibition have resulted in a few new multiplex chains—including Silverbird, Ozone, and Genesis-Deluxe—but nothing like the model of affordable neighborhood cinemas that many film enthusiasts have in mind. While the government's unveiling of its 200-million-dollar Entertainment Industries Intervention Fund marked an ostensible return to certain frameworks of state sponsorship (akin, perhaps, to Senegal's short-lived Société National du Cinéma, established in 1973), only one filmmaker—the aforementioned Tony Abulu—has thus far benefited, raising painfully familiar questions about the efficacy of state involvement in cultural affairs. For the most part, despite the derivative aspirations that persistently surround it, Nollywood remains *sui generis*—a self-supporting African success story.

Emerging as a popular art—what Karin Barber famously defines as "syncretic, concerned with social change, and associated with the masses"—Nollywood rejected the prohibitive costs as well as the European high-art associations of celluloid film in favor of video technologies; avoided the protracted distribution dramas of a *Countdown at Kusini* by establishing speedy circuits of VHS and VCD dissemination, largely via marketers operating in southern Nigeria, and largely according to infrastructures of media piracy (including large-scale dubbing suites) that were already in place; and managed to develop a star system that would eventually guarantee extensive audience interest across the globe.[10] Singular in so many ways, Nollywood has extended its "rebel" status to the development of certain theories of stardom, which, solidifying around the turn of the twenty-first century, have taken transnationalism as a given, generating icons whose performance styles, semiotic structuring, and sheer sex appeal have been oriented, at once, to West Africa and the diaspora. As Alessandro Jedlowski argues, Nollywood "developed not in a vacuum but within a system of media transnationalism," making it a key source for the study of mobile star images.[11] Jonathan Haynes suggests just how these images have managed to emerge in the dauntingly diverse contexts of southern Nigeria, where a number of otherwise divergent ethnic groups share an investment in "the importance of individual destiny, individual spiritual force, and, therefore, individual dynamism and individual achievement as social values."[12]

Nollywood's relatively organized methods for producing and publicizing icons are not immune to controversy, however. They coexist with flourishing occult imaginaries that often attempt to guard against the kinds of isolated success stories of which stardom consists, primarily by pathologizing what seems an unaccountably self-sustaining prosperity. Precisely because the path to global movie stardom—and thus to potentially endless riches—is so obscure, Nollywood's star system is frequently the reviled target of what Jean and John Comaroff have called "occult economies," even as Nollywood films regularly embrace those economies stylistically, narratively, and thematically. The mystical flip side of the sort of secular gossip that seeks to shame Nollywood stars by accusing them of everything from bleaching their skin to sleeping their way to the top, occult economies tend to suggest that, given the conspicuous absence of a practical, communicable formula for becoming famous, icons like Omotola Jalade-Ekeinde and Genevieve Nnaji must be in league with demons. Nollywood's distinct "Afromodernity"—to borrow another term from the Comaroffs—is such that its stars must constantly negotiate a range of contradictory demands characteristic of the postcolony. Discursively intricate, reliant upon a range of personality types, and untethered to any formalized factory for the production of glamorous images, Nollywood's star system evokes Achille Mbembe's argument that what typifies life in places like Nigeria and Ghana are the "distinctive ways identities are multiplied, transformed, and put into circulation." Nollywood stardom thus concretizes Mbembe's concept of the postcolony as a "dramatic stage" on which subaltern performers must confront the contradictions of modern life, including the manifold failures of state and private agents, new technologies, and religious revivals.[13] The history of Nollywood's star system offers an important reminder that a recent, hybridized example like *Doctor Bello* suggests both stasis and change, both "old" and "new" Nollywood. *Doctor Bello*'s diverse funding sources might recall *Countdown at Kusini*—and Abulu's use of 35-mm film might represent a perversion of some of Nollywood's foundational, format-specific mandates—but its complex use of Nigerian star images occasions the kind of African visibility that even the likes of Ossie Davis and Ruby Dee could not possibly have eclipsed.

Crucial to *Doctor Bello*'s complex intertextuality are the film's Nigerian stars, especially Genevieve Nnaji and Stephanie Okereke. Abulu's star-specific references to Nollywood are perhaps too plentiful to list, but they include Nnaji's numerous, elaborate costume changes, which, in addition to providing a complex combination of modern and traditional styles of dress, also reflect Nnaji's well-known, off-screen identity as a fashion designer, whose label St. Genevieve donates the bulk of its proceeds to African child welfare programs. Unlike *Countdown at Kusini*, which seemed to give only Davis and Dee their iconic due, *Doctor Bello* uses its own transnational status to explore the intersections of Nigerian and American acting styles, star images, and approaches to publicity. Within the latter category, Vivica A. Fox's decision to skip the Lagos premiere of *Doctor Bello* stands out not as a personal failure or a sign of disrespect, but rather as an indication of certain, longstanding American production protocols: Fox, as a prominent member of the cast of the sitcom *Mr. Box Office*—a first-run syndicated series that in 2012 received an order of 100 episodes, prompting a rather grueling shooting schedule and the near-sequestration of its stars—simply could not fly from Los Angeles to Lagos. No less busy than Fox, *Doctor Bello*'s most prominent Nigerian performers are part of an industry that, since the establishment of the Afro-Hollywood Awards in 1996, and especially since the production of Kingsley Ogoro's groundbreaking *Osuofia in London* in 2003, has made room for stars' global travel, inspiring promotional events throughout West Africa and the diaspora. Industrial design is not the only, or even the most powerful, determinant of transnationalism for Nollywood stars, however. Since funds for production and promotion remain scarce, official forms of international publicity—far-flung junkets set up by individual Nollywood producers—are relatively rare. Far more common are the events that Nollywood stars set up themselves and that feature them in a range of capacities (performer, fashion designer, screenwriter, director, reproductive rights activist, NGO leader, diplomat, scholar, novelist, journalist, corporate brand ambassador, environmentalist, and educator) and in a range of locations around the world.

Nollywood stars "become" transnational not through contact with Hollywood performers and production funds, as a superficial consideration of *Doctor Bello* might suggest, but instead through individual, itinerant, industrially sanctioned agency; through fluency in multiple African and European languages; through an extreme facility with contrasting accents; through far-reaching philanthropic activities; by joining forces with some of the least seemly but most visible agents of transnationalism, such as major corporations; by directly engaging with the Hollywood star images that continue to flood West African markets; and, perhaps most importantly, by maintaining an emphatically antiessentialist, self-pluralizing approach to Africa and Africans. Performing in Nigeria just sixteen years after independence, Ossie Davis and Ruby Dee could not help but dominate the iconography of their film. More than thirty years later, Nigeria's cinema stars are so visible, so powerful, and so far-reaching that they demand extensive attention. I argue that the discipline of star studies, as developed within film and media studies, needs to be reconceived to suit the performers who have shaped, strengthened, and circulated Nollywood cinema across the globe. I scrutinize the films, publicity tours, award ceremonies, corporate contracts, reality television series, and debates about nation, race, ethnicity, language, religion, and culture that continue to impact Nollywood stardom both at home and abroad, arguing that Nollywood stars are ambassadors of bricolage wherever they go.

Here, I seek to redress two of the most common ways of reading Nollywood's prolific performers, which represent divergent yet equally false and insidious assumptions. One approach, familiar from Western publications (most notably *Time* magazine), suggests that Nollywood operates, as do its stars, in an imitative capacity, "aping" Western trends without comprehending the consequential cross-cultural, transnational politics of the process. The other, ostensibly inverse approach, familiar from African cultural critics, is to view Nollywood's stars as being rooted exclusively in local configurations—of art, of culture, of commerce; thus restricted to southern Nigeria, Nollywood stars are seen as, at best, having nothing to say to the world beyond their alleged borders, and, at worst, as being benighted black Africans, beholden to tradition and to tribalism. A committed study of Nollywood stardom provides the opportunity to confront such alarmingly consistent figurations, and in the process develop new ways of theorizing cinema stardom from within African and diasporic popular cultures. What would a theory of cinema stardom look like if it began from Nollywood and not Hollywood?[14] This book takes up that question in tracing the complexities of Nollywood's star system—the first to have developed with African film performers on the African continent.

QUESTIONING ESSENTIALISM

It is through some extremely adaptable stars that Nollywood has managed to address many of the tensions of multiculturalism—what Stam and Shohat define in terms of an "obvious cultural heterogeneity" that combines "multiple ethnicities, languages, and religions."[15] It is instructive that the authors waste no time in citing Nigeria as a key, almost prototypical example of a multicultural country, one characterized by over 500 languages and over 250 ethnic groups, of which Hausa, Yorùbá, and Igbo are the largest. To this day, the official Nigerian narrative of multiculturalism tends toward a tacit investment in environmental determinism, with the arid north seen as the site of an essentialized Hausa culture, the oil-rich southeast that of an allegedly unified and impregnable Igbo identity, and the equatorial southwest the "natural" home of an oft-stereotyped Yorùbá people. From these generalized geographical considerations come assumptions about ethnic boundaries—dividing lines that have long been exploited in Nigerian political life and popular culture. In his analysis of Nollywood's "trans-ethnic ethic," Akin Adesokan acknowledges that "some aspects of Nollywood filmmaking are segmented along ethnic and regional lines," but he also recognizes the aesthetic, commercial, political, and philosophical consequences of cross-cultural collaborations, particularly those that depend upon performers.[16] In a series of notable, star-driven cases, Nollywood has managed to subvert local expectations by, for instance, casting Yorùbá performers in Igbo roles, or vice versa, thereby demonstrating not simply the transformative potential of several top talents, but also a broadly antiessentialist approach to screen acting, in which the self-pluralizing, stereotype-shattering tendencies of some savvy performers see them migrating from one medium to another—from, say, reality television programs to Nollywood films—and from one culture to another. Arguing that Nollywood is "best understood in the context of coexistence" in multiethnic Lagos, Adesokan cites the star images of, among others, Richard Mofe-Damijo (or RMD) and Liz Benson, both of whom have parlayed their "surprise" appearances in Yorùbá films into advertisements for Nollywood's "inclusiveness."[17]

Other scholars have suggested the extent to which Nollywood relies upon its stars to embody pan-African ideals. Peyi Soyinka-Airewele argues that multiculturalism is "reflected in Nollywood cinema through the movement of actors between African countries and the mixing of languages, names, cultures, and featured locations in a manner that has transformed the way audiences conceptualize borders and boundaries."[18] According to the author, Nollywood films tend to "unveil a multidimensional, heterogenous landscape of Africa, away from the Hollywood model that imagines a blur of unrelenting sameness."[19] Nollywood's *Internet Love* (Yomi Adejumo, 2012) offers a compelling illustration of Soyinka-Airewele's point. In the film, Barbara Ukattah plays a Nigerian woman who impersonates a Zimbabwean in order to win the affections of a Nigerian-American man. In her mind, this man, being Westernized, must be thoroughly contemptuous of fellow Nigerians but sexually curious about other black Africans; he would, she reckons, surely prefer a woman who says she's from Harare to a "razz Naija girl" (what, in her lowest self-estimation, she believes herself to be). In other words, *Internet Love* imagines a diasporic Nigerian who has internalized white America's simultaneous fear of Nigeria and objectification of an abstracted Africanity. Ukattah must portray a young performer who herself attempts to embody a Zimbabwean, with predictably dizzying results.

In order to profitably explore the antiessentialism of Nollywood films and of Nollywood stars, it is first necessary to outline some of the permutations both of essentialism and of its opposite, since they jointly suggest a range of responses to Nigerian multiculturalism. Essentialism is hardly a universal concept; it must be contextualized historically, politically, and culturally. Broadly speaking, it concerns taxonomy: essentialism, as Diana Fuss argues, "is most commonly understood as a belief in the real, true essence of things, the invariable and fixed properties which define the 'whatness' of a given entity."[20] Essentialism was, of course, central to the operations of colonialism, permitting, for instance, British colonizers to essentialize themselves—along white supremacist lines—as ideologically coherent agents of empire, while at the same time essentializing colonized populations according to a racist, primitivist rubric. Throughout the immediate postindependence period, however, essentialism was employed to "explain" the resistance of certain ethnic minority groups to various processes of nation building, particularly in Nigeria.

Historically, there have thus been two general strains of essentialism—what might be described as essentialism "from above" and essentialism "from below." To this day, a Western-authored, Africa-focused essentialism might subsume ethnic particularities under a totalizing, pessimistic, and altogether condescending conception of Nigeria and Nigerians. With an eye toward Nollywood stardom, such essentialism might manifest in an inability—or in a conscious refusal—to distinguish between the differing approaches to acting of, say, Igbo and Yorùbá performers; in the process, this approach would surely fail to recognize the antiessentialism of an Igbo star who agrees to play a Yorùbá role (or vice versa), and it would likely dismiss the significance of the thick accents of certain stars for whom Yorùbá is a foreign language, or who learn a few lines of Igbo phonetically. Oge Okoye, a major star, has often suggested that there is no such thing as an authentic accent in any language, thus drawing attention to the social construction of phonetics. Her theory was put to the test, however, when she had to speak Yorùbá for Fathia Balogun's *Street Girls* (2012), her much-publicized debut in the Yorùbá sector.

While Okoye's Yorùbá is audibly, even comically different from that of the native speakers who are her costars in the film, little is made of her bizarre accent as the narrative progresses. One character, Dabira (played by Balogun), complains only when Okoye's Clara replaces a few Pidgin phrases with their rough Yorùbá translations. For Dabira, the leader of a group of armed bank robbers, Pidgin is the preferred vehicle of "street speech"—far more appropriate to "thug life" than classical Yorùbá. When she criticizes Clara—curtly asking, "Is it necessary for you to speak Yorùbá?"—it is not because Okoye's Yorùbá is so "bad," so heavily accented, but because it is not Pidgin. The irony, however, is that Dabira's Pidgin is hardly free of a Yorùbá influence, just as the Pidgin in Kenneth Nnebue's *Living in Bondage* (1992) bears more than a few traces of the Igbo language, anticipating the diverse, creolized Delta dialects of the Nollywood classic *Domitilla: The Story of a Prostitute* (Zeb Ejiro, 1997). In *Street Girls*, Okoye's obvious lack of fluency in Yorùbá is no more a structuring narrative influence than is the appearance of a white American actor in the role of a Ghanaian farmer in *Elmina* (Emmanuel Apea Jr., 2010), a melodrama that for Jane Bryce exemplifies a certain tendency in West African popular cinema—a tendency to interrogate identity and the politics of representation, to honor novelty and difference without necessarily citing them as such.[21] If defiantly "deaf and blind" casting practices merit little to no narrative attention in a range of Nollywood films, they are nevertheless central to star-driven publicity: Okoye's surprise appearance in *Street Girls* earned her considerable coverage in the popular press, with numerous Nigerian newspapers touting the star's "Igbo-to-Yorùbá" trajectory.

In celebrating Okoye's "crossover" case, it is unclear whether the press is upholding inclusiveness and heterogeneity as ethnically specific traits. As this example suggests, there is often a fine line between essentialism and antiessentialism: arguing that there is no single, "essential" Yorùbá accent or worldview, while conceding the existence of a Yorùbá ethno-linguistic group, threatens to present that group as strictly resistant to cohesion and coherence—as essentialized in its fluidity. I attempt to avoid such an interpretive catch-22 by detailing the efforts of Nollywood stars who, in a variety of ways, emphatically self-identify along ethnic lines, but whose actions—both on and off the screen—suggest a principled commitment to change (rather than continuity), adaptability (instead of fixity), and transnational mobility (as opposed to a nation-state-based essentialism, a way of "being Nigerian" for local as well as global consumption). That is not to say that there is no such thing, among Nollywood's antiessentialist stars, as Nigerian pride. But the very transnationalism that Nollywood requires—the globetrotting narratives that it generates, the peripatetic publicity circuits that it inspires—compels stars to consistently confront nationalism with pan-Africanism, Nigeria's political borders with a transhistorical ethnic expansiveness, and their own acting styles with a variety of techniques and traditions. Performing the mobility of an ethnic identity, which works to de-essentialize that identity by tracing some of its pan-African and diasporic iterations, becomes a compelling way of engaging transnationalism.

If there is such a thing as an essentialism "from below," it is perhaps best described in Gayatri Spivak's concept of strategic essentialism—the means through which the subaltern subject can gain political legitimacy, consciously employing simplifying tactics and proffering a false unity and consistency that is yet rhetorically effective. If radical forms of antiessentialism range from postmodernism's aggressive relativism to Stuart Hall's description of the decentering of identity (through which "we are confronted by a bewildering, fleeting multiplicity of possible identities"), then a more measured conception of antiessentialism is offered by Tariq Modood, who, following Wittgenstein, writes that "we do not have to be browbeaten by a dogmatic antiessentialism into believing that historical continuities, cultural groups, [or] coherent selves . . . do not exist."[22] In applying Modood's understanding of antiessentialism to the subject of Nollywood stardom, I hope to suggest a way of reading the industry's star images in ways that respect both their differences as well as their shared responsiveness to social forces—their collective capacity to shift over time and across national contexts. In my reading, Nollywood star personae are rooted in specific local and regional formations (of nation, ethnicity, culture, language, and religion) while at the same time remaining conducive to the kinds of changes that transnational travel can occasion, and that tend to nourish notions of "good acting." For instance, the Ghanaian Van Vicker has frequently portrayed Nigerian-born men—including native Igbo and Hausa speakers—in his Nollywood films, suggesting that antiessentialism can manifest as opposition to national determinism (in which the nation-state defines an individual identity, thus preventing it from illustrating other, alleged national cultural traits). In this case, the refusal to essentialize Vicker as broadly African, which permits an awareness of his Ghanaian rather than Nigerian roots, leads to a pronounced appreciation for his acting talents in press accounts of his Nollywood performances, which suggest a successful cross-cultural trajectory—a Ghanaian's conscious creation of complex, ethnically discrepant Nigerian characters.

Famous for having played an American role (and for having convincingly approximated a bland American accent) on the Ghanaian television series *Sun City* (2003), Vicker frequently self-identifies as a global citizen whose late father was white and Dutch and whose mother is Ghanaian and Liberian. (For his part, the Nollywood star Jim Iyke—born James Ikechukwu Esomugha in Libreville, Gabon—famously self-identifies as pan-African, as does the Desmond Elliot who was born in Nigeria to a Yorùbá father and an Igbo mother, and the Ramsey Nouah whose father is Israeli and whose mother is Yorùbá.) Vicker's openness to global travel has not threatened to efface his Ghanaian identity, and his nationally inflected use of Twi (particularly in the 2012 Ghanaian film *Joni Waka*, which he produced and directed) informs his star image. Vicker cannot be essentialized as Ghanaian—a reading that would posit the impossibility of his ever impersonating a Nigerian or an American—but that does not mean that Ghana lacks relevance to his stardom; in fact, Ghanaian national pride appears to be a structuring influence on his career. Like his fellow Nollywood stars, Vicker is not shackled by national or ethnic specificities, but he does not deny the centrality of those specificities to his personal processes of self-fashioning. That those processes have generated a dizzying assortment of cross-cultural imitations in his Nollywood films speaks not simply to the sheer diversity of West Africa but also to Vicker's willingness to take risks as an actor. Affirming Ghana, and honoring Twi, makes for a Vicker whose antiessentialism steers clear of the sort of postmodernist extremism that would radically decenter his identity.

NOLLYWOOD IN AFRICA

In examining the global flows of Nollywood stardom, this book alternates between considerations of two distinct types of transnationalism: minor and major. An itinerary defined by hegemonic (usually corporate) structures as well as by an orientation toward the West (especially such "First World" metropolitan centers as New York, London, and Paris), major transnationalism describes Nollywood's relationship to the global North, including the Hollywood that, for instance, helped produce *Doctor Bello*. By contrast, a minor transnationalism—a trajectory defined by the relations among nation-states in the global South, or among exclusively minority populations across the global North—describes Nollywood's responsiveness to, and ongoing reception in, multiple West African countries (especially Senegal, Sierra Leone, and, as Van Vicker's stardom demonstrates, Ghana). Minor transnationalism provides a powerful reminder that Nollywood is not (as the American popular press would have it) strictly interested in borrowing from Hollywood or in imitating Tyler Perry movies (a preposterous suggestion that *Time* magazine has offered with apparent impunity).[23] In fact, Nollywood must contend with a cultural diversity that is much closer to home—that has led, for instance, to a certain grassroots resistance to video among Sembène-fixated Senegalese cinephiles, or that guarantees multidirectional public controversies in response to a Ghanaian actor (Majid Michel) playing a Nigerian terrorist (in Pascal Amanfo's 2013 Nollywood film *Boko Haram*, later retitled *Nation Under Siege*). Nollywood's transnationalism, then, is not limited to relations between Nigeria and the West.

Individual Nollywood stars, hailing from different cultural, political, religious, and linguistic pockets of West Africa, consistently enact, by necessity, the antiessentialism that Suzanne Gearhart suggests is crucial both to practical and philosophical experiences of transnationalism. Indeed, as anatomized by stars, a variety of ethno-linguistic groups represent the "different cultural strands within national life" that in Gearhart's analysis "do not necessarily need to be kept separate *or* tied into one single knot.

Instead, each can contribute to . . . a cultural project that asks something more or better of us instead of merely returning to us what in cultural terms we already know or have."[24] The fluid movement between Igbo and Yorùbá identities that Nollywood stars so often enact, which can be considered a form of minor transnationalism unto itself (especially considering its inflections in Benin and Cameroon), also suggests a certain resistance to Western prescriptions, to the boundary-creating and border-enforcing legacy of colonialism, and certainly to a racist, vernacular American view of black Africans as being all alike. Star-driven antiessentialism suggests, then, a response to or expectation of Nollywood's global reception, signaling an orientation toward the diaspora, but also, more locally, a means of resisting tribalism.[25]

In tracing the persistently antiessentialist transnationalism of Nollywood stars, I remain dedicated to detailing ethnic specificities. Just as postcolonial theory should be as committed to exposing the lasting legacies of colonialist oppression as to imagining limitless spheres of influence for the postindependence subject, any attempt to locate an antiessentialist project in contemporary Nigeria must consider the precise ethnic, cultural, religious, and linguistic contexts out of which that project develops.[26] Perhaps Funke Akindele's character puts it best in the film *Lady Gaga*: believing herself to be "capable of anything," she successfully mimics, over the telephone, a foul-mouthed white American. This performance-within-a-performance signals a remarkable confluence of actress and role: the Funke Akindele who emphatically identifies as Yorùbá—and whose publicist, as I discuss in chapter 2, is tasked with disseminating to the Nigerian popular press the Yorùbá-specific justifications for Akindele's business decisions—is also known for her impressive range as an actress. She has earned acclaim for playing a handful of Igbo roles, and in *Lady Gaga*, she even goes so far as to pull off a spectacular cross-cultural imitation. Afterward, in a soliloquy, her character places this imitation in its proper context, drawing attention to the way that Yorùbá phonetics facilitate impersonation and proudly declaring herself to be "boundless." It is hardly paradoxical, then, to look at antiessentialism against the backdrop of ethnic identity, as I do in this book. In fact, as Akindele's star image reminds us, it is often cultural specificity that provides a springboard for the free play of identity. Addressing this topic, Akin Adesokan argues that numerous Nollywood films "constitute and are constituted by concrete aesthetics of cross-cultural identity, even while they bear signs of cultural specificity."[27] This complex double structure—this tension between obviousness and ambiguity—provides a kaleidoscopic yet rigorous lens through which to examine Nollywood stardom.

Another example of an ethnic particularity leading to the perceived limitlessness of a Nollywood star persona is that of Igbo widowhood, which by tradition requires the shaving of the widow's head. Within the well-publicized context of Nollywood's star system, the portrayal of Igbo traditionalism doesn't simply provide Igbo actresses with the opportunity to honor their roots; it also gives actresses of all backgrounds and identities a chance to demonstrate their willingness to renounce vanity for a role. The publicity potential of this process is especially pronounced when a Yorùbá performer shaves her head in order to portray an Igbo character. In this instance, the specificity of Igbo traditionalism highlights both the off-screen deployment of a performer's "contrasting" Yorùbá identity as well as that performer's admirable commitment to an antiessentialist conception of acting. Her Yorùbá identification does not prevent her from accepting an emphatically Igbo role, and her fabled beauty does not limit her physical expressiveness: she can go bald on screen, Igbo-style. For her, a Yorùbá ethnicity can be both hyper-specific—part and parcel of her public identity, of her singular star image—and responsive to radical transformations.

NOLLYWOOD IN THE WEST

One of the most common temptations in Western accounts of Nollywood is to view the industry—in keeping with its cheekily derivative but well-entrenched name—according to an assumed orientation toward Hollywood cinema. Within this view, only dominant global agents can give Nollywood any degree of meaning—as if Nigeria remains locked in what Frantz Fanon called "the colonized mind," a blindly mimicking impulse rooted in neurotic feelings of cultural inferiority.[28] A 2013 *Time* magazine piece declaring Nollywood superstar Omotola Jalade-Ekeinde one of the one hundred most influential people in the world casually defines Nollywood—presumably for an exclusively Western readership—in terms of an alleged affinity with certain Indian and American cinematic styles: "Think Bollywood via Tyler Perry."[29] While such a directive has its broadly explanatory value—especially given Nollywood stars' promotional activities along the very same Atlanta church circuit that continues to influence Perry's films—it is blind to Nollywood's singularity and, in many ways, it is remarkably inaccurate (and dare I say racist?), to boot. As Brian Larkin and Carmen McCain have amply demonstrated, it is northern Nigeria's Hausa-language film industry—not southern Nigeria's Nollywood—that has embraced Bollywood for its generic and iconographic approaches. (Bollywood-style musicals are plentiful in the north, not in Nollywood.)[30] Surely the *Time* writer (Richard Corliss) wished to suggest that Nollywood now rivals Bollywood in terms of its annual filmic output—which is certainly true—but his analogizing style suggests one of the dangers of defining Nollywood in terms of transnationalism.

A far more productive approach is to examine the efforts of Nollywood stars to remain in conversation with a range of Western cultural forms, either directly (through interviews and a variety of public appearances) or indirectly (by portraying characters who, say, listen to Lady Gaga or openly imitate Nicki Minaj). Over the past two decades, Nollywood stars have complicated, if not quite eradicated, certain stereotyping tendencies of Western media, which often entail the assumption that Africa is enmeshed in miserable political, social, psychic, and somatic circumstances—that all Africans are oppressed, depressed, and physically ailing. As agents of powerful, complex counter-narratives, Nollywood stars routinely appear on CNN and the BBC, but also on local television programs like Atlanta's *Talk Time Africa*, providing appealing alternatives to alarmist or paternalist figurations.

The assumption that itinerant African art forms—and itinerant African film stars—must necessarily contend with Western condescension and objectification would seem to ignore the fact that there are thriving African diasporic communities in Europe and the United States. When an African cultural form such as a Nollywood film travels to, say, Atlanta, and is screened in private Nigerian-American homes there, is it faced with direct supercultural pressures? Perhaps not. In its global circulation, then, Nollywood stardom complicates the conventional models of resistance, translation, and cooperation that often characterize North-South relations, precisely because the phenomenon so often finds powerful and much-publicized contexts of reception in Atlanta, Houston, New York, Chicago, and Washington (not to mention Paris, London, Toronto, Rome, and Berlin).[31] Nollywood stardom suggests the extent to which "minor" cultures matter to local formulations of the global, as well as to the ongoing performance of transnationalism "from below."

ACTING TRANSNATIONALISM

In this book, I am as concerned with the artistry of acting as I am with the semiotics and political economy of stardom, just as I am equally committed to tracing transnationalism in both its major and minor iterations. I look at a series of specific performance strategies as well as at the broader processes of meaning-making occasioned by (among other professional practices) publicity appearances, photo shoots, and sponsorship deals. This book is thus as much a study of the mechanics of acting as of the phenomenon that Richard Dyer famously identifies with the phrase "structured polysemy." Indeed, Dyer's concept offers a crucial means of contesting the notion that film stars are uninvolved in the construction and maintenance of their own images—that they are somehow unaware of the ways that their meanings are made to circulate globally. Conceptually, "structured polysemy" suggests an antiessentialism that does not threaten to devolve into a radical, identity-denying postmodernism. It describes the extent to which stars who seem impossibly adaptable and itinerant are in fact rooted in rather well-defined historical, ethnic, cultural, and industrial contexts—contexts that they can appear to transcend through the hard work of deliberate image construction as well as through the transporting potential of brilliant screen acting.

This book is not a collection of capsule biographies, but it does bring biographical facts to bear upon readings of individual films, a variety of star personae, and the debates about Nollywood that thrive in West Africa and the diaspora. "Biography does not trump labor," argues Amy Lawrence. "We should not assume that [a personal narrative] has a necessary, constant, or legible effect on [a star's] work as an actor."[32] Heeding Lawrence's caution, this book uses biography sparingly, primarily as a text created through complex circuits of publicity in West Africa and the diaspora—circuits that include Nigerian and American television talk shows, for instance, as well as fan magazines in Ghana and South Africa, and film festivals in Paris, Rome, and London. Writing about the relationship between stardom and biography, James Naremore argues that "human figures in a film are received in three different ways: as actors playing fictional characters, as actors playing 'themselves,' and as facts in a documentary." This book considers all three perspectives of reception, suggesting their transnational, star-activated permutations. In the process, I embrace an eclectic intertextuality, taking stars' publicity appearances (whether conditioned by biography or distorted through certain corporate objectives) as seriously as the films that depend upon and extend their complex images. In Nollywood, an individual star persona is not reducible to a film or even to a series of films; part of my purpose in offering a history of Nollywood stardom is to show how the platforms for iconicity have expanded exponentially since the early 1990s. In explaining the way that a star's meanings can accrete over time and with the aid of new technologies, Naremore defines the star image as "a complex, intertextual matter, owing not only to the actor and her or his previous roles, but to the filmic qualities of microphones, cameras, editing, and projection; it derives as well from narratives written about the actor in publicity and biography and thus becomes a global category."[33]

Historically speaking, academic studies of stardom, which typically comprise accounts of American and/or European stars, have not had to bear the burden of proving that their human subjects are, in fact, famous; most proceed from the assumption that their readers will unquestioningly accept that the star images they describe are actual and operable—that Marlon Brando is "an icon," that Marilyn Monroe is "a legend," and so on. To say that a study of Nollywood stardom simply does not have that luxury is, of course, to presume a primarily Western readership. Certainly names like Halima Abubakar, Stephanie Okereke, and Omotola Jalade-Ekeinde are hyperfamiliar in southern Nigeria, spanning multiple language communities and reminding each that local and even global stardom is possible for Nigerian women. That said, Western ethnocentrism—including and especially the sort of ethnocentrism that is sadly typical of star studies—is such that any account of Nollywood stardom must carefully elucidate the extent to which, at the very least, local and global audiences recognize Genevieve Nnaji or Ramsey Nouah as stars. This process of elucidation must combine close readings of individual films and of their associated publicity texts (from Nigerian print and online newspapers and fan magazines to posters, VCD cases, and YouTube videos) with the sort of field research that involves tracking the circulation of star images and discourses, interviewing moviegoers about their favorite performers and how they have come to know them, and even witnessing firsthand the promotional activities of individual Nollywood stars in West Africa and the diaspora.

From Dakar to Cannes to Atlanta and beyond, I have been present in a range of locations where Nollywood stars have sought to introduce themselves to global audiences, displaying a diversity of strategies for acting transnationalism. That phrase, which recurs throughout this book, refers to the fact that Nollywood stars actually *enact* transnationalism, performing literal border-crossings while promoting their films and public personae. But it also refers to a more figurative framework, one in which stars suggest—both within the boundaries of fictional characters and in their actual, off-screen lives—a variety of ways of responding to globalization. From a star-making embrace of the eponymous phone in the *BlackBerry Babes* trilogy, to a complete capitulation to Lady Gaga's aggressive global appeal, to principled, resistant critiques of Beyoncé and Rihanna, Nollywood stars play a range of roles that themselves respond to Western cultural and economic imperialism as much as to local practices of media reception. But stars are equally committed to communicating their differing understandings of transnationalism through the maintenance of a whole host of personae—through the execution of affective strategies that do not necessarily depend upon literal transnational travel. From Oge Okoye's widely publicized interest in securing dual citizenship for her children to Omotola Jalade-Ekeinde's appreciation for "homey" Ghanaian recording studios (as articulated on her African reality television series *Omotola: The Real Me*), Nollywood stars constantly and consciously employ their own understandings of transnationalism in ways that further define their polysemous star images.

To the casual observer, the sheer agency of Nollywood stars can seem remarkable. Stephanie Okereke veers from villainous roles to saintly ones, pausing in between for a lead performance in a light comedy—and all in the span of just a few months. At first glance, it seems to be Okereke alone who is in charge of this constant alteration of her image—who has made possible this prodigious juggling of performance styles. Upon closer inspection, however, it becomes possible to view the intensely prolific Nollywood film industry itself as the source of a diversity of performance options. Simply put, the sheer abundance of films produced annually might make shape-shifting easy—might even *mandate* that stars move rapidly from project to project, without becoming too concerned with the lack of continuity among the characters they play. Nollywood stars tend to describe the industry's famously tight shooting schedules—as well as its equally well-known proliferation of projects—as pleasurably challenging. Indeed, such is the interpretive approach of Toyin Alausa in the documentary *This is Nollywood,* as she seeks to contextualize the pride she takes in performing. Asked how she "juggles so many scripts," Tonto Dikeh, another major star, says, "A job is something you have to love. For me . . . coming from reality television . . . having character after character is a gift."[34]

In its ever-altering iterations, Nollywood stardom helps—as remains so crucial from an African-studies standpoint—to combat the racist notion that a black African can only ever "be" one thing, can only ever embody a single (and singular) "type." The odious issue of essentialism is one that does not dog white Western stars, and those are the performers who most often appear in academic studies of stardom. (Of the dozens of talents analyzed in Dyer's book *Stars,* none are black, and nearly all are American.) Complaining that Jennifer Aniston is constantly playing the same role—saying that there is a definite Aniston type and that the performer herself never deviates from it despite her in-demand status—is not necessarily to draw attention to her whiteness; it does not threaten to essentialize her as the embodiment of an allegedly racially specific psychic limitation. On the other hand, to suggest that Halima Abubakar is always performing a near–nervous breakdown in all of her films—that her characters are seemingly always on the verge of emotional collapse—can seem dangerously close to an Afro-pessimist pronouncement, one that asserts a black African woman's essential inability to change or grow, even on the screen. However, a close look at Abubakar's specific choices *as an actress,* and at the many meanings of her image *as a star*—a reading strategy that this book repeatedly advocates—reveals a far wider range of character types than can be seen in the reductive (and not uncommon) positioning of the performer as the essence of African emotionality.

Through its remarkable productivity, Nollywood has constituted a kind of acting school for its stars. As Jonathan Haynes suggests, while the industry does not always honor the discrete script, it never ignores the importance of acting, encouraging improvisation both by necessity (as when a script simply does not exist) and by artistic preference (because the best performers are capable of generating considerable excitement through sheer self-invention).[35] Given Nollywood's multilingual status—its shifts between, say, English and Yorùbá, or (less commonly) between Igbo and Ibibio—improvisation can reveal, among its star practitioners, varying commands of any one of a number of languages. Onookome Okome has argued that the seminal *Living in Bondage* did more than simply convince filmmakers of the viability of video technologies; in Okome's account, it also proved the importance of "expanding the linguistic and cultural base" of Nollywood, primarily by embracing flexibility at the levels of dialect and performance.[36] One of Nollywood's most common dialects, Pidgin, might appear to be an equalizer, a great leveler—a democratizing linguistic approach that provides the impression not simply that stars are like each other but also that they are like everyone else in anglophone West Africa. But this perspective on Pidgin is blind (or, as it were, deaf) to phonetics—to the way that diverse stars inflect even a shared, vernacular language with a range of accents—as well as to the fluidity of the idiom itself. As Nollywood films from *Living in Bondage* to *Domitilla* demonstrate, "Pidgin" describes a complex, occasionally incompatible collection of creolized dialects even within southern Nigeria—a complexity that stars often anatomize, both on and off the screen. Simply put, Funke Akindele's Pidgin is not Oge Okoye's Pidgin; the Pidgin of *Show Bobo* is not that of *Street Girls*; and so on. There is no single Pidgin among Nollywood stars, just as there is no single physical performance style: Halima Abubakar often uses her hands in a series of elaborate, dazzlingly expressive gestures, spreading her ten fingers as if to ward off the masculinist inanity that so often surrounds her, or slicing the air with her nails during moments of rage. By contrast, Uche Jombo, in playing some similar roles (wealthy, well-educated, urban businesswomen who are unlucky in love) has a habit of hiding her hands from the camera, and using only her face, neck, and shoulders to modulate various states of emotion.

Dyer identifies such physical gestures as crucial performance signs, but he also traces a twofold approach that I have adopted in examining Nollywood star acting. Dyer distinguishes between—and describes the importance of combining—sociological and semiotic approaches to the study of stardom. The sociological approach addresses the ways that stars are relevant to, partly constitutive of, and partly constituted by their societies; the semiotic approach suggests the ways that stars function within filmic, journalistic, and promotional texts. Dyer writes, "You need to know what kind of thing a text is in society in order to know what kind of questions you can legitimately pose of it, what kind of knowledge you can reasonably expect it to yield."[37] That is why I situate Nollywood stardom in its various national, ethnic, cultural, linguistic, and religious contexts, while exploring the transnational movements of individual, polysemous star images and asking what those images say not only about West Africa but also about the region's diasporas. The subject of the following six chapters, Nollywood stardom is an effective vessel through which to redress Western misrepresentations of Africa and Africans, and to gain an expansive understanding of the political economy of star images in the age of globalization. Nollywood stars illuminate an important argument that Mojúbàolú Olufúnké Okome and Olufemi Vaughan make about West Africa's "transnational encounters"—specifically, that such encounters are "vibrant, complicated, and dynamic, providing new definitions of homeland and diaspora, tradition and modernity, citizen and subject, and gender and generation." Indeed, the authors could be describing Nollywood stars when they suggest that West African migrants are "remarkably innovative and adaptive to rapidly shifting conditions," due not to some essentialized African pliancy but to the unique, improvisatory pressures that, in Achille Mbembe's reading, define the postcolony.[38] Nollywood stars perform postcolonial adaptability in ways that make them key sources for a grounded understanding of such phenomena as globalization, multiculturalism, creolization, and the corporate restructuring of African sectors from health to telecommunications. Nollywood's careful, controversial, and at times contradictory development of a thriving star system marks the first time that an African film industry has actively sought agents of awareness beyond liberationist, colonial, and griotic frameworks.

STRUCTURE

In this book, I argue that the study of Nollywood stardom can facilitate efforts to expand the parameters of scholarship on southern Nigerian films, partly by showing how the Nollywood industry relies on its remarkably diverse performers to promote its products and politics, both at home and abroad. By calling into question false and often condescending assumptions about black African identities, Nollywood stars also combat the stereotyped renderings of their industry, its politics, and its peoples. Chapter 1 confronts academic star studies—a primarily Western, Hollywood-focused scholarly discipline—with the Nollywood phenomenon, while exploring the development of the industry's star system across multiple media platforms.

Classical film theory is rich in assessments of the extent to which traditional, darkened spaces of commercial public exhibition facilitate audience identification with on-screen stars. Far rarer are allusions to the ways that home viewing might affect identification and desire. While scholarship on this subject is scant, it is possible to identify three pertinent paradigms: privacy (understood as individual or small-group spectatorship in a limited, usually domestic setting); screen size (examined across ever-evolving platforms, from television to laptop to smartphone); and autonomy (largely defined as the private spectator's capacity to stop and start a text at will, or to pause, rewind, or fast-forward it, exercising an individualized power over media that has the potential to undermine or redefine stardom). These three paradigms can and frequently do overlap, especially when confronted with the matter of format quality—with the failure-prone materiality of videotape, for example, or with the relatively limited storage space of the VCD. In chapter 2, I investigate the matter of materiality—of format specificity—and its effects on Nollywood stardom, suggesting that dominant ways of reading VHS and VCD as low-quality media leave little room for discussions of viewers' enjoyment of stars, whose well-established, ever-legible personae can transcend (or at least survive alongside) audiovisual distortions, from extreme signal loss to a mildly jittery image. Increasingly essentialized as formats of and for the global South, VHS (which has long since obsolesced in the West) and VCD (whose use has largely been limited to the non-West) are the primary material storage formats for Nollywood films; neither is of a technically high quality; yet both have witnessed—and both have helped to develop—Nollywood star images, making them crucial objects of analysis.

In chapter 3 I turn to the corporate identity of Nigerian telecommunications superpower Globacom, first as filtered through Nollywood's *BlackBerry Babes* trilogy and finally as evidenced in its star-centered promotional practices, asking what happens to an antiessentialist stance—and to the stars who so often embody that stance—when corporate goals confront local modes of resistance. Globacom's dominant yet contested role in West

Africa's diverse media landscapes makes the corporation a key source for the study of Nollywood stars' sometimes vexed migrations. The semiotics of star-centered Globacom print ads is part of the fabric of chapter 1. In chapter 3, my main focus is on the Globacom-created controversies that Nollywood stars have been called upon to diffuse—but that they often end up exacerbating, largely on account of their complicated personae. Chapter 3 also examines the moving-image advertisements that carry, and further complicate, Nollywood star images via Globacom's numerous and increasingly far-reaching services. I take a close look at the star-studded *BlackBerry Babes* trilogy (Ubong Bassey Nya, 2011–2012) in terms of its complex, indirect depiction of its stars' off-screen (and sometimes contradictory) relationships to corporate globalism. The trilogy's ambivalence about Globacom is evident in its attempts to balance an anticorporate stance with quiet yet passionate pronouncements about the wonders of information technologies. A satire about brand loyalty, the trilogy uses such stars as Oge Okoye, Tonto Dikeh, Mary Remmy, Karen Igho, and Eniola Badmus to enact different ways of using mobile phones—phones that Globacom "brings to life" with its data plans, and that these specific stars have helped to sell through their diverse off-screen activities.

If the *BlackBerry Babes* trilogy attempts to make satirical sense of the relations between Nollywood stars and corporate globalism, then Ubong Bassey Nya's follow-up film *Lady Gaga* (2012), the subject of chapter 4, offers its own way of understanding media piracy in the age of globalization by using the intertextuality of stardom to interrogate copyright; American media and economic imperialism; and local, ethnically differentiated Nigerian methods of media reception. If the *BlackBerry Babes* trilogy offers an allegorical depiction of Nollywood's star system (and of the industry's many Globacom brand ambassadors), then *Lady Gaga* deals with a more explicit evocation of global stardom's component parts: in the film, Oge Okoye's character channels the Lady Gaga who is a daily presence in southwestern Nigeria, eventually pirating her whole persona and achieving untold success.

In this book, I have selected a series of films that centralize stardom in some way, whether through satire and allegory (as in the *BlackBerry Babes* trilogy), or by engaging with off-screen debates about fame in today's Nigeria (in films as otherwise far apart as Afam Okereke's *Beyoncé and Rihanna,* Charles Inojie's *The Price of Fame,* and Lancelot Oduwa Imasuen's *The Celebrity* and *Last Celebrity*). Still other films, like the four-part *Lady Gaga,* are explicitly about media stardom, making them especially relevant to the study of Nollywood's complex and ever-shifting star system—a system that, for a whole host of reasons, has been largely resistant to the development of child stars. Chapters 5 and 6 consider the past, current, and potential future contours of child stardom in Nollywood, tracing debates that span West Africa and the diaspora. In these final two chapters, I examine Nollywood's complicated billing practices, noting that, in countless cases, child performers are not credited even when they are clearly the leading players of their films. If the decision to bill an adult star by her maiden and not her married name often suggests a certain, perhaps nostalgic respect for her early screen accomplishments (and also, at least potentially, a progressive refusal to honor the traditionalism of a gender-specific name change), then the refusal to credit children at all speaks to the confused and frequently fraught status of child stardom in Nollywood. I consider several films that rely heavily upon actual child performers, but I also detail the growing West African and diasporic backlash against Nollywood's apparent predilection for casting adults in youth roles—a predilection that can have productive career consequences (as in the cases of the diminutive actors Osita Iheme and Chinedu Ikedieze), or that can turn a film, as well as an age-inappropriate performer, into a laughingstock.

I close the book by considering the subject of youth stardom against the backdrop of West Africa's child-welfare movements and with an eye toward the explosion of regional interest in Miley Cyrus, Justin Bieber, Selena Gomez, and other, globally circulating Hollywood "teen talents." In the end, Nollywood will continue to redefine the terms and conditions of global film stardom, whatever the efforts of a persistent Western imperialism, proving the ongoing importance of examining a star system that has developed on the African continent. What Alessandro Jedlowski refers to as Nollywood's "creole aesthetic formula"—one marked, as Édouard Glissant might have said, by the meeting of local and international influences—means that the industry's star personae are "intrinsically cosmopolitan," and they deserve to be studied as such.[39] Indeed, these stars suggest a dynamic set of responses to

Manthia Diawara's impassioned call for the development of a West African regional imaginary—one that would "promote the circulation of goods and cultures" beyond the confining or outmoded prescriptions of the nation-state, supporting the maintenance of mobile identities.[40] "Modern popular arts have the capacity to transcend geographical, ethnic, and even national boundaries," writes Karin Barber.[41] So do Nollywood stars, as the following pages attest.

1

From Yorùbá to YouTube

Studying Nollywood's Star System

When Nollywood star Omotola Jalade-Ekeinde was shooting the VH1 drama series *Hit the Floor* in February, 2013, she started live-tweeting from the set, describing the Paramount lot and calling her colleague Kimberly Elise "a beautiful Method actor." That tweet in particular seemed to say so much all at once: that a Nollywood star can thrive when 8,000 miles from home and filming scenes with an American costar; that she can classify that costar's performance style according to what is perhaps the most revered model of realist acting; that she can join forces with a fellow woman of color in order to furnish a reflection of global "girl power" (the tweet came with the hashtag "GirlsRock"); and that she can define her own ever-evolving identity as a truly boundless one. This tweet alone displays the notion that Nollywood's star system well equips its constituents to achieve expansive success. Omotola Jalade-Ekeinde has, as she says, "the power" to infiltrate American popular culture; the proof is in the Instagram photos that she provides—the charming self-portraits of the Nigerian star weaving her way through a Melrose Avenue lot with the legendary Paramount banner as a backdrop.

When a star like Omotola travels to Hollywood, she demonstrates the possibility of respecting Nollywood's specificity—its celebrated self-development outside of state support and foreign subsidies—while simultaneously linking it, via the visibility of stardom itself, to production sites in

Los Angeles. VH1's *Hit the Floor* may not represent a Hollywood-Nollywood coproduction in the conventional economic sense, but it still makes use of a performer whose star was born within the boundaries of southern Nigerian films. Conceivably, Jalade-Ekeinde's travels to Hollywood help shed light upon the singularity of Nollywood without necessarily introducing a qualitative dimension or suggesting a hierarchical relationship between the two industries. If Nollywood develops star performers whose identities become so widely known and so wildly popular that Hollywood begins to take notice, and if such stars as Jalade-Ekeinde accept acting gigs in Los Angeles, then Nollywood and Hollywood do not necessarily converge in typical ways. VH1's *Hit the Floor* is not, after all, an international coproduction; it remains very much an American project. But one of its performers is a Nollywood legend.

FROM TELEVISION TO "CINEMA": BILLING VIDEO STARS

In focusing on Jalake-Ekeinde's actions in Hollywood, I am perhaps getting ahead of myself. How, after all, did the actress become a star in the first place? What is her persona's special significance in Nollywood, and how does the industry develop stars more generally? Such questions are rarely asked in scholarship on Nollywood, if only because the matters of narrative, aesthetics, economics, and access—not to mention of nation, region, race, and culture—have been so pressing. But one could easily argue that without stars, such industrial factors simply *would not* matter, precisely because Nollywood, as popularly defined, would not really exist. "Evidence of a Nigerian star system dates back at least as early as 1992," writes Stefan Sereda, "apparent in the opening credits of the best-selling *Living in Bondage*."[1] While he does not elaborate, Sereda is right to look to on-screen credit sequences for evidence of stardom in operation. Indeed, *Living in Bondage* functioned, in part, to publicize a host of well-known Nigerian television stars as, suddenly and specifically, movie stars, using its opening-credit sequence to signal a new set of professional terms for Francis Agu and Kanayo O. Kanayo, among other beloved performers. Broadly speaking, the politics of billing, in which one performer's name will inevitably appear before (or larger than) another's, can lead to illuminating superimpositions—"juxtaposed graphic signifiers of stardom and success," to quote Lisa Kernan.[2]

The significance of the on-screen (opening or closing) credit sequence should not be underestimated. Jonathan Gray argues that such sequences serve "to create genre, character, and tone," but surely they also function to foreground stardom, literally showing who comes first in the panoply of performers.[3] The one-name-after-another crawl of a credit sequence is perhaps the clearest textual indication of a hierarchy of actors and actresses—of a behind-the-scenes star system with demonstrable on-screen effects (such as, for instance, a performer's precise role and time spent in front of the camera). Anyone who regularly watches Nollywood films has surely had to sit through more than a few elaborate, impossibly prolonged opening-credit sequences in which superimposed performers' names slowly fade in and out, or in which such names become legible through digital pixels that explode into different directions in order to make way for the next credit.[4] Such sequences usually end, as in Western media, with the identification of the director, reflecting Nollywood's auteurist culture and also inviting auteurist analyses. But they also, invariably, illuminate particular pecking orders among performers, some of which might seem surprising.

Consider, for instance, the case of *Emotional Crack* (Lancelot Oduwa Imasuen, 2003). In this film, Stephanie Okereke plays the lead role, that of Crystal, a battered housewife who has an affair with her husband's mistress, Camilla (Dakore Egbuson). Despite the fact that Okereke has by far the most screen time, her name appears fourth in the opening credits, reflecting a stardom that was, for the performer, nascent in 2003 and easily eclipsed by that of three others (two of whose names appear before the film's title): Ramsey Nouah (who plays Crystal's abusive husband, Chudi), Patience Ozokwor (popularly known as Mama G, who plays Crystal's protective mother, Magdalene), and Dakore Egbuson. Befitting images that were well-established and widely celebrated by 2003, Nouah and Ozokwor are the two above-the-title stars, and Egbuson is the performer whose name appears immediately after the words "Emotional Crack" but before Okereke's credit.

Viewed today, in the wake of Okereke's ascension to the ranks of Nollywood's most prolific and itinerant writers, directors, and performers, the opening credit sequence of *Emotional Crack* might seem strange and somewhat misleading as an entrée into the narrative's breakdown of characters. Okereke, however, has frequently been at the center of similarly odd or inaccurate billing practices: in the opening credits of Teco Benson's 2002 thriller

Terror, the words "Introducing Stephanie Okereke" are superimposed over a shot of her character typing away on an office computer; Okereke, in fact, began acting in 1997 at the age of fifteen, when she appeared (albeit in relatively small roles) in multiple Nollywood films. An equally deceptive credit occurred in 2009, when the first posters advertising the Nigerian theatrical release of Izu Ojukwu's *Nnenda* gave Okereke fourth billing, after the male stars Francis Duru, Ramsey Nouah, and Uti Nwachukwu, despite the fact that Okereke (who was by then a major international star) plays the prominent title role. Suggesting a level of sexism incommensurate with *Nnenda*'s feminist narrative (the film follows an intrepid activist as she seeks to reform orphanages), the initial, controversial posters also signaled an opportunistic attachment to reality television: Uti Nwachukwu, who received billing above Okereke despite his comparably scant screen time and short Nollywood résumé, had represented Nigeria on the third season of *Big Brother Africa*, becoming a fan favorite and later winning the series' fifth season, titled *All-Stars*. But was it really a movie-style stardom that Nwachukwu had earned with his reality-TV victory or just a reasonable degree of name recognition and an associated commercial cachet? As Julie Wilson argues, reality television stardom represents a culturally debased yet readily salable phenomenon, one that is frequently defined against a more "genuine," intricate, or intelligent cinema stardom. When reality stars attempt to shift toward this more respectable echelon, they are often stymied by the publicity circuits that, in Wilson's words, "do not primarily work to construct a broader star image" for each of the individuals in question, and that prefer to function within limited rhetorical constructs ("the 'good girl,' the 'scheming bitch,' the 'average joe,' the 'homophobic jock'"). Publicity for reality TV thus acknowledges that the format's stars must "play roles"—that each is compelled to "perform an identity"—but it does not, generally speaking, allow for much flexibility, in contrast to more searching coverage of bona fide film stars.[5]

In Nigeria, the culturally denigrated status of reality-TV stardom is arguably a function of the reality format itself rather than a reflection of television's "lesser" status vis-à-vis cinema, in large part due to the longstanding lack of extensive moviegoing opportunities for Nigerians. Within the nation's particular postcolonial circumstances, the small screen has always been an acceptable place for stardom, if only because it has often seemed like the *only* place, the *only* available medium. However, the television stardom that served to publicize *Living in Bondage* as a repository of professional acting talent, with its roots primarily in scripted dramas (such as the 1990s soap opera *Checkmate*, starring Francis Agu), is not the same as that which would influence the billing of *Nnenda*. Nowadays, Nollywood producers are less likely to turn to local soap operas than to a plentiful crop of globally popular reality television programs in order to select some already-famous faces—some widely publicized if relatively untested talents. In fact, Nollywood's growing reliance on reality television for a roster of ready-made stars has transformed the opening credit sequences of numerous films into promotions not simply for the stars themselves but also for the TV programs out of which they first emerged. Nwachukwu, Karen Igho, and Tonto Dikeh are three major Nigerian stars whose earliest Nollywood credits centralized their reality-TV credentials, often in openly celebratory ways. The 2008 film *The Celebrity* (Lancelot Oduwa Imasuen), for instance, features the following on-screen credit, stylized typographically through various fonts and colors, and ending in an exclamation mark: "Introducing Ofunneka Molokwu of *Big Brother Africa* as Esther!"

If reality television, however widely consumed, is also, and simultaneously, widely denigrated throughout Nigeria—a point that Wole Soyinka made in his extensive keynote speech at FESPACO in 2013—then Nollywood producers would seem to be responding unapologetically to a pronounced popular appetite for the format's stars.[6] Perhaps, in employing such hyperbolically celebratory credits as the one quoted above, Nollywood films that rely upon reality-TV stars also work to defuse or preempt a public backlash, implanting the notion that such stars, whose names appear alongside those of the industry's legendary leading lights, are themselves worthy of considerable esteem. But to what extent are they professional performers? With what thespian tools are they able to act for the camera? It has become increasingly difficult to argue that the star of a reality-television franchise like *Big Brother* is ever unaware of the mechanisms of the franchise's production and transnational dissemination. Indeed, the structures of monitoring that feature so prominently on *Big Brother* and that lend the franchise its name lead inevitably to contestants who "play to the cameras," but who also, as competitors, seek to out-act each other. This call to consciously perform was especially pronounced during Uti Nwachukwu's season of *Big Brother Africa*, on which he was pitted against contestants from Ghana, Malawi,

Uganda, Zimbabwe, Mozambique, Botswana, Zambia, Tanzania, Kenya, Ethiopia, Angola, and South Africa, each of whom sought to suppress a "personal secret" as part of the season's effort to further mystify the boundaries among a wide range of African national "traits." For Meryl Shikwambane, a South African contestant forced to feign a lack of worldliness (in alleged contrast to an "expected" South African cosmopolitanism), that secret involved a steamy affair with an unnamed Namibian celebrity; for Tatiana Dos Santos Durao, a contestant from Angola, it entailed a refusal to reveal the extent of her singing talent, so that she could pass herself off as "simple" and unaffected, and experientially far from the thriving popular cultures of her native Luanda.

Nwachukwu, for his part, attempted to hide his intense affection for Britney Spears—a fandom that complicated his professed allegiance to the "purity" and singularity of southern Nigerian popular culture. As a Britney fan hailing from Lagos, Nwachukwu exemplified a reception practice that is transnational as well as transcultural. That it represented his mandated secret on *Big Brother Africa* suggests that it is still capable of surprising those with fixed notions of Nigerian national identity (and of associated local reception practices). If multiple modes of mobility are necessary for Nollywood stardom, then the hybridity of Nwachukwu's fandom—the devotion both to "Naija culture" as well as to Britney Spears—would seem to position him as being at least partly suited to a film industry so famously committed to expansive pop sensibilities. After all, Britney posters abound in Nollywood films, particularly in those that take place on university campuses and that feature aspirational young women who self-fashion—often across strong national, ethnic, cultural, and class boundaries—while oversized images of the American pop star stare approvingly down at them. For instance, in *Jénífà* (Muhydeen S. Ayinde, 2008), Funke Akindele's title character (née Suliat), in attempting to transform herself from a strictly Yorùbá-speaking "razz village girl" into a post-ethnic campus diva, finds a measure of inspiration in the Britney posters that adorn the walls of various dorm rooms, reflecting a relatively mutable American star persona (spanning Spears's somewhat discrepant adolescent, young-adult, and post-"meltdown" phases). In the case of Uti Nwachukwu, however, a real-life reliance on Britney Spears as a source of encouragement is not, in itself, enough to establish him as a Nollywood-style star, as the *Nnenda* credit controversy makes clear. There, the issue was less Nwachukwu's reality-television origins—less his one-time role-playing "as himself"—than his résumé's restriction to *Big Brother Africa*. If his public persona has not yet undergone a series of shifts, it is due not to Nwachukwu's refusal to "reinvent" it (à la the maneuverable Ms. Spears) but instead to the scarcity of his major film roles, a preponderance of which would, in the ever-evolving Nollywood, demand consistent refashioning.

BEYOND "MERE CELEBRITY": CONSTRUCTING CINEMA STARDOM

There are, according to cliché, two types of film performers—those who, like Nwachukwu, appear to play themselves, and those whose fame rests upon a capacity for change.[7] In cinema studies, however, there is a strong yet surprisingly underexposed subfield devoted to bridging the gap between these two perceived types. It goes by the name "star studies," and its central tenets are as follows: film stardom is a discursive construction developed and maintained through a variety of semiotic means; an individual star persona is mutable (albeit in often subtle ways and regardless of personal or corporate protestations); and the operations of a so-called star system provide an important window through which to look not simply at a series of film texts but also at entire film industries.[8] In Nollywood, some of the top stars might seem equally unalterable, enshrined in typecasting and consistently associated with the genres that they have helped to develop—such as, in the case of Okereke, the lesbian-themed campus drama (in which young, female-identified university students explore same-sex desire).[9] For Okereke—an especially in-demand and relatively well-paid actress—that genre represents only one facet of the kaleidoscopic Nollywood, whose producers, she maintains, "reward" her by permitting her to pursue a whole host of performance modes (from comedy to drama to just about every imaginable hybrid in between).[10] Simply put, an industry as dizzyingly productive as Nollywood would seem to need a certain, stabilizing degree of standardization, but with productivity comes possibility—innumerable chances to change as a performer and to evolve as a star, even within seemingly fixed generic confines.

Perhaps no Nollywood star better exemplifies this expansive potential than Liz Benson. Mere months after starring in *Glamour Girls*, Benson rose to new prominence by playing three significantly discrepant roles in a single film—Chika Onukwufor's 1995 melodrama *True Confession,* written and produced by Kenneth Nnebue. Benson's capacity to portray various ages, gender identities, and temperaments is characteristic of the talents of Nollywood's top stars; through Benson's performances *True Confession* offers a crucial distillation of the industry's pronounced yet understudied openness to change. Stars literally embody this openness, physicalizing diverse aspirations and appearing as hypervisible ambassadors of adaptability. However, as Jonathan Haynes suggests, Nollywood's immense annual output both requires and is the direct result of an "imitative and generic" process that Haynes, Onookome Okome, and Karin Barber have all linked to commercialized African popular arts in general—to the precise material conditions that tend to prescribe standardization and repetition.[11] Since star studies, as a discipline, endeavors to elucidate what Marsha Orgeron calls the "multiple mediations"

of stardom—including those that seem "unextraordinary, or even... shamefully unworthy," such as salacious news items planted by producers for the purposes of publicity—it can serve, in the context of the seemingly monotonous Nollywood, to clarify the complex industrial permutations that depend upon, and extend, powerful public personae.[12] At the same time, star studies can shed light upon the widely disseminated idea that Nollywood stardom is open to all Nigerians, both local and diasporic, and that stardom is the result of labor, rather than some amorphous sense of exceptionality.

The career of Stephanie Okereke offers considerable insight into the efforts of Nollywood stars to expand the parameters of their public images. If Nollywood producers indeed honor Okereke by offering her a variety of gigs, such a strategy is neither constant nor qualitatively consistent. When her options are scarce or seem unsavory, Okereke, who has a master's degree from the New York Film Academy, simply creates her own opportunities, bypassing traditional Nigerian funding sources to produce her own scripts. In 2008, for instance, Okereke wrote, directed, and starred in *Through the Glass*, a romantic comedy set in southern California about a freewheeling young man who discovers an abandoned infant on his doorstep. He enlists the help of his Nigerian neighbor (played by Okereke) to cope with the stress of caring for a child. Shot in Carson, California, and distributed internationally by Okereke's own company, Next Page Productions, *Through the Glass* premiered at a gala event at Hollywood's Pacific Design Center, received well-publicized theatrical bookings in Europe and Australia, and earned a Best Screenplay nomination at the African Movie Academy Awards. In seeking to further diversify her star image, Okereke turned to graduate school in New York City, financing sources in Houston and Atlanta, production in the greater Los Angeles area, and red-carpet premieres on no fewer than four continents. *Through the Glass*, which was screened out of competition at the 2010 Cannes Film Festival, would later become the first Nigerian feature to open commercially at a Swiss cinema. Back in the United States, Okereke received an award of recognition from the California Legislature and the city of Carson. Citing her "truly global stardom," the award honored Okereke

Facing. Figure 1.1. "You work to be what you're not": Toyin Alausa on the labors of "transformative" Nollywood stardom. *Image courtesy of California Newsreel.*

for shooting her film on location and thereby giving a boost to the Carson economy.

Crucially, in writing the screenplay for *Through the Glass,* Okereke managed to create a character unlike any she had previously played—a wise Nigerian expatriate who, in coming to the aid of a sheltered, ethnocentric American, teaches him to appreciate a "Naija cuisine" that includes egusi soup and pounded yam. Screenwriting provided an opportunity for Okereke to adjust her own global image, and it remains a major means through which a wide range of Nollywood stars can systematically transform their personae, providing new avenues for their performative talents. Like Okereke, the actresses Uche Jombo and Funke Akindele are also major Nollywood screenwriters. Jombo has frequently collaborated with writer-producer Emem Isong, most notably on the script for *Games Men Play* (Lancelot Oduwa Imasuen, 2006), in which Kate Henshaw's Tara, a young production assistant for a popular television talk show (whose imperious host is played by Monalisa Chinda), must research men's dating habits for an upcoming episode. Suspecting that some of the best stories can be found close to home, Tara eventually meets with her pregnant twin sister, Tracy (played by Jombo), whose unfaithful husband (Jim Iyke) is a self-described sex addict, unashamedly attached to his young mistress, Angel (Dakore Egbuson).

While Henshaw has the juiciest role—and while Chinda delivers a delicious impersonation of a bombastic, Oprah-style talk-show host—Jombo brings a welcome calm to much of the movie, infusing her early scenes with a strong sense of Tracy's quiet integrity. Eventually, however, the character snaps, albeit in a believably modulated way. When an emboldened Angel visits Tracy at the latter's office complex (where she is a top executive with numerous employees), she finds, to her surprise, that Tracy is unwilling to engage in a cat fight. Instead, she sits behind her vast desk, remaining silent and stock-still as she listens to Angel berate her for being "fat" and therefore "unfit" for the role of wife. "You don't do your husband justice," Angel says, shamelessly goading Tracy and hoping for an emotional eruption from the other woman—the kind of violent outburst that would warrant retaliation. The strong-willed Tracy does not stoop to Angel's level, however; she does not give her husband's mistress the satisfaction of seeing her squirm. Later, however, she bravely confronts said husband with a single, shaming complaint. "I can take about anything from you," she says, "ranging from your late-night comings to your cheating, but what I will *not* have is being insulted in my office, right in the presence of my workers, by your idiot of a mistress." When the husband, Taiwo, attempts to defend himself, Tracy preempts his protestations by declaring, "It's obvious that you don't have any respect for me." Leaving Taiwo to cope with the emotional mess that he himself has created, the rejuvenated Tracy walks confidently away.

Even within the confines of a single film script and in the service of a single character, Uche Jombo managed to establish a series of discrepant performance modes for herself, extending from the mostly mute yet always facially expressive calm of Tracy's earliest scenes to the vocal dynamism required for the dramatic diatribes of the film's denouement. Paying close attention to the emotional range that a Nollywood star displays within a single film provides one way of highlighting that star's relative immunity to typecasting. In Jombo's case, this tactic depends upon a recognition of the star's own writing ambitions—of her willingness to create, in the scripting stage, a multidimensional role for herself, one that was both unlike her previous roles and also impossible to pin down, to pigeonhole on its own terms. Tracy is all but unclassifiable, neither silent housewife nor vengeful harridan, and neither completely acquiescent nor fully unforgiving. She is, as Tracy herself points out, "a woman with many selves," and a complex inner life that Jombo, as an actress, communicates wordlessly, through her ever-expressive eyes. (Watch the way they convey Tracy's untold knowledge of the "games men play" during a meeting with her patronizing, chattering sister, Tara; notice, as well, the way they stare threateningly ahead, unblinking and utterly disbelieving, as Angel outlines Tracy's alleged shortcomings.) Fittingly, Tracy shares some screen time with Chinda's Abby Davis ("Yes, *that* Abby Davis—the big star, the talk-show host," as Tara puts it in her voice-over narration). As the host of "Abby's Corner," a popular television program, Abby has a platform from which to dispense advice to the women of Lagos, whom she collectively positions with the pronoun "you." However, while this proverbial you "may not know about a new and truly sociopathic" form of infidelity, it is not as if Abby, in her private life, is particularly enlightened on the topic. In melodramatic fashion, Abby fails to heed her own advice, and exhibits an embarrassing lack of knowledge of the subjects that she herself addresses on her show. That is largely because, as Tara declares in voice-over, Abby is a mere mouthpiece, a figurehead—the show's on-screen star, not its well-informed, behind-the-scenes researcher, a role that Tara has proudly and professionally assumed. In her personal affairs, the otherwise confident Abby must contend with her hustler boyfriend, Richmond (Mike Ezuruonye), as well as with his money-hungry "woman on the side," Tayo (Ini Edo), who hopes to acquire some of Abby's vast wealth.

As the complicated character of Abby makes clear, Jombo and Emem Isong were not interested in turning Tracy into their script's only multidimensional woman. Apart from the obvious professional and experiential discrepancies, the principal distinction between Abby and Tracy lies in their divergent responses to the knowledge of infidelity. While Abby must maintain, for the sake of her show, a front of unremitting omnipotence that contrasts with her private pain and surprise over the misdeeds of men, Tracy is able to openly acknowledge her own ignorance, and then work to expunge it once and for all. As she acquires more information—a wider awareness of Taiwo's mendacity—Tracy becomes increasingly confident, a self-styled "survivor" who is able to "bounce back from abuse." Two years later, Jombo would write an entirely different character for herself—the neurotic diva of *The Celebrity* (Lancelot Oduwa Imasuen, 2008), who is, in many ways, Tracy's opposite. Where Tracy, in *Games Men Play*, is modest and deferential before becoming powerfully, justifiably denunciatory, Nnene, in *The Celebrity*, is arrogant and accusatory from the start—and also a drunk who yet manages, in her occasional moments of sobriety, to cogently describe the obstacles to emotional stability that she daily faces as a major public figure, a woman whose every move is charted and commented on. The source of the character's extremely low self-esteem, however, is never clarified, but it appears to be related to the culture of gossip that characterizes public and private responses to Nnene's celebrity. That last word, in particular, is itself a factor in Nnene's tarnished pride, for she is not, as she laments, a "true star" but instead a "mere celebrity," which means—in terms that have been central to academic star studies—that she is "famous for being famous," rather than for being a talented, self-constructing, salaried performer. In relation to her education and career, Nnene is considerably more than, say, a Kim Kardashian or a Paris Hilton, but her celebrity makes her long to be "something better."

Crucially, Nnene recognizes that fame, for her, will not go away. As a well-known lawyer for a public relations firm—and as a woman whose low self-image is widely recognized among her "fans," who publicly lament her lack of success in securing fidelity from a young footballer—Nnene hopes to transition into a career as a Nollywood film actress. In her estimation, she is already famous, already the subject of gossip, so why can she not also be a Nollywood star? By Nnene's reckoning, such a star is inevitably analyzed by a broad public, but she is also respected as an actress rather than derided as a celebrity—acclaimed for her performance skills instead of condemned as a "simple solicitor." The deliriously depressed and self-deluding Nnene hopes to give up the law for an "easier" pursuit, which she believes Nollywood stardom to be, thus demonstrating a level of ignorance incommensurate with her friends' sophisticated understanding of "what it takes to make it in acting." At the same time, however, Nnene clearly understands that a culture of gossip "comes with the territory" for Nollywood stars—that such stars are scrutinized, sometimes in unseemly ways. She also accepts that transformative acting is a precondition for prominence in Nollywood's star system.

With this requirement in mind, Nnene decides to get her feet wet by disguising her voice and impersonating an invented persona—a growling, wheezing woman named Miss Duke. It is as this fictional character that Nnene calls the television studio where her close friend, Jess (Omotola Jalade-Ekeinde), serves as the host of a popular talk show—a live daily broadcast that requires Jess to dispense advice to the lovelorn. Like Monalisa Chinda's Abby Davis in *Games Men Play*, however, Jess is too busy fretting over the lives of others to see that she herself is in need of some assistance, particularly in the romance department. When Nnene phones the show, as part of a segment connecting Jess with "real people," she hopes not only to successfully enact a new, fictional persona but also to convey her own pressing questions about life and love. Nnene, in dropping her voice to a low, broken, raspy register, may sound like someone else—may acoustically embody this "Miss Duke"—but she is still inextricably Nnene, down to her desperate desire to know what to do about the men who do not love her. Jess, the consummate professional, humors her, helping to maintain the illusion that she is indeed speaking to "Miss Duke"—a stranger who is decidedly unlucky in love. Later, however, Jess encounters Nnene outside of the studio. Giddy over her transformative performance, Nnene first announces her dream of becoming "an actress in one of those Nollywood films," then confesses to having "played a role" for Jess, as the depressed Miss Duke. "So . . . did you know it was me calling your show?" she asks, grinning. "Of course I knew it was you!" replies the cruelly condescending Jess. "I don't know any other girl with such low self-esteem!"

If Nnene's own "pathetic" personality type shines through any performance, however technically successful in terms of vocal mimicry, then Jess' triumph as a talk-show host is that her professional self-presentation is all but impregnable. However chaotic her private life may be, onscreen she is the very image of implacability, a doyenne doling out advice. Where she errs, however, is in directly addressing her equally famous friends during her broadcasts, gazing into the camera and declaring Nnene to be "in need of help." If Chinda's lordly Abby Davis, in *Games Men Play*, evokes Oprah, then Omotola Jalade-Ekeinde's somewhat more accessible Jess suggests the Wendy Williams who, on her globally syndicated television talk show, similarly engages her famous acquaintances through direct appeals (for instance, chiding Mary J. Blige for appearing in a disastrously misconceived Burger King commercial in 2012). Jess, on her show (titled *Emotions with Jess*), employs two modes of the second-person pronoun "you," shifting effortlessly from the "you" of nonspecific collective address to the "you" of a more personalized approach. In the sequel to *The Celebrity*, titled *Last Celebrity* (Lancelot Oduwa Imasuen, 2008), Jess becomes increasingly ambitious as she embraces her own professionalism at the expense of her friendships. At one point, with Nnene at home watching, Jess affects concern and, leaning forward, says to the camera, "I have a special message for you, Nnene. I hope you are listening to me." Describing her as "one of my best friends," but also as a woman who is "always making excuses for her man," Jess positions Nnene as a victim of low self-esteem and, significantly, as a public figure "relevant" to the rest of Jess's viewers (who comprise that other "you"). Addressing Nnene through a live television broadcast, Jess asks, "Now, why do you have to make excuses for your man, or even say you're sorry when you've done absolutely nothing wrong? Trust me; that is so, so wrong. The minute you start to do that, something is amiss; something is definitely wrong." The repeated use of the word "wrong" amounts to an insistent shaming tactic, an incantatory way for Jess to berate her friend without the possibility of that friend fighting back, or otherwise interrupting.

At this point in Jess's monologue, the diegetic camera—that of the television show itself—cuts to a close-up of Jess's feet, then slowly pans up her bare legs to end, finally, on a standard shot of her face. Such a baldly objectifying trajectory is the result of the male camera operator's combined lust and incompetence, and Jess knows it, although it is a measure of her professionalism that she does not let this distasteful knowledge impinge upon her composure, does not let it destabilize the illusion that she is utterly unperturbed, coolly supplying guidance to her alleged friend. Addressing Nnene, Jess, who is seated on a green leather sofa, flanked by yellow flowers, and with an opulent red-and-blue velvet curtain behind her, says, "However you want to be treated in your relationship totally depends on you. You want some respect, demand it. And don't you forget to give it!" The film then cuts to Nnene, seated in her living room, watching Jess on her television set and shaking her head in drunken defeat—a far cry from the Tracy who, in *Games Men Play*, does not need to be told how to command respect.

Consciously avoiding typecasting by writing many of her own scripts, Jombo has created a collection of dramatically discrepant characters, no two less alike than Tracy and Nnene. In 2011, Jombo established her own production company, Uche Jombo Studios (UJS), where she collaborated with writer Rita C. Onwurah on the screenplay for *Damage* (Moses Inwang, 2011), which focuses on a woman (played by Jombo) who is both a victim and a perpetrator of spousal abuse. The first in a series of UJS-produced films about contemporary social problems, *Damage* gave Jombo a unique opportunity as an actress: the challenge of portraying a smart, self-aware woman who willingly enables a toxic relationship and who "gives as good as she gets." *Damage* deviates from an earlier Nollywood depiction of spousal abuse: 2003's *Emotional Crack*, whose central character, Stephanie Okereke's Crystal, is quite the opposite of Jombo's Sarah, both in professional style as well as in personal temperament. Where the well-educated Crystal is strictly a victim, reluctantly fighting back only through words, the crass, spoiled Sarah throws as many punches as she receives, and even instigates several scenes of sheer battery, at one point throwing a large vase at her husband's head. Crystal's spouse, Chudi, openly, even proudly spouts gender essentialist notions, claiming that Crystal's occasional expressions of independence are "unnatural"; he wants her to remain stereotypically subservient to him, like "a good Nigerian woman." ("I will teach you to be a housewife!" he shouts while slapping her.) After learning that Crystal has secretly applied for—and accepted—a job at a prestigious Lagos accounting firm, Chudi explodes, and Crystal is forced to stand up for herself. "You just want to degrade me and keep me in the house like a piece of furniture?" she asks, defending her decision to use her advanced degrees and seek employment. "Yes," replies Chudi, who beats her to the point of bruising her face, rendering her, as she says, "unsightly."

By contrast, Taiwo (Kalu Ikeagwu), Sarah's husband in *Damage*, resents his wife's financial reliance on her wealthy family, and wishes she would get "a real job," one whose tasks might require more than "doling out daddy's money to various charities." Despite his disgust over Sarah's class background, Taiwo is perfectly willing to "show her off" to the public, even when her body bears the telltale signs of spousal abuse. Taiwo himself sports some visible, wife-inflicted wounds, and while several subsidiary characters in *Emotional Crack* complain about the way that the bruised Crystal looks ("He's practicing his boxing skills on your face!" exclaims the character's mother), few friends of Sarah and Taiwo are actually aware of the extent of their marital problems, preferring instead to invest in the image of conjugal bliss that they present to the public. *Damage* begins, in fact, with this socially prominent couple's red-carpet arrival at the fictional "Recognition Awards." Seated in the back of a stretch limousine, Sarah and Taiwo are slated to accept a "couple of the year" prize from a glamorous collective composed of the most prominent Nigerians. Like Nnene, Jombo's character in *The Celebrity* and *Last Celebrity,* Sarah is "famous for being famous"—not a movie star but a socialite. However, while Nnene's "fans" know all about her disastrous romantic entanglements, Sarah's "public" is blind to the abuse that she both suffers and inflicts—hence the "couple of the year" award that is so naively presented to her and to Taiwo.

The event that centralizes this award is a typically splashy affair, reminiscent of a Nollywood movie premiere. Indeed, within a mode of sheer self-reflexivity, *Damage* shows several Nollywood stars (among them Osita Iheme and Chinedu Ikedieze) arriving on the red carpet, posing for pictures, stopping to sign autographs and to submit to interviews with various Nigerian print and television outlets, generally conferring glamour and excitement upon the occasion. (At one point, Jombo's longtime collaborator, the producer-screenwriter Emem Isong, arrives to receive a prize of her own—a kind of lifetime achievement award celebrating her contributions to Nollywood movies.) Inside their stretch limo, however, Sarah and Taiwo are not pleased, partly because they know that, as mere socialites, they're out of their depth among Nollywood's power players. They also, however, know that they would be accepting their "couple of the year" award under false pretenses. "I guess there's no point in going after all," Taiwo admits, to which Sarah replies, "Yes, because it would be a lie." The film then flashes back six months to the morning when Taiwo dragged Sarah down one flight of stairs, and she pushed him down another. Throughout the remainder of the film's narrative, Sarah demonstrates both her self-respect and her self-delusion, defending her right to "hit back" but also failing to foresee the harm that her violence will continue to cause as her two young children struggle to evade their parents' toxic relationship. At the film's U.S. premiere in Atlanta, Jombo described the singular significance of Sarah in her panoply of Nollywood film protagonists, calling the character "an original"—a complex and contradictory figure created first through Jombo's screenwriting efforts and later through a performance style that did not shy away from revealing the less savory aspects of Sarah's personality. From the contrasting Tracy and Nnene to the all-but-unclassifiable Sarah in *Damage*, Jombo has written as well as acted her way toward a multidirectional star persona.

Quite apart from the matter of deliberate performative development, however, is that of the "accidental" persona shift, which can occur even when performers and producers agree to provide something comfortingly familiar—something standardized and redundant. In other words, the unstable, ultimately productive meanings that Jonathan Haynes links to location shooting—to the documentary value of a "background" reality, caught on the fly by itinerant cameras—are not the only sources of unexpected variations in seemingly constant plots and themes.[13] Similarly unplanned patterns of signification can accrue to the stars who (occasionally by contract, but most frequently by informal agreement) must promote their films in a range of venues for a diversity of audiences throughout West Africa and the diaspora—and who, in any case, often experiment as performers, even within the confines of "franchise" roles.[14]

If, as Karin Barber contends, consumers are as instrumental as producers in keeping African popular arts alive, then those Nollywood films that focus on stardom conceivably satisfy their audiences in unique ways: as a series of Ghanaian and Nigerian theater managers have suggested over the past few years, such films can "flatter" filmgoers by furnishing an "insider" feel—appearing to obliterate the boundaries between production and consumption, between "backstage" processes and the onscreen representations to which they give rise.[15] They can also, on an even simpler level, confirm for filmgoers what they already know, particularly if they read those print and online publications that address the central components of Nollywood's star system. These components include the promise that anyone can become a star, and that the hard work of self-promotion is universally practicable. Reflexive, star-driven films about stardom itself—of which there are seemingly endless examples—tend to suggest that Lagos, Nigeria is not unlike Los Angeles, California: a metonym not merely for movie glamour but also for unceasing industrial activity and the shared consciousness of stars and their fans.

PRACTICAL MAGIC: THE BASIC INFRASTRUCTURE OF FILM STARDOM IN SOUTHERN NIGERIA

Plastered throughout Lagos, audition notices—typically eight-by-ten paper sheets upon which is printed information about when, where, and for what films one can "try out"—often seek to fill minor or even non-speaking roles, but they also tend to identify the allegedly democratic aspects of Nollywood's star system. In June, 2011, for instance, a much-mimeographed, far-reaching flier for a "contemporary religious movie set to star Oge Okoye," whose producers were "looking for patient cast members," promised that "stardom can come for anyone," since "all it takes is a simple start." Indeed, the age span identified as the most desirable, twenty-five to fifty-five, would seem so vast as to embrace a variety of adult "types," and upholding "patience" appears to suggest a rather broad, fulfillable set of expectations; after all, who could not claim to be patient, at least on occasion? Such seemingly egalitarian assurances are not necessarily reflective of the reality of Nollywood's star system: since the industry is still so young, so too are the stars who emerged as such during the late 1990s, including Genevieve Nnaji, Ramsey Nouah, Desmond Elliot, and Omotola Jalade-Ekeinde, not one of whom needs to be "phased out" for having aged. Indeed, each is now more popular than ever, as evidenced by his or her employment records, iconic presence on Nigerian magazine covers, and participation in diasporic modes of publicity (Jalade-Ekeinde, for instance, recently made *Time* magazine's list of the 100 most influential people in the world, and shortly thereafter appeared as herself on VH1's *Hit the Floor*). If the films that they have most recently completed offer any indication, Nnaji, Nouah, Elliot, and Jalade-Ekeinde are all still expected to portray young romantic leads, although iconic actress Uche Jombo, who is still in her thirties, has suggested the pressures that come with aging (particularly for women)—pressures that Jombo, as a prolific screenwriter, has woven into her work, especially *The Celebrity* and its sequel. Indeed, Jombo's professional identity as a "multi-hyphenate"—an actress-director-producer-screenwriter—is hardly rare in an industry whose budgetary restrictions have long required individuals to perform numerous duties on film sets, often for a single, fixed fee.[16]

When Jombo and Funke Akindele—to take just two prominent examples—write scripts about Nollywood stardom, and eventually embody those scripts' central characters, it is difficult for audiences not to see certain connections between performer and role. In fact, searching for such connections—a process aided and abetted by such Nollywood-centered magazines as *FAB*, *African Vibes*, *Reading Bridges*, *Complete Fashion*, *Exquisite*, *Flair*, *Totally Whole*, and *Nollywood Divas Awards Magazine*, which routinely publish both behind-the-scenes accounts of Nollywood film productions and intimate interviews with individual stars—can constitute a distinctly pleasurable activity. While magazine profiles, like printed audition notices, would seem to privilege the literate (and thereby limit the level of egalitarianism involved), the proliferation of "candid" star photographs, in the popular press as well as on promotional posters, television, and the internet, helps to identify certain star-specific "personal" traits that can then be tested against the very same stars' on-screen self-representations.[17]

As dramatized in a climactic sequence in *Last Celebrity*—in which Jombo's Nnene expresses her concerns about aging in the face of "fresh new talent" (a monologue that Jombo wrote)—considerable competition for film stardom comes not necessarily from the ranks of "real people" but from the commodified, heavily promoted realm of African reality television.[18] For example, in the third installment of Ubong Bassey Nya's now-iconic *BlackBerry Babes* trilogy (2011–2012), Karen Igho, formerly a contestant on *Big Brother Africa*, makes her Nollywood debut. Identified in the opening credits as "Karen Igho of *Big Brother Africa*," she plays a rural outsider hoping to scheme her way into the inner circle of the film series' titular women—an ultraglamorous group of BlackBerry fetishists, each of whom is played by a major star (from Oge Okoye to Tonto Dikeh) willing to provide a winking awareness of her own public persona, contributing to the complex reflexivity of the series itself. Now a bona fide film star—a status solidified by the widely publicized, cleavage-baring dress that she wore to the 2013 Africa Magic Viewers' Choice Awards, which further complicated her public persona (even to the point of rendering it intensely controversial)—Igho symbolizes not simply the longstanding synergy between Nollywood and Nigerian television, but also the very promise that is at the heart of the global reality-TV genre: that "real people," picked from a crowd, can become stars fit for the front pages.[19] That Igho has managed to translate her reality-TV renown into a thriving film career has much to do with her persona's visible maneuverability: a Google image search for "Karen Igho" yields an astonishing assortment of fashions, hairstyles, and makeup choices, not to mention an array of readily distinguishable film characters. If Igho has succeeded in transcending the "trashy" echelons of "mere celebrity" to become something more than a reality-TV star, then she has clearly labored for the opportunity.

In Nollywood, stardom alone does not guarantee a high salary for film appearances. While precise figures are impossible to come by, owing to the informality of an industry where bookkeeping is not a priority, it is important to set a few plausible parameters. Published accounts, both popular and academic, tend toward hyperbole, either arguing that Nollywood stars are fabulously wealthy or dismissing the possibility that they receive adequate compensation for their work. For the vast majority of stars, the truth appears to be somewhere in between. Nevertheless, a conspicuously popular, longstanding approach in Nollywood studies is to highlight the alleged disjunction between narrative and reality, and thus between character and performer, with the effect of suggesting that stars routinely lie about their incomes, boasting in the manner of a charismatic 419 schemer for whom true affluence is but a masquerade. Writing in the mid-1990s, Wole Ogundele argued that Nollywood actors "are nowhere near half as rich in real life as the characters they play"—a true enough assertion at the time of *Living in Bondage* and *Glamour Girls,* but one that makes no distinction between an unknown performer and a bona fide star.[20] In the years since, as earnings have gradually gone up, the presumption that Nollywood stars are poor has persisted, almost to the point of cliché. In 2008, at the nadir of Nollywood's crisis of overproduction, Nigeria's *Tell* magazine responded to an equal and opposite cliché—namely, the gossip-driven notion that stars are corruptly comfortable—by publishing a series of rather condescending suggestions for allegedly vulnerable, penurious performers: "Nollywood actors need to be continuously encouraged, guided, and exposed." More importantly, according to the magazine, they need to be weaned off the assumption that they can "become rich overnight," accepting instead that the "ambition to make professional films, and not the inordinate quest for wealth at all costs, should be the compelling [motivation]."[21]

Again, the refusal to distinguish between stars and the little-known performers who routinely play minor roles creates considerable confusion. Is *Tell* suggesting that Nollywood stars (as distinct from mere actors) are misleading influences on the newcomers who hope to match their levels of success? Or is the magazine saying that *all* Nollywood performers are pathetically underpaid—and perhaps pathetically hopeful about effecting positive, remunerative changes? In reality, with the average Nollywood budget reaching a mere 10 million naira (65,000 US dollars), even the most popular stars cannot expect to command more than 5 million naira (or 32,000 dollars) per movie.[22] Since in-demand stars like Okereke, Nnaji, and Jalade-Ekeinde can make up to two dozen films in a year—one of the obvious economic as well as creative perks of so prolific an industry—their annual salaries can rise to 120 million naira (or 741,000 dollars). Such figures represent only a small slice of a lucrative pie, however; they do not reflect the range of rewarding options for top stars: endorsement deals that run the gamut from the telecommunications sector to the sports world; paid television, red-carpet, and nightclub appearances; and increasingly common Hollywood gigs (like Jalade-Ekeinde's special appearance on VH1's *Hit the Floor*). Investigating the abundance of professional opportunities available to individual stars—beyond those associated with film acting—is not merely one of the mandates of star studies; it is also a way of answering basic questions about compensation and exposure.

Of course, the constant creation of new vocational options for Nollywood stars can make studying the industry seem even more daunting, but it also presents practical challenges to the producer who hopes to promote a film on the basis of a stable star persona. I was struck by this dilemma when tracking the theatrical exhibition of Niyi Akinmolayan's 2010 science-fiction film *Kajola*. One of the film's stars is Desmond Elliot—frequently a sympathetic romantic lead, the beating heart of over 200 popular films. In keeping with this hyper-familiar persona, the official posters for *Kajola* (designed by Adonis Productions) presented a warmly beaming Elliot, his face far more prominent than those of his costars. There were two problems with this presentation, one being that Elliot is not, in fact, the film's star, and the other being that the supporting role that he plays is, surprisingly, a villainous one. As a power-hungry leader in a dystopian future Nigeria, Elliot delivers a transfixing performance in *Kajola*, but his rather misleading appearance in the project's promotional materials suggests a certain reluctance (on the parts of producers) to advertise star-based change—although, ironically, such reluctance only irritated audiences who, in complaints filed with Silverbird and Ozone theater chains, described being "deceived" on multiple levels.[23] The infamous case of *Kajola*—the first (but far from the last) Nollywood film to be unceremoniously ejected from Nigerian multiplexes—complicates the familiar assumption that, from a basic economic standpoint, Nollywood *needs* consistency from its performers, that an unvarying star identity is a useful, even indispensable source of product differentiation, a way of attracting and maintaining audiences. In relation to Elliot's role in *Kajola,* audiences apparently wanted not "more of the same" but rather truth in advertising—an acknowledgement of Elliot's range as an actor, which could double in this instance as an accurate entrée into a new and challenging film.

Elliot's villainous *Kajola* character is compelling, in part, for its remarkable deviation not simply from the typical Elliot role but also from the typical Elliot biography, which upholds his offscreen status as "a wonderfully warm and loving family man."[24] Detailing the affective differences between Elliot's *Kajola* character, a man who articulates his own, devilish ideas about marriage and fatherhood, and the Elliot who, according to the "Father's Day Edition" of *Genevieve* magazine, "adores" his four kids, as well as his wife of many years, suggests a specific reception practice that star studies has long centralized.[25]

Recent attempts to "internationalize" star studies have incorporated comparative analyses of Hollywood and Bollywood, but they have largely ignored Nollywood, leading to a vast gap in the scholarly literature on stardom.[26] Most practitioners of academic, film-focused star studies, from Richard deCordova to Martin Shingler, have used Hollywood's internationally renowned, longstanding, but frequently mutating, star system as a template for analyzing the modes of publicity and of personality-shaping adopted by emerging national cinemas.[27] These familiar methods of analogizing remain valuable, but the specificity of Nollywood stardom suggests new ways of theorizing the relationship between Hollywood and African cinemas. Retaining the traditional focus of star studies on the intertextual materials, such as magazine articles and filmed public appearances, that shape a star's idiosyncratic identity and that strengthen that identity's relationship to the star's specific film industry and culture, it is possible to posit that the appearance of a star system in southern Nigeria over the past twenty years has been a uniquely transmedial phenomenon. Simply put, Nollywood's star system emerged in an era of proliferating media platforms, meaning that the complex coexistence of various popular technologies and modes of publicity has been the chief condition of possibility for stardom in southern Nigeria, rather than, as in Hollywood, an eventual, often legally and ideologically fraught option.

In Nollywood, a global, transmedial model of stardom sees performers engaging in promotional activities throughout West Africa, in venues that often require the use of multiple languages: Yorùbá, Igbo, Nigerian Standard English, Pidgin, and many more. Accents are of equal importance, particularly as a means of garnering popular acclaim for performers' linguistic and phonetic facilities. Beyond a star's shape-shifting circulation among Nigeria's thirty-six states, however, and even beyond her travels into, say, Sierra Leone and Ghana (two Anglophone African countries in which Nollywood products remain remarkably popular), there is the matter of transcontinental media flows—especially those that take Nigerian films and their stars into such diasporic locations as London, Paris, Atlanta, and Houston. Paying close attention to stars' promotional activities—a move that star studies centralizes—can yield insights into Nollywood's specific transnational victories, such as its growing popularity on satellite television channels in the United Kingdom and on the Africa-wide network Africa Magic, which originates with M-Net, South Africa's first pay-TV company. It can also, as these references to cable and satellite suggest, offer insights into the cultures of media convergence in which Nollywood plays an increasingly significant part.

In many ways, Nollywood stars have become emblems of transmediality. As soon as they have achieved star status and are therefore immediately recognizable to vast Nigerian and diasporic audiences, Nollywood performers are often recruited to promote converging media platforms, most notably VHS, VCD, DVD, analog broadcasting, and broadband digital distribution. Since December 2011, Nollywood Love, a Lagos-based online entertainment company, has been acquiring the distribution rights to thousands of Nigerian films, uploading them for viewing on a dedicated YouTube channel that boasts nearly half a million subscriptions.[28] Since its inception, Nollywood Love has relied upon Nollywood stars to promote the company. Significantly, the resultant YouTube commercials, like those for Nollywood Love's later, phenomenally popular incarnation as iROKOtv.com, provide stars with opportunities not merely to define and publicize Nollywood according to the industry's own convergent paradigms, and within the global purview afforded by the internet; they also provide opportunities for stars to practice and promote their own, diverse acting techniques.

The element of surprise embedded in these strategies is resonant with broader efforts to present Nollywood stars as capable of astonishing their audiences. Sometimes, these efforts are as explicit as the online iROKOtv ads in which a star will employ the phrase "I bet you did not know that . . ." and then complete it with a personalized declaration, such as "I speak Pidgin" or "I can use a British accent." Such ads would appear to speak not to a Nigerian audience, for whom linguistic and phonetic variations are the facts of everyday life and for whom Pidgin remains prevalent, but to diasporic audiences for whom the social realities of Nigeria—and the associated shape-shifting talents of Nollywood stars—might seem surprising. Indeed, Nollywood star images have been crucial cross-generational tools for Nigerian-Americans worried that their children lack an awareness of Nigerian cultural practices.[29] Furthermore, in a 2011 interview with journalist Christian Purefoy, Jason Njoku, the managing director of Nollywood Love, made clear that his company's ads—especially its star-centered YouTube videos—are oriented almost exclusively to the diaspora, mostly owing to the realities of media infrastructures in Africa and to the relatively limited availability of broadband services in Nigeria.[30] However, Njoku also stressed the significance of clarifying Nollywood's contours for the unenlightened "West"—an ironic reversal of the classic colonialist and neocolonialist terms whereby Africa is seen as the site of sheer ignorance and as the object, as Brian Larkin has argued, of efforts to promote media literacy.[31] Nollywood stars are now engaged—explicitly through their internationally circulating promotional activities—in teaching non-Nigerians to dispense with the sort of essentialism that led, for instance, to a recent CNN special report declaring the Nigerian accent the world's fifth sexiest, as if a nation of 175 million could possibly yield a single speech pattern.[32] The transnational task of Nollywood, beyond but immediately related to the matter of commercialization, is, according to Jason Njoku, to "define" the phenomenon for its diasporic audiences. It is instructive that Njoku's company has attempted to do so not through film clips or auteurist discourses but instead through stars.

The complex and affirmative promotional activities of Nollywood performers are not limited to the internet, however. With increasing frequency, such performers are being asked to promote cable, satellite, and mobile-phone technologies, especially those with roots in Globacom, Nigeria's powerful and far-reaching telecommunications company. In June 2012, Globacom hired four major Nollywood stars—Desmond Elliot, Ali Nuhu, Uche Jombo, and Ini Edo—to appear in a series of magazine ads for Glo Gista, the company's new prepaid mobile phone plan. "Gist without limits," the tagline for Glo Gista, appears on all of the ads, beneath or beside unique pairings of Nollywood stars—pairings that are not limited by filmic precedents but that the ads nevertheless identify as belonging to "the Nollywood tradition." In other words, the ads show stars who pose in ways that exceed the performative boundaries of their most famous film appearances, and next to stars with whom they have not shared much screen time. For instance, in his ad, instead of posing with fellow Ghanaian and frequent screen partner Nadia Buari, actor Van Vicker appears alongside Nigerian actress Uche Jombo. Significantly, the Vicker-Jombo pairing, in which the two stars pose as lovers aboard a cruise ship, suggests several key points about the mutually supportive promotional agendas of Globacom and Nollywood. To begin with, the image serves as a reminder that a performer's membership in Nollywood's star system is dependent upon the films that he or she makes and certainly not upon the nation of his or her birth. That is why the Ghanaian Van Vicker, who has made several prominent Ghanaian films but whose success in Nollywood rivals that of Nigerian heartthrob Ramsey Noah, is identified as a "Nollywood star" in his Glo Gista ads.[33]

In his cruise-ship setup, Vicker is being embraced from behind by Uche Jombo, whose girlish smile suggests a strong emotional counterpoint to the intensely dissatisfied, romantically unsuccessful attorney she plays in *The Celebrity,* or the quietly dignified, proudly independent executive of *Games Men Play.* Of all the Nollywood stars pictured in the Glo Gista ads, Jombo is the sole producer-actress-screenwriter—a woman whose industrial power and self-fashioned feminism are further belied by the aforementioned flirtatious pose. This is not to say that the Glo Gista ads are engaged in strengthening gender-specific stereotypes but rather that they work to further the sense of performative diversity that is so central to Nollywood's star system. Like Nollywood Love and iROKOtv ads, they represent yet another attempt to portray Nollywood stars as transcendently talented—as capable of meticulously assuming a variety of guises. It is worth stressing, then, that a film like *Games Men Play* showcases a far less flirtatious Jombo than the one who appears in the Glo Gista ads. Jombo's strong, self-assured Lagosian executive must combat both her husband's manipulative, mendacious ways as well as those of his malicious mistress—a far cry from the woman who caresses Van Vicker's chest and shoulders and smiles brightly in the Glo Gista ad.

Corporate gigs therefore furnish visible avenues through which even the most adaptable of Nollywood stars can further complicate their public images. If Jombo's own scripts have provided her with opportunities to portray a wide range of character types, they have not yet centralized the sort of sheer "girlishness" that Globacom requested in employing the star as a brand ambassador, and that, as a means of making her seem more "accessible"—less a distant, detached, globally circulating screen icon than an easily approachable "everyday" Nigerian—succeeded in expanding her stardom. If millions of Africans know Jombo through, say, *Games Men Play,* then millions more have surely seen the transnational Globacom billboards on which her face so prominently appears; those who have been exposed to both may well marvel at the emotional contrast between the high-powered, "mature" Tracy and the grinning, cruise-ship "girlfriend." A consummate star, Jombo has clearly worked, in a variety of capacities—actress, model, producer, screenwriter, brand ambassador, and activist—to inspire wide recognition of her adaptability. If the multiple platforms for Nollywood stardom all tend (with varying degrees of persuasiveness) to suggest that labor—something that anyone can conceivably perform, and that here includes the hard but familiar work of linguistic, phonetic, and facial flexibility—is at the center of Nollywood's

Figure 1.2. The empowering intersection of Nollywood stardom and Nigerian corporatism: brand ambassador Funke Akindele exhorts Globacom subscribers to "rule your world."

star system, then occasionally a film breaks free of this consensus to indicate that something amorphous is behind iconicity, something exceptional that cannot be taught.

"WHAT IT TAKES TO MAKE A STAR": NOLLYWOOD'S REFLEXIVE, FAME-FOCUSED FILMS

Toward the end of Tchidi Chikere's *Efficacy* (2006), a romantic melodrama starring Stephanie Okereke and Desmond Elliot, a woman named Lucia Jacobs (Okereke) asks herself why she and no other Nigerian woman in sight is so "special," so capable of commanding male attention. She answers her own question in voice-over—through a subjective narration that occurs throughout the film, privileging Lucia's point of view. Lucia, it seems, is more "alive" than other women—or so she tells herself. Determined to overcome her rural origins and succeed in the big city, Lucia might initially seem to represent yet another example of the familiar Nollywood village girl who attempts to make good in Lagos. Having decided that she is an instrument of God and that her mendacious, status-seeking ways must end, Lucia hastens to tell a successful businessman named Mr. Duke (Elliot) that she has lied to him about her own background. Duke, however, already knows of her talent for deception, having seen her present a range of personae during a special television program. Lucia, who has been taking advantage of Duke in the days since his Jeep splashed muddy water on her white dress, and who has been telling him that she's unemployed, in need of food, and afraid of Lagos, is in fact a popular television reporter whose interview series *PM Express* is based upon the Ghanaian MultiTV program of the same name. It is through *PM Express* that Lucia comes into closest contact with other Lagosian women, interviewing those she meets on the street for a special report on sex addiction, and coming to discover that she can interpret their responses and mimic their deliveries, as well. While it fills her with professional pride, such a facility for shape-shifting does not sit well with Duke, who is upset to discover not merely that Lucia is gainfully employed but also that she manages to imitate both "urban" and "rural" ways of speaking and dressing, and to express both religious and secular understandings of the world. Thriving in the fertile middle ground between apparent polar opposites and occasionally combining them, Lucia is a woman whose imitative acting talent, tied as it is to her "obvious life force," makes her a star.

Such a shapeless conclusion might be perfectly permissible within the boundaries of a film's melodramatic narrative, but it will not suffice as an explanation for why certain Nollywood performers achieve star status. Strictly at the narrative level, *Efficacy* presents an outmoded model of media stardom, one that masks the actual, industrial determinants of actorly success in today's West Africa. While Lucia believes herself to be "simply gifted" —blessed with a talent that is beyond her control—she is played by a woman who has had to work in a range of contexts, promoting her films while finding new platforms for her stardom. What is exemplary about *Efficacy*, a film whose theories of media stardom seem quaint and archaic, is that it stands in stark contrast to more recent efforts to dramatize the harsh practical determinants—and potentially harsh consequences—of Nollywood success. Such films as *Show Girls* (Afe Olumowe, 2011) and, to a more oblique degree, *The Celebrity* focus on an audition process that is especially taxing for women, since it requires them to compromise their "sincere" romantic relationships by sleeping with casting directors—or, at the very least, by self-sexualizing, serving up an image of confident eroticism for the exclusive delectation of men. For its part, *Show Girls* occasionally cross-cuts between two crucial locations: the private home where five young women live and discuss their dreams of media stardom, and the casting suite where those dreams are frequently dashed. At one point in the film, a pair of male casting directors appear to tire of their sexist, objectifying ways, though they do not repent. Rather, they simply fail to notice the umpteenth woman to bump and grind before their casting couch, preferring instead to stare at each other as they discuss the day's events. The aspiring actress, whose dancing skill fails to merit much appreciation, ends up asking the casting directors why they're so inattentive; the men respond by suggesting that female supplicants are beginning to blur for them; they can no longer distinguish between, say, a young woman and an old woman, or a beautiful woman and an ugly one. "A woman is a woman," says one exhausted executive, as the actress stands before him, panting and sweating, her rear end the focus of a low-angle shot.

Full of misogynist cruelty, the moment is a metacommentary on the repetitive nature of many Nollywood devices—on the all-too-recognizable recycling of scenes and sequences within individual films. It is also, like the female protagonist's professional trajectory in *Efficacy*, an instance of a film's narrative contradicting the determinants of stardom that actually operate in Nollywood. In *Show Girls*, a female film star is selected at random and only because a casting director is too fatigued to "tell the good women from the bad," especially since, to him, they all resemble one another. The film forces the spectator to watch—and to become, like the on-screen casting directors, potentially inured to—a seemingly endless series of wordless audition routines in which women simulate stripping. However, the five Nollywood stars who play the film's aspiring performers (Amanda Ebeye, Mary Lazarus, Kiera Hewatch, Moyo Lawal, and Cynthia Ihebie) are far from interchangeable, each having come to the film with her own culturally and industrially specific image. Collectively, they suggest a stark contrast to the casting directors' allegations of indistinguishable femininities. The *Show Girls* spectator *can* tell these women apart, and rather easily; the misogynist casting directors are rendered foolish for failing to appreciate female performers' discrepant efforts; and the five aspiring talents continue to occupy the kinds of close-ups that not only invite identification but also evidence the women's brilliantly different styles of facial expressivity. Ebeye, for instance, has perfected a wide-eyed double take that is both comic and tragic—both a means of expressing innocuous surprise and sheer, sanity-questioning confusion—while Hewatch, whose confident character believes herself to be "destined for Nollywood superstardom," offers the locked jaw and fearsome gaze of a genuine egotist.

If *Show Girls* suggests that myopic misogyny makes luck the only available determinant of stardom for women, then the film's mode of production—its entrenchment in the Nollywood industry—suggests an obvious alternative. Indeed, even the most cursory consideration of the discrepant professional trajectories of Ebeye, Lazarus, Hewatch, Lawal, and Ihebie would disclose a model of Nollywood stardom that depends not upon luck but instead upon various promotional activities in Nigeria and the diaspora. For instance, in the summer of 2013, Ihebie sought to further diversity her star image by submitting a video entry to the MTN series *Project Fame West Africa*, a music-competition program not unlike *Nigerian Idol*. Submitting herself as a so-called "wild card" entry, Ihebie single-handedly demonstrated the flexibility, the openness to new platforms, of Nollywood stardom.[34] Lest her film *Show Girls* seem completely misleading, however, it is important to point to a particular scene that pivots on an accurate, evocative reference to an actual Nollywood star. Having failed to find work as an actress, Ihebie's Bianka turns to another mode of self-expression—dance. Spending her free moments in a huge Lagos studio—a space whose vastness recalls that of a factory and whose occupants are all aspiring performers—Bianka emerges one afternoon to find a caged bird, an African grey parrot, amid the shrubbery outside. Stopping to gawk at it, Bianka begins to slowly and sympathetically feed the bird through the bars of its cage, in a shot that lasts well over one minute. The scene's meaning is unmistakable, offering a strong indication that *Show Girls* does not share the misogyny that it repeatedly invokes: the abused, unappreciated Bianka is but a caged bird—imprisoned both by her own ambitions as well as by the men who would like to limit her mobility, to serve her up for show.

She meets two such men at a casting call for which she is utterly unprepared. Believing herself to be auditioning for a dance role in a music video, Bianka tells the casting directors to play a cassette tape that she has brought along—a recording of "Wiz Party," a popular single from Nigerian Afrobeat artist WizKid's debut album *Superstar* (2011). Wearing a purple miniskirt and shimmying provocatively to lyrics that describe a magnetically glamorous woman, Bianka ends up performing a lap dance for one of the casting directors, who waits until the music has stopped to tell her that she's "on the wrong track." Not only has the illiterate Bianka failed to read the precise casting call—the notice identifying the exact purpose of the audition process—but she has also neglected to furnish her name. "It's Bianka," she blurts, "Bianka Jalade." She then explains that her surname is but a stage name—"adopted from Omotola Jalade, my idol." In response to this confession, the two male casting directors laugh mercilessly, as if to suggest that Bianka offers a comically pathetic contrast to Omotola the celebrated movie star. There is one person present who does not laugh, however—the only woman running the casting call, who sits at the long desk where the two men are doubled over with their derisive chuckles. This woman does not speak; she simply glares at her sophomoric colleagues, admonishing them with eyes that appear to understand the significance of Bianka's strategies of empowerment, her modeling herself after the inspiring, iconic Omotola. Whatever this woman's own emotional response to Bianka's act, however, she is unable to deny that the task at hand is to hire an actress, not a dancer—and that Bianka, with her desperately sexy "stripper moves" and apparently hilarious allegiance to a major Nollywood star, has distracted from it. "But I also act!" Bianka interjects, hoping for another chance, self-inventing on the spot. "I am an *actress*." Choosing to believe her, one of the casting directors hands Bianka a script, but, being illiterate, she cannot read it—cannot perform the lines that appear on its pages. Confessing her illiteracy, she explains that she has had "no formal education," no access to books or to teachers. "But I speak well. I can learn languages and change accents like *that*," she says, snapping her fingers to signal the speed of her adaptability. "I also speak six Nigerian languages, and three international—English, Spanish, and Mandarin." Assuring the casting directors that she can learn anything phonetically—including the lines of a multilingual Nollywood script—Bianka would seem to be positioning herself as a potential Nollywood star, but the doltish male casting directors, being so myopic, turn her down. "I'm sorry," says one of them, "I can't take a chance on you. This script is important, and the project is international, with multiple sponsors." So Bianka, having simulated a striptease, confessed her illiteracy, and all but begged for a chance to become a Nollywood star, must leave the room—but not before denouncing the casting

Figure 1.3. Prominently displayed on the original VCD cover, the tagline of Afam Okereke's *Beyoncé & Rihanna* (2008) assures the consumer, "The only way to stardom is talent." *Collection of the author.*

directors for their sheer misogyny, for a cruelty that, in the future, they "won't be able to afford."

As its obvious feminist consciousness indicates, *Show Girls* is not entirely fantastical; it is hardly immune to some brutal industrial truths. In the documentary *This Is Nollywood* (Franco Sacchi, 2007), director Patience Oghre describes Nollywood's frequently demeaning, flesh-baring audition process, and the film itself substantiates her claim by showing an open call at which a male star, Desmond Elliot, is present to confer authority, provide inspiration, and legitimate the alleged "star search." What we see, however, is closer to the colloquial conception of a Hollywood or Broadway "cattle call," at which women flash flirtatious grins in the hope of attracting attention. The film makes clear that this is not, in fact, the search for a star, but the means through which a relatively minor role is cast. Nevertheless, as Elliot's presence attests, the promise of stardom is dangled for women who appear to be as hopeful and as naive as some of those in *Show Girls*. At a later point in *This is Nollywood*, however, several established female stars describe their thrill in playing people different from themselves, recalling the power of mutability—of versatile acting styles—to construct complex star images and to telegraph such productive complexity through a range of promotional venues in Nigeria and the diaspora. Perhaps the most condensed depiction of this investment in mutability and masquerade can be found in the aforementioned ads for Nollywood Love and iROKOtv.com. If only a relative handful of Nollywood stars have appeared in these ads, then that is because many stars are contractually obliged to shoot more than one. In most cases, these multiple appearances provide individual stars with opportunities to use a range of fashions, accents, and even languages.

That Nollywood Love and iROKOtv ads employ Nigerian Standard English as well as Pidgin, Yorùbá, and Igbo speaks to their eagerness to address as many Nigerians as possible—a fairly familiar commercial move. However, an individual star's use of a range of accents, adoption of different costumes and hairstyles, and "personalized" insertions cannot be as easily explained. Undoubtedly, iROKOtv ads provide meaningful platforms for stars' self-expressions, showcasing their diverse acting talents and collective capacity to embody a range of identities. But the ads also serve to reinforce stars' *specific* personae: Ogo Okoye, an actress who routinely self-identifies as a British as well as Nigerian citizen, and who has defended her decision to give birth to her children in London rather than Lagos, employs both British and Igbo accents in no fewer than four iROKOtv ads. Moreover, she speaks Pidgin in an ad uploaded in January 2012, grinning to telegraph her sheer delight in her own vocal talents.

In keeping with Nollywood's need to fashion marketable distinctions among its stars, Okoye is often described—and often presents herself—as the polar opposite of Genevieve Nnaji. A longtime critic of famous Nigerians who voluntarily emigrate, Nnaji told CNN in March 2011, "I never diss my own country." Such divisions attest not simply to the diversity of Nollywood stars but also to the absence of any accepted form of Nigerian patriotism; Okoye proudly identifies as a citizen both of Nigeria *and* of the diaspora (she was, in fact, born in Britain), while Nnaji frequently declares her exclusive allegiance to Africa—a declaration that Nnaji dramatizes and expands in her 2011 film *The Mirror Boy,* Obi Emelonye's account of a mother who moves her teenage son from London to The Gambia, counseling him to accept that he's African and that he "should be proud of that." In her interview with CNN, Nnaji made clear the strong connections between the Afro-optimist politics of the film and her own "personal position," and yet she has played a whole host of characters who are, to put it mildly, ambivalent about Nigeria, if not mired in an outright Afro-pessimism.

Nigerian press accounts of Nollywood stardom frequently identify and celebrate such complex connections between performers and their roles. Local reports often complicate a seemingly unvarying star biography by centralizing the discrepant performance techniques displayed in the star's Nollywood films, further discrediting the notion that Nollywood fandom needs any sort of stabilizing consistency in the face of the industry's vast annual output. Moreover, it is possible to track the formation of certain Nollywood filmmaking cycles by considering the widely publicized intersections and contradictions between stars' on- and offscreen experiences. For instance, as reported in the Nollywood trade press and on a range of West African websites, the "private" trials and tribulations of Stephanie Okereke might suggest a fated recapitulation of the pain that she has expressed in her most melodramatic films, but they are also, more often than not, explicitly positioned as having generated some popular Nollywood subgenres, in which other stars have profitably appeared. When NigeriaFilms.com reported on the injuries that Okereke sustained in a major car accident in 2005 (while on her way to the African Movie Academy Awards), it also focused critical attention on the creation of a cycle of Nollywood films that appeared to take inspiration from Okereke's story and from her stardom.[35] In a similar vein, the magazine *African Vibes* published a postaccident account of Okereke's popularity, providing insight into the star's eagerness to "keep [her fans] guessing" by exploring the fine line between fiction and biography.[36] Okereke has not, however, reenacted her accident on screen, and (thus far) her only filmic reference to the car crash that nearly ended her life is the cane that she carries in *Efficacy*—the walking stick that helps her to maneuver through the film's many outdoor locations, and that her character, Lucia, never discusses. In declining to narrativize the cane, the makers of *Efficacy* lend it an open meaning. It may well be Lucia's much-needed physical support or a mere prop for her hectoring, self-dramatizing performances—something that she can shake at Duke, as she does at one point. Whatever its diegetic function, however, the cane was clearly required for the recuperating Okereke, who needed to learn to walk again after her accident. There it is in *Efficacy*—a tall, skinny, stark reminder of the star's near-death experience.

If car crashes abound in Nollywood films, taking or complicating the lives of countless characters, then certain examples are clearly traceable to Okereke's accident, particularly given their star-centered spin. Far removed from, say, the Benin highway disaster that claims the life of a major male character in *Little Angel* (Dickson Iroegbu, 2003) is the car accident that scars the face of Oge Okoye's glamorous Salome in *Show Girls,* an obvious allusion to Okereke's personal tragedy. When Okereke was slated to play the role, Salome, as written, was supposed to suffer not a disfiguring crash but, instead, a series of romantic and professional disappointments, which would together compel her to reevaluate her position as the host of the highly rated but poorly reviewed television program *The Salome Show*. After Okereke's accident forced her to drop out of the film, however, the role of Salome was reconceived to suit a less nebulous dilemma, one centralizing the question of whether a well-known and widely visible star can possibly "reenter the public eye" after a (literally) scarring tragedy. Like Monalisa Chinda's Abby Davis in *Games Men Play,* and like Omotola Jalade-Ekeinde's Jess in *The Celebrity* and *Last Celebrity,* Salome is a haughty talk-show host known for mistreating her underlings. However, in contrast to her counterparts, and particularly as played by Oge Okoye, Salome is spectacularly bad at her job, securing high ratings for her show only through various backroom deals and by dangling the delicious possibility of "coming completely undone" during a live broadcast. Crucially, Salome creates the impression that she is sexually desirable primarily by requiring those around her to diminish their own attractiveness. When she catches her assistant, Shelby (Amanda Ebeye), applying makeup to her young and beautiful face, Salome reprimands her: "I don't know how many times I have told you that it is unacceptable to do all that to your face in this office!" Ironically, Salome's injunction against makeup comes back to haunt her after her car accident, when it quickly becomes obvious that no amount of cosmetics can possibly conceal her facial scars, which include large, teardrop-shaped gashes on both cheeks.

Shot while Okereke was recuperating, *Show Girls* would appear to represent a fictionalized effort to explain the star's sudden and conspicuous absence from Nollywood movies. Faced with what one character cruelly calls the "uglification" of her body, Salome must make a choice: remain hidden from public view or return to the brightly lit soundstage on which her television program is shot. "*The Salome Show* is seen on four continents," she reminds her colleagues, and, with its extensive and multinational corporate sponsorship, the program's global "flow" cannot be interrupted, even for the course of a few days. "The show must go on," agrees an associate producer who hatches a plan to replace Salome, if only temporarily. When Salome consents and selects Shelby as her stand-in, the young and inexperienced assistant balks at the thought of superseding her boss (thus suggesting that she is not nearly as unassuming as she appears—that she indeed dreams of "one day becoming a bigger star than Salome," as she later admits). With Salome ceaselessly complaining about her facial scars, Shelby is finally forced to take over for her, at first ineptly and then with an increasingly confident, transfixing style that leads critics to claim that the former production assistant has singlehandedly "breathed new life into the otherwise boring *Salome Show.*" In outlining Shelby's gradual, mindful process of acquiring the tools of a talk-show host, the film demonstrates that stardom can be achieved through hard and systematic work, proffering a believable star-as-laborer model that operates in express contrast to the star-centered theories of *Efficacy*, a melodrama that upholds luck and exceptionality as the only possible determinants of success (especially for "scheming" women).

When the disfigured Salome sees that Shelby has gained an even greater viewership for *The Salome Show* than she ever could, she confronts her former employee, angrily accusing her of having "stolen" or at least "smudged" her stardom. "You're trying to take the shine off me!" Salome shouts, in the process acknowledging that a well-entrenched media stardom is reproducible, and even, as Shelby has ably demonstrated, surpassable. Cynically suggesting that "that's show business," Salome soon resigns herself to the loss of her career. She adds, in her most sagacious mode, "It's politics—the whole thing can get very political." Shelby, then, should watch her back.

That Salome, whose assistant usurps her stardom, is herself a sort of stand-in for Stephanie Okereke is perhaps unsurprising, particularly given Okereke's preproduction involvement with the film. There is, however, a crucial difference between a character-based homage and a star substitution. To what extent, then, is Oge Okoye recognizable as Okereke's replacement—as the actress selected to step in for the indisposed star? In the absence of behind-the-scenes insights, how might the film's spectator perceive the various diegetic and extratextual levels at which *Show Girls* engages with one of Nollywood's most shocking real-life calamities? At the time of her recuperation, the facts of Okereke's accident were largely limited to the sphere of gossip—to "junk journalism," as Carmen McCain calls it—and *Show Girls* surely contributes its own, unseemly level of conjecture.[37] Far from a sympathetic portrayal of a suffering star, the film suggests an opportunistic, hyperbolized engagement with that star's "private" situation; perversely, it presents her loss of beauty and, subsequently, of fame, while simultaneously rejecting the supposed singularity of her onetime talent. Okereke, however, bounced back from her accident with her beauty and acting technique very much intact, as she demonstrated in the nine starring roles that she played in 2006 alone. In 2008, using a series of still images of her facial scars and complicated convalescence, she even produced an autobiographical essay film that she screened at the Hollywood premiere of *Through the Glass*.[38]

Whatever the film's moral infelicities vis-à-vis Okereke's accident and recovery, it is clear that *Show Girls* is far from accurate in detailing other aspects of the star's own "story," furnishing a famous protagonist whose vanity exceeds her willingness to "soldier on." Still, the general contours of Okereke's biography, and the broad contexts of her career, remain distinctly readable in *Show Girls*, making the film a risky (if ungenerous) representation of some of the more tragic aspects of an actual star's reality. In Nollywood films, references to such real-life performers are rarely so direct, however. Industry tensions surrounding star-centered reflexivity—of the sort described in Carmen McCain's article "Video Exposé"—came to a head in 2006, when producer John Nkeiruka Nwatu, responding to the concerns of several prominent performers, decided to provide a disclaimer in the opening credits of the film *The Price of Fame* (Charles Inojie, 2006). According to Nwatu, such high-wattage stars as Genevieve Nnaji, Ramsey Nouah, and Omotola Jalade-Ekeinde had become "dangerously" central to Nollywood narratives, not as on-screen performers but as reflexive points of reference, prompting the inclusion of the following text in the opening credits of *The Price of Fame*: "The names of characters and places used in this film have no representation of any place or anybody living or dead. Any resemblance thereof is a matter of coincidence."

Credited to producer Nwatu, this disclaimer would appear to indicate a refusal to engage in any way with the documented realities of Nollywood's star system. It would seem, that is, to represent a desire to dilute a recognizable stardom through satire or allegory—to turn *The Price of Fame* into an indirect commentary on some of the industry's real-life icons. However, as Carmen McCain suggests, there are several striking intersections between the film's characters and their living Nollywood counterparts—connections that can hardly be deemed subtle or coincidental, given the plot's general resemblance to Genevieve Nnaji's life and career (albeit as filtered through gossip). With its double structure of distance from actionable scandal-mongering (a distance primarily conveyed through a disclaimer rich in pseudo-legalese) and proximity to "legitimate" star biography, *The Price of Fame* suggests some of the possible pitfalls, or discursive contradictions, in Nollywood's fictionalized efforts to furnish "insider" information about its own star system. At what point do these efforts begin to rankle their real-life sources, and why do the lives of actual stars appear to infiltrate even those films that promise to be free of factual influence? Nollywood's star-centered films appear to complicate Karin Barber's reference to the diverse "realisms" produced through the interactions of African popular art and "everyday life"—of mediated representations and "lifelike ordinary individuals"—precisely by demonstrating that emphatically *unordinary* figures are nonetheless subject to quotidian experiences (staring repeatedly at a small television screen, as in *The Celebrity* and *Last Celebrity*) and to embodied tragedies (a devastating automobile accident in *Show Girls*).[39] Nollywood stardom, in all of its lifelike registers, thus constitutes a source as well as a mode of realism for countless Nollywood films. It is almost as if *The Price of Fame*, for its own part and despite protestations to the contrary, proves the thematic and narrative significance of the industry's leading lights: to represent any side of the struggle for success in southern Nigeria is, inevitably, to draw upon the empirical examples of Nnaji and company.

2

Glittering Video

Format, Fashion, and the Materiality
of Nollywood Stardom

There is a moment on Omotola Jalade-Ekeinde's reality television series, *Omotola: The Real Me,* when the Nollywood star addresses the intense public backlash against the dress that she wore to the 2011 Grammy Awards in Los Angeles. Making history as the first Nollywood star to grace the Grammy red carpet, Omotola caused quite a splash in a black-and-white, sequined sheath dress, albeit for all the "wrong" reasons: form-fitting around the chest, waist and hips, Omotola's sleeveless costume was said to accentuate both her best and worst physical features, making her seem, as one Nigerian publication put it, "too much the mother of four that she is"—too, in a word, womanly.[1] While the star on her reality TV series acknowledges the "backlash against the backlash"—the discourse of Afrocentrism and self-empowerment that promotes appreciation for "big black bodies"—she also makes an important point about her Grammy appearance, noting that it was live, "in the flesh," and subject to countless far-flung flashbulbs.[2] It was not, in other words, a well-regulated, formally constructed scene from a movie. In the glare of live coverage, it laid bare Omotola's "real" identity, allegedly giving the lie to her persistent on-screen portrayals of young adults.

On the aptly titled *The Real Me,* Omotola seeks to "raise the curtain" on both her private identity and her public persona, sharing some of the daily particularities of her roles as wife and mother as well as the ongoing construction of her stardom. "You will get to see everything," Omotola promises the series' viewer. "What we are doing is very real. It's basically my whole life. The parts where I'm taking care of the kids, the parts where I'm taking care of the home, the parts where I'm working, the parts where I'm yelling."[3] Belonging to a global tradition of putatively warts-and-all reality television programs, *The Real Me* can be read as an emphatic advertisement for antiessentialism and self-pluralization, especially since its star subject consistently avers that "there isn't one single Omotola," just as there will never be "one single Nigeria."[4] Presented with the possibility that a star-centered reality television program might actually undermine stardom—demystifying a distant, glamourous persona by "dragging it down to earth" and overexposing it—Omotola notes that, in the age of media convergence, no one medium can matter more than another. Defending the debased mode of reality television, she says simply, "It's another form of entertainment, and I am an entertainer."[5]

Tellingly, throughout *The Real Me*, the performer extends her own, proudly antiessentialist stance to an endorsement of the diverse platforms for Nollywood stardom—not only broad categories such as cinema, television, and music, but also specific storage technologies such as CD, VCD, and VHS, none of which has the power to circumscribe a star's talent, beauty, or "meaning." If the materiality of Omotola's grainy VHS appearances makes her age (a mere thirty-three at the time of her Grammy appearance) less starkly visible than the live glare of the red carpet, then that does not mean that it in any way limits her glamour or paralyzes her identity. Quite the opposite, in fact: as *The Real Me* makes clear, a star's keen awareness of the format specificities of her various projects can permit her to transcend the perceived constraints of any one medium or material. After all, a VHS cassette might deteriorate—as all analog media inevitably do—but its very existence attests to the wide relevance of the star "contained" on the magnetized tape therein, whose image has demanded duplication and dissemination via a range of historically specific formats, including unfashionable but relatively affordable videotape.

In one episode of *The Real Me*, the series' star must "work around" the technical limitations of a recording studio in Takoradi, Ghana, where she remains confident that the sheer force of her personality—her warmth as a performer—will "shine through" any format-specific distortions, like grainy images or scratchy audio. Throughout her television series, Omotola indicates that one of Nollywood stardom's key contributions to world culture has been to embrace and transform the alleged insufficiencies of the global South's "lesser" media technologies and production facilities. If Nollywood as an industry is widely known for having made the most of the materials at its immediate disposal during the acceleration of structural adjustment in the early 1990s—namely, low-cost VHS cassettes rather than expensive, "artful" celluloid film—then Nollywood stars should themselves be seen as having shifted popular prejudice against ostensibly deglamourizing media technologies.[6] What other film industry has witnessed the birth of a bona fide, far-reaching star system on so "lowly" a format as videotape? "Perhaps nothing reduces the grandeur and majesty of technological achievement more than its breakdown and failure," suggests Brian Larkin, but Nollywood's iconic performers demonstrate the durability of stardom even amid technical interference.[7]

Borrowing from Larkin's work as well as from Lucas Hilderbrand, whose book *Inherent Vice* develops an aesthetic theory of analog video, I advocate an approach to the materiality of Nollywood films that dispenses with what might be termed technological snobbery. Not merely rooted in the recognition of remediation—of high-definition digital video's alleged improvements upon VCD and especially VHS formats—technological snobbery inevitably entails *cultural* snobbery, bleeding into xenophobia and media imperialism. Essentialized as non-Western formats, VHS and VCD have been redefined by antiessentialist stars, literally carrying those stars' images throughout West Africa and the diaspora, in spite and in many cases because of their technological limitations. Looking into Nollywood's pre-internet, pre-satellite past—into the period before Africa Magic and iROKOtv—I consider what material storage formats "do" to Nollywood stardom, and what Nollywood's transnational stars have done to them. If Nollywood's audiovisual quality is so "bad," then how have the industry's stars managed to emerge as ultra-glamorous icons? No other film industry in the world has developed a bona fide star system using only VHS and VCD. The significance of this singular victory is my subject here.

In the visual arts, format is fashion: performers must "wear" the materiality of the media in which they appear, and precisely how they do so often speaks volumes about their differing personae and acting styles. From the lionizing glamour of 35 mm film to the homey intimacy of jittering video-

Figure 2.1. Styled like "a glamor goddess of the Golden Age of Hollywood cinema," Omotola Jalade-Ekeinde appears in an ad for her reality television series *Omotola: The Real Me* (2012–).

tape, format specificity can shape stardom in several ways, but it need not limit it. In this chapter, I trace the expressive dialectic between format and fashion, arguing that Nollywood stardom cannot be contextualized without paying close attention to the material specificity of VHS and VCD—two allegedly low-quality formats that nevertheless represent the inaugural storage forms for Nollywood stardom.[8] The global introduction of the VCD in 1993 coincided with the completion of Nollywood's "founding" film—Kenneth Nnebue's two-part Igbo melodrama *Living in Bondage*, which was famously shot and distributed on videotape.[9] Nollywood's adoption of the VCD in the late 1990s coexisted with its continued use of VHS: both formats were cheap, convenient, and easy to reproduce, but they also shared certain storage limitations as well as a relatively lusterless audiovisual landscape, and they have lasted well into the so-called digital era. Together, they represent the originating formats for Nollywood stardom, and they should be studied as such.

In addressing VHS, both its "low" audiovisual quality and gradual obsolescence, I hope to evoke Kenneth Harrow's theorization of trash as ranging from "such concrete things as waste management and toxic dumping" to "the tropes and styles that borrow from the rubbish bins, trash heaps, [and] garbage cans of the world."[10] VHS is, increasingly, *in* these trash piles, but it is also *of* them—and it always has been. That is because VHS is not simply an object but also a *source* of obsolescence, threatening both to dilute star images through generation loss and to destabilize the Nollywood industry through the sheer ease of its pirated duplication. Addressing these issues, Carmela Garritano argues that "[t]he technology, or medium, of the text is not incidental to its symbolic life," and while I have generally dispensed with the terms "video movie" and "video film" (partly for the sake of space and style), I share Garritano's belief in "the singular importance of video technology to the history of African popular video." I also, in the present chapter especially, share her "emphasis on video as a medium that generates particular material conditions at the level of the artifact" and as "a form of technological mediation and commodification that is different from film."[11] As Larkin makes clear, technologies "have their own material shape and design" and thus "do not simply enact the relations of ideology."[12] VHS was not simply affordable for Kenneth Nnebue in the early 1990s—a mere hand-me-down from the West. It was also a specific format with which he was well acquainted, and that could accommodate his artistic vision. Despite contemporary Western assumptions, "trashy" technologies like VHS and VCD are not blindly embraced in the global South, and their deficiencies are not necessarily bad. "Bad" is very much in the eye of the beholder, as Nollywood never ceases to illustrate.

In its vibrant, multifaceted dimensions, Nollywood stardom forces us to reconsider the assumption that shoddy, low-fidelity formats such as VHS and VCD are somehow hostile to glamour—that they're utterly inimical to charisma, mysterious magnetism, and even physical beauty, bringing big stars in line with "ordinary people" by shrinking their dimensions and obscuring their sharpest contours. Such assumptions span global popular writing on videotape's distortions, but they can also be found in less condemnatory accounts of the home-video aesthetic, as well as in self-conscious celebrations of VCD's vernacular use-value in the global South.[13] In all such approaches, aesthetically substandard formats are positioned as antithetical to "genuine" stardom, either because they can help to "make everyone a star" (in the case of the portable camcorder) or because they deteriorate (in the case of the VHS cassette, which exhibits generation loss when reproduced and which, as an analog format, naturally degrades during playback, and particularly when paused, rewound, and fast-forwarded). Because Nollywood's star system originated and solidified with videotape, it presents a forceful challenge to the typical critical take on analog materiality. Working from the Hollywood model—wherein major stars like Jane Fonda and Shirley MacLaine embraced videotape during the later stages of their careers, long after achieving fame in the dimensions of 35 mm film and long after losing their youthful beauty—scholars have tended to view low-fidelity formats as accessible adjuncts or commercial afterthoughts to cinema stardom.[14] Usually seen as secondary—both temporally and qualitatively—to the more glamourizing effects of celluloid, VHS was in fact the foundational format of Nollywood stardom.

In this chapter, I investigate the haptic aspects of VHS and VCD, as well as those of the costumes that stars wear both on the screen and in their live, "in-the-flesh" appearances, taking seriously the metaphor of format as fashion. I argue that, in studying the materiality of stardom, it is necessary to move fluidly among investigations of the star body (especially in relation to the perceptible markers of age), star fashions (especially at the intersections of film characters and "authentic" off-screen personae), and star formats (especially Nollywood's inaugural—and all too corruptible—VHS cassettes and video compact discs). The present chapter, in other words, examines the development of an embodied, fashion-forward Nollywood stardom against the backdrop of VHS and VCD, a pair of technically low-quality storage formats that have become increasingly associated with the quotidian, the pornographic, and the pirated, both globally and at the local level of southern Nigeria.[15] If such associations would seem antithetical to "true" film stardom—to its licit, larger-than-life qualities—they have nevertheless been powerless to prevent Nollywood's most prominent performers from achieving iconic, hyper-fashionable status.

A range of Nollywood stars have worked both with and against certain historically specific technological limitations and have ultimately countered the crippling effects of lackluster VHS and VCD visuals through elaborate and expressive costuming, using format-specific opacity to the advantage of their aging faces. Forced to appear via the "old" formats of VHS and VCD—to bear and to "wear" them, as it were—several "old" Nollywood performers have become notorious for portraying children and young adults, presumably under the assumption that VHS and VCD, while hardly "glamourizing" in the traditional celluloid sense, can through their very lack of visual clarity obscure the physical evidence of age. At the same time, these formats have inspired stars like Omotola Jalade-Ekeinde, Rita Dominic, and especially Genevieve Nnaji to experiment with bolder and more legible costumes—dresses and accessories that can survive, as expressive objects, the formal wear and tear of VHS reproduction and VCD bootlegging—and to take their own fashion-forward glamour beyond the boundaries of video, to the live clarity of the red carpet as well as to the glossy pages of popular magazines. Long after they had been deemed obsolete in the Western world, VHS and VCD continued to help "old" Nollywood stars seem new—fresh, fashionable, and fit for the pantheon.

LIVING VIDEO

In praising the panoply of technologically mediated arenas for Nollywood stardom, Omotola Jalade-Ekeinde joins a growing list of Nigerian public figures who are embracing such "old" formats as VHS, and not simply out of a certain techno-fetishism or hipster nostalgia. Obsolete in the global North, videotape survives in the global South, and even those who work within new digital platforms—particularly the hosts of Nigerian web series and Africa Magic specials—tend to express a certain respect for analog technologies. The *G-Bam Show*, a Globacom-produced Nigerian television program that focuses on entertainment and technology, frequently features video mash-ups whose footage combines VHS, VCD, and DVD recordings. *G-Bam*, a variety show whose hosts, Illrymz and Isio de la Vega, are young and hip, is geared to appeal to young people. Its video mash-ups can be seen to serve an instructive function, teaching youth viewers about the material effects of pre-digital formats. The series' inaugural episode—which aired on the NTA (Nigerian Television Authority) network at 8:00 p.m. on Saturday, February 20, 2010—features Nollywood star Rita Dominic in a range of roles and, instructively, in a variety of formats, beginning with a VHS clip from her first film (Aquila Njamah's 1998 *A Time to Kill*) and including 16 mm and 35 mm footage as well as a so-called "digital short" in which Dominic, as herself, visits a health spa. Each clip exhibits a different Dominic: impossibly young in one and more "mature" in another, her image (and voice) must also contend with the discrepant qualities of the various media formats involved in star construction. Significantly, the smoothness of Dominic's expressive speaking voice survives the distortions of a degraded VHS soundscape, remaining resonant amid audible crackles and between moments of unintended muteness, but her striking face must compete with the celluloid-specific scratches and spoilage visible in the revived 16 mm prints.

A similar bricolage effect is at work in the Nollywood film *Across the Niger* (2004), Izu Ojukwu's account of the Biafran War.[16] In a historiographic gesture, Ojukwu used Windows Movie Maker to approximate a "celluloid aesthetic," imposing scratches, splotches, and the flickering destabilization suggestive of a well-worn 16 mm print—precisely the kind of print that an itinerant documentarian might have produced in 1967, when *Across the Niger* takes place. The "Film Age" effects that Ojukwu borrowed from Windows Movie Maker are strictly suggestive of celluloid wear and tear, but since *Across the Niger* was shot on video, and reproduced on tape, any VHS copy is going to exhibit a dizzying array of distortions, with an artificially rendered, celluloid-style spoilage coexisting with various, inevitable forms of video interference. The sum of its imperfect material lives, *Across the Niger* illustrates Hilderbrand's point that "each [media] format has a specific aesthetic of failure"—a unique way of decaying—and it is instructive that Ojukwu uses these discrepant elements to emphasize lead actor Kanayo O. Kanayo's truly transmedial star persona.[17] The opening image of *Across the Niger*—a low-angle shot of Kanayo as his character engages in a solitary salute to his beloved yet troubled country—not only introduces the spectator to the film's mixture of simulated and incidental distortions; it also evokes Kanayo's rich history as a performer, his stardom's having spanned celluloid, television, VHS, and digital productions—a history that the lionizing low-angle shot seems to celebrate.

Across the Niger is an unusual Nollywood film, but its visible amalgamation of media formats is characteristic of contemporary, star-centered Nigerian television programs—particularly the *G-Bam* broadcast that so lovingly curates Rita Dominic's major multimedia appearances. While the analog home-video aesthetic of Dominic's *A Time to Kill* only grew grainier—more quaint and archaic—in the dozen years separating its initial release from the retrospective *G-Bam* broadcast, it is important to point out that the latter was analog, as well. Even at the start of the twenty-first century's second decade, all Nigerian television broadcasting was analog.[18] While compilation programs like *The G-Bam Show* attempt to reveal the aesthetic as well as affective differences between discrepant media formats, their position on Nigerian television effectively prevents them from crafting a convincing hierarchy between analog and digital, between old and new. *G-Bam* might look back upon Rita Dominic's stardom by bringing together a variety of clips—some far sharper than others—but its own status as a grainy analog broadcast defends against any techno-condescension, marking its media archaeology as a fan gesture, a product of love, desire, and respect. Where an American high-definition digital program might use an analog aesthetic as the butt of a visual joke—distancing analog media as a means of promoting its own, modern audiovisual qualities—*The G-Bam Show*, like Omotola Jalade-Ekeinde herself, sees Nigerian stardom as amalgamating, by necessity, a variety of formats, and to the benefit of iconicity. *G-Bam*'s lack of disdain for VHS is fitting, since part of the point of the series' first episode is to show that Rita Dominic has been a star "since day one." If Dominic did not require digital formats in order to become famous, then *G-Bam* clearly does not require an exclusive reliance on hi-def in order to, as its tagline suggests, "reach out to you."

The refusal to take a presentist approach to media stardom in southern Nigeria—the sort of approach that would denigrate or dismiss the early, VHS-based work of certain Nollywood icons—is not simply a function of infrastructural conditions that make analog rather than digital (or VCD rather than high-definition) formats altogether necessary, even during the second decade of the twenty-first century. In fact, appreciation for these formats, which the Western world has deemed obsolete, appears to be an active ethos. Nigerian television is currently loaded with love letters to analog media—with video mash-ups that bridge the gap between past and present, and with so-called "lifestyle" series, like *The G-Bam Show*, consistently and movingly inserting stars into the equation. Now that Nollywood, broadly defined, is over twenty years old, retrospectives are popping up all over the place. Throughout the Nigerian television landscape are odes to some of the low-cost, low-fidelity platforms that, in the absence of artful (and expensive) celluloid, helped to make full-blown Nollywood stardom possible, as *G-Bam* puts it, "in the first place." Television personality Toke Makinwa currently cohosts, with celebrity photographer Yomi Black, a star-centered series entitled *VHS*, which outlines the future of Nigerian entertainment while acknowledging its past. Tellingly, it does this by combining reviews of new Nigerian YouTube sensations with reflections on old analog hits.[19]

Even outside of Nigeria, African media platforms have lately promoted appreciation for VHS and VCD, particularly from the perspective that such allegedly low-quality formats can actually be used beautifully, and in ways that resist the prescriptions of Western culture. One need not be a VHS fetishist to recognize that the format's "flawed" specificity can sometimes seem artful, even hauntingly expressive (as in Abderrahmane Sissako's use of a gray and grainy VHS aesthetic for the Islamic funeral service that ends *Bamako* [2006]). Moreover, low-fi, low-priced technologies—the VHS and VCD formats so central to Nollywood history—need not be confined to considerations of cost. They need not be reduced to their shared, allegedly democratizing capacity to turn some of the victims of structural adjustment programs into bona fide moviemakers. They can, in fact, enable considerations of aesthetics—the kind that leave a presentist technological determinism in the dust.

In Nollywood studies, VHS and VCD are rarely at the center of aesthetic considerations, prompting instead a focus on the more practical matters of mass production and access. As Haynes points out, Nollywood remains "an extraordinary example of the sort of coping mechanism that keeps Africa alive: out of the impossibility of producing celluloid films in Nigeria (because of economic collapse and social insecurity) came a huge industry, constructed on the slenderest of means and without anyone's permission."[20] Viewed from this perspective, analog and low-fi formats become the affordable agents of an African popular art—the devices of convenience that preclude aesthetic shaping. When Haynes, for instance, writes that Nollywood is "cruelly constrained in its material circumstances," he suggests the extent to which VHS and VCD are seen as retrograde formats—aesthetically pernicious and altogether limiting, but nevertheless the vessels for wide distribution.[21] Celebrations of Nollywood tend to position the industry in terms of the transcendence of technological limitations. Viewing VHS and VCD through a grudging acceptance of their affordability and practical applications, however, threatens to preempt acknowledgment of the formats' productive relationship to Nollywood stardom. It also denies their potential for aesthetic sophistication—a sophistication that Sissako incorporates into *Bamako*, shifting from an elegant celluloid to a "cheap" yet expressive VHS aesthetic for narrative, thematic, and affective purposes. Denigrating hand-me-downs (as the odious French lawyer does throughout *Bamako*) suggests a clear contribution to Afro-pessimism, defined in this instance as the belief that Africa and Africans will always be beholden to yesterday's devices—to the detritus of the West.[22] That said, a purely appreciative account of VHS and VCD might appear to deny the possibility of technological expansion in Nigeria, suggesting a problem common to broader (usually Western-authored) efforts to embrace adversity.

While VHS and VCD are not nearly as denigrated locally in Nigeria as they are throughout the West (where VCR production has long since ceased and where VCD was never a widely adopted commercial format), a culture of suspicion still surrounds those media technologies that—like analog devices in general—can seem metonymic of breakdown. Haynes beautifully evokes the inherent failure of VHS—the format's relative sensitivity and lack of durability—in describing the fate of "a videotape that has spent a week out in the tropical sun on a hawker's shelf and is then played on a machine full of Harmattan dust."[23] Improper storage, combined with the environmental specificity of southern Nigeria, conspires to further define the VHS format, to the detriment of whatever sounds and images—whatever stories and performances—it was intended to contain. In addressing the materiality of VHS in Nigeria, Brian Larkin has considered the dialectic of depreciation and piracy, highlighting the Nigerian experience of "cheap tape recorders, old televisions, videos that are the copy of a copy of a copy to the extent that the image is permanently blurred, the sound resolutely opaque."[24] Already shoddy, VHS is made worse through illegality, degrading with every illicit duplication. As Lucas Hilderbrand argues, practices of piracy can serve a democratizing function, making media more widely accessible than "official" distribution circuits typically allow.[25] But piracy's overwhelmingly negative, illicit associations have helped to position Nollywood—around which bootlegging is rampant—as a strictly rebel industry rooted in crime and carelessness, one whose leading material formats are indistinguishable not only from breakdown but also from theft.

It is against this popular understanding of piracy that Nollywood stars, working with the industry's top writers and directors, have devised methods for expanding the term to cover "persona stealing" (the subject of chapter 4 of this book). Forced by crushing poverty to listen to her idol, Lady Gaga, on low-quality, pirated recordings, the protagonist of Ubong Bassey Nya's 2012 melodrama *Lady Gaga* (played by Oge Okoye) justifies her scratchy, discordant, utterly tone-deaf singing voice as an imitation of a specific, substandard, pirated recording—the only kind of recording that she has ever known. As an actress, Oge Okoye thus works to mimic—to embody—the materiality of "bad" media; the dingy VCD format of the film, made considerably worse through pirated duplication, offers a further comment on this process. Tellingly, Okoye's character comes to cynically embrace piracy as "the only option" in southern Nigeria. Renouncing live singing, she finally achieves stardom by "stealing" Lady Gaga's whole persona and lip-synching to such songs as "Telephone," "LoveGame," and "Bad Romance."

As *Lady Gaga* suggests, any attempt to document the development of Nollywood's star system must pay attention, at every opportunity, to the materiality of media, but also to the embodied aspects of stardom itself—to the matter of how the star's physicality functions both within specific formats and in conscious response to them. *Lady Gaga* rather reflexively demonstrates that a format's materiality has a bearing on stardom and that stardom can effectively redefine it as more than just a set of technical specificities. Star studies, as a discipline, has often addressed the relationship between flesh-and-blood performers and the "properties" of the media in which they appear, but such accounts have almost always presupposed celluloid film (and 35 mm at that). They range from Edgar Morin's pessimistic view of celluloid's transformative potential, in which Morin posits that "cinema does not merely de-theatricalize the actor's performance" but also "tends to atrophy it," to Barry King's investigation of the dialectic between celluloid materiality and certain corporeal characteristics.[26] King suggests that, for the staunchest advocates of stage acting over screen acting, the intimacy afforded by cinema—as well as the relative clarity of 35 mm film—limits human expressive potential, prohibiting multiple modes of impersonation and reducing performers to their physical essences. Not simply glamourizing, celluloid is in this conception clarifying, capable of promoting "typage"—the theory from Soviet cinema in which physicality stands in for entire social groupings, uncovering the "essential" connections among the members of a particular social class. As outlined by King, such theories of celluloid's specificity serve as reminders that VHS and VCD are not the only formats said to "dilute" a performer's skill or circumscribe a star's iconicity. King, for his own part, advocates "a qualified technological determinism," noting that technology "always represents a complex of potential uses," and that the body—in contrast to essentialist, physiognomy-focused assumptions—is always open to multiple, divergent interpretations.[27]

It is instructive that King segues from technological to corporeal considerations, ultimately investigating what he calls "the cultural economy of the human body." That is because the body, like technology, must be contextualized historically, culturally, and even geopolitically. After all, when it was introduced in 1993, VCD was officially declared "a technology fit for a poor cousin in laggard, developing countries instead of cutting-edge economies." It was reserved, in other words, for the global South—essentialized as a Third-World technology.[28] It was therefore against this corporate, Eurocentric backdrop that Nollywood stars developed their own on-screen performance methods. If, as a low-cost, low-quality format, VCD was deemed "essentially" Third World and if VHS was placed in the same category following its obsolescence in the West, then the antiessentialist techniques of Nollywood stars suggest a specific, collective response to condescending assumptions about what certain technologies can achieve vis-à-vis performance. As Shujen Wang points out, VCDs, which are relatively easy to duplicate, have long symbolized resistance to Western cultural imperialism—a point that *Lady Gaga* explores through its depiction of the VCD-based pirating of Western products (particularly music videos). For Wang, formats that flood the global South because of their affordability—formats whose very saturation reflects local economic hardships—can be turned, through bootlegging, against the West.[29] But they can also, as Nollywood demonstrates, make stardom more mobile, and their very technological inferiority can help to "prove" the talent, beauty, and glamour of the performers who survive it and emerge as icons in spite of it. If, as Wang suggests, Chinese piracy has satisfied a local appetite for movie stars even while literally diluting their images, then Nollywood's origins on VHS and VCD have depended, from the start, upon a durable stardom that can transcend technological manipulation.

With distortion so visibly a part of low-fi formats, cinematic realism would seem to be beyond Nollywood's reach. But such an assumption only strengthens technological determinism while denying the impact of stars as well as the specific aesthetic and affective contributions of VHS and VCD. To begin with, it is naïve to think of realism as ever being rooted in the invisibility of the cinematic apparatus, despite the protestations of classical Hollywood and of screen theory, and it is just as naïve to assume that audiovisual clarity necessarily inspires the spectator's suspension of disbelief. Furthermore, the notion that corruptible, fuzzy formats like VHS and VCD are, by definition, never suggestive of realism is plain wrong: as James M. Moran points out in his book on home video, these formats have long "been valued as immediate, literal, and naturalistic," in contrast to the "contrived, synthetic, and analytic" associations of celluloid and of high-definition digital platforms.[30] Tellingly, filmmaker Okey Ogunjiofor, who worked with Kenneth Nnebue on *Living in Bondage*, has consistently upheld the connection between Nollywood and so-called "personal tapes" (VHS recordings of private functions such as weddings and anniversaries), suggesting that the former "inherited" the technologies, aesthetic codes, and cultural associations of the latter.[31] For video historian Caetlin Benson-Allott, an analog or "low-def" video aesthetic often connotes "personally significant events," and I would argue that this very connotation, which extends to southern Nigeria (especially as evidenced in the many pro-analog video mash-ups on

The G-Bam Show), has afforded Nigerian audiences a closer, more intimate connection to Nollywood stars, as well as an appreciation for the recognizable naturalism of the home-video aesthetic.[32] Having come of age in an era of structural adjustment, without access to traditional movie theaters or exposure to celluloid film, many of Nollywood's fans know only what Benson-Allott calls the "postcinematic experience of spectatorship"—as well as, by implication, the "postcinematic" experience of stars.[33]

If, owing to their technological limitations as well as to their accessibility to users, VHS and VCD are connotative of a kind of naturalism—generative of the so-called home-video aesthetic—then that does not mean that Nollywood stars are free to flout the determinants of realist acting, safe in the assumption that the industry's formats will do their work for them. When Nigerian publications praise Genevieve Nnaji for her naturalism, or Jim Iyke for his sheer believability, they rarely mention format, preferring instead to abstract star performance from a film's specific—and alterable—audiovisual conditions. An approach to the analysis of acting that pays attention to VHS and VCD, however, might do well to consider the mutually reinforcing relationship between the "immediate, literal, and naturalistic" associations of home video and the equally "naturalistic" performance styles of some of Nollywood's biggest stars. James Naremore describes naturalism, in acting terms, as "that mode of theatrical representation which claims that the external aspects of the individual, his or her utterances, behavior and appearance in everyday settings, gives a privileged access to personal and collective realities."[34] When the actor Johnpaul Nwadike, playing an aspiring rapper in *Lady Gaga*, softens his voice to a near-whisper to deliver somber lines about the harsh socioeconomic realities of southern Nigeria, and then declares in a bellow that he's going to "escape to the United States," he not only demonstrates his vocal and emotional range as an actor; he also employs some of the codes of naturalism, wherein the volume of one's voice corresponds to the subject of one's speech, in order to suggest a broader experience of what his character calls "Naija in the here and now."

Such tonal variation also serves a practical purpose in the face of format specificity: if low-fidelity reproduction causes the soundscape to crackle or to lose some audibility, then Nwadike's choices, which integrate speech acts with expressive bodily movements and postures, can maintain a level of legibility that owes everything to the actor himself. To cite a personal spectatorial experience, I once purchased (in, of all places, a beach market in Yoff, Senegal) a VCD version of a VHS dupe of *Lady Gaga* that betrayed considerable wear and tear. While the format's deficiencies worked to the advantage of the film's plot and especially to its themes, resonating with the diegetic piracy's production of a "crackling" *Lady Gaga*, they also served Nwadike's acting style—and vice versa. While audible distortions made it difficult to hear Nwadike's speech during his character's more depressed moments, the general meaning of these scenes still came through, owing to the actor's capacity to project despair and to suggest, through his slumped posture, bowed head, and barely moving lips, that a lack of aural clarity had been his original intention. Likewise, Nwadike's shouting, with its accompanying facial contortions, remained readable even amid degraded audio—although I would eventually need to turn to a technically improved version of the film, available on iROKOtv-PLUS, to hear all of its dialogue.

Nwadike's embodied acting, and its capacity to ensure that dramatic meaning survives what Hilderbrand calls "the degenerative materiality of videotape," extends beyond format specificity into the star's public appearances, which have lately called attention to Nwadike's "in the flesh" presence in the United States.[35] Nollywood's star system, with its orientation toward publicity, has helped to cement the association between the "real" Nwadike and his itinerant *Lady Gaga* character: when Nwadike traveled to Los Angeles on a publicity tour in 2013, the Nigerian magazine *Diamond Celebrities* followed him, and when, shortly thereafter, he made a special appearance at the Tabernacle Baptist Church in Atlanta, his diasporic fans helped to promote Nwadike's presence through numerous social media platforms (including Twitter, Instagram, and Facebook).[36] Fittingly, Nwadike's trip to the Tabernacle entailed a session in which the star could "press the flesh," shaking hands with members of the congregation and further reinforcing his live, embodied presence in the diaspora. Since Nwadike's public persona so emphatically encompasses travel to the United States, his globetrotting role in *Lady Gaga*—as well as in several other recent Nollywood films—can remain readable as such even across hazy, degraded media formats. In other words, the knowledge that Nwadike often "escapes" to the United States can inform those *Lady Gaga* scenes in which his melancholy character mumbles his eagerness to "flee Nigeria"; when the mumbling becomes completely inaudible in bad dupes of the film, Nwadike's specific stardom can "authorize" an accurate reading of the character as oriented toward the diaspora.

Transatlantic travel is, of course, expensive, and Nwadike's much-publicized actions might threaten to position him as impossibly privileged—and thus an unrealistic embodiment of collective Nigerian experiences. But it is precisely the low-fi aspects of Nollywood's principal formats that can guard against some of the grandiose and spendthrift associations of Nwadike's star persona, bringing it back down to earth, as it were. When Nwadike travels to the United States—a pricey venture in itself, as anyone who has booked a Lagos-to-Atlanta flight can attest—shots of his urban shopping sprees tend to show up on Instagram, and evidence of his acquisition of bling are tweeted, and not merely by Nwadike himself. But if we take VHS and VCD to connote what Moran calls "the intimacy of home mode conventions," then it is also possible to view the codes of Nollywood's video aesthetics (which typically involve a single camera and include a preponderance of close-ups, long takes, and "real-time" shooting) as helping stars to suggest "the quotidian realism of everyday life."[37]

Paying close attention to format specificity—to a VHS or VCD aesthetic—can serve the further purpose of complicating the conventional critical assumption that Nollywood is almost pathologically invested in depicting upward mobility at the expense of any kind of realism. Stars can—and do—remain glamourous and iconic even amid the distortions of low-fi formats, but the aesthetic components of those formats, which are so famously connotative of intimacy and accessibility, have helped Nollywood maintain a productive balance between stardom and domesticity and between ravishment and realism. As Naremore makes clear, movie stars must, almost by definition, suggest such a delicate balance, combining unreachable extravagance with more attainable ordinary qualities, "because they function both as ego ideals and as common folk with whom the audience can identify"—hence the provocatively paradoxical title of Ty Burr's book on movie stardom, *Gods Like Us*.[38] With its homey associations, video conceivably helps Nollywood stars relate to their local audiences; so does the television set, computer, or laptop screen that invariably "carries" Nollywood's video images, literally bringing them into the viewer's domestic space. As Moran points out, such small screens deemphasize spectacle, strengthening the link between mediated representation and live spectatorship and creating a certain continuity between star and "regular" person.[39] As Jonathan Haynes suggests, Nollywood films—and by extension Nollywood stars—"are not at home" in high-priced, largely inaccessible festival venues, where they are projected (at a further loss of visual clarity) upon giant screens.[40] And as Rita Dominic has declared on *The G-Bam Show*, most stars "like being in your living room," where they can appear to "belong" to the daily habits of their audiences, imbuing the domestic sphere with a range of exciting and even glamourous experiences and being transformed in turn by the quotidian conditions of private reception.

Such a description, with its semiotic underpinnings, makes Nollywood stars sound remarkably close to a Brechtian conception of acting—and for good reason. According to Naremore, Brecht's radical modernism was always antiessentialist. Naremore notes that, "instead of expressing an essential self," the anti-realistic Brechtian player "examines the relation between roles on the stage and roles in society, deliberately calling attention to the artificiality of performance, foregrounding the staginess of spectacle, and addressing the audience in didactic fashion."[41] The effectiveness of performance, therefore, need not always be rooted in realism—in the embodied "naturalness" of the actor (as advocated, for instance, by Stanislavsky). As Naremore points out, a Stanislavskian method is committed to recovering and expressing a performer's "authentic" self, therefore suggesting the method's close kinship with psychoanalysis. Brecht's conception of acting, by contrast, offered an investment in semiotics—in a performer's capacity to make clear a shared understanding of society, through all of the readily readable symbols associated with the state, its citizens, and their customs. For Moradewun Adejunmobi, Nollywood's diverse local audiences are connected by a unique appreciation not for any one thematic approach but rather for the supreme adaptability of Nollywood stars, Nollywood film narratives, and even Nollywood's aesthetic choices—antiessentialism remaining a key connection between stars and their fans in contemporary Nigeria.[42] However, the matter of format specificity—of analog video's particular, often artless, de-glamourizing look and feel—can conspire to define acting as broad or as bad even in the absence of a Brechtian aesthetics. So can stardom itself, rendering doubly suspect the sort of film that endeavors to embrace realism.

NOLLYWOOD AND NATURALISM

Film theorists have long debated the relationship between a star's iconicity and the strictures of realism. For many, the semiotics of stardom—the individual star's all-too-recognizable traits—not only trump a documentary-style "authenticity"; they also ensure that the already familiar devices of documentary will lose their association with verisimilitude. The star persona is so strong—and so obviously constructed—that it can obliterate the truth claims of the filmic devices with which it comes into contact, creating spectatorial cynicism about all efforts to showcase "the real." The star's polished performance (both of fictional character and of professional, public self) suggests that quality acting, coupled with sheer iconic familiarity, can overtake and render pathetic even the most assiduously realist of film styles.

Historically, however, so-called bad acting has posed an even bigger problem, with critics citing the wooden performances of nonprofessionals in a wide range of films, from the Italian neorealist classics *Paisan* (Roberto Rossellini, 1946) and *Shoeshine* (Vittorio De Sica, 1947) to the semi-documentary *Medium Cool* (Haskell Wexler, 1969).[43] However, even those critics who appreciate such (non)performances—who believe that documentary devices can offer all the aid they need—still reject the relationship between stardom and realism. Gilberto Perez, for instance, argues that, in the context of Italian neorealism, documentary techniques "[went] a long way toward giving the performance" that a nonprofessional could not possibly provide on his or her own. Perez does not see the same thing happening for stars, however: "The neorealist nonprofessional becomes identified with the character he or she plays. With a movie star it is the other way around: each character he or she plays becomes identified with the movie star."[44] While Perez concedes that "the movie star and the neorealist nonprofessional are icons that alike arise from the index"—that "alike depend on the camera's documentary image"—he separates the star from the "everyday" individual, using two familiar case studies: Greta Garbo (the performer around whom Roland Barthes constructed his famously appreciative account of the cinematic close-up) and Maria Pia Casilio (the "ordinary" young woman who plays the maid in De Sica's 1952 film *Umberto D.*). For Perez, "the particulars of Casilio's face take their place among other documentary particulars in a world of everyday reality, whereas the particulars of Garbo's face inhabit from movie to movie a world of Hollywood make-believe."[45]

Can the same be said of the Nollywood context? Is it possible to distinguish between Nollywood's nonprofessionals and its seasoned stars? One of the most insidious effects of the downplaying—and outright denigration—of Nollywood performances is the maintenance of the racist, essentialist myth of the unprofessional African. As the Americo-Liberian writer and politician Edward Wilmot Blyden made clear at the height of British colonialism in West Africa, attempts to essentialize Africans as lazy and resistant to professionalism have their roots in a fantasy of performance. For British colonizers, this often meant that their own egotism and individualism, which they publicly and proudly enacted on a daily basis, blinded them to the behavioral distinctions among members of colonized populations, producing the impression of a unified and inherently unproductive workforce.[46] Blyden, writing in the early years of the twentieth century, cited two reasons for the alleged inefficiency of African laborers: alienation, by which he meant an existential crisis occasioned by the confusions and contradictions of colonialism, and a conscious, politicized resistance to exploitation. In both cases, for Blyden, deliberate and exacting processes of self-fashioning—of acting—operated as forms of protest against British colonial dominance. "Laziness," defined in racist ways by the colonizers, was occasionally performed in calculated ways by the colonized, thus representing an act of resistance.

Today, racist assumptions about a "natural" black African laziness are apt to be at the unspoken heart of objections to Nollywood. Such objections can be heard in the university classroom, from students who breathlessly wonder why "the acting is so bad," but who occasionally answer their own questions by indignantly asserting that Nollywood performers "don't try hard enough," that they "don't do the work" required of any thespian, and that they "don't care" or "can't contribute" to the production of imagined realities. In teaching courses in which these kinds of comments crop up, I tend not only to express my own intense disagreement with the generalized assessment of Nollywood acting as "bad"; I also attempt to elicit from my most irate, anti-Nollywood students some justifications for their blanket rejections. When, as often happens, students respond by saying that Nollywood acting "is just like soap-opera acting," I remind them that soap-opera acting requires a considerable degree of professionalism, that soap stars (especially in a U.S. network-television context) typically perform their roles rapidly and without the luxury of rehearsal time. They can scarcely be considered "lazy." American soap stars whose series shoot every day of the week are, of course, not unlike the Nollywood stars whose films are produced on equally tight schedules and who often make well over a dozen movies a year, memorizing lines with a proficiency that would put anyone to shame.

This vocational connection can enable a more nuanced account of Nollywood's widely alleged resemblance to soap operas (a category that includes local television productions as well as Mexican, Brazilian, and Argentinian telenovelas), but so can the industry's video aesthetics. Videotape's specific effects on acting have rarely been suggested, let alone studied in detail. It is clear, however, that videotape technologies—along with VCD and DVD formats—have helped to inspire the creation and maintenance of qualitative distinctions between celluloid cinema, on the one hand, and television and its related home-viewing platforms, on the other. Such distinctions—through which acting often is upheld as "better" in celluloid—can operate even when a celluloid film is transferred to VHS, a format whose inevitable distortions and degradations offer their own transformative aesthetics, as Lucas Hilderbrand has suggested. The sort of signal loss that literally destabilizes Sharon Stone's much-paused leg-parting in VHS rental versions of *Basic Instinct* (Paul Verhoeven, 1992), which represents a rather well-known example, potentially undercuts Stone's performance considerably, and not merely by effacing her much-touted on-screen nudity. Such videotape distortions can, in this case, dilute Stone's practiced glamour, giving her performance an aura of amateurishness. Stone, however big a star and however skillful an actress, simply cannot control the notoriously unstable formal qualities of videotape; they, in many ways, control her—largely because, in contrast to Nollywood stars, she was expected to appear primarily on celluloid, in American multiplexes with huge screens. "Perfection"—both of sound and of image—was doubtlessly presupposed. After all, *Basic Instinct* was a big-budget Hollywood film. Was anyone on set, back in 1992, to tell Sharon Stone how to compensate for eventual video distortions—how to anticipate them, how to use them as an actress? "We experience videotape meaningfully, materially, and erotically," writes Hilderbrand, and our own actions as consumers (handling and playing cassettes, for instance) affect general audiovisual aesthetics as much as specific acting styles. However, as Nollywood demonstrates, such styles can develop amid a sophisticated awareness of format specificity, supplying a mode of resistance to the alleged limitations of the so-called Third World—as well as, for good measure, a contrast to Hollywood that yet manages to consolidate movie-star glamour.[47]

In arguing that videotape "changes not just what we can watch but also how we do so," Hilderbrand asks, "Would it be too much to say that we see differently when we see something recorded on video?" Widely understood to be de-glamourizing—or, at the very least, not nearly as glamourizing as 35 mm film—video formats, in Hilderbrand's analysis, are typically viewed in terms of access alone, as a means of making media widely available to consumers, qualitative audiovisual distinctions be damned. This, too, has been typical of approaches to Nollywood—the so-called "popular" or "people's" industry, which famously offers an abundance of low-cost (and often low-fidelity) recordings to consumers, almost exclusively for the purposes of home viewing, including in video parlors whose private trappings include wooden and plastic partitions, a limited number of seats, and a general, homey coziness. This model of the popular, combined with an aesthetics of access, persists into the digital age. According to Hilderbrand, "the transition from analog to digital implies dematerialization and loss-free reproduction. At least in theory. In practice, digital formats compress and malfunction too," and in ways that threaten to dampen stars' glamour and redefine the effects of their acting techniques.[48]

Historicizing Nollywood stardom means, therefore, engaging with the specificities of the industry's formats—from analog to digital—but also with the differential ways that those formats function in the United States and Nigeria. Nollywood's aesthetics of access—part and parcel of its general, low-cost, anti-celluloid ethos—has material effects on stardom. This is particularly true in instances of VHS bootlegging. A notoriously common practice among consumers of Nollywood products, bootlegging only exacerbates the audiovisual problems associated with videotape. Hilderbrand cites "the white noise, the jittery image, the unnatural colors, the grain, the momentary loss of signal that triggers the blank blue TV screen or the flash of tracking" as being among the formal properties of bootleg tapes, and it is important to point out that the practice of VHS bootlegging persists throughout southern Nigeria even into the era of broadband digital distribution; indeed, a growing number of films from the first ten to fifteen years of Nollywood's development are being digitized from bootleg VHS duplicates—which is why some of iROKOtv's heavily publicized "classic" videos display many of the messy formal properties that Hilderbrand identifies as being specific to videotape.[49] Like Hilderbrand, Brian Larkin has lingered on the experiential effects of poor-quality, low-fidelity video renderings, although Larkin focuses largely upon northern Nigeria's Kannywood contexts. He writes, "Pirate videos are marked by blurred images and distorted sound, creating a material screen that filters audiences' engagement with media technologies and [a] new sense of time, speed, space, and contemporaneity," and also, I would add, acting and stardom.[50]

Given the material and aesthetic limitations of the formats in which their work most frequently appears, how can Nollywood stars ever acquire what might be called a "cinematic" glamour? One could argue that, in Nollywood's lo-fi context, publicity appearances become extremely important, as stars can use the real time of the red carpet event to enact a series of glitzy personae, without worrying about what might happen to such personae through the vagaries of video formats. Or one could turn to Laura Marks, who argues that those formats that are often defined as bad or as artless, such as video, in fact glamourize their visual and aural objects, turning technical flaws into invitations to imagination. Marks writes,

> Part of the eroticism of [video] is its incompleteness, the inability to ever see it all, because it's so grainy, its chiaroscuro so harsh, its figures mere suggestion... But haptic images have a particular erotic quality, one involving giving up visual control. The viewer is called on to fill in the gaps in the image, engage with traces the image leaves.[51]

Marks's focus is on video pornography, but her point about "bad" formats being uniquely appealing applies to Nollywood, as well, which is not, of course, to say that Nollywood cinema is like pornography or to link it back to its stereotyped rendering as a wholly low cultural form. It is instead to suggest that non-celluloid Nollywood films, which constitute the vast majority of the industry's products, offer stars both the exciting sense of liveness and of presence so widely associated with video, while at the same time, through inevitable distortions (especially of audio), giving them a distanced, otherworldly quality that is entirely conducive to stardom. Marks suggests that, when watching a low-quality video, "your natural impulse to stare is heightened by the difficulty of figuring out exactly what is going on [on the screen]. The effect is like a striptease. Now you see it, now you don't. And your imagination will inflame you more than a realistic picture could."[52]

Even in Nollywood's rapidly digitizing contexts, poor quality persists, though nowhere more obviously than in the sphere of sound. As images get sharper, sonic obstacles remain—alternately too loud and too soft and sometimes absent altogether. Such acoustical imperfections are usually attributed to rushed shooting schedules or to the kinds of professional inadequacies that can lead to a poorly placed boom microphone, for instance. But whatever their source, such imperfections can, as Marks suggests of grainy video, invite fantasy. Anyone who regularly watches Nollywood films knows that the sound might cut out at any moment, making for a somewhat suspenseful viewing experience. In watching (and listening to) Nollywood films whose soundscapes are patchy, I find myself not only frenziedly adjusting the volume on my television set or laptop, but also projecting onto the films themselves, attempting to fill their narratives with the words that I cannot hear but that I can infer from various contexts. I will often long to hear a performer's precise words for the purposes of comprehending his or her character's story, but I will also take the opportunity to ponder the (literally untold) possibilities implicit in star performances. When Rita Dominic's voice cuts out but her lips still move, I can imagine that she is slipping into the posh British accent that she often employs (and that alienates some of her fans); when Halima Abubakar is similarly bereft of a soundtrack, I can suppose that she is using the soft speech that she reserves for her most seductive moments; when Funke Akindele loses her language, I let myself think that she's inserting some Yorùbá words into an otherwise English-only project. The possibilities are endless. The level of spectatorial agency that the flaws of low-fidelity technologies afford is clearly conducive to the sort of active fantasizing that star systems solicit.

Nollywood's technological "limitations" are not merely markers of populism or of self-starter pride; they are not merely evidence of a resistance to the formalist pretensions of celluloid art films and cultures. They are also generative of new ways of engaging with moving images. Larkin alludes to this phenomenon by defining the Nollywood industry's "material and sensorial effects on both media and their consumers," describing how low-quality

VHS and VCD, which, I would add, are the sources of so many YouTube and iROKOtv videos, shape Nollywood's products, enabling them to "take on cultural value and act on individuals and groups." What Larkin describes as "the dialectic of technological breakdown and repair" ends up "impos[ing] its own cultural experience of modernity."[53] As Carmen McCain suggests, one of the best sources for understanding this subject is a Nollywood film narrative itself—the sort of narrative that focuses, in self-reflexive fashion, on the complex production and reception of video content.[54] For some films, depicting video culture means deconstructing star personae.

THE AGE OF NOLLYWOOD

When director Mahmood Ali-Balogun cast Genevieve Nnaji, Joke Silva, Barbara Soky, Alex Usifo, and other "old" Nollywood stars in his widely publicized 35 mm melodrama *Tango with Me* (2012), a proliferation of Nigerian press accounts began suggesting several connections between cast and format. If the advanced age of Ali-Balogun's stars could be likened to that of celluloid itself—with both performers and format fighting against obsolescence—then a certain qualitative distinction could be read into this connection, as well. If, as one publication put it, "older is better," then Ali-Balogun was wise to use both "old" stars like Nnaji, Silva, Soky, and Usifo, and an "old" format like 35 mm film, foregrounding a far-reaching respect for "elders."[55] For *The Vanguard*, the project represented Ali-Balogun's willingness "to give the old faces a chance to excel again," which the newspaper read as "a clear indication of his strong desire, not only to raise the bar" through the use of 35 mm film, but also to simultaneously "encourage the return of the once-popular faces in Nollywood."[56] Nigerian press coverage of the production of *Tango with Me* thus represents an extensive effort to interpret the materiality of a Nollywood format according to the corporeality of Nollywood stars. For its part, *The Vanguard* works to promote as much sympathy for celluloid as for fading performers—a sympathy dependent not upon sentimentality per se but instead upon an awareness of the quality of archaic forms. If 35 mm film faces global annihilation at the hands of high-definition digital formats, then senescent stars face replacement by a fresh crop of talents; and if digital formats are not nearly as "artful" as celluloid (an interpretation that FESPACO, for instance, has helped to uphold in West Africa), then new performers may be far less accomplished than their predecessors.[57] The irony, of course, is that Ali-Balogun's old faces are hardly very old at all.

Now in its third decade, Nollywood presents some immediate, intractable challenges to the study of styles of acting and systems of stardom. To begin with, the industry is far too young to offer evidence of even an informal apprenticeship system—the kind that might require respected talents to pass along the secrets of their trade to members of a younger generation. As James Naremore argues, such systems tend to function for the purposes of professionalization; those that spanned the nineteenth century and the first half of the twentieth, in an American theatrical context, contributed to the maintenance of professional continuity.[58] But beyond this high-minded interest in intergenerational proficiency, there are practical matters to consider, as well. While a performer's proudly competitive spirit is often said to expand with age, the telltale markers of time are tough to deny, or to ignore, even—perhaps especially—when plastic surgery enters the equation. In representational media such as cinema and television, the requirements of realism are frequently far more extreme than in live theater, making it all but impossible for an aged man to, say, play a young romantic lead. However, if that aged man is a star, and if he has managed to develop a recognizable style of acting, then he can impart that style to a younger, up-and-coming performer, not merely as a capitulation to the cycle of life but also as a means of strengthening his legend.

Amy Lawrence explores this subject in her book on Hollywood actor Montgomery Clift, noting that the legendary Broadway star Alfred Lunt, secure in his own stardom and uninterested in actively competing with Clift, conferred his own performance methods upon the much-younger actor.[59] Through Clift, Lunt inadvertently helped turn the mid-twentieth-century Hollywood star system into a major agent in the survival of specific Broadway styles. In contrast to Lunt, who made only a handful of movies, Hubert Ogunde and Moses Olaiya Adejumo, two titans of the Yorùbá Traveling Theater, became prolific filmmakers in middle age: Ogunde consistently played the powerful priest Osetura in a distinct, audience-pleasing style, reliant on his charismatic gap-toothed smile, and Adejumo regularly played the uniquely comedic Baba Sala, employing an exaggeratedly deep voice for moments of stress and sometimes speaking with his trademark pipe dangling from his mouth, creating an amusingly syncopated speech.[60] The extent to which Ogunde and Adejumo have influenced younger performers—much in the manner in which Lunt influenced Clift—remains to be seen, however. While Adejumo's son Muyiwa has remade some of his father's films within the Nollywood rubric, shooting on video and marketing both online and through traditional vendors, he has not been terribly successful, partly because his efforts to extend his father's legend can seem naked attempts to create his own, but mostly because the youthful Muyiwa, with his baby face, scarcely resembles the Baba Sala so beloved in Nigeria, producing a perplexing contrast.

If Muyiwa Adejumbo is competing with his iconic father, then he must also compete with actors his own age, especially if he is to move beyond the confines of Baba Sala fandom—a reality that compelled the actor to enter the music industry in 2006, in a bid to diversify his image. With Nollywood still so young, constant competition among generationally equivalent stars remains a defining characteristic of the industry, as well as a further obstacle to the development of an apprenticeship system. However, if Nollywood is not yet old enough to witness the replacement of aging, venerated performers with fresh, young talents, then it is surely mature enough to avoid letting, say, a forty-year-old actor portray a teen. While the well-established Genevieve Nnaji remains, at the level of looks, sufficiently youthful to tackle child roles, her longstanding familiarity as a Nollywood star renders such performances problematic, particularly when they are embedded in dramas that require considerable degrees of realism.

Nnaji's occasional portrayals of teenage characters, however, point to one of Nollywood's most significant interventions in global discourses of stardom, particularly those that problematize the aging female body. "Aging women on the screen are not just old," argues E. Ann Kaplan, "they are usually bad. Indeed, in women age and badness appear equivalent, as if the very refusal to slip quietly into oblivion—as patriarchal ideology demands—is problematic." This gender-specific assessment spans scholarship on stardom, but it is clearly culturally specific, as well. "Western culture," Kaplan concludes, "does not know what to do with old women."[61] If Nollywood is not yet old enough to be forced to figure out "what to do" with aging female stars (who, plucked from obscurity as women in their late teens and early twenties, are still, for the most part, well under forty), then it must nevertheless meet the needs of those narratives that focus on children.

While it is by now axiomatic that Nollywood is almost allergic to child stardom—a subject whose complexities I explore in chapters 5 and 6—it is perhaps equally obvious that the industry's willingness to cast women in their thirties (such as Nnaji) in the roles of teenagers speaks not to a lazy flouting of the "rules" of realism but, rather, to an investment both in women's lasting beauty and in their transcendent acting talents. In other words, if Nnaji can play a teenager (as she did at the age of thirty, in Tchidi Chikere's 2009 film *Free Giver*), then that is not merely because she can look like one. It is also because she can act like one, providing performances of such sheer charm and such transportive power that few could possibly condemn them as "unrealistic." Consider, for instance, a key scene from *Free Giver*, in which Nnaji's character, Mary Ann, is so impoverished that she cannot pay her school examination fees. Tossed from her classroom, she collapses on the sidewalk outside, and finds within minutes that her tearful face has attracted the attention of a rather handsome middle-aged man, who emerges from his black BMW to assist her. Squatting down beside her, the man asks her why she's crying, and she replies that she cannot afford school. Saddened to hear of her penury but inspired by her stated wish to be a good student, the man counsels her to dry her eyes and takes her back to the heartless principal who cruelly rejected her.

Seated in the principal's office, listening to her new friend promise to pay all of her fees, Nnaji's Mary Ann is alternately confused, chagrined, grateful, frightened, and excited. As an actress, Nnaji expertly telegraphs each emotion while subtly suggesting the significance of Mary Ann's age. For instance, Nnaji slouches slightly to suggest youthful shyness. To suggest what Mary Ann's benefactor, Gius (Zack Orji), calls "schoolgirl nerves," Nnaji grips the character's backpack, holding it to her breast as if it were a comforting stuffed animal or doll. To suggest the kind of naked excitement that quickly culminates in embarrassment, Nnaji smiles slightly, her eyes fixed on the floor, and then grins broadly—a move that might seem unwarranted, considering that Mary Ann mentions her mortification, but that nevertheless rings true. Nnaji knows, in other words, that for children an awareness of embarrassment is sometimes a reason to keep on smiling; the dawning of shame is not always sobering. Abashed at her own giddy response to Gius's gratitude, Nnaji's Mary Ann makes a face—wrinkles her nose in displeasure—before baring all of her teeth in a charismatic smile, as if powerless to correct the expression that caused her embarrassment in the first place, making it more pronounced in the process. Mary Ann's broad smile is directed at the floor—a sign of her lasting shyness. Addicted to grinning, she's still somewhat afraid of adults.

Nnaji never permits Mary Ann to seem remotely womanly. As an actress, she never ceases to express the character's childishness, and she is ably assisted by the style of the film itself. The opening scene, for instance, shows Mary Ann seated amid a sea of girls, all awaiting their qualifying exams. This long shot uses casting as well as costuming to contribute to the sense that Nnaji, as Mary Ann, is "just one of the girls"—to lift a line from a later scene in the film, when the ambitious and intelligent Mary Ann is modestly attempting to present herself as ordinary. In casting actual children, director Tchidi Chikere provides a space in which Nnaji's chameleonic qualities can emerge. In *Free Giver*, Nnaji the star is initially subsumed under a sea of kids, in a democratic gesture dependent, in part, upon dress. Uche Obiora, who designed the film's costumes, has all of the girls—including Nnaji's Mary Ann—wearing red uniforms with long skirts and short sleeves, and white trim at the collar. Moreover, these uniforms have padded shoulders, making even the smallest of the girls seem sturdy, and bringing all of them further in line with Nnaji's adult physicality.

The plot of *Free Giver* begins when the principal (played by C. O. C. Nze) calls three students to the front of the classroom. One by one they stand, in the order in which the principal identifies them. Last is Nnaji's Mary Ann, who rises slowly, then wobbles cautiously between the rows of desks, eventually making her way to where the other girls stand, their hands clasped in front of them as they await the principal's verdict. He tells them that they are to be removed from school for their inability to pay the required fees, and he takes the opportunity to berate them in front of their classmates—to shame them publicly. "We are not running a charity organization!" he shouts. "You cannot sit for the exam until you have paid the fee in full!" Listening to his words, Mary Ann winces. Nnaji gives the character egregiously bad posture—the sort of spine-bending stance that suggests the iconic Mary Pickford of *Rebecca of Sunnybrook Farm* (Marshall Neilan, 1917), or the equally iconic Lillian Gish of *Broken Blossoms* (D. W. Griffith, 1919) and *True Heart Susie* (Griffith, 1919), and that serves as a physical shorthand for chagrined youth. But if, as the references to Pickford and Gish attest, Nnaji's gesture seems antiquated—an overly obvious expression of vulnerable girlhood—it is excused, in large part, by the narrative context in which it appears. It telegraphs youth, yes, but it is a justified gesture, given the shaming techniques that surround it. As the principal continues to shout, Mary Ann continues to implode, her stomach bending until she is practically touching her toes.

Another factor helps Nnaji blend in with the girls, as well as with the lesser-known adult women who play a few of them (including the two who stand next to Mary Ann, representing her fellow penniless students). That factor is make-up—or, more accurately, its absence. Nnaji is, at first, all but unrecognizable *as* Nnaji, and not necessarily because she is so believably performing girlhood. Her face, which is often heavily made up in films (especially the iconic *Sharon Stone* series) as well as in publicity materials, is untouched here—naked. Kingsley Nwoke, who did the make-up for *Free Giver* (including for Mary Ann's later, post-school scenes), gave Nnaji very little to work with for the film's first section. The fact that the actress is nearly unrecognizable at the start of *Free Giver* is good for the film, as well as for Nnaji: it grounds Mary Ann in the reality of a Lagosian classroom and not in the glamourous semiotics of stardom. It also serves as a reminder that stardom itself—even for someone as seemingly exceptional as Nnaji—must be constructed, often from scratch, and often using something as seemingly simple as eye shadow.

Beyond Pickford and Gish, Nnaji's performance as the teenage Mary Ann evokes that of another ultra-glamourous woman of color: Diana Ross. In the early sequences of *Lady Sings the Blues* (Sidney J. Furie, 1972), Ross plays Billie Holiday as a young girl living in a Harlem brothel, her back hunched from sheer shyness, her face free of the glamourizing makeup that will later give Billie what one character calls "the look of greatness"—and what audiences can recognize as a key constituent of Ross's own star quality. Especially striking about Ross's characterization of the young Billie Holiday is her capacity to suggest that the little girl knows more than a bit about sex—that, when confronted by a violently desirous man, she can well read the meanings of each lascivious lip movement. That is what makes the film's famous rape scene so powerful: it begins with a girl who knows what is coming.

In *Free Giver*, Nnaji is equally able to express a girl's growing dread of middle-aged male desire. The film's opening sequence is disturbing not simply because the principal publicly denounces three impoverished schoolgirls whose financial failings are beyond their control, but also because he later attempts to solicit a range of services from them in return for providing the examination fee himself. If his school is, as he says, not a charitable outfit, then it is certainly a site of questionable exchanges. Threatened with expulsion, one of the moneyless girls begins to flirt with the principal, her face fractured into discrete units of meaning by a series of extreme close-ups that isolate first a confident smile, and then a pair of flared nostrils, and finally an enticing wink. If the camerawork in this instance does part of the performer's work for her, telegraphing licentiousness by abstracting her face into a series of come-hither signals, it stays relatively far away from the principal, who in a reverse medium shot is seen adjusting his posture—from powerfully erect to boyishly bowed—and scratching his cheeks to suggest the dawning of desire, the persistence of an itch. Seemingly satisfied that this girl is going to give him what he wants, he lets her stay. In turning his attention to Mary Ann, however, he notices at once that she is far less assertive. Still hunched, still hesitant to make eye contact, Mary Ann comes across as a bundle of nerves—and as pre-sexual, to boot. Part of the effect of Nnaji's slouched posture is that it keeps her breasts from view. By bending, she forces her uniform to billow—to swell outward in a way that conceals the contours of her adult body. It is this very womanly body that has so often been at the center of debates about Nollywood stardom, representing a test case in efforts to define success, sex appeal, and even ethnicity. In the industry's star system, a woman's shape can say more than she may want it to.

DRESSING LIKE A STAR

The matter of the Nollywood star body has long been a subject of intense local interest, and it has often focused on women's breasts. At the Africa Magic Viewers' Choice Awards in March 2013, Nnaji took to the Victoria Island red carpet wearing a white dress with a low-cut neck that extended to her stomach, exposing considerable portions of her breasts. Like the iconic, plunging-neckline Donatella Versace dress that Jennifer Lopez wore to the 2000 Grammy Awards, Nnaji's outfit was designed to show off her body and also to stir up debates about the boundaries of fashion. At Africa Magic's Eko Hotel event, Nnaji was not alone in sporting such a revealing dress: both Funke Akindele and relative newcomer Karen Igho wore outfits whose necklines, while not nearly as low-cut as Nnaji's, still managed to barely conceal their nipples.

In the cases of such established, indeed legendary stars as Nnaji and Akindele, the choice of a racy dress can be seen as part of a well-earned process of experimentation. With little left to prove, Nnaji and Akindele can try out new, potentially risky public personae, testing a series of off-screen performance styles that can serve the further purpose of confirming their chameleonic qualities. From pathetically shy schoolgirl in *Free Giver* to boldly breast-baring, red carpet luminary, Nnaji gets to run the gamut. Nollywood's narrative diversity facilitates such shape-shifting, but so do the increasingly varied public events that seek to celebrate the industry's stars—events like the Africa Magic Viewers' Choice Awards and even the African Movie Academy Awards, both of whose Nigerian locations speak to the dominance of Nollywood films and Nollywood performers in all pan-African celebrations beyond FESPACO.

If Nnaji's public emergence as a fashion maven marks a definitive departure from her convincing depiction of a modest schoolgirl in *Free Giver*, it does not exactly differ from her screen persona as she elsewhere expresses it. In films as otherwise far apart as *The Mirror Boy* (Obi Emelonye, 2011), *Ijé* (Chineze Anyaene, 2010), and *Tango with Me* (Mahmood Ali-Balogun, 2012), Nnaji portrays glamourous heroines whose trendy costumes often exceed the boundaries of plot, recalling Stella Bruzzi's argument that clothing "exists as a discourse not wholly dependent on the structures of narrative and character for signification."[62] In *Tango with Me*, Nnaji's costumes seem to belong strictly to the star and not to her character, Lola, a "down-to-earth" dance instructor. Lola's spectacular white wedding dress is both a large-bust as well as a drop-waist number, drawing attention to Nnaji's breasts in spite of her character's self-proclaimed "modesty," and accentuating the star's slim figure in spite of Lola's fear of being fat.

Such contradictions highlight, in the case of *Tango with Me*, the significance of stardom over character, and of glamour over realism. Beyond her elaborate wedding dress, Lola's clothes rarely seem to be in the character's price range, and they most effectively act as reminders of Nnaji's off-screen identity—of the fact that the star has her own clothing line, St. Genevieve, whose proceeds go to charity, and which supplied costumes for the film, as for Nnaji's *Ijé*. Rather unbelievably, Lola has a vast collection of elegant dresses from which to draw on any given day. This depiction of sartorial plenitude may be out of the range of realism for a story about "a simple couple" (to quote the film's British trailer), but it is not beyond the boundaries of Nnaji's stardom. As expressed through her multiple public appearances, and especially at red carpet premieres and award ceremonies, such plenitude makes possible Nnaji's many, much-discussed costume changes. But it does more than simply telegraph her fashion-forward status or augment her well-developed glamour. It also shows Nnaji's star persona to be amenable to a range of styles, further divorcing it from the stereotype of a Nollywood that provides and even requires sameness and repetition.

In *Tango with Me*, Lola's costumes seem extensions of Nnaji's stardom. They seem, in other words, to confirm that Nnaji is in fact a star, and one whose image requires the frequent costume changes that exceed the limitations of narrative alone. Glamour appears to matter more than adaptability, however, if glamour is defined through dress and if adaptability means occasionally embracing low-cost uniforms (as well as effecting a sartorially specific cross-ethnic trajectory, as in the Igbo Nnaji's portrayal of the Yorùbá Lola). Only once does Lola wear a simple, oversized white T-shirt—the sort that has helped to cement Oge Okoye's reputation as "the people's star." In Nnaji's case, the white T-shirt simply signifies Lola's lowest point, her awareness of her husband's reliance on psychobabble to explain and excuse his deficiencies. However, as soon as things begin to look up—as they eventually do—Lola sheds the white T-shirt and returns to the pricey, sexy loungewear and cocktail dresses that she has previously preferred. The irony is that these dresses have already demonstrated their failure to sexually arouse Uzo (Joseph Benjamin), Lola's enervated husband, or even to satisfy the man's general aesthetic tastes. Their revival thus seems less a requirement of plot—and less a reflection of character psychology—than a means of meeting the needs of Genevieve Nnaji's specific stardom, which, unlike that of Okoye, often requires unbridled, fashion-forward glamour.

In analyzing the Maciste films of Italian silent cinema, Jacqueline Reich suggests that multiple costume changes may satisfy a performer's artistic ambitions as well as signal her potential popularity among a wide range of spectators.[63] The star who dons a diversity of dresses can therefore feel as if he or she is putting on a series of masks, in keeping with a venerable theatrical tradition. Since each specific costume can carry socially, culturally, ethnically, economically, and even religiously specific connotations, it can also speak directly to or for a discrete audience "type." In the Nollywood context, such circuits are remarkably complex, considering the cultural pluralism of Nigeria, but that has not prevented them from finding public expression through the centralizing of dress. Efforts to promote collective pride in Nigeria's diversity have often involved fashion, as Toyin Falola and Matthew Heaton have pointed out. The Second World African Festival of Arts and Culture (FESTAC), held in Lagos State in 1977, famously showcased the dance and acting performances of a range of troupes from across Nigeria, but it also placed the troupes' costumes on prominent display at various stations, offering them up as indices of Nigerian diversity—as ready reminders of the fact that there is, has never been, and can never be a single Nigerian style. In using fashion to further the aims of antiessentialism, FESTAC "clearly illustrated the wealth of Nigeria and buttressed Nigerian aspirations to be recognized as a leading representative of black and African affairs in the international sphere." While FESTAC raised pressing questions about the lasting clashes between Négritude and nationalism, it nevertheless used Nigeria's own diversity, and the celebratory manner in which it could be publicly presented, as a template for respecting the range of "issues relevant to the black and African world."[64]

Nollywood's deployment of sartorial diversity, both on screen and off, does not simply reflect Nigeria's multiculturalism; it also deconstructs and even redefines it. For instance, tensions between Yorùbá and Igbo cultures persist as plot points in Nollywood films (including *Tango with Me*), but such tensions tend to be transformed—even subverted—through fashion. As far back as Tunde Kelani's groundbreaking film *Thunderbolt: Magun*, depictions of anti-Igbo prejudice have used female beauty, partly as constructed or accentuated through costumes, in order to question the assumptions underlying that prejudice. In *Thunderbolt*, for instance, the Ifá priest, operating within a specifically Yorùbá system of divination, is surprised to discover that the film's protagonist, Ngozi (Uche Obi-Osotule), is Igbo. When asked why he is so surprised, the biased *babalawo* replies that he did not think that an Igbo woman could possibly be so beautiful, or so elegantly dressed. Other figures in the film, whose main plot impetus is interethnic conflict, concur, declaring that Ngozi is different from "a typical Igbo woman" because she dresses so well. Kelani and screenwriter Femi Kayode (who also wrote *Tango with Me*) thus employ sartorial stereotypes in order to suggest the inanity of anti-Igbo prejudices—the kinds that can seem both classist and sexist.

Because her most prominent roles arrived when Nollywood's star system was not yet advanced—when, that is, red-carpet events were rare, and when individual marketers had arguably the most say in constructing a performer's identity for public consumption—Uche Obi-Osotule was not able to extend Kelani and Kayode's antiessentialist conception of fashion into any major, extra-filmic appearances. Nevertheless, at the time of *Thunderbolt*'s production, the intertextuality of her star image was sufficiently rich to infuse the film with a variety of meanings and associations, suggesting an important yet surprisingly understudied subject. While Kelani's *Thunderbolt* is among the most discussed Nigerian films—one of the few that regularly receives mention in scholarship on Nollywood, despite Kelani's outspoken ambivalence about the industry—no one has yet considered the influence of Obi-Osotule's stardom. She made her film debut in 1996, playing the lead role in Chico Ejiro's *Onome*.[65] As the title character, Obi-Osotule (billed as "Uche Osotule") combines the no-nonsense practicality of a young woman born in Ajegunle, an impoverished district of Lagos, with the wide-eyed vibrancy of someone who hopes and perhaps expects to one day escape the slums. A melodrama, *Onome* trades in misunderstandings, missed connections, and painfully poor timing, culminating in a series of tragedies, including the protagonist's contracting an ominously unnamed, sexually transmitted disease. Five years later, Uche Obi-Osotule would play a similarly afflicted character in *Thunderbolt*, suggesting that Kelani had seen *Onome*, and that he cast her at least partly on the basis of it, perhaps counting on a powerful intertextual connection. Acclaimed as an AIDS allegory, Kelani's *Thunderbolt* gains further meaning and poignancy from its star's previous performance in *Onome*.

A remarkable actress whose work forms a complex pattern of associations, Obi-Osotule has been a victim of several false assumptions about Nollywood acting—assumptions that would never fly if applied to, say, the Hollywood context. For example, in the edited collection *Nollywood: The Video Phenomenon in Nigeria*, Pierre Barrot writes, "Uche Obi-Osotule is so caught up in her character [in *Thunderbolt*] that she frequently bursts into real tears, with no hint of artificiality, and by doing so manages to convey an irresistible level of emotion."[66] Though presumably well-intentioned, such a comment seems dangerously close to an essentialist conception of African women, which, in this case, sees them as being constitutionally incapable of distinguishing between reality and fantasy—between self and role. Moreover, it represents a problem that is quite common in studies of acting—namely, the inference of a psychic process from a filmed performance, and the attribution of a so-called "authentic" (rather than "faked") emotion to an individual whose job is to create characters using the familiar vocabulary of affect, which includes, of course, the shedding of tears. How, exactly, does Barrot know that these tears are "real"—that Obi-Osotule is "really crying" in Kelani's film? While Barrot's book is, as a whole, devoted to celebrating Nollywood's unique modes of resistance to Afro-pessimism, the author's one comment about acting—or, rather, non-acting—hardly seems a reflection of Afro-optimism. By stripping Obi-Osotule of her professional identity as a conscious and meticulous performer—by denying her the title of "actress"—Barrot relegates her to the realm of reflexive emotionality.

She has not had many chances to combat such a misplaced approach, but this may be changing. While *Naija Parrot* has named her one of "nineteen faded and outdated Nollywood stars who are no longer relevant in the industry," the *Nigerian Voice* has revealed that her retreat from films represented a conscious decision to "step away from fame" in order to focus on family life and to become a successful author of children's books.[67] In a wide-ranging interview with Azuh Amatus, the star, whose name is now Uche Mac-Auley, referred to writing as her "first love," and explained that, after a failed (and quite public) marriage to Nollywood producer Obi Osotule—a marriage that famously produced no children and that caused many to question the couple's fertility—she found herself committed to a new, much-younger man whose generation, she claimed, experiences fewer gendered pressures.[68]

While the star's ex-husband was once publicly dubbed "the man who cannot make a woman pregnant," her current husband, Solomon Mac-Auley, has attempted to preempt such prejudiced criticisms by openly describing his marriage as a joint artistic rather than baby-making venture.[69] He runs a company that publishes children's books, including his wife's, and in 2009, he directed the activist documentary short *Violence Against Women*—part of his ongoing efforts to raise awareness about the disturbing effects of misogyny on its victims, and to demonstrate his personal separation from masculinist stereotypes. In 2010, he directed the feature film *In a Lifetime*, which focuses on the efforts of four women, all from the same family, who struggle to break free of misogynist social prescriptions—and who eventually succeed, thanks not to divine intervention (as in a more familiar Nollywood trope) but to the influence of a character played by Uche Mac-Auley in a much-anticipated return to the screen. While it is important to heed Oyèrónkẹ́ Oyěwùmí's warning against applying Western conceptions of gender to non-Western (especially multicultural Nigerian) contexts, it is possible to perceive a feminist project in Uche Mac-Auley's film, and particularly in her performance.[70] In a further indication of the star's conscious participation in her own image's construction and manipulation, Uche Mac-Auley co-wrote the screenplay for *In a Lifetime* and coproduced the project with her husband. No helpless non-professional whose onscreen tears are unbidden and uncontrollable (as in Barrot's conception), Uche Mac-Auley remains a major, politicized force both in front of the camera and behind the scenes.

Thunderbolt, her breakthrough film, suggests a conservative or "traditionalist" Yorùbá project, but only to those who fail to recognize its exposure of the sort of misogyny that tries to hide itself in the guise of a "natural" cultural custom. For Barrot, the film's concluding sequence, in which Yorùbá fetishism reigns supreme while Western-style medicine flounders, "seems to be a concession by Tunde Kelani to his Yorùbá public, the majority of whom are raised within traditional belief systems."[71] It is equally possible, however, to read *Thunderbolt*'s interventions in a prejudiced Yorùbá traditionalism—interventions that count upon the capacity of the film's female star to sympathetically enact a cross-cultural trajectory, a process of "passing" as Yorùbá while "being" Igbo—as representing its most significant theme, its ultimate "message." The star's effectiveness as a performer, and Ngozi's power as a character, together transcend the film's Yorùbá-centered "moral," recalling Stefan Sereda's comment that while many Nollywood films "adopt a cautionary pedagogical stance, their main messages [can be] undermined by counterbalancing diegetic voices that at times present compelling arguments."[72] The Igbo Ngozi presents just such a voice, and it is far louder—especially because spoken by a young star—than that of the Ifá whose shaming cultural chauvinism the film seems, at times, to share, if only as a concession to cliché. Considering the vigilant role of the National Film and Video Censors Board, whose actions during and after the production of *Thunderbolt* Barrot outlines, the film's eleventh-hour, religiously inflected righting of wrongs can be seen simply as a sop to convention.

Figure 2.2. As Ngozi in Tunde Kelani's *Thunderbolt* (2000), Nollywood star Uche Obi-Osotule (now Uche Mac-Auley) asserts her strength. *Image courtesy of California Newsreel.*

The Ifá's triumph is practically a mandated ingredient. As such, it does not really linger in the memory. What does is the image of Uche Mac-Auley (then Uche Obi-Osotule) looking perplexed when presented with the smug men who reject her Igbo identity, telling her that she's either "too beautiful" or "too well-dressed" to be anything but Yorùbá. What lingers as well is the success of this one character—a success that is inseparable from that of the actress who plays her—in embodying the markers of a culture different from her own. As Akin Adesokan points out, Ngozi is hardly delusional— hardly capable of blurring the line between reality and fantasy; she represents, in Adesokan's words, "a fully aware self," and she proudly declares, at one point, "I, Ngozi, am an Igbo girl."[73] She is played by a star whose own public identity has long been rooted in an activist stance regarding women's rights, and whose self-transformations—from actress to screenwriter to producer to author of children's books—have offered further evidence of Nollywood stardom's supreme adaptability. Her specific persona proves the importance of looking at Nollywood films—even widely familiar, seemingly ideologically stable ones like Kelani's *Thunderbolt*—through the lens of stardom.

Cross-cultural performances of the sort that *Thunderbolt* centralizes are remarkably common in Nollywood's star system, but they do not always follow familiar formulas. When Oge Okoye made her first Yorùbá-language film in 2012, she confessed to having previously held negative assumptions about Yorùbá productions, telling the *Vanguard* that she'd believed the many stereotypes linking Yorùbá culture to a lack of professionalism as well as to a general disregard for the aesthetics of moving images.[74] Press accounts of the making of the film, whose title in English is *Street Girls* and whose plot revolves around four young women who must turn to armed robbery when their salaries as street sweepers are slashed, focused almost exclusively upon the project's capacity to educate the Igbo Okoye.[75] The recipient of a chieftaincy title for her contributions to Igbo culture in Enugu State, Okoye is one of several Igbo stars who have made films almost exclusively in English.

Joining her on that list is Genevive Nnaji. If, in the film *Tango with Me*, a baggy T-shirt hides Nnaji's body and dampens her glamour, then it does so largely in order to signal her character's momentary listlessness and depression—as if only a cheerful, fulfilled woman could possibly want to dress up. However, that oversize T-shirt helps Nnaji to further manipulate her image, much as her child role in the film *Free Giver* offered an opportunity to expand her performative repertoire. The de-glamourizing, desexualizing, and even de-gendering T-shirt not only offers, in visual terms, "a new Nnaji"—variety and adaptability remaining watchwords in Nollywood's star system. It also gives her a chance to enact a new role: suffering wife. Waiting for her husband to acknowledge her pain following a gang rape, Nnaji's Lola lounges in her living room, re-experiencing the desire that she first felt on her wedding night, and then just as quickly reverting to a state of depression brought about by the awareness of her husband's physical and psychic shortcomings. Nnaji the fabled beauty plays the role without a hint of indignation—without so much as a flicker of surprise at having been rebuffed. While the absence of egotism marks the sympathetic Lola as a familiar Nnaji "type," the character's marital context created a new challenge for the actress—as did the film's horrific rape scene, the aftermath of which leaves Lola floundering. Nnaji, in *Tango*, lets Lola weep without a hint of self-pity, and she resists the easy pathos of a self-infantilizing performance style. Lola, in fact, could not be further from Nnaji's *Free Giver* character, the teenage Mary Ann. In both films, Nnaji's costumes help to construct the characters, but the effectiveness of both performances lies with the actress alone.

One of the major features of Nollywood's star system involves not simply its orientation toward off-screen glamour and the publicity potential of the red carpet appearance, but also its development of sartorial diversity among women as well as men. Ramsey Nouah, Desmond Elliot, and Van Vicker are among the male stars who routinely wear unbuttoned, torso-baring shirts to premieres—although, instructively, Nigerian newspapers and Nollywood fan magazines both tend to question whether such sartorial choices can seem "tacky," rather than (as with women's plunging-neckline dresses) "alarming" or "immoral."[76] While film premieres and award celebrations tend to require that all stars "dress up," these events cannot possibly regulate the range of expressions available to the stars who, as in Hollywood, maintain relationships with major, ever-evolving designers and who employ personal stylists. If Nnaji and Okoye, to take just two examples, can surprise their fans—and perhaps surpass their own expectations—by donning ever more daring dresses during public appearances, then so too can their film characters create and modulate a range of identities through costuming.

Consider, for instance, the film *Girls on Fire* (Okey Zubelu Okoh, 2013), which follows the foibles of four young women who share a house in Lagos. Having failed both professionally and romantically, the women are faced with destitution—until one, Zoe (Ihuoma Nnadi), hatches a plan: in exchange for payment, she will sleep with married, middle-aged women, all of whom happen to be closeted lesbians. The plan proves so successful that Zoe's housemates soon catch wind of it, eventually joining her in, as one character rather crudely phrases it, "eating older women." As the four women's fortunes increase, their costumes change: Oge Okoye's Irene, who, in keeping with Okoye's relatable image, has dressed mostly in sweats and in the occasional oversize T-shirt, suddenly shows up clad in an expensive evening gown. Adaeze Eluke's Chloe, who was a lab technician until she quit over a colleague's imperiousness, discards her bland professional attire for bright colors and low-cut cocktail dresses; she even begins wearing an expensive "Afro" wig. Last but not least, Eve Esin's Lauren pours herself into the kinds of cleavage-bearing outfits that make her ex-boyfriend—a tiresomely self-aggrandizing young man who was dumb enough to dump her—sick with lust and longing.

Girls on Fire is a comedy about the free play of identity. As such, it provides innumerable outlets for the talents of two established stars (Oge Okoye and Funke Akindele, who plays the Okoye character's Yorùbá-speaking sister), as well as considerable testing ground for three emerging ones (Nnadi, Eluke, and Esin). Evidence that Nollywood's star system functions both to strengthen familiar personae as well as to produce new luminaries can be found in the film: it is the young, enterprising Zoe who, as played by Ihuoma Nnadi, inspires Okoye's Irene to "think big" and to "dress for success." Since Okoye is a major star, her character's complete capitulation to the ministrations of Nnadi's Zoe can be read as an endorsement of a relatively untested young talent. If Zoe's glamourizing tactics work on Okoye/Irene, then one can be certain that the actress who gives Zoe such vibrant life has a fine future in Nollywood films. This somewhat surprising approach to selling Nnadi's star qualities suggests a reversal of the familiar Hollywood route, wherein an icon plays Pygmalion to a neophyte—both on-screen and, presumably, off. (Think of the well-established Gregory Peck romancing the fresh-faced Audrey Hepburn in *Roman Holiday* [William Wyler, 1953], or even the luminous Diana Ross, in *Lady Sings the Blues,* brilliantly improvising her way through scenes with the young Richard Pryor, and all but ensuring that Pryor would have a major screen career.) Though Okoye's Irene is, in *Girls on Fire,* supposed to be "just one of the ladies," Okoye herself can never be. Though her understated acting helps Irene to blend in with the others, Okoye is always recognizable as Okoye; the body of the star is still present, and it is a powerful reminder of all that has come before—in Okoye's case, over 100 films and countless, kaleidoscopic public appearances. "Actors' bodies are presented to be read," writes Amy Lawrence, "but what their bodies express is an inescapable doubleness—the actor's body making legible the character's physical and mental state."[77]

As the four women of *Girls on Fire* enjoy their newfound riches—as well as the advanced glamour that such riches have afforded them—they post photos to Facebook, watch Nicki Minaj music videos in an imitative mode (with Irene openly celebrating Minaj's many self-transformations), and discuss their collective adaptability. Each of the four is, in fact, no less adept at persona-shifting than is Minaj, who represents, in this film as in several others, a Western woman of color whose capacity to assume a variety of guises is upheld as one of many models for Nollywood stardom. With her elaborate wigs and weaves, her wildly inventive costumes, and her general penchant for surprising her fans, Minaj represents a handy analog for Nollywood's star system. She appears, in *Girls on Fire*, by way of a plasma television set that plays her videos, but she's a more pervasive presence than that, providing the film with a considerable degree of self-reflexivity: by studying her, Lauren, Irene, Zoe, and Chloe create a space in which appropriation and experimentation lead to glamour and success; they suggest, in other words, the many avenues—of fashion, of performance style, and of off-screen demeanor—through which Okoye has achieved stardom, and through which her juniors (Esin, Eluke, and Nnadi) can attempt to travel if they crave her level of fame. If Nicki Minaj's status as a Western star raises uncomfortable questions about American cultural imperialism, her identity as a woman of color helps, perhaps, to circumvent or at least leaven them. And if Minaj's shape-shifting proficiency threatens to be seen, in essentialist terms, as the "natural" domain of the "deceptive" black woman, then the level of dedication and deliberation with which the protagonists of *Girls on Fire* embrace the vagaries of fashion—the consistently conscious manner in which they construct and manipulate identities—demonstrates that essentialism is often only in the eye of the biased beholder.

By imitating an American icon whose self-transformations already reflect their own, the stars of *Girls on Fire* engage in a complex, kaleidoscopic process that Nicole Fleetwood has described as "the performance of hypervisibility." For Fleetwood, "hypervisibility is a performative strategy for black female cultural producers, one that emphasizes the faulty notions of a 'visual truth' of blackness by representing excess and fantasy."[78] In the Nigerian context, the performance of hypervisibility is not simply constitutive of stardom; it is also a means of questioning and subverting the received wisdom that, say, an Igbo woman (like Oge Okoye) can only ever be one thing, can only ever enact one identity. Fleetwood develops the concept of "excess flesh" in order to "redress how black women are represented and constructed as having/being 'too much' in relation to the ideals of white femininity." But while "excess flesh enactments... operate differently" in a range of national, cultural, and economic contexts, they always require an audience.[79] In appreciating Nicki Minaj, the protagonists of *Girls on Fire* are always performing for each other—as well as for Funke Akindele's Ashake, the barefoot, Yorùbá-speaking villager and sister of Irene, who arrives to reveal just how much of a willful self-construction Irene's urban glamour really is.

True to the insistent antiessentialism of Nollywood's star system, Ashake's significance is not restricted to the film's narrative; it also extends into the extra-textual realm of casting. Funke Akindele is, famously, Yorùbá—so famously, in fact, that her publicist is tasked with informing the popular press of the deeply rooted, Yorùbá-specific reasons for the star's actions and decisions. For example, when rumors that Akindele was pregnant began circulating in the summer of 2012, her publicist stepped in to announce, once and for all, that the star would not be discussing the state of her womb.[80] Akindele's refusal, as relayed through an intermediary, hardly represented a calculated attempt to inspire curiosity and attention. Instead, it reflected Yorùbá proscriptions against publicly addressing the topic of reproduction. As Oyèrónkẹ́ Oyěwùmí points out in *The Invention of Women*, "In Yorùbá cultural logic, biology is limited to issues like pregnancy that directly concern reproduction," making a public declaration of reproductive status not only culturally incongruous but also dangerously close to an essentializing tactic.[81]

Akindele's respect for Yorùbá conventions remains strong in spite of —or perhaps because of—her stardom. Nollywood's investment in antiessentialism is hardly at odds with Akindele's strong Yorùbá cultural identity. In helping to shape her stardom, Nollywood projects do not always work to strengthen or even to indicate that identity. While Akindele has made several dozen Yorùbá-language films, she has also appeared in nearly as many English-language projects—including *Girls on Fire*, a film whose antiessentialism leads not merely to mimicry of Minaj among the eponymous media consumers, but also to a specific casting practice that deliberately links, through a depiction of sisterhood, the Yorùbá Akindele and the Igbo Okoye. In this case, Yorùbá culture becomes the "origin" of Okoye's character, giving the actress a performance opportunity somewhat like the one that marked Uche Mac-Auley's work in *Thunderbolt*, but that ups the ante considerably on Kelani's intertribal Ngozi: here, an Igbo actress must pass as a Yorùbá villager passing as an Igbo city girl. Even before Akindele's Ashake shows up—in theatrical, illusion-shattering fashion—there are some subtle, canny clues signaling Irene's roots. One such clue is costume—particularly the pre-success sweats that the listless Irene prefers, and that have elsewhere made Okoye seem accessible (rather than intimidatingly glamourous in a high-fashion manner). If these baggy sweats—like Nnaji's oversize white T-shirt in *Tango with Me*—help to make the transition into expensive, "sexy" styles of dress seem more impressively extreme, then they also, in their capacity to "de-gender" the body, serve as reminders of one of Oyěwùmí's key points about Yorùbá cultural tradition: that within that tradition, and prior to colonization by the West, "gender was not an organizing principal." According to Oyěwùmí, "The social categories 'men' and 'women' were nonexistent, and hence no gender system was in place" in precolonial Yorùbá society. In other words, "gender has become important in Yorùbá studies not as an artifact of Yorùbá life but because Yorùbá life, past and present, has been translated into English to fit Western patterns of body reasoning."[82] If, without exactly presenting herself as genderless, a star like Funke Akindele still manages to resist these patterns (even telling off a reporter at the 2012 Hip Hop World Awards for daring to ask if she was pregnant), then so too does a Nollywood film like *Girls on Fire*, in which it is only the (closeted) Yorùbá character who feels comfortable in loose, de-gendering sweats—at least until financial success frees her to adopt high fashion and a fully feminine masquerade.

In addressing Nollywood's ongoing interest in Igbo-Yorùbá relations, it is worth pointing out that many of the industry's biggest stars claim an Igbo ethnic identity, and often participate in efforts to promote Igbo culture. At the same time, however, there appears to be considerable pressure for Yorùbá performers to adopt Igbo names and guises if they wish to exit the Yorùbá filmmaking sector to become stars in English. However, even though the Yorùbá sector is rumored to offer notably lower compensation for performers than do English-language projects, many (like Funke Akindele) remain committed to their Yorùbá roots, frequently returning to make Yorùbá films. That the Yorùbá sector is less than lucrative for performers would seem to be an open secret in southern Nigeria; it is a reality that one Yorùbá star, Eniola Badmus, attributes (in an admittedly essentialist manner) to Yorùbá culture itself—to the fact that Yorùbá people "help each other, sometimes without a fee being attached." The Yorùbá filmmaking sector is hardly immune to the appeal of stardom. As Badmus has said, Yorùbá films routinely "create household names." The stardom that develops in the Yorùbá sector, however, is not necessarily dependent upon the publicity potential of a fat salary. By contrast, Igbo performers who work in the English sector are often publicized according to their paydays, with press headlines labeling one or the other the highest earner in Nollywood. Such economic distinctions tend to inspire qualitative ones, as well, in keeping with the essentializing techniques of tribalism. For instance, when she was just beginning to work in the English sector, Badmus was asked by producers to adopt an Igbo surname. Her response? "I told them I would not sell my birthright."[83]

Like Akindele, Badmus has been a significant crossover success, earning the affectionate nickname "Gbogbo Big Girl"—a Yorùbá-inflected reference to her physical size, as well as, in colloquial Nigerian terms, her youthful mobility and gregariousness. The hardworking Badmus even has a role in *Girls on Fire*. She plays Patience, a Yorùbá woman with limited English-language skills whom the titular figures hire as their maid (and punching bag). Patience strikes up a friendship with the pot-stirring Ashake, and the scenes that feature both Badmus and Akindele are small classics of grand theatricality—of broad acting and brilliant physical humor. They're comic tributes to the pair's Yorùbá roots; the performers' rapport is undeniable and irresistible, recalling their inspired work in *Jénífà*, in which Badmus plays a bold "big girl" who teaches Akindele's title character how to attract wealthy men. Worlds apart from Patience, Badmus's character in *Jénífà* is an urban sophisticate—a swaggering, heavily made-up hustler whose T-shirt reads, "I get prettier every day and I can't wait until tomorrow!"

Like *Jénífà*, *Girls on Fire* depicts multiple modes of media consumption. The eponymous housemates mesh best when dancing to Western music, but Nicki Minaj is not their only source of inspiration. The film further rejects a race-based essentialism by having its title characters watch the white pop star Ke$ha on television. Like Minaj, Ke$ha is well known for her elaborate costumes, ever-changing hairstyles, and colorful, glitter- and sequin-studded make-up. But her persona lacks something that Minaj's has embraced, and that further links the latter star to the Nollywood context: phonetic adaptability and experimentation. In describing her decision to periodically adopt an English accent, Minaj has consistently cited Melanie Brown (aka Scary Spice) as a phonetic model. In other words, Minaj made a conscious choice to imitate not a white Brit but, instead, another woman of color. In a 2012 interview with *The Guardian*, Minaj discussed studying Brown's face as it was engaged in producing an English accent, and confessed to later copying Brown's physical mannerisms as well as her speech.[84] When Minaj shifted from African American Vernacular English to a posh, British-accented English during a broadcast of *American Idol* in 2013, she inaugurated a new phase in her public persona, one dependent upon a notably new phonetic. Like Nollywood's top stars, Minaj has managed to suggest the significance of vocal adaptability not merely for the purposes of performing scripted roles but also in order to signal the diversity of black identities worldwide. Minaj, moreover, was born in Trinidad, another former British colony—a factor that gives her shape-shifting a special resonance within a broad Afro-diasporic experience. With her keen awareness of her own complex national, cultural, ethnic, and linguistic backgrounds, and with her willingness to reinvent herself, it is no wonder that Nicki Minaj is now a reference point for Nollywood films and for Nollywood stars.

Oge Okoye, Stephanie Okereke, Halima Abubakar, and Rita Dominic are among the Nollywood icons who use British accents, especially offscreen. In *Girls on Fire*, however, Okoye's character is too invested in passing as a citified Igbo woman to worry much about a British accent. Besides, Irene must keep up with her housemates, all of whom change costumes as often and as quickly as they change personae. Their overtly attention-seeking actions, through which they attempt to locate their "new" (but never "true") selves, recall bell hooks's point, in "The Oppositional Gaze," that subjectivity requires visibility—that self-fashioning, perhaps paradoxically, depends upon the eyes of others.[85] *Girls on Fire* might be dismissed as mere "fluff"— and more readily so than most Nollywood films—because each of its characters, in falsely acquiring riches and new clothes, works at times to resemble a "video ho," displaying the same portions of belly and side-boob that have rendered controversial so many Nollywood stars' red carpet costumes.[86] However, if such costumes can reflect not knee-jerk exhibitionism but instead a rather savvy decision to publicly question the strictures governing Nigerian femininities, then so, of course, can the literal self-exposure of the eponymous *Girls on Fire* fuel a sense of Nollywood as committed to destabilizing the social prescriptions surrounding active, visible women.

For Nicole Fleetwood, such processes of destabilization depend upon the self-conscious hypervisibility of black women. Fleetwood writes, "Such artistic practices privilege the performative component of visual narratives and in so doing turn excess flesh into a strategic enactment and not a being unto itself."[87] If Nollywood stars are always performing, always juggling a variety of guises—both on-screen and off—then it is important, indeed appropriate, to see them as participating in their own personae's construction, and not as capitulating to the demands of an objectifying industry or as being limited by the meaning-making potential of media technologies. One of the defining characteristics of Nollywood's star system is its warm embrace of risk-taking women; another is its capacity to create links between their personal cultural risks and the challenges of on-screen representations. The Igbo but famously British-friendly (and, indeed, British-born) Oge Okoye playing a Yorùbá villager who pretends to be city-born and city-bred is but one example of a Nollywood star—and a Nollywood film—facing these challenges head-on. If they threaten at any moment to become illegible, there is always fashion to fall back upon; a costume change can always signal a paradigm shift. With its focus on the foibles of a quartet of Lagosian housemates who help themselves to the comforts of clothes, *Girls on Fire* brings to mind Stella Bruzzi's comments about another depiction of the friendship of four women of color—Forest Whitaker's *Waiting to Exhale* (1995). Bruzzi writes that, in Whitaker's film, style and identity require "appropriating diverse elements from anywhere and giving them a new, fluid, relaxed intonation." When the function of fashion is "not confined to the construction of a stable, identifiable image," then it becomes an indispensable tool in the strengthening of antiessentialism—a task that an African American movie landmark shares with Nollywood's ongoing, star-centered project.[88]

The protagonists of *Girls on Fire*, with their vastly different backgrounds but collective commitment to self-fashioning, recall a point that Moradewun Adejunmobi makes about Nollywood itself. In her words, it is precisely because Nollywood videos emerged "at a time of extreme social instability created by the vagaries of military rule and the haphazard economic policies pursued by the government" that they "do not appear to fix the audience at a specific point on the social hierarchy."[89] For Adejunmobi, Nollywood's audiences are "loosely connected not by ethnic solidarity, or even by class, but by shared interests in projects of individual enrichment."[90] If such a statement makes Nollywood sound a lot like the popular stereotype of a social media platform—a lot like the Facebook whose use is said to make everyone

Figure 2.3. Nollywood's real-life "girls on fire," Kate Henshaw, Rita Dominic, Uche Jombo, and Funke Akindele, promote their reality television series *Screen Divas* (2013), which follows their efforts to empower African women to prevent domestic violence and to resist limiting social prescriptions.

a star—then that is perhaps fitting. Facebook, Twitter, and Instagram have not simply expanded the parameters of Nollywood stardom. They have also inspired new narratives in Nollywood films—even entire subgenres devoted to the theme of connectivity. At the same time, the Nigerian telecommunications giant Globacom has been relying upon more and more Nollywood stars to spread its complicated and increasingly controversial corporate gospel. What happens to their images in the process is not what might be expected. West African social realities, along with the unpredictable limitations of technologies, are always waiting in the wings.

3

A Mobile Glow

Nollywood Stardom and Corporate Globalism

A woman proudly hoists a BlackBerry in what appears to be a promo for the phone but is in fact a poster for a film. In another image, the same woman is holding a similar phone, only this time the ad has nothing to do with a movie. It is a flyer for a particular cell-phone service plan, and it first appeared on the pages of *The Punch*, a popular Nigerian newspaper. In yet another image, the woman's face is rendered in cartoon form for the cover of Nigeria's *Y! Magazine*—a cover whose upper right-hand corner is comprised of an ad (couched as a contest) for the BlackBerry Bold 5. Beneath the ad, but above the illustrated face, is a quote. It comes from Hillary Clinton: "You have just one life to live. It is yours. Own it, claim it, live it, do the best you can with it." What Clinton's words are doing on a Nigerian magazine cover—and at the precise meeting point between a Nollywood star and a cell phone—is hardly obvious. Upon closer consideration, however, the Clinton quote seems entirely appropriate, even indispensable. It speaks volumes, not only about Nollywood's star system but also about that system's growing relationship to a specific form of corporate globalism.

The three advertisements described share a pair of common threads: an iconic BlackBerry phone and an equally conspicuous Nollywood star, Tonto Dikeh. The first ad is for the 2011 film *BlackBerry Babes*, director Ubong Bassey Nya's satirical take on the so-called "campus film," one of Nollywood's most popular genres. *BlackBerry Babes* follows six self-proclaimed "university girls"—and downright BlackBerry fetishists—as they compete to claim the mantle of "Most Technologically Sophisticated." For them, social progress—at both micro and macro levels—has everything to do with connectivity. They not only believe that their multiple BlackBerry phones bespeak high fashion and magisterial status; they also describe the devices' capacity to connect them with the wider world—with what one girl describes as the "life outside of Nigeria." Of the six young women, Tonto Dikeh's character, Vivienne, is perhaps the most invested in ideals of globalism. Appearing within the boundaries of so reflexive a film, Dikeh's Vivienne represents a fitting confluence of performer and role, given that the star has been a prominent advocate of pan-Africanism and also of efforts to "sell" Nollywood overseas.

In the second of the ads described above, Dikeh's use of a BlackBerry is a clear indication of the popularity of her character in *BlackBerry Babes*—as well as of the film itself. Deploying Dikeh as an instantly recognizable (albeit unofficial) ambassador for BlackBerry, the ad has her touting her upcoming appearance on *The Big Friday Show,* a weekly production of MTV Base Africa that airs on Nigeria's Silverbird Television (STV). An example of the type of transnational horizontal integration increasingly central to media conglomerates, MTV Base Africa, which has its roots in the American Viacom Inc., its principal production facilities in South Africa, and some of its major broadcast audiences in Ghana and Nigeria, "needs" Dikeh's BlackBerry to help spread the word about its programs, particularly via text. "Message your friends," reads Dikeh's ad, "and let them know about *The Big Friday Show.*"

The image of Dikeh holding a BlackBerry is more than just a nod to one of her most beloved films. It is also a reflection of her role in promoting Nollywood across the African continent—and, implicitly, across the globe. All at once, the ad attempts to sell Dikeh's tech-friendly star image, the MTV Base Africa series that has often promoted that image (as well as, by extension, the Nollywood industry itself), and also the telecommunications superpower that both sponsors *The Big Friday Show* and is a major force in making cell-phone culture—what *BlackBerry Babes* and its sequels so mercilessly satirize—such a recognizable presence in Nigerian everyday life: Globacom. When Dikeh wields a BlackBerry to "spread the word" about a promotional television appearance, she provides reminders of her own star persona, of Globacom's transmedia presence, and also of the company's controversial capacity to make telecommunications a familiar term throughout West Africa.

The *Y! Magazine* image of Dikeh that brings together a BlackBerry contest and Hillary Clinton is even more complex. To begin with, Dikeh appears, in illustrated form, as a broad caricature, suggesting that her "real" face is so recognizable, indeed iconic, that it can survive cartoon distortions. Even more parodic than those distortions is the generic framework in which they appear: an old-fashioned, American-Western-style "Wanted" sign that cheekily "criminalizes" Dikeh and suggests that the "reward" for her capture can be found on page forty of the magazine. On that page, in fact, is a glossy color image of the actual, corporeal Dikeh wearing an elegant evening gown and posing rather seductively—reward indeed.

While the BlackBerry's presence on Dikeh's magazine cover might be dismissed as a mere capitulation to commerce—a reflection of the publication's reliance on advertising support—it is clear that Dikeh's own image renders it distinctly appropriate, even inevitable. This is, after all, Dikeh the BlackBerry Babe, whose public, on- and offscreen uses of the phone have helped to cement her iconicity, just as her own persona has helped to popularize the BlackBerry in Nigeria. Who better to herald a sponsored magazine contest for a BlackBerry Bold 5 than the woman whose possession of just such a phone gives her character a glamorous, near-legendary quality in Ubong Bassey Nya's film trilogy? And who better to help rescue that trilogy from the accusation that it feeds negative stereotypes of Nigerian femininity than Hillary Clinton? Appearing at the juncture of Dikeh and a BlackBerry, Clinton's quote not only mediates between the two icons but also acts as a reminder of the goals of female empowerment that so many Nollywood stars espouse. Exhorting her fans to make the most of their lives and to connect with others, Clinton sounds remarkably like the Dikeh who, in *BlackBerry Babes,* attempts to better herself through online social networking, saying, "My life is my own—I can be anyone—and the world is literally at my fingertips." Such an utterance is, of course, also a reminder of the antiessentialism, the self-pluralization at the heart of Nollywood's star system. But *BlackBerry Babes* and its sequels satirize that system, as well as a general culture of appreciation for smartphones that often feeds both classism and nationalism,

Figure 3.1. At the intersection of a Clinton quote and a BlackBerry ad: Tonto Dikeh, one of the stars of Nollywood's *BlackBerry Babes* trilogy, appears in cartoon form on the cover of Nigeria's *Y! Magazine*. December, 2012.

suggesting that resistance to commodity culture can, through parody, coexist with a certain demystification of Nollywood stardom.

This chapter examines the comically self-referential *BlackBerry Babes, Return of BlackBerry Babes* (2011), and *BlackBerry Babes Reloaded* (2012)—three multipart films (all directed by Ubong Bassey Nya) that together address the topics of telecommunications and brand loyalty. In exploring this particular film cycle, I reflect upon the role of Nollywood stardom in promoting the intensely controversial yet immensely successful Globacom, and vice versa. A corporation whose transnational reach openly relies upon stars' glamor and popularity, Globacom threatens to reposition such stars as overpaid, overexposed, and oblivious to the cultural, social, psychic, and even bodily effects of wireless technologies. Throughout West Africa, Globacom is viewed with considerable ambivalence. On the one hand, the corporation has—like Nollywood itself—surmounted tremendous economic and cultural obstacles to become a leading media force. On the other, it has become—again like Nollywood—so successful, so dominant, as to eclipse or preclude alternatives to its products and practices. While it is possible to praise Globacom's capacity to promote mobile telephony in West Africa, it is difficult to avoid recognizing the aggressiveness of the corporation's growth, its delimiting of certain avenues for accessing media content (as well as its increasing role in creating such content), and its perceived imposition of particular Nigerian corporate ideals upon the rest of West Africa.

PROMOTING MOBILE TELEPHONY

In examining Globacom's role in developing both Nollywood stardom and mobile telephony, it is perhaps best to begin with *BlackBerry Babes*. The film opens with a high-angle shot of a highway on which a car has broken down, its former occupants standing in frustration as they await assistance, and as fully functional cars rush past. This omniscient establishing shot seems a curious way of beginning a film whose title is *BlackBerry Babes*, but it serves as a reminder of what Brian Larkin has called "the dialectic of technological breakdown and repair"—a dialectic that carries a special resonance in Nigeria.[1] The inoperable automobile set against a series of speeding vehicles is a clear visual indication of the coexistence, in late modernity, of advanced technological utility and sheer, oppressive stasis. "Breakdown and failure are, of course, inherent in all technologies," writes Larkin, "but in societies such as Nigeria, where collapse is a common state of technological existence, they take on a far greater material and political presence."[2] In the case of *BlackBerry Babes*, the opening allusion to the promise of functionality and the coincident experience of breakdown is not really "about" car culture. Rather, it prepares the spectator for the film's true subject: an imperfect yet all-powerful, "locally grown" mobile telephony.

The emergence of Nigeria as an information society has hinged on the success of telecommunications technologies. In the literature on the politics of connectivity, bona fide information societies are largely limited to advanced nations—those of the global North. The question of whether developing countries—those of the global South—can be considered information societies has created a clear dichotomy between production and consumption. Accordingly, those countries that produce communications media are most frequently positioned as information societies, while those in which "mere" consumption is the only available experience of new technologies are assigned a lesser status, one in keeping with familiar frameworks for ignoring the so-called Third World. But even before Globacom's emergence helped introduce a communications-based paradigm of Nigerian technological production—a veritable Africanization of IT—some scholars suggested that the remarkably diverse uses of communications tools throughout the African continent in fact destabilized the familiar separation between technology's production and its consumption. As Mike Powell has noted, Africans' capacity to recast communications technologies—whether via piracy or through more licit means—has long been underestimated.[3] Why not assume that new, resistant ways of engaging with media can make a country like Nigeria a prototypical information society, even apart from the corporate contributions of Globacom?

Given its political history, Nigeria offers an instructive case study in technology's adaptable relationship both to state power and to civic society. Beginning in the colonial period, communications technologies tended both to consolidate and express political hegemony. Larkin writes of the way in which technological development became, in itself, "a necessary spectacle of colonial rule," one that positioned premodern tradition as its "lesser" opposite.[4] Larkin's conception of the "colonial sublime," through which he theorizes the subjugating function of "unimaginable" new technologies, turns from a description of bridge and railroad construction to extended considerations of two separate but related media—radio and cinema. Larkin concludes that, in Nigeria's postcolonial present, communications technologies are being "constantly reinvented, constantly recycled" in ways that both confirm Nigeria's interactions with the wider world and showcase its resistance to Western theoretical assumptions.[5]

Historically, perhaps the single most contentious communications technology in Nigeria has been the telephone. Both in its landline and wireless configurations, the telephone has managed to shape a vast array of social spaces—some obvious and others surprising. In exploring the post-independence connections among technology, the state, and civic society, Ebenezer Obadare helpfully tracks the development of telephony in Nigeria, noting that the telephone "has been an index of social stratification" as well as a means of connecting Nigerians with relatives forced by economic hardship to emigrate from the country. In uniting family members across vast geographical distances, the telephone has served simultaneously as a welcome communications tool and a reminder of limited opportunities in Nigeria's domestic economy. The need to use a phone for familial contact is itself a function of the dispersions of globalization—what Obadare calls the "swelling" of the diaspora.[6] At the same time, this specific communications need is inseparable from Nigeria's inability to generate employment opportunities, particularly for young people who must, in response, repair elsewhere.

In *BlackBerry Babes* and its sequels, cellular phones are praised not for their potential to connect "vococentric" family members but rather for their utility in linking users to "the entire internet"—and thus to strangers throughout the world. Astonishingly, at no point in the trilogy is a lead character seen speaking into a cellular phone. Instead, the trilogy's protagonists operate their BlackBerries in strict silence, while texting each other or typing into the interfaces of Twitter, YouTube, Google, and Facebook, among many other websites. This insistence on the BlackBerry's specific status as a smartphone—this valorization of the device's diverse computing capabilities and advanced connectivity—is not simply a way of showing that the trilogy's characters are media-literate. It is also a reflection of the way that, in Nigeria especially, practices of telephony have long coexisted with debates about civic society's self-politicizing web presence. In the days of dial-up internet, the telephone represented a precondition for access to the online realm—an association that would only intensify in urgency during the regime of General Sani Abacha. When Abacha was in power in the mid-1990s (a period that witnessed Nigeria's positioning as a pariah state in international affairs), growing opposition to his regime ran parallel to an increased, if still relatively limited, popular use of the internet as a tool of protest—thus anticipating the "wired" social advocacy of the Arab Spring, and allowing the West to perceive that the average Nigerian was never reducible to Abacha's despotism. Obadare writes of the extent to which Abacha's regime viewed information technologies as threats to military rule. In a desperate effort to maintain dictatorial control, Abacha not only closed down Nigerian telephone and IT centers but also "contemplated banning the internet or at least blocking popular access to it," all in order to "asphyxiate civil society by denying it the critical oxygen of information and communication."[7] The technological breakdown imposed by Abacha, rooted as it was in the tyranny of military rule, reflected the persistent (and by now clichéd) connections among new media, politicized self-fashioning, and protest. But Abacha's efforts to limit access through systematic oppression cannot hold a candle to the kind of breakdown that, as Larkin argues, is inherent in all technologies—and that corrupt (or simply inadequate) telecommunications providers have long conferred upon the Nigerian media landscape.

If, as Obadare suggests, "new technologies of communication, in particular mobile telephones, appear to expand the existing territory of public expression," then it is often as "combined causes and instruments of protest." In Nigeria—and, indeed, throughout West Africa—popular recognition of growing corporate chicanery, coupled with lasting cynicism surrounding government corruption, has called into question the operations of various telecommunications providers, particularly Globacom. At the same time, popular protests against poor but pricey telecommunications services have proliferated, and on September 19, 2003, something extraordinary happened: in Obadare's words, "mobile phone subscribers in Nigeria took the unprecedented step of switching off their handsets en masse," thus demonstrating the capacity of a communications technology to protest the very problems that it embodied. For many, these problems included poor reception, impossibly high tariffs, and constantly changing contract terms. While the privatization pressures associated with structural adjustment programs were partly culpable, many Nigerians saw a more specific state failure in the weakening of the National Communications Commission (NCC), which by the early years of the twenty-first century had become almost completely unable (or simply unwilling) to regulate telecommunications companies, having long since capitulated to a general climate of neoliberalism.[8]

While the NCC would eventually acquire the habit of fining cell-phone service providers (including Globacom) for their myriad corporate failings, questions about the commission's effectiveness in curbing corruption—or even in halting the kind of media imperialism that a successful, globalizing telecommunications company can impose—have yet to be answered. At present, it is clear that while all independent Nigerian service providers have generated controversy, each has erred in its own specific way. Obadare notes that, during and after the mobile-phone boycott known locally by its numerical date (9/19), protesters "were eager to draw parallels between the activities of the phone companies and those of the oil companies in . . . conniving with the state to undermine the interests of the Nigerian public."[9] With the emergence of Globacom, however, such protesters would have even further justification for making such a claim—and would confront new and persistent pressures against doing so. Globacom is owned and operated by the Michael Adenuga Group, which also consists of Conoil, an oil exploration firm.[10] Founder and CEO Michael Adenuga is himself something of a Nigerian celebrity, a billionaire who advocates Nigerian national pride—as well as, tellingly, resistance to negative, corruption-centered stereotypes—through his numerous public appearances and in print, television, and online ads for Globacom.[11]

While Obadare mentions Adenuga's corporation, his essay was written several years before Globacom became the top telecommunications provider in West Africa, not to mention a globalizing force whose capacity to tempt controversy has only grown stronger in the second decade of the twenty-first century. Obadare notes that Globacom, which began operations in Abuja in August 2003, mere weeks before the 9/19 protests, emerged as a corporation whose domestic ownership was (and still is) promoted as a reason for its respect for Nigerian consumers, although such respect may well be imaginary at best, the product of a certain discursive construction. Globacom's first corporate victory was to adopt a per-second rather than per-minute billing option for its subscribers. Since the per-minute system, which as a rule "rounded up" (thus forcing subscribers "to pay for the whole of the next minute for calls that exceeded the previous minute even by a second"), was at the heart of the 9/19 protests, Globacom's implementation of a per-second system was widely seen as a reason for its sudden popularity—and as the cherry on the cake of its acclaimed indigeneity.[12]

It is by fashioning himself as a celebrity of sorts—and, of course, by co-opting beloved Nollywood stars as brand ambassadors—that Adenuga seeks to preempt or contradict criticism of his corporation's practices. For while Globacom has vastly improved service quality and lowered prices for its subscribers, such improvements have come at a cost. For starters, the corporation's success has meant fewer options for consumers—no small matter when considering that Globacom has, in recent years, had a major hand in producing media content, much of it confined to the format of reality television and made widely available through its expansive service plans. Since such plans have spread throughout West Africa, Globacom raises difficult questions about the limits of indigenous pride and the potential of a widely successful company to remake an entire region in its own image.

Interpretations of Globacom that view the corporation as unscrupulous and even imperialist have long been available to West Africans. As early as 2006, when Globacom was still an emergent force (and not yet a metonym for African corporate hegemony), the Nigerian brand expert Uche Nworah observed that "Adenuga and his scions" were "gradually painting Nigeria's business landscape green, the color of their cash-cow brand, Globacom."[13] Several years later—and with Nworah himself no longer a distanced, critical observer but, suddenly, a Globacom brand manager—Adenuga's corporation is still dipping into its green paint, but its brush has by now cut across many thousands of miles, marking Globacom as a truly transnational force. As such, it has been met with multiple modes of resistance—but so too have Nollywood stars (and, of course, Nollywood films). If deregulation leads to privatization, and if privatization makes a Globacom-style multinational possible in the first place, then such a multinational's specific corporate image must be tailored to the perceived needs and prejudices of an array of consumers, many of them separated by nation, ethnicity, class, culture, language, and religion.

If sheer performative adaptability has been a hallmark of Nollywood stars—with individual talents speaking multiple African languages, employing vastly different accents in English, and generally moving among a diversity of ethnic and cultural guises—then it makes sense that a rapidly globalizing corporation would co-opt their mobile identities. Nollywood stars did not invent Globacom's performance-centered advertising strategy; they simply gave it a greater flexibility. From the beginning, as Obadare points out, mobile telephony has produced, if not required, a certain star system in Nigeria, with individual corporations bearing the public identities of a variety of Nigerian icons, from beloved musicians to a much-feared military dictator. It was General Abacha who, in 1994, "tried to hijack the benefits of . . . privatization and commercialization" by "creating his own cell phone company," to which he tied his likeness—an illustrated portrait that flatteringly removed Abacha's familiar facial scars.[14] While Abacha's scheme failed, and while his self-serving sentiments were further effaced by the return to civilian rule in 1999 and the "democratic" auctioning of mobile licenses in 2001, Globacom, which won its own bid in 2003, initially relied upon a similar structuring of stardom in order to sell its services. But Adenuga has wisely moved well past Abacha's all too fascist model of godlike iconicity by inviting the participation of a whole host of Nollywood stars, shifting from the dictatorial associations of the singular image to the more egalitarian flavor of multiple faces. In their Globacom ads, Nollywood stars promote mobile telephony, as well as the range of experiences—from texting to internet browsing to television watching—that a smartphone can provide. In their movies, too, such stars tend to celebrate wireless technologies, in ways that both obliquely and directly suggest their connections to West Africa's top telecommunications provider.

GLOBACOM'S SUPRANATIONAL STARS

As indicated in a series of star-centered ads from 2012, the phrase "without limits" is central to Globacom's corporate mission, in terms both of technology and of transnational reach. One image features Nollywood's Desmond Elliot, his gaze directed outward and his finger pointing in the same direction, as he smiles beside the question "Are you ready to experience a world without limits?" That the ad promises a boundless world rather than simply an expansive Nigeria or West Africa is instructive; it also resonates with the rhetoric of the *BlackBerry Babes* trilogy, in which the central characters, glued to their Glo-enabled phones, celebrate their direct contact with "all the world"—and very rarely with one another. (Examples of this approach include Tonto Dikeh's Vivienne declaring, "I can reach the world faster with a BlackBerry Touch," and "A Facebook app is how I stay in contact with the rest of the world.") While the stars of the *BlackBerry Babes* trilogy all hail from Nigeria, they represent a remarkably diverse bunch—Nigerian-American, Nigerian-British, Igbo, Ibibio, Yorùbá. If in their dialogue exchanges they sound like Globacom ads, it is scarcely accidental. Van Vicker has himself suggested that even those Nollywood films that do not receive funding from Globacom (such as the *BlackBerry Babes* trilogy) nevertheless paint a flattering portrait of the corporation, either because their stars are Globacom brand ambassadors or because any reference to connectivity requires, within a realist rubric, the crediting of Nigeria's most technologically adept and economically successful service provider.[15] If, in other words, a film that features cell phones does not mention Globacom, then it might as well be science fiction. "Nollywood films, notably, care little for realism," argues Jane Bryce, but the *BlackBerry Babes* trilogy, in its capacity as satire, betrays what Bryce has called a "preoccupation with actual social conditions and political events." Bryce's formulation refers to the hybridized Nigerian newspaper fiction of the 1990s—the writings that "supplied the means of 'softening' such 'hard' issues as political repression and economic exploitation through a process of fictionalization and parody."[16] One of Bryce's chief points is that the coincident emergence of Nollywood and newspaper fiction offers a reason to see the two forms of popular culture as equally committed to providing a realist basis even for extreme, satirical exaggeration. Of course, this realist basis can serve either as a target for the discontent (as in Okey Zubelu Okoh's 2013 film *Girls on Fire*, which, in detailing the all-too-common experience of unemployment, uses it as a launching pad for a wild, partly juju-influenced gay-for-pay scheme) or, perhaps less frequently, as a source of national pride amid depictions of caricatured criminality. In the case of the *BlackBerry Babes* trilogy, a certain, credible respect for Globacom pervades the antic proceedings—a respect that is rooted in the corporation's success in combatting the corruption of its rivals, and in making mobile telephony a reality for millions of Nigerians.

So fraught has been the history of the cell phone in Nigeria that the achievements of Globacom cannot be taken for granted. By reminding their audiences of Globacom's existence and of its victories, films that are not strictly "about" the corporation work to promote, in familiar Nollywood fashion, pride in Nigerian economic achievement. Yomi Adejumo's *Internet Love* (2012) and Ifeanyi Ogbonna's *Fazebook Babes* (2012) both define social media in expressly Nigerian terms, upholding Facebook, Twitter, and Instagram as the "beneficiaries" of Globacom—as sites that, through the corporation, gain Nigerian users. That these users either insist upon employing strictly pseudonymous personae (as in *Internet Love*) or engage in overtly criminal activity (as in *Fazebook Babes* and its sequel, *Fazebook Lovers*) does little to limit a common framing device that upholds Globacom as "the great connector." If the occasional Nigerian elects to operate illicitly, then surely Globacom cannot be blamed. Indeed, as Shedrach John's earnest *Fazebook Babes* theme song makes clear, the driving force behind Nigerian criminals is not Globacom, and not an essentialized national immorality, but, instead, a historically specific paucity of opportunities for economic advancement. When the women of Ifeanyi Ogbonna's film find that, on Facebook, truth-telling gets them nowhere—that, in light of persistent global stereotypes, they are better off self-identifying as Americans than as Nigerians—they realize that criminality, their only way of earning money in "today's Lagos" (where driving a public bus proves both risky and unremunerative for the two protagonists), represents the next logical step in an increasingly cynical progression. Similarly, in *Internet Love,* Globacom is a source of pride for characters who must nevertheless concede that it is not much of a job creator for "everyday Nigerians"—that it seems more a symbolic than an actual, practical victory for the Nigerian economy. It can connect young women with "the wider world," but thereafter leave them ill-equipped to move beyond some demoralizing circuits of commerce and chicanery.

In describing Nollywood's efforts to depict the consumerist excitement of city life, most scholars cite the industry's obsessive rendering of car culture—the shots of pricey automobiles that seem tacit advertisements for particular manufacturers and models. For Lindsey Green-Simms, such images suggest not simply a familiar commodity fetishism, but also an orientation toward the promise of upward mobility—one that need not depend upon "hard work, education, and individual merit."[17] If the automobile, as a symbol both of proud modernization and of possible corruption, tends to signal a certain ambiguity surrounding commodity culture, then so do information technologies. On the one hand, such technologies conceivably place Nigeria and Nigerians in contact with the wider world; on the other hand, however, they hold the potential to democratize fraud by making its mechanisms accessible to anyone with an internet connection.

If, in the *BlackBerry Babes* trilogy, an incorruptible approach to the internet is largely limited to Eniola Badmus' Apollonia—an abused, overweight young woman whose smartphone literally puts her in touch with effective empowerment strategies—then it is still presented as an ever-available option for all Nigerians. Resisting essentialism, the trilogy revels in the satirical extremism of its titular, tech-savvy schemers, presenting their fraudulent activities as conscious choices rather than as "natural" or "inevitable" ones. At the same time, through frequent endorsements of the democratic potential of information technologies—endorsements that even the most corrupt, self-serving characters make—the three films manage to similarly rescue Globacom from the perils of essentialism, marking it as a corporation with a clear conscience and the capacity to self-correct.

Praising Globacom serves a stereotype-shattering function in the *BlackBerry Babes* trilogy, in that it links the corporation not to some familiar notion of corruption but instead to the self-bettering strategies of its central characters. If some of those characters succumb to the impulse to "do evil," it is only because they want to and not because some indecipherable, "essentially Nigerian" inner voice is compelling them to. On one level, the trilogy seems to offer yet another instance of Nollywood's general fascination with "deadly dames." On another, it may appear to traffic in technological determinism—in the notion that a BlackBerry can make a good girl "go bad." But on still another level, the trilogy can be viewed as a response to the sort of stereotyping in which Western media is enmeshed. If all three films directly employ the Nigerian-as-scammer stereotype, then they do so through the exaggerations of satire, presenting a group of women whose only thoughts are of BlackBerry phones. Asked if she'd like to go out on a date, Tonto Dikeh's Vivienne responds by brandishing no fewer than four phones, declaiming in the face of her would-be seducer, "Mister, in my hand here I have the BlackBerry Javelin; I have the BlackBerry Bold 1; the BlackBerry Bold 2; and I also have the BlackBerry Curve. And if I was to get anything new for myself, obviously it would be something higher than what I have here, which is the BlackBerry Bold 3. So if you really want to talk to me, you'll get me the BlackBerry Bold 3, with a four-year internet connection. Then and only then can you actually, really talk to me."

A preposterously long-winded answer to an extremely simple suggestion, Vivienne's speech not only signals the film's satirical approach; it also alludes to one of the specific, hard-won successes of Globacom—the only Nigerian telecommunications provider powerful enough to promise a four-year subscription. Nigeria's 9/19 protests were partly devoted to pressuring service providers into extending their plans. With renewal rates so outrageously high in Nigeria, companies were offering contract periods of as few as four weeks, forcing subscribers to pay an arm and a leg for services that were extremely spotty to begin with. When Globacom entered the picture in 2003, it promised to change all of that, and one of its earliest ad campaigns assured potential subscribers that their access to the internet would "not be interrupted"—whether by bad reception, prohibitively high tariffs, or fleeting contracts. No wonder Vivienne is dreaming not of a date but of a four-year telecomm subscription.

Vivienne's hyperbolically pro-BlackBerry speech does not seem any more preposterous for offering an understandable (if implicit) appreciation for Globacom. If a culture of principled support for telecommunications pervades the *BlackBerry Babes* trilogy, it never becomes so pronounced as to seem egregiously propagandistic. Nor does it ever edge toward a sentimental earnestness—partly because its chief agent, Apollonia, is played by Eniola Badmus, whose star image and specific acting strategies are equally resistant to manipulative techniques. Indeed, in a promotional image for the trilogy, it is Badmus who makes the strongest impression, staring quizzically, even threateningly at Tonto Dikeh, and thereby challenging the seductive gazes of Dikeh and costar Karen Igho. Additionally, as an actress, Badmus is not afraid to make a fool of herself—or to fall on her ass, as she does at the very beginning of *BlackBerry Babes Reloaded*, when a terrifying motorcycle ride tosses her into a puddle of mud. Furious because her BlackBerry has been ruined, Apollonia screams at the motorcycle's driver, a young man whose apparent pique at having given a lift to this less-than-glamorous lady is what allows him to let her fall—and what prevents him from helping her up. As Apollonia bellows at anyone who will listen, she sounds not like someone for whom a BlackBerry is everything—the ultimate material acquisition—but

Figure 3.2. Tonto Dikeh, Eniola Badmus, and Karen Igho appear in an iROKOtv ad that asks, "Who are the BlackBerry Babes?" Note the use of the BlackBerry's logo and corporate orthography.

rather like a woman who has been pushed around (literally) for too long. In this instance, an uncorrupt appreciation for a smartphone is hardly sentimentalized; it stands for an abused woman's hard-won self-empowerment. The trilogy's resistance to mawkishness extends into dramatically different areas, however, as when the glamorous Vivienne is schooled by the wise sugar daddy she's hoping to con and who denounces her "addiction" to her BlackBerry. Defending her use of the phone, Vivienne condescendingly declares that what she's doing "is called social networking. It's how I stay in contact with the rest of the world. And with fashion!" As befits a film star, Dikeh the celebrated fashion plate proves that last statement to be true: her Vivienne dons a series of elegant dresses (all designed by the trilogy's talented costumier, Ogo Okechi), and the character's glamour is so extreme that the other characters are compelled to comment on it, treating Vivienne as if she, too, were a star. Only the character's professorial sugar daddy is unimpressed, saying, "I bought you one phone, and in less than a month, you said it was out of fashion. Then I bought you another one, and you soon said the same thing! Life is not about models of phones."

That may be true, but the *BlackBerry Babes* trilogy makes clear that beneath its star-driven, satirical extremism is a very real and all-too-recognizable West African media environment—one in which a growing telecommunications corporation experiences both an untold prosperity and, outside of Nigeria, a nagging resistance. As a Globacom spokesperson, Van Vicker has publicly addressed the corporation's success in improving cell-phone signals and expanding West Africans' access to television and the internet, but he has also sought to assuage regional (especially Ghanaian) concerns about the corporation's dominance. Vicker suggests that Globacom's "respect" for Nollywood stars, whose work tends to promote pluralism, is a function of its investment in all West Africans, saying, "I believe in Glo, because they are Africa's biggest telecommunications network, and I know Glo believes in me, as well." A Nollywood star's Globacom contract signals, in other words, a mutually supportive relationship, rather than the exploitation of a beloved public figure by a major corporation.

When asked how he understands the specific link between his own star image and the corporate identity of Globacom, Vicker emphasizes the fact that, for a film star, a Globacom contract offers a two-way street: "There is a lot that I can gain from Glo, and a lot that Glo can gain from me." In response to the difficulties that the corporation has faced in Ghana, Vicker upholds stardom as its prime promotional tool. While he concedes that Globacom's executives "need people to push their brand" in his home country, he does not see this as being an impossible task. While Vicker highlights his own success in promoting Nollywood in his native Ghana, he allows for the possibility that others will be equally able to establish a regional consensus about the quality of "something that comes from Nigeria." Such comments offer an obvious analogy between Nollywood and Globacom, wherein both are upheld as Nigerian answers to regional needs. If these needs are often met with resistance—from fans of celluloid African art films at FESPACO, for instance, or from Ghanaians who hate the Globacom masts being erected in their backyards—then stars can always step in, changing moods and minds. Vicker's view holds that what Nollywood stars have done for the negative image of video films—improving it with talent, beauty, and an indefinable "it" factor—the very same stars can do for a corporation that some Ghanaians have called corrupt. These stars' promotional goals are achievable, according to Van Vicker, because Globacom's executives "know talent": "The [stars] that they have selected will do a good job in communicating to their countries what Glo intends to do."[18] In other words, amending Globacom's divisive international image may well be as easy as enlisting stars.

THE EMPOWERING BLACKBERRY

In attempting to mask its national, cultural, and infrastructural specificities with the generalized ideals of pan-Africanism, Globacom continues to use a range of Nollywood stars as icons of glamour, modernity, and mobility, thus raising key questions about what Nollywood stardom might mean when circulated outside of Nigeria, and via advertisements for a series of profoundly politicized telecommunications services. Simply put, Nollywood stars take political risks in joining forces with Globacom, but controversy is hardly a hindrance to stardom; if anything, it can serve to strengthen it, altering its meanings in significant ways. (As Tonto Dikeh once said on an episode of *The Juice,* "I'm controversial because I'm extremely good at what I do . . . and I'm extremely good at what I do because I'm controversial.") When considering Globacom's effects upon individual Nollywood stars, and vice versa, it is important to also examine popular Nigerian representations of mobile telephony—representations that offer some not-so-subtle endorsements of Globacom. However much it may parody the youthful fetishization of its titular phone, the *BlackBerry Babes* trilogy does not denounce mobile technologies themselves—party because such technologies constitute platforms upon which star identities can be built, and through which Nollywood films can themselves achieve increased global visibility.

Allegorizing the widely reported rivalries of Nollywood stars by casting them as competitive BlackBerry fetishists who each use the phone for self-serving (and openly "image-creating") ends, the *BlackBerry Babes* trilogy offers a cheeky take on celebrity culture and its attendant "techno-fetishism" —what new media theorist André Nusselder defines as the belief that "technologies disavow the limits of ordinary life and provide us feelings of pleasure by opening up a realm of seemingly unlimited possibilities."[19] By depicting the free play of identity that a BlackBerry phone can afford, the trilogy offers a running commentary on some of the terms and conditions of Nollywood stardom, including the imperative to enact, both on-screen and off, a diversity of identities. While such performative pliability is arguably a precondition for film stardom in any industrial context, Nigeria's remarkable ethnic, cultural, linguistic, and religious diversity makes constant shapeshifting even more necessary for stars—something that the *BlackBerry Babes* trilogy acknowledges both at the narrative level as well as through specific casting and acting choices.

In *BlackBerry Babes, Return of BlackBerry Babes,* and *BlackBerry Babes Reloaded,* the Yorùbá superstar Eniola Badmus appears as a rural, semi-literate outsider who must adapt to life in Lagos, largely by engaging with what one Igbo character approvingly calls "mobile mania"—the rampant desire to use cellphones (especially BlackBerries) as indices of class and social status. Since Badmus, in speaking English, not only exaggerates her Yorùbá accent but also offers the Pidgin words and phrases that her "betters" reject, and since her malapropism-prone character is constantly mischaracterizing the BlackBerry as "BlackBoogie" (and Facebook as "Bookface"), she seems an unlikely candidate for the kind of tech-savvy glamor that the others exude. However, it is an indication of the BlackBerry's powerfully transformative potential—and of Badmus' adaptable talents—that the subjugated Yorùbá character, once in possession of a smartphone, starts to stand up to her tormenters, offering a series of impassioned speeches in defense of her class as well as her weight (Badmus the "Gbogbo Big Girl" is no svelte starlet), and wearing a variety of trendy jeans, high-heeled shoes, and custom wigs.

The presence of the Yorùbá Badmus in the *BlackBerry Babes* trilogy is not simply a testament to the star's popularity; it is also a reflection of the theme of transcendence through technology. In particular, Badmus' character, Apollonia, is able to transcend her rural background as well as the persistent problem of tribalism in Nigeria. For Apollonia, ownership of a BlackBerry phone is a prerequisite for social acceptance. If such acceptance is not quite complete—if the technologically mediated eradication of tribalism does little to alleviate the pressure to be thin and pretty—then the smartphone, with its handy apps and internet connection, can link Apollonia to the self-help discourses that she so desperately desires. After becoming acquainted with a series of global efforts to promote women's acceptance of their own varied and variable bodies—efforts that she discovers and participates in through social media—Apollonia is miffed to learn, in the trilogy's final film, that her conventionally glamorous acquaintances hate her Facebook profile picture, calling it "ugly" and "a bad advertisement for a Facebook page." Apollonia, in hearing these words, is first confused, and finally indignant. After all, her Facebook profile picture is of her own face—hers and nobody else's—making it, to her mind, the clearest possible marker of her public identity. "Isn't that what Facebook is for?" she asks—is the site not designed for direct self-representation? The other girls laugh at Apollonia's alleged ignorance, highlighting her childlike refusal of the temptation to "better herself" through fabrication—through a "false" Facebook profile photograph (of another person, perhaps, or of an idealized avatar). Apollonia, however, firmly resists the pressure to "sanitize" and "glamorize" her own image for the purposes of social media acceptance, saying, "My face is me—my page is mine—and I won't change a thing."

In this final film in the trilogy, *BlackBerry Babes Reloaded*, the titular figures join a high-end prostitution ring that relies on Twitter and Facebook to find, court, and co-opt clients. When Apollonia learns of their new profession—and of the vast sums of money that it generates—she wants in. However, in requesting membership in the prostitution ring (evocatively called the Wet Angels Elite Club), Apollonia sets herself up for some brutal bullying, asking, "Is there anything you girls can do that Apollonia cannot do?" In response, the others laugh, with Tonto Dikeh's character cruelly pointing out that, while each Wet Angel is "a figure eight," Apollonia remains "a *big* figure eighteen." Flustered, Apollonia reverts to a familiar comic neologism, as she protests that her "Bookface pictures are fine." With a faltering voice, she adds, "On Bookface, I am desirable."

To this, the other girls laugh, and one of them takes it upon herself to shout, "No! Your pictures are ugly—*very* ugly!" Tonto Dikeh's character (renamed Cyrene in this film, to reflect her ascension to the Wet Angels Elite Club) is the cruelest of the group, not only labeling Apollonia "a pig" but also calling attention to the Yorùbá woman's signature linguistic misstep: "How many times have I told you? It's Facebook, not Bookface. How in the world will anyone ever understand you?" Seconds later, she adds, again addressing Apollonia directly, "Your brain is too myopic for the sophisticated thing you carry in your hand. It's never going to work. Just drop it!"

To Apollonia, however, "it" is not an act; she cannot "just drop it." The BlackBerry that she possesses, and that exposes her to innumerable strategies of self-empowerment, is also what emboldens her to talk back. Outlining her understanding of mobile technologies—of a whole host of BlackBerry apps as well as of a wide variety of website interfaces—Apollonia manages to command a certain respect from her tech-savvy listeners. But even though they come to accept that she has "surmounted" her rural Yorùbá roots in order to competently enter what Cyrene calls "smartphone culture," the Wet Angels still resist Apollonia's proud declaration of her own sex appeal. One of them adopts a condescending tone to say simply, "Apollonia, accept that you must lose some weight to look like us." Apollonia responds to this comment with an unchecked rage: "I should lose weight?! Lose weight and disfigure myself just because I want to join your club?!" Calming down considerably, she concludes with what she calls a statement of self-respect—one that also reflects her growing awareness of the world's social and sexual diversity: "There are many men who would die for what I have," she says, in a voice so firm and so clear that the others cannot possibly critique it. Tellingly, the triumphant Apollonia, whose BlackBerry brings her a new confidence as well as a crucial capacity for change, has the scene's last word.

If the *BlackBerry Babes* trilogy treats the titular phone as a kind of joke —a semi-magical seed whose consumption can be life-changing, a bit of juju unto itself—then it also reserves some room for earnest appreciation, especially as the phone is shown to connect its users not only to each other but also to new social possibilities, employment opportunities, and global trends. At the same time, the film's cheeky, self-reflexive presentation of Nollywood's star system, which uses the creation of acclaimed "BlackBerry Babes" allegorically, leaves plenty of space for sincere testimonials, particularly as the transcendent talents of Eniola Badmus permit her character to subvert expectations and traverse ethnic, linguistic, class, and cultural boundaries. As the nearly ten-hour trilogy progresses, it becomes increasingly difficult not to see Apollonia as a stand-in for Badmus herself, so close is the character to the star's defiantly plus-sized public persona. If the BlackBerry phone helps Apollonia circulate and celebrate her own image, then Nollywood's star system has certainly afforded Badmus a similar set of opportunities.

As the *BlackBerry Babes* trilogy demonstrates, employing allegory in order to satirize Nollywood's star system scarcely undermines that system; instead, it only serves to strengthen it, and to promote appreciation for stars' brilliantly differentiated, always-evolving identities. But this type of representational tactic cannot resolve the contradictions—or defuse the controversies—at the center of stars' corporate connections. Of the trilogy's titular babes, several are played by stars who have received Globacom sponsorship—meaning that the corporation has used their various images to help promote its products and policies, compensating them both monetarily and with the increased visibility that comes with a big endorsement deal. In general, the task of a Globacom "brand ambassador" is to promote the corporation's identity in a range of West African national spaces. But such spaces might not be as easily traversed as those of southern Nigeria, and Nollywood stars might not be equipped to ease the regional tensions produced by Globacom's corporate dominance—a dominance that more and more West Africans appear to be regarding as a form of media imperialism.

The transnational saturation of star-centered Globacom advertisements leaves little doubt that West African viewers of *BlackBerry Babes* see its stars through the lens of corporate globalism. The film and its sequels might expose the inanities of consumerism, but they can only present the theme of connectivity in a positive, self-consciously modern light. This is partly because their stars have, at various times and to differing ends, signed Globacom endorsement deals—corporate contracts that preclude negativity in the depiction of communication technologies. For a Globacom-sponsored performer to portray even a subtly anti-technology stance might reflect negatively upon the corporation, which by now is so dominant in West Africa as to be synonymous with telecommunications in general. Thus the *BlackBerry Babes* trilogy, dependent as it is upon stars who—like so many others—tend to maintain close ties to Globacom, can satirize cellphone fetishism but cannot critique telecommunications.

If this particular tightrope pays dividends for Nollywood star images, allowing them to swing between the poles of parodic consumerism and a proud, technologically mediated self-transformation, it does not necessarily preempt negativity altogether, suggesting that Globacom's corporate position—at least in relation to on-screen representation—omits concern for certain persistent, egregious stereotypes of urban Nigerian women. In *Black-*

Berry Babes and its sequels, these women become increasingly committed to con artistry, using their smartphones to seduce and destroy unsuspecting men. At the same time, in a series of especially telegraphic asides, they describe the beauty of connectivity, thus turning into spokeswomen for information technologies—and, in the process, contributing to the reflexivity of a film series whose stars have been among the glamorous faces of a telecommunications superpower.

SATIRIZING MOBILE MANIA, RESPECTING CONNECTIVITY

If the wildly successful *BlackBerry Babes* trilogy has its detractors, they are largely limited—at least in the realm of online Nollywood reception—to self-identified Nigerian feminists who claim to be fed up with the industry's depiction of devious, status-seeking, sexually promiscuous young women. As one user wrote in the comment section of the first film's iROKOtv page, "I really wish at times [that] black women could stop being portrayed as gold-digging women. It really creates a bad stereotype, and then men approach us all as though we are money-hungry people. [We] need more Nigerian movies that portray strong independant [sic] black women, who aren't so promiscuous."[20] This particular comment inspired a series of responses that echoed its sentiments, thus creating a space for a feminist denigration of *BlackBerry Babes*. In a similar vein, the online Nollywood fan magazine Bella Naija furnished the chagrined headline "'BlackBerry Babes'—What Does This Movie Say About Us?"[21]

However admirably invested in resisting stereotypes, such responses tend to misread the film, which functions, like its sequels, not with a straight-faced essentialism but rather with satire very much in mind. In her own reading of "principled" anti-Nollywood approaches, Jane Bryce provides a powerful caution: "If many of the roles given to women appear to be 'negative,' we should not make the mistake of reading them literally. Rather than looking for a one-to-one relationship with reality, we need to read Nollywood as part of the [postcolonial] 'crisis of representation,' and its modes of signification as a dramatization of that crisis."[22] Bryce argues that it is "both futile and anachronistic to ask [Nollywood] to offer 'positive' representations of women or anyone else"—and one might profitably add Oyèrónkẹ́ Oyěwùmí's suggestion, in *The Invention of Women,* that the exportation of

Western feminism represents nothing less than a neocolonialist practice, a piece of imperialism unto itself. Bryce's brand of resistance to literal-mindedness pays pleasurable dividends for a reading of the *BlackBerry Babes* trilogy. Simply put, it is obviously a satire of consumerism to show a woman's willingness to die for a smartphone or to depict the wildly contagious avarice that leads to a fraudulent prostitution ring called the Wet Angels Elite Club (whose cheeky name alone should single the filmmakers' comedic distance from their subject). In Northrop Frye's well-known analysis, satire is a process whose "moral norms are relatively clear" and whose author "assumes standards against which the grotesque and absurd are measured."[23] While BlackBerry ownership remains on the rise in Nigeria—even as the company is ceding considerable ground to the iPhone and Android in other parts of the world—the depiction of an unadulterated BlackBerry lust is what shifts Ubong Bassey Nya's films from the realm of socioeconomic realism to that of sheer comic exaggeration. Such a shift is hardly a one-way process, however. It is more of a shifting back and forth—an oscillating between sincerity and fakery, realism and extremism. After all, as James Naremore suggests, self-reflexive, star-driven films often "hover between techniques of social documentary and satiric fantasy," the better to highlight their stars' fantastical accomplishments, but also their entrenched positions in the machinery of a real-world movie industry.[24]

Based on an absurdist story by Sylvester Obadigie, whose Nollywood credits (as both writer and producer) include numerous films about the Nigerian entertainment scene, Ubong Bassey Nya's screenplay highlights the improbable monstrosities of "mobile mania," but it also leaves room for Eniola Badmus' Apollonia to transcend (whether through childlike guilelessness or mature activism) the culture of mendacity and betrayal at the center of the narrative. Nya's authorship is especially pertinent to a consideration of the *BlackBerry Babes* trilogy, since it starts with Obadigie's screwball story, in which the BlackBerry phone is an oracle that can point to peace as well as to doom, and in which women literally trip over each other in order to reach it. But as Obadigie's own credits suggest, he has long been invested in representing Nollywood's star system through exaggeration and allegory. In 2008, his prose story about the surprising private lives of (fictional) Nigerian public figures became the basis for Lancelot Oduwa Imasuen's film *The Celebrity*, which itself shifts between a self-conscious, exaggerated evocation of its own stars' public personae and an apparently heartfelt tribute to their remarkable talents.

Each entry in the *Blackberry Babes* saga might profitably be described as a cinematic roman à clef, given how legibly it connects its fictional characters to the public personae of the stars who play them. Like satire, the cinematic roman à clef requires a certain level of audience knowledge, raising important questions about the reception of Nollywood's most reflexive films. To a spectator who is unaware of, say, Tonto Dikeh's history of promotional appearances, would her BlackBerry Babe be as comical a reminder of some of the corporate contexts for Nollywood stardom—or even as clear a depiction of Dikeh herself? In describing the roman à clef, Sean Latham suggests that the mode's effectiveness relies upon a tacit contract between author and reader, meaning that it "ultimately depends for definition on the conditions of its reception and circulation." Capable of passing as fiction, a text leans toward the roman à clef "only through the introduction of a key that lies beyond the diegesis itself," and whose possession can confer pride (and a certain "snobbish pleasure") upon those who "share in [a] text's gossipy delights."[25]

Latham's assessment of the empowering potential of the roman à clef suggests a fresh way of comprehending Karin Barber's famous claim that African popular arts are constituted as much by producers as by consumers. Extended to the Nollywood context, Barber's claim would seem to signal the capacity of Nigerian consumers to keep the industry afloat through a variety of idiosyncratic distribution, exhibition, and reception practices. But seeing the star-centered reflexivity of certain Nollywood films as specifically satirical, one can observe a major comedic avenue through which Nollywood reaches out to its audiences, and through which its audiences can make sense of stars' omnipresent corporate promos. In his book on film comedy, Geoff King suggests that satire expresses a constant tension between outright absurdity and muckraking commitment. "It shades at one end into broader and generally 'safer' comic forms. At the other, it reaches into darker realms, beyond that usually considered to be comic." King is quick to point out, however, that "not all satire is oppositional in relation to its place of production, as a subversive undercurrent."[26] In the case of the *BlackBerry Babes* trilogy, the tensions of satire are both extreme and ever-present, at once threatening to the public images and corporate contracts of its stars and wildly celebratory of their acting skills and self-promotional talents. At the same time, a certain satirical dialectic renders the trilogy simultaneously pro- and anti-BlackBerry—both invested in the capacity of lawful telecommunications services to improve Nigeria's global image and allergic to the absurd lure of commodity fetishism. It is by considering the place of the audience in relation to the text, however, that one can best perceive the function of satire. Through the *BlackBerry Babes* trilogy, that function is not to give offense necessarily—not to condemn Nigerians for ever investing in telecommunications technologies—but perhaps to honor a certain exasperation with the saturation of Globacom and of the BlackBerry phones that its services nourish, and to acknowledge some of the pains of media imperialism without providing a deadly didacticism.

There is a remarkably persistent assumption, among Western print critics, that African popular cinema in general—and Nollywood in particular—will unthinkingly assimilate anything new or popular, anything with a demonstrable (and preferably American) cachet. Hence the now-prominent notion that the *BlackBerry Babes* trilogy is, according to countless iROKOtv user comments, "Nollywood's 'Social Network'"—that is, an African adaptation of David Fincher's critically acclaimed 2010 film about the founding of Facebook.[27] Again, the specter of essentialism emerges to circumscribe Nollywood: if it is Nigerian, then it must be an American wannabe.

Rather than view it as a tripartite remake of *The Social Network*, I read the *BlackBerry Babes* trilogy as being deeply satirical—not so much a tribute to but a takedown of American media imperialism. When the tech-savvy campus ladies, like the brainy Harvard boys of Fincher's film, convene in the dormitories to debate the uses of Facebook, they not only emphasize their own racial, national, and gendered differences from the American lads, proudly declaring the social media site a "platform for black Nigerian women," they also articulate a truth that Mark Zuckerberg (as played by Jesse Eisenberg) cannot quite concede: that Facebook, more than just a simulacrum of social acceptance ("Like a final club, except we're the president."), in fact provides a measure of practical advancement for low-income users, helping them to get hired, get married (to wealthy men, in the *BlackBerry Babes* trilogy), and generally get "ahead." This use of Facebook for economic advancement is entirely plausible; what pushes it toward the satiric is that it is the site's *only* available use in the *BlackBerry Babes* trilogy, prompting Apollonia—

the lone voice of reason—to wonder what is so wrong with her "simple" Facebook profile page, which she believes to be an accurate reflection of her appearance, habits, and hobbies. Upon closer consideration, however, Apollonia's seemingly reasonable, familiar use of Facebook may well suggest an uncritical capitulation to the site's publicized terms and conditions, to its well-regulated "official" determinants. If Facebook, with its growing global hegemony, is going to push its way onto the university campuses of southern Nigeria, then certain Nigerians—like the BlackBerry Babes—may want to push back, cynically redefining Facebook as a tool through which to finagle American funds (one woman receives a monetary advance from an American "sugar daddy"), and generally rejecting Zuckerberg's more utopian claims about the social network's worldwide legitimacy.

Articulating the *BlackBerry Babes* trilogy's satirical take on social media is important not merely because it helps to further disentangle Nollywood from the odious assumption that, as a popular African industry, it is unaware of the critical, metatextual tools of satire. Doing so also throws into stark relief the sudden bursts of sincerity that serve to celebrate Nollywood stars, the tech-savvy characters they play, and also, by extension, a telecommunications corporation like Globacom, whose operations have dramatically expanded Nigerians' access to mobile services. The distinctions between satire and sincerity can be seen throughout the trilogy, especially when characters transition from a maniacal, even murderous investment in their phones to a more distanced, reflective perspective—a transition that requires the cultivation of an acting style that can veer between broad comedy and quiet contemplation. If this style suggests, more specifically, a certain alternation between Brechtian and Stanislavskian models of acting, then it is not by accident. Indeed, in the *BlackBerry Babes* trilogy, as elsewhere in Nollywood's engagements with celebrity and consumer culture, Stanislavsky is mentioned directly. Characters who crave success in the public sphere know that they need to perform certain roles, and that performance itself, if rooted in subjectivity—in a psychologized specificity—can be immensely satisfying. From *Last Celebrity* to *Efficacy* and beyond, Method acting (Stanislavsky as filtered through Lee Strasberg) is upheld, both as a source of narrative inspiration as well as through the evidence furnished by Nollywood star performances. An even more obvious evocation of Stanislavsky is offered in a single shot from *BlackBerry Babes*—a shot that recurs in *Girls on Fire* and that shows

Stanislavsky's famous book *An Actor Prepares* propped up on a table in a Lagos living room.[28]

If, in Nollywood films, characters frequently read Stanislavsky, then so do the stars who play them. Several of the industry's biggest names, including Bukky Ajayi, have studied the Stanislavsky technique in London. The actress Nse Ikpe-Etim, who stars in Kunle Afolayan's 2011 film *Phone Swap*, describes her reliance on Stanislavskian methods when preparing to "immerse" herself in a role:

> I follow the school of thought of Konstantin Stanislavsky, [who] is the father of Method acting, and also Stella Adler. I also believe in the spirituality of acting. So when I get a script, apart from what my director is planning to draw for me, I go to the drawing board, I imagine a lot of things. I dig up experiences which might not be my own, things I have heard, and I create the character. Acting is not exactly doing what the director wants you to do.[29]

If Ikpe-Etim's statements offer an endorsement of Stanislavsky's lasting appeal, they also suggest the extent to which his teachings empower performers to create their own characters, regardless of directorial intent.

There is, however, another production factor that threatens to impinge upon a performer's creative process: corporate sponsorship. In *Phone Swap*, that factor forces the film's stars to serve as mouthpieces for Globacom and BlackBerry: the former provided much-needed production funds, while the latter withheld support despite the entreaties of producers, who carefully and conspicuously weaved the BlackBerry brand into the narrative anyway, hoping for an eleventh-hour subvention.[30] Given this setup, as well as the fact that director Kunle Afolayan is a Globacom brand ambassador, the 35 mm *Phone Swap* can be seen as a glorified commercial for two prominent, convergent corporations. This appears, in fact, to be the preferred interpretation among Nigerians who find the combined corporate hegemony of Globacom and BlackBerry to be, in a word, repellent. In his review of *Phone Swap*, Augusta Okon does not hold back, writing, "I found [the film] rather overbearing with [its] inability to wittingly conceal the direct import of product placements of sponsors (Globacom, BlackBerry)." In other words, even at the level of mise-en-scène, *Phone Swap* is an obviously sponsored affair—one whose makers simply could not resist "shoving it in our faces." For Okon, "the [BlackBerry] ads subtly showed during the rolling of the opening credits" could not possibly prepare for the propagandistic deluge to come, with the film depicting "the joys of Globacom" through numerous avenues: showing "Glo Zone, [the] sale of Glo recharge cards by Afolayan [in a director's cameo] decked in [Globacom's] sales apparel," as well as countless Globacom promotional kiosks. In Okon's view, these and other images all screamed, in Globacom's corporate voice, "'Hey, guys, we sponsored this movie . . . halla!'"[31] In her review for Africa Magic, Peju Akande seconds Okon's sentiments, suggesting that *"Phone Swap,* as has become typical of most Nigerian films that get corporate sponsors, bores the audience with Globacom green. Sometimes, the movie proceeds like an hour-long advertisement for [the corporation]. Such [an] inordinate amount of time is spent advertising Glo that the movie could as well have been renamed: *Glo Phone Swap.*"[32]

Similar charges can of course be leveled against the *BlackBerry Babes* trilogy, at least with respect to its obsessive elevation of the titular smartphone brand. But as *Phone Swap* demonstrates, an endorsement of BlackBerry is often synonymous with an endorsement of Globacom. While Afolayan's film represents the convergence of the two brands for funding and promotional purposes, the general, mutually supportive relationship between BlackBerry and Globacom is so obvious in Nigeria as to extend well beyond *Phone Swap's* particular production structure. In the *BlackBerry Babes* trilogy, which did not receive official corporate sponsorship, the matter is often as simple as a character saying that without Globacom her BlackBerry would not be able to function, since Glo "gives good reception." At other points in the trilogy, characters openly acclaim Globacom for "bringing internet to the Black-Berry"—as well as for bringing Nigerian television to the internet.

There is a moment in the trilogy's first film when Oge Okoye's Damisa realizes that she has missed a live broadcast of *Big Brother Nigeria,* a popular reality television series, part of the global *Big Brother* franchise. Out running errands, Damisa was away from her sixty-inch flatscreen television set when the evening's episode aired. Upon returning home, she uses her BlackBerry to call Tonto Dikeh's Vivienne, hoping that the other woman will be able to fill her in on what she missed. She learns not only that the episode was highly entertaining but also that she need not have missed it at all—that she could easily have watched it even while out running errands. Vivienne, the film's most tech-savvy character, knows all about Globacom's 3G services, which promise the sort of high-speed internet connection that facilitates live-streaming video—including mobile TV. That Damisa is so down about

Figure 3.3. Nollywood's Nokia Babe? Mary Remmy promotes iROKOtv's Nokia app. April, 2013.

having missed an episode of *Big Brother Nigeria,* and that she perks up as soon as she's reminded of all that can be seen on a BlackBerry screen, suggests that the sequence is an unsubtle advertisement not just for the smartphone but also for the Globacom that (allegedly) grants it such an exciting and varied life. It is no accident that Damisa's traditional television set remains blank—dead—while she speaks by phone to her friend. With the diversely functional BlackBerry a blazing object in the foreground, the embarrassingly retrograde television remains ensconced in the lonely, lifeless background—a pathetic reminder of times past.

When *BlackBerry Babes* touts television as a newly mobile medium, one no longer confined to an unwieldy, stationary set, it celebrates more than just the BlackBerry-Globacom connection. It also alludes to—and endorses—the off-screen persona of one of its stars, Mary Remmy, who plays Kaisha, the urbanized, glamorized, and witheringly condescending cousin of Apollonia, who resents that she "shares blood" with the Badmus character. Since

2012, Remmy has been the face of an iROKOtv app that promises to "bring your favorite stars straight to your fingertips"—that, in other words, does precisely what Dikeh's Vivienne claims is possible in an era of extensive media convergence. Thus far, however, the iROKOtv app is exclusive to Nokia phones, suggesting that an awareness of Remmy's off-screen promotional activities can complicate the apparent brand loyalty of the *BlackBerry Babes* trilogy, reinforcing its status as broad satire (rather than a corporatized paean to a particular smartphone). For spectators who are aware of it, Remmy's Nokia-friendly star image suggests an obvious, even preferable alternative to BlackBerry mania.

Within this regime of reflexivity, Damisa's specific obsession with *Big Brother Nigeria* is no small matter: it prepares the way for the trilogy's third film, which features, as its opening credits effusively declare, "Karen Igho of *Big Brother Africa*!" If, throughout the trilogy, the convergence of Globacom and BlackBerry signals the "obviousness" of a corporate synergy that exists in the real world, then the fusion of Nollywood and reality television, which arrives via Karen Igho, suggests a certain star-making strategy—an effort to turn Igho from a onetime *Big Brother* contestant into a bona fide film star. *BlackBerry Babes Reloaded*, like its predecessors, seems well aware of its stars' offscreen corporate gigs, but also of their general experiential trajectories. Igho's character, Anwuli, is, like Igho herself, a self-described "village girl" who hopes to "make good" in the big city. While Anwuli eventually and at a considerable personal cost becomes a BlackBerry Babe, Igho herself has long since served as one: BlackBerry is, along with Globacom and Coca-Cola, one of the official sponsors of *Big Brother Africa*, requiring the series' contestants to appear in commercials, and thus to function as committed mouthpieces for its corporate identity. Karen Igho's public image, then, has always centralized her connections to BlackBerry culture, lending a sense of inevitability, or at least of symmetry, to her appearance in the *BlackBerry Babes* trilogy.

If Eniola Badmus has frequently and approvingly quoted Apollonia on Twitter, then Igho has similarly used the social networking site to suggest her various personal and professional affinities with Anwuli. Beyond the broad matter of corporate sponsorship, the similarities between Anwuli's statements in *BlackBerry Babes Reloaded* and Igho's real-life tweets are remarkably close, with both using the phrase "grass to grace" (an alliterative distillation of a village-to-city trajectory)—a phrase that Igho often turns into a hashtag on Twitter.[33] Igho's presence in the trilogy thus offers a further indication of its sheer self-reflexivity, but also, on occasion, of its satirical bent. If Igho often describes her "tough" upbringing and "rough road" to stardom (tweeting, for instance, "I wasn't born with a silver spoon but I eat with one now"), then the rural Anwuli similarly expresses her own desire to better herself, to move "beyond the village."[34] However, in keeping with the trilogy's tendency toward satirical exaggeration, Anwuli schemes like Lady Macbeth, making life a living hell for those around her (and particularly for her manipulable male lover) as she hungrily pursues ownership of the latest BlackBerry device. The vengeful, acquisitive Anwuli thus gives Igho a chance to demonstrate her acting range—and perhaps to transcend the limitations of reality-TV stardom, of a sympathetic image developed within the family-friendly confines of *Big Brother Africa*.

If the *BlackBerry Babes* trilogy is attuned to what one character calls "the gifts of Glo"—to the fact that multiple media industries can, via a single Globacom subscription, converge on a single BlackBerry phone—then it is also alert to the happiness that such convergence can bring, and not merely to the Damisa who wants to watch *Big Brother* on something other than her huge, housebound television set. For Vivienne, speed and synergy can "make the world a better place"; a Glo-enabled BlackBerry can "connect everyone." Throughout the trilogy, characters openly praise their smartphones but also, by implication, the Globacom that enjoys several exclusive arrangements with BlackBerry. These apparently earnest, celebratory moments stand out precisely because they constitute interruptions in the overarching satire, but also because they assiduously link the trilogy's protagonists to actual Globacom brand ambassadors.

When a close-up of a Blackberry phone (literally) shows what that phone can do, its users approvingly describe their Globacom accounts, noting that, without a Glo subscription, they simply would not be able to talk, text, and "visit the internet." When Apollonia buys a dummy phone whose only function is to sit atop a Blackberry retail counter and advertise the brand, she must be instructed in the acquisition of service plans—in the fact that Glo "gives phones life" through its subscriptions. Such moments suggest a pronounced pedagogical function that is inseparable from a sincere appreciation for what a BlackBerry—and by extension Globacom—can "do." If much of Ubong Bassey Nya's trilogy is devoted to the deliberately ridiculous shenanigans of the *BlackBerry Babes* themselves—who at one point kidnap their professor, photograph him in "compromising positions" (using, of course, their smartphone cameras), and blackmail him in order to receive solid A's—then the sequences of consumerist pedagogy not only stand out but also seem like commercials for BlackBerry as well as for Globacom, raising key questions about the trilogy's relationship to product placement.

Perhaps the most powerful indication of a satirical self-reflexivity arrives in the first film, when the aforementioned professor is delivering a lecture entitled "Propaganda and Public Opinion." Too fixated on their phones, the students do not hear a word. But the gist of the lecture is this: there is a fine line between an "accidental" endorsement and a conscious propagandizing, and the latter is least likely to be well received. The professor, Dr. Mukoro (played by Oliver O. Peters), asks his students if they can identify the difference between propaganda and public relations. They cannot, of course, because they do not even try, so distracted are they by their BlackBerry phones. For Dr. Mukoro, however, the difference is nonexistent—it is a trick question. Like any corporate public-relations strategy, a traditionally defined propaganda technique "concentrates on matters of the heart and mind"; it makes people "feel" and even "consciously believe" that they need, rather than want, a product. The irony, of course, is clear, as Dr. Mukoro faces a sea of students who have bought into BlackBerry culture at the expense of their education. In his smug focus on false consciousness, Mukoro is not unlike the eminent professor in Tunde Kelani's *The Campus Queen* (2003), who lectures his students on the differences between tradition and modernity: "So many years after independence, the African elite has refused to go back to the people, to their culture; we have decided to abandon the people." Inadvertently aligning himself with a blinkered elite through the use of the word "we," the professor manages to put his foot in his mouth, prompting criticism from his students. However, it is precisely because she is not glued to a cell phone that one young woman can expose the professor's hypocrisy, standing up to declaim, "Sir, you're an advocate of culture, but there you are in front of us, in these fantastic Western suits, with a gorgeous tie!" It is difficult to imagine a similarly Marxist response from the BlackBerry Babes.

The Campus Queen sees university life as the nexus of Nigerian sociopolitical developments, acquiring a documentary quality through Kelani's use of actual theater departments whose members lend the film their own forms of political cabaret. By contrast, it is primarily through a depiction of the futility of schooling that the *BlackBerry Babes* trilogy exposes its own satirical extremism. In *Return of BlackBerry Babes,* a secondary school student catches "BlackBerry fever," using the money that her parents intended to go toward her school fees to pay instead for a new phone. When a school official finds out, she attempts to shame the student, saying, "Buying a BlackBerry is no way to repay your parents' sacrifices." In response, the girl screams, "If you ever tell anyone what I've done, I will kill you!" Perplexed rather than threatened, the official replies, "You'll kill me? Over a BlackBerry phone?" Shaking her head—as sure a sign of incredulity as of sanity—the woman laughs and walks away. It is clear from this moment, as well as from numerous others, that the *BlackBerry Babes* trilogy does not endorse "mobile mania" per se. But it nevertheless reveals—largely through Eniola Badmus' Apollonia— the positive, self-empowering uses of a BlackBerry phone. Even if it did not gesture toward the phone's genuine use-value, however, the trilogy would still end up propagandizing on its behalf. As Dr. Mukoro points out in his lecture, presence is propaganda, a product's sheer visibility rendering it desirous regardless of its contexts, and simply because it is constantly on display.

By this logic, the *BlackBerry Babes* trilogy is guilty of helping to popularize the eponymous phone. This is precisely how the British blog Mediolana has read it, suggesting that the trilogy provides both "observation" and "prophecy." On the one hand, the three films seem responsive to Nigerian social realities—particularly to the fact that "Nigerians have embraced the mobile telecoms era with a gusto that is almost scary, running in their tens of millions to secure contracts with the likes of . . . Globacom." On the other hand, the trilogy, in obsessively showcasing the BlackBerry itself, all but guarantees the product's lasting market success (at least in Nigeria). The Mediolana profile has its problems (among them a distinct cultural chauvinism that allows the author to express "shock" that a colleague managed to "sit through" *BlackBerry Babes*), but it is among the most incisive Western popular assessments of the complex relationship between the trilogy and "telecoms culture." Almost despite itself, Mediolana manages to praise Nollywood—first in backhanded fashion (calling *BlackBerry Babes* formulaically spellbinding, whatever that may mean), and finally by noting that Nollywood represents "nothing less than the future of capitalism itself." The comment's bombast is tempered through the subsequent listing of three salient factors that make *BlackBerry Babes* so prescient a case study: its "market responsiveness" (the audience-triggered process of producing sequels, of generating a bona fide filmic cycle); "profitability" (proven economic success across multiple distribution platforms, from VHS and VCD to DVD and streaming video, coupled with "fair" licensing arrangements and the need for "relatively little capital investment"); and "aspirational values" (the social and market pressures that *BlackBerry Babes* expresses "with only some irony," and that inevitably work to instill in audiences a desire to own the eponymous phone and to subscribe to Globacom). To Mediolana, which ignores the widespread pirating of *BlackBerry Babes* and its sequels, the trilogy suggests that Nollywood's power players "have identified a popular idea and milked it to the hilt at a speed which puts economic agents in virtually every other film market . . . to shame."[35]

Among this litany of "revolutionary" factors, perhaps the most debatable is the assertion that the *BlackBerry Babes* trilogy operates "with only some irony." As I have been arguing, the trilogy is, in a variety of ways and for disparate reasons, blisteringly satirical, from start to finish. Of course, irony and satire are not necessarily the same, but in the case of the *BlackBerry Babes* trilogy, satirizing Nollywood's star system is a process that depends upon a steady supply of irony. For instance, at the very moment when a minor male character is complaining about the saturation of cell phones and celebrities, his own mobile device begins to ring—and not with just any tone, but with the spoken words "Yo, it's Wiz Boy!" This parodic ringtone offers an obvious, amusing reference to WizKid, the Nigerian teen star whose hit song "Holla at Your Boy" features the lyric "Yo, it's your boy Wiz!" Other examples of irony-in-action similarly satirize stardom: when, in *BlackBerry Babes Reloaded*, the men who run the Wet Angels Elite Club are initiating a new member, the film flashes back (via a lap dissolve) to the moment when Tonto Dikeh's Vivienne was vetted and deemed "special"—in possession of a "flawlessness" and "star quality." This self-reflexive flashback sequence also reveals that *The Glo Soccer Academy*, one of many Globacom-sponsored reality television programs, is playing on a traditional set in the background, distracting several of the men who are tasked with anointing Vivienne. Satirizing Nollywood's star system by showing the vetting process established by some comically sleazy men, *BlackBerry Babes Reloaded* also signals a fissure in its own and in its stars' support for Globacom. After all, if Glo is more apt to invest in reality television than in Nollywood fiction films—if *The Glo Soccer Academy* can distract from the development of a "flawless" female star—then perhaps the corporation's true priorities are far removed from the realm of movie glamour, whatever its past successes with *Phone Swap*.

Of course, true to the trilogy's challenging nature, *BlackBerry Babes Reloaded* soon complicates its initial presentation of reality television as distracting "background noise" by introducing former TV personality Karen Igho as Anwuli, a character whose eagerness to become a BlackBerry Babe mirrors Igho's own efforts to become a bona fide film actress (rather than someone who simply "plays herself" in front of documentary television cameras). *BlackBerry Babes Reloaded* is obviously ambivalent about reality television. On the one hand, the film situates reality TV as a "lesser" form of popular culture; Tonto Dikeh's character insists on watching Nollywood movies instead—and always with a box of popcorn that reinforces her preference for a classically "cinematic" experience. This is particularly ironic given Dikeh's own history: like Igho, she got her start on reality television, appearing in 2005 on the Nigerian competition series *The Next Movie Star*. While Igho, in fact, won her season of *Big Brother Africa*—a victory that furnished several sponsorship deals, public relations and career management contracts, and of course considerable exposure—Dikeh was named a mere runner-up on *The Next Movie Star*. True to her divisively eccentric image, however, Dikeh has claimed that the "loss" was what she in fact wanted all along. As with a *Big Brother Africa* victory, to win *The Next Movie Star* is to receive further, ostensibly star-making contracts. But as the fraught history of mobile telephony in Nigeria clearly indicates, some contracts are crueler than others. Dikeh has claimed that not winning *The Next Movie Star* is what, ironically, allowed her to jump-start her Nollywood film career. "I didn't want them to manage me," she confesses. "Them" in this case refers to the particular management team that the series' producers contracted to represent the eventual winner—a team with its own, limiting ideas about how best to develop a Nollywood career. "I didn't want to be in bondage," Dikeh states, with her usual bombast. "I wanted to be a free bird, explore the industry, and be successful. I didn't want management at that particular time."[36] If, in Dikeh's case, a reality television series provided crucial early exposure, independence— from formal contracts as well as from talent managers—paved the way for an entirely self-determined success, and for a hard-won, unheralded entrée into Nollywood's star system.

Perhaps, then, it is less ironic than simply appropriate for her *BlackBerry Babes* character, Vivienne, to prefer Nollywood films to "trashy" reality television shows. After all, Dikeh, while never denying that *The Next Movie Star* gave her the "small push" into public life that she needed, has apparently resisted looking back, becoming one of Nollywood's biggest stars. In *BlackBerry Babes* and its sequels, her character may keep up with *Big Brother Nigeria*, but she is clearly more interested in promoting mobile television—telling Oge Okoye's Damisa to "watch on the go"—than in upholding the reality mode per se. This preference is clear when she sits, popcorn in hand, to watch a Nollywood film on the biggest screen she can find—which, tellingly, happens to be her traditional television set. There is the sense that, for Vivienne, the convenience of a portable BlackBerry screen is what makes watching *Big Brother Nigeria* worth her while—that, in other words, she simply would not watch it in a more conventional manner, on the expansive TV screen that she reserves for "big" Nollywood movies. (In a further reflection of self-reflexivity, the film that she watches on her living room television set features a series of "cat fights" of the kind that appear throughout the *BlackBerry Babes* trilogy, and that have led to the morally prescriptive anti-Nollywood stance that Jane Bryce addresses.) However much Vivienne might despise it, though, reality television remains a veritable fount of future film stars; the proof can be seen in Dikeh herself, as well as in Karen Igho's intense, star-making performance as Anwuli, the most potently mobile of the trilogy's tech-savvy aspirants.

Perhaps the *BlackBerry Babes* trilogy wants to have its cake and eat it, too—wants, that is, to poke fun at mobile mania while endorsing smartphones and Globacom. Perhaps it wants as well to bash reality television while simultaneously relying on the publicity potential of a *Big Brother* winner making her major Nollywood debut (hence the opening credit that exclaims, "Introducing Karen Igho of *Big Brother Africa*!"). Perhaps it maintains a love-hate relationship with Nollywood's star system, at once allegorizing it as a "pimp school" where girls become glamorous, avaricious women and stressing, through sheer self-reflexivity, the considerable cultural contributions of Oge Okoye, Tonto Dikeh, Mary Remmy, and perhaps especially Eniola Badmus—the "Gbogbo Big Girl" herself. That gender-segregated list belies, however, the trilogy's interest in the way male stars are shaped in Nollywood. In keeping with its generally satirical approach, the first film telegraphs this masculine interest through a joke: in its second and third scenes, *BlackBerry Babes* makes prominent use of Muna Obiekwe, one of Nollywood's top male stars, and suggests his centrality to the narrative to come. Obiekwe, however, has disappeared by the film's third scene—not to return until much later in the trilogy. His elimination is not quite a *Psycho*-style disposal of a major star—but it is close, and just as cheeky. It offers a welcome, satirical commentary on Nollywood's alleged "overuse" of women. As Jane Bryce points out, "women's bodies and the performance of femininity" are "among [the] most powerful signs" not simply in Nollywood but also in "all cinema." Noting Nollywood's orientation toward female consumers, Bryce suggests the specificity of an industry where "films are, most frequently, made by men for a female-dominated audience and defined by masculine heteronormative assumptions."[37] Of course, the *BlackBerry Babes* trilogy was directed by a man—and written by one, too. But assuming that male authorship somehow "distorts" female experience is to underestimate the power of women's star images to shape even the most sexist narratives; it is also, of course, to underestimate the frequency and power of improvisation—a performance technique to which Jonathan Haynes has referred in attempting to define Nollywood's productive differences from, say, mainstream Hollywood practice.[38]

The authorship of stardom is not simply a matter of performance style or of an intertextuality that accrues from the memory of multiple characters. It is also embedded in a sign system that assimilates publicity stills, print advertisements, interviews, red-carpet appearances, charity work and, increasingly, tweets, Facebook updates, and YouTube commercials. If the seemingly contradictory *BlackBerry Babes* trilogy really does want to have and eat its cake, then that is hardly problematic for Nollywood star images, which are already invested in seemingly opposed ideals, in empowering idiosyncrasies and ever-shifting strategies of self-fashioning—in, that is, the general objectives of an antiessentialist, self-pluralizing approach. One could argue that it is in the very nature of media convergence and of multi-platform stardom to embrace change, but numerous Western stars maintain ideologically rigid images across a range of media platforms, which to some consumers makes them seem even more admirably, comfortingly consistent or coherent.[39] One could also argue that viewing Nollywood stars as uniquely changeable is itself an essentializing tactic—or, at the very least, a way of saying that Nigerians just happen to be fickle, inconsistent, sociopathic. But the *BlackBerry Babes* trilogy helps to suggest ways of viewing the changeability of stars as a response to specific Nigerian social, corporate, and political—not to mention ethnic, gendered, and economic—pressures. Globacom might be good for Nigeria and Nigerians—after all, it did improve signal quality, succeed in lowering costs and extending contracts, and it has become an African economic powerhouse—but there are those who would resent its regional dominance, as well as the impression that certain Nollywood stars have sold out by endorsing the corporation. The *BlackBerry Babes* trilogy concedes that Globacom can enable the bad as easily as the good; that reality television can stupefy its viewers while also uncovering talented people (like Tonto Dikeh and Karen Igho); and that Nollywood stars can seem competitive as well as cooperative.

If the near-Hitchcockian elimination of Muna Obiekwe suggests that even Nollywood's biggest male stars are disposable, it does not indicate that they are interchangeable. However, in addressing the close connections between certain Nollywood stars, the *BlackBerry Babes* trilogy offers another nod to Hollywood's famed "master of suspense"—or, at the very least, to one of his beloved tropes: the doppelgänger. Throughout the trilogy, the mirroring of characters provides considerable narrative excitement, raising compelling questions about identity theft, eroticized imitation, and dangerous interchangeability. But such an approach is founded, by and large, upon the well-known physical and professional similarities between actual sets of Nollywood stars. Oge Okoye's Damisa, for instance, belongs to a group of Lagosian university women who wield their BlackBerries for fell purposes, and she is constantly pitting herself against her contemporaries, comparing styles of dress and even particular behavioral tics. To belong to this so-called "BlackBerry League," one must share a set of stylistic preferences (straight weaves are in, Afros out, and short skirts trump long pants), but Damisa the queen bee is paranoid about being imitated, afraid that someone will steal her singular thunder. Damisa's principal competitor (and ostensible friend), Vivienne, is played, in a striking bit of casting, by Okoye's younger rival—and relative lookalike—Tonto Dikeh. In their 2012 film *Miss Queen*, the two stars do not share screen time. Here, however, they're almost always together.

True to its satirical self-reflexivity, the trilogy does not stop with the women's physical resemblance. Indeed, it addresses their overlapping star images from multiple perspectives, including those of romance and fashion. In Muna Obiekwe's first scene in *BlackBerry Babes*, he's attempting to pick up Dikeh's Vivienne. His ploy does not work, however, and, rebuffed, he reluctantly returns to his actual girlfriend—Okoye's Damisa. After Obiekwe's disappearance, the film shifts from a depiction of erotic doubling to focus instead upon the matter of identity theft—something that the internet facilitates but that competitive stars can, in their own ways, just as easily enact. As characters, both Damisa and Vivienne are occasionally engaged in stealing men's credit card information. But by the end of *Return of BlackBerry Babes*, only Damisa has been caught. We see her being hauled off by Interpol agents attempting to crack down on internet crime. Knowing that she's going down for a misdeed that her "friend" has similarly committed, Damisa collapses emotionally. As performed by Oge Okoye, the character's breakdown is remarkable—a show-stopping feat of superlative acting—and it is matched by the intensity that Tonto Dikeh brings to the ruthless Vivienne.

The scene that precipitates Damisa's downfall involves a collision between Damisa and Muna Obiekwe's character, Duke, her onetime lover, mentor, and co-conspirator. Furious at Damisa for her treason (she has branched out on her own, becoming a bona fide BlackBerry Babe beholden to no one), Duke screams insults. Damisa, in response, is calm, even contemplative. She says, "One problem I have with you is this: you underrate me a lot. For how long have we been rocking it together? One year and nine months—let's just call it two years. And you think that's not a long enough time for me to have picked up vital lessons from a master? Give me a break!" Damisa laughs in the face of her former beau and sudden foe, whose misogyny is such that he simply cannot comprehend how his ex-girlfriend has managed to break free of him. This extended scene gives the trilogy an opportunity to make something perfectly clear: its criminal women were "created" by criminal men—molded, in star-system fashion, into a cadre of glamorous performers, all eminently capable of deceiving their "fans" (as Duke euphemistically refers to the victims of fraud, who have permitted themselves to be "taken in" by beautiful, talented women). When Damisa tells Duke that she has had to "put Vivienne in her place," it is impossible not to think of the professional rivalry between Okoye and Dikeh—of the hierarchical nature of Nollywood stardom.

When Vivienne finally enters the room, she and Damisa immediately get into a physical fight so intense that it sends them tumbling out into the courtyard, where the Interpol agents are waiting. Before they seize Damisa, however, the male agents watch as the two women take turns pinning each other to the ground, wrestling-style—a process that provides a clear visual commentary on the way stardom works, with one talent being "on top" at a particular time, while another must accept her own (perhaps temporarily) subjugated position. This seems precisely the reading that the film wishes to elicit, since in the preceding scene Damisa addresses the "give-and-take" between her own public image and that of Vivienne—only to assert her supremacy by saying, "I'm up, and she's down." (In response, the cruel Duke says, "For now.") Literally acting out this competitive process, Damisa and Vivienne are constantly exchanging roles in a type of street brawl—until Interpol closes in.

Flashing his badge, one agent announces that he's after Damisa only. Vivienne, who throughout the fight has been calling Damisa a thief—accusing Damisa of having stolen her men, her money, and her "entire identity"—suddenly points at the other woman and shouts, "That is her! That is Damisa!" Dikeh delivers these lines as if they were cathartic—as if uttering them were a purgative drug, restoring Vivienne's ego and making her feel more powerful than ever. Held from behind by a couple of cops, Vivienne leans forward as if extended by a bungee cord, crying out that she has finally "won." "What have I done?" asks Damisa, feigning bewilderment just as her hands are being cuffed behind her. "What have you done?!" Vivienne screams, in a mocking voice that Dikeh makes increasingly shrill, almost to the point of unintelligibility. "What have you done?! You have duped all the men in Lagos! That's what you've done!" Again, the question of deception is central to the women's exchange. But the Vivienne who denounces Damisa for being duplicitous is, of course, herself guilty of equivalent crimes. Vivienne, in other words, is only performing innocence—as well as principled pique—by saying that she is "nothing like" Damisa. However, as she is being placed under arrest for "international fraud," Damisa declares that Vivienne is "an accomplice." In so doing, she unwittingly provides Vivienne with another opportunity to act. Contradicting her earlier claims about Damisa's duplicity, which clearly telegraphed the women's close relationship—their intimate knowledge of one another—Vivienne suddenly says, "I don't know her! I do not know her!" But Damisa, realizing that Vivienne will only keep on repeating this line—protesting her innocence and ignorance in a strident manner—furnishes some believable details, declaring, "We type together, we do everything together!" Finally, the Interpol agents catch on: these women have been in cahoots, jointly using "false" Facebook pages in order to solicit men from around the world—a new sort of 419 scheme that serves as a social-media preamble to the illegal acquisition of credit-card numbers. The film ends with both women being taken, under considerable duress, to the police station.

The criminal give-and-take between Vivienne and Damisa, coupled with their parallel but differently enacted destinies, might suggest a certain singularity in Nollywood cinema, but Oge Okoye and Tonto Dikeh are not the only Nollywood performers whose faint physical resemblance belies contrasting acting styles. Well known for their congruent beauty and alleged competitiveness, Yvonne Nelson and Jackie Appiah were cast in the title roles in *Sisters at War* (Frank Rajah Arase, 2014), a Ghanaian film that shrewdly exploits their status as star lookalikes, but that allows them ample narrative space in which to develop polar characterizations. Lest this seem a strictly "feminine" phenomenon, however, it is worth noting the frequency with which certain male stars are aligned with one another, both in press coverage and in film narratives. Khing Bassey and Van Vicker, both Nollywood heartthrobs, have played vastly different characters, but their equivalent allure tends to create its own overriding meanings—particularly in films that present them as "half-castes," emphasizing their light skin and biracial identities. In *BlackBerry Babes Reloaded*, Bassey appears in a dual role—as Elvis, the corrupt solicitor for the men who run the Wet Angels Elite Club (which Vivienne, rechristened Cyrene, joins after her release from prison), and as "The Boss," the shady figure who secretly runs the whole show. The joke is that the beautiful Bassey, with his Vicker-like baby face, does not seem remotely threatening—and, indeed, both he and Vicker are rarely called upon to make much mayhem (beyond the melodrama of romance) in their movies. But Vicker is very much a leading man, while Bassey is still a supporting player. The latter actor's lack of prominence in *BlackBerry Babes Reloaded*—not to mention his lack of love scenes—sets him apart from Vicker the lady-killer, in spite of his close resemblance to the Ghanaian icon. At one point in the film, a fraudster-cum-pimp casually mentions that Bassey's character resembles "a certain movie star"—a teasing, if implicit, reference to Vicker that is meant to shame the seemingly asexual Elvis with a reminder of how erotically far removed he is from his famous lookalike. Vicker, as one of his Globacom ads puts it, is "fine" (meaning gorgeous) and given to "planting kisses" on his costars. Bassey, in *BlackBerry Babes Reloaded,* is comparatively chaste.

While the striking resemblance between Okoye and Dikeh plays out on screen in the first two entries in the *BlackBerry Babes* trilogy, the connection between Bassey and Vicker is only implicitly called upon in the final film. In offering "inside" jokes about the men's physical resemblance, *BlackBerry Babes Reloaded* relies upon audience knowledge—of Vicker, of discourses of male glamour, of star-centered competition and differentiation—in order to "activate" its satire. If, as Karin Barber so famously suggests, popular arts are equally constituted by producers and consumers, then Nollywood's frequent use of satire should not be seen as remotely surprising to those who view the industry as popular (in the sense that Barber intends).[40] That is because satire, as Geoff King points out, is often dependent upon expansive audience knowledge—of its precise textual operations, certainly, but also of its cultural justifications.[41] While some satirical targets are far more obvious than others, satire itself is a process that involves a constant negotiation between text and audience. In the case of the *BlackBerry Babes* trilogy, the spectator needs to be aware of diverse star images in order for certain jokes to work—in order for comically ironic meanings to be made. This is true, of course, for self-reflexivity more generally, and stardom, given its diverse visibility, is perhaps uniquely suited to smoothing the relationship between text and audience.

Without an awareness of the complex, corporatized star images that it references, the *BlackBerry Babes* trilogy might seem little more than a saucy romp. Globacom's saturation in West Africa has meant, however, that the region's spectators have routinely been exposed to the corporation's use of Nollywood stars—even if "only" through the impossible-to-miss billboards that are being erected with increasing frequency, especially in urban Nigeria and Ghana. So even if they have not seen the Nollywood films that have helped to shape corporate-sponsored star images, it is quite likely that such spectators would still be able to perceive the extreme, satirical self-reflexivity so central to the *BlackBerry Babes* trilogy. Globacom's use of Nollywood stars, rather than erasing or precluding those stars' filmic successes, serves to clarify their images for those who do not watch many films—and to expand them for those who already recognize that the industry's on-screen performers are impressively adaptable. If stars' corporate connections make them controversial figures throughout West Africa, then controversy alone is not an obstacle to stardom, as Tonto Dikeh has made abundantly clear. And if the *BlackBerry Babes* trilogy becomes a kind of commercial not just for the title phone but also for Globacom itself, then Globacom repays the film in a unique way. By helping to make Nollywood star images so visible throughout West Africa, the corporation all but guarantees that audiences will "get" the trilogy's self-reflexive jokes.

Love it or loathe it, Globacom has only managed to strengthen Nollywood stardom. When individual talents, performing in character, imitate their extra-filmic advertising images, they not only demonstrate a keen awareness of the ways that these images have been structured for corporate purposes; they also raise the possibility that they are critical of such structuring (self-awareness so often seeming synonymous with self-critique). As *BlackBerry Babes* and its sequels demonstrate, the strengthening of Nollywood stardom often means the strengthening of Nollywood cinema, not only because an iconic star can lend considerable glamor and power to a narrative but also because a burnished iconicity can help to generate a productive, pleasurable self-reflexivity. Moreover, Nollywood's status as a popular film industry—its requisite responsiveness to its own fans—suggests a reason for flattering such fans by making them feel part of a particularly knowing, stardom-savvy group. It also helps to clarify one reason why the *BlackBerry Babes* trilogy relies upon approving references to Globacom. The corporation's celebrated capacity to connect its subscribers while providing them with a steady supply of star images not only helps the trilogy's characters learn about glamour and various strategies of self-fashioning; it also, conceivably, helps the trilogy's fans to remain committed to Nollywood. The loyal domestic audiences that constitute ongoing funding sources for Nollywood films are also, increasingly, Globacom subscribers. Both as film fans and as smartphone users, these audiences are always in touch with star images. Stardom itself can hook them, and a Globacom connection, with its star-centered promotions, can keep them.

Like stars themselves, Globacom must constantly negotiate between good and bad publicity—must navigate the often fine line between success and scandal. In 2012, a Globacom marketing executive committed suicide in Ibadan after alleging that he'd been bullied by his colleagues.[42] At the same time, the corporation intensified its efforts to curb the spread of Islamist terrorism by promoting "unity through connectivity"—and offering a special service plan for Ramadan.[43] In executing its wide-ranging public relations plans, Globacom has continued to use Nollywood stars to promote its pan-Nigerian—and increasingly pan-African—objectives, and the ethnic, linguistic, and religious diversity that these stars represent has helped the corporation to present itself as socially progressive. The Nigerian public has tended—with the conspicuously criminal exception of the Boko Haram that routinely blows up Globacom's telecommunications masts—to accept that the corporation reflects a new, allegedly unified (or at least unifying) Nigeria, but also, simultaneously, a diverse West Africa.[44] Approval abounds on the blogosphere, with numerous Nigerians writing of the synergy between Globacom and the star personae that the corporation so widely employs. For instance, an August 2011 entry on the blog GistMania sets out to "prove" that the corporation is opposed to tribalism, providing a list of twenty-one brand ambassadors and their ethnic identities. "Mike Adenuga sees beyond your tribe," the author writes of Globacom's CEO, "as attested to by the workers in his companies"—who include, in this case, several Nollywood stars.[45] However, in a telling indication of the adaptability and tribal indeterminacy of such shape-shifting stars, the otherwise confident blogger places question marks next to the parenthesized ethnicities of no fewer than four of the twenty-one names (including Ramsey Nouah, whose father is Israeli and whose mother is Yorùbá, and Jim Iyke, who was born in Gabon). If Globacom appears to be forward-thinking, then that is perhaps because its sponsored star images often seem so borderless—equally liberated and liberating.

The persistent problem of tribalism is often the derided target of attempts to celebrate stars' mobile identities. An adaptable iconicity is never apolitical in Nollywood, and the efforts of the *BlackBerry Babes* trilogy to compare and contrast, in self-reflexive fashion, its own stars' personae suggests a certain commitment to a broadly antiessentialist agenda. As the cases of Oge Okoye and Tonto Dikeh—as well as of Khing Bassey and Van

Vicker—indicate, even a relative physical resemblance cannot culminate in a semiotic equivalence. Like Globacom, the *BlackBerry Babes* trilogy seems to understand something about Nollywood stardom—namely, that diversity remains its watchword. When, in the trilogy, ironic doubling tactics extend to the connections between on- and offscreen personae, they equally contribute to the sense that even ethnically "similar" stars are in fact dramatically different—impossible to pin down.

Consider, for instance, the way in which the trilogy mobilizes and complicates an emphatically Yorùbá identity: Eniola Badmus passionately upholding, as the Yorùbá Apollonia, the BlackBerry's capacity to improve lives seems a lot like the Funke Akindele who, as an official Globacom brand ambassador, promotes the corporation's alleged role in resisting tribalism. In her Globacom ads, Akindele not only expands her star image by adopting a range of costumes, hairstyles, and makeup choices; she also represents one of several Yorùbá performers who have joined their Igbo counterparts in endorsing Globacom—often in the same ad. In February 2013, Globacom unveiled a promotional image of the Yorùbá Akindele joining BasketMouth (one of Nigeria's top comics) to sell Globacom's Glo International Top Up Card, with its promise of connectivity "across America, the UK, and Canada." The official advertising image shows Akindele and BasketMouth against the telling backdrop of the American Statue of Liberty, united through their professional dress and possession of BlackBerry phones. With her straight wig, bright-blue eyeshadow, and maroon lipstick, this Akindele looks almost nothing like her most famous film characters—and certainly nothing like the Yorùbá Badmus. In proudly pointing with one hand to the BlackBerry that she holds in the other, Akindele seems to be celebrating the device's transformative, connective potential. By contrast, her costar BasketMouth is looking down at his phone as if shocked—and a bit disturbed—by its power, in a manner reminiscent of the way in which many of the men of the *BlackBerry Babes* trilogy are humbled and bewildered (rather than emboldened and glamorized) by the BlackBerry's revolutionizing capacities.

For fans who know the films and performances of a Globacom brand ambassador, a star-centered telecomm ad can contain pleasurable surprises. In response to the promotional image described above, *African Movies News* published a passionate appreciation of the "inspired" union of Akindele and

BasketMouth. The piece goes on to celebrate the shared capacity of Akindele and Rita Dominic to "transform" themselves in their separate Globacom ads, noting that while the typically vivacious Akindele can "tone it down" for her ads, the contrastingly calm, "aristocratic" Dominic can offer a "kinky go-all-out display." The maneuverability afforded by a Globacom ad can therefore serve to extend and even redefine Nollywood stardom. As *African Movies News* argues, "little was known of Rita and Funke's deep sense of humor beyond the snippets they portray sometimes in movies," and, while I would contend that Akindele, an inspired comedienne, shows more than mere "snippets" of humor in her films, I agree with the assertion that Globacom ads furnish seemingly infinite performative possibilities—that they can go so far as to "surprise" stars' fans.[46] Such ads offer opportunities for Nollywood stars to shine in vastly different ways, and in so doing they contribute to the already productive intertextuality of the stars' films.

In the case of the *BlackBerry Babes* trilogy, a far-reaching intertextuality is inseparable from a sheer, ironic self-reflexivity. Director Ubong Bassey Nya seems well aware of his stars' varying offscreen promotional gigs, permitting them to rather insistently perform their corporate identities within the narrative boundaries of the trilogy. They do so by occasionally reproducing some of the Globacom ads in which they have appeared, assuming the poses that have helped sell the corporation's service plans or paraphrasing the taglines that they have uttered in television commercials as well as on the radio. The *BlackBerry Babes* trilogy might seem crassly propagandizing—an extended advertisement for BlackBerry and Globacom—but its complex star performances suggest that the situation is not so simple. So, of course, does satiric self-reflexivity—most amusingly apparent when Dr. Mukoro lectures his BlackBerry-obsessed students on the manipulations of corporate and even "entertainment-based" propaganda. Throughout the trilogy, Tonto Dikeh and Mary Remmy can (as Vivienne and Kaisha, respectively) allude to their dissimilar off-screen identities—to Dikeh's diverse BlackBerry gigs and to Remmy's contrasting connections to Nokia—while simultaneously suggesting a shared dependence on Globacom, the service provider that "gives phones life." The corporation itself can, in creating its dazzling ads, use Nollywood stars in ways that will resonate with their filmic personae, pushing them to expand their performance tools while referring back to the Nollywood products that made them famous in the first place. The particular chicken-or-egg, epistemological conundrum that the *BlackBerry Babes* trilogy presents is, of course, central to its cheeky appeal: for audiences who have been exposed to Globacom ads, the question of what came first—the acting strategies embedded in the ads or the ones that the same stars employ throughout the trilogy—is part of a unique, intensely pleasurable process of active reception that puts stardom at its center.

4

When Stars Collide

Lady Gaga and the Pirating of a Globalized Persona

Despite Tonto Dikeh's boastful claims of complete autonomy, star-making remains a collaborative process. So, of course, do attempts to dramatize individual star personae. In 2011, several of the talents behind the *BlackBerry Babes* trilogy reunited for a project called *Lady Gaga*.[1] As he had done with film pitches dating back to the days of *The Celebrity*, Sylvester Obadigie wrote a treatment—a prose story that would serve as the basis of a screenplay; Ubong Bassey Nya, who would eventually pen that screenplay, signed on to direct; and Oge Okoye, who had played Damisa in *BlackBerry Babes* and *Return of BlackBerry Babes*, signed on to star. The celebrated trio was back— only this time they were committed to cribbing from the life of Lady Gaga. Knowing that they would need not only trusted colleagues but also the kind whose talents could turn a black Nigerian woman into a walking reference to a white American music star, they enlisted three key people: make-up artist Matthew Alechenu, who had helped Eniola Badmus transform into a glamorous, lipstick-loving city girl in the *BlackBerry Babes* trilogy; costumier Ogo Okechi, who had designed and supplied that trilogy's trendy dresses; and Austine Erowele, whose thematically relevant song "BlackBerry Babes" had given the three films a further, jaunty self-reflexivity. Together, these six collaborators would generate a melodrama about the fine line between piracy and fair use—a four-part film about a globalizing media phenomenon that both supports and subverts that phenomenon, in inimitable Nollywood fashion.

At its heart, *Lady Gaga* is about a village girl with big dreams, who goes to the city in a last-ditch effort to make them come true. It offers, in other words, a fairly familiar Nollywood formula. But it also offers Lady Gaga herself. Viewed through a VCD collection of her music videos (pirated from an official box set), Gaga appears at several crucial moments in the film that bears her name. Dancing across a tiny television screen, she seems to be providing careful instructions to the village girl who believes that she shares the American's hyper-specific talents—and who even comes to believe that she is the second coming of the superstar herself. If everyone around her laughs at her pretensions, then she can take comfort in the fact that Gaga, too, was once called crazy. And when she is feeling especially neglected—lost and alone—she turns to the Gaga whose image is available everywhere, even in a remote village in Nigeria.

If extensive audience knowledge is crucial to the satirical success of the *BlackBerry Babes* trilogy, then it is somewhat less central to the operations of *Lady Gaga*, which grounds its narrative in the articulated biographical contours and visible creative contributions of a young American named Stefani Germanotta. Better known by her stage name Lady Gaga, Germanotta is an explicit source of narrative inspiration for Oge Okoye's character, who is also named Stefani—a fact that for her helps to blur the line between the two women. The Nigerian Stefani, who views fashion as performance art, is often suspected of being a prostitute, and she is sometimes accused of being a man. In her mind, the fact that Gaga has herself faced similar charges only cements the pair's connection.

After being told that she is "not woman enough" to sexually service the men of her village, Stefani repairs to the small room that she shares with her mother, and it is in this room that she watches—and dances to—the music video for Gaga's "Telephone" (featuring Beyoncé). Crucially, this is the video in which, as part of a narrative preamble to the song, Gaga is escorted to a small prison cell by two butch female guards who proceed to undress her, remarking afterward about the condition of her genitalia. "I told you she didn't have a dick," mutters one woman. "Too bad," responds the other. A knowing nod to Gaga's own public image, which is often deemed insufficiently or falsely "feminine" ("tranny" being the slur of choice for the star's gender-essentialist detractors), the dick joke signals the extreme self-reflexivity of the "Telephone" video: here is a performer so seemingly comfortable in her own body that she can expose it to the scrutiny of the camera; here as well is someone so confidently self-aware that she can poke fun at her own "controversial" qualities, which include a capacity to suggest gender inversion—or, more transgressive still, genderlessness. For Oge Okoye's bullied Stefani, Gaga is an inspiration on multiple levels.

The four-part, over four-hour film *Lady Gaga* is a crucial case study in the way that Nollywood stardom has adapted both in relation and in resistance to Hollywood models. Ironically, it is only by blurring the lines between Okoye's Stefani and the "real" Lady Gaga that Ubong Bassey Nya's melodrama manages to address key differences between Nigerian and American conceptions of sex, gender, film acting, live performance, and more. In *Lady Gaga*, the lines that blur are at once biographical, sartorial, sexological, musicological, performative, and even psychic, suggesting that some inchoate post-racial, post-national position has been mobilized to unite a black Nigerian and a white American. However, this is not quite the case: *Lady Gaga* presents Nigerian sociopolitical conditions as being so specific as to preclude a lasting connection between African and American star images, and it raises the nagging matter of copyright protection, which in this case forecloses a fusion between the black Stefani and her white idol, whose songs Stefani sings publicly, for a profit, without permission.

In depicting a Nigerian woman's efforts to become an American pop personality, *Lady Gaga* tests the limits of Nollywood stars' antiessentialist, self-pluralizing strategies. When racial binarism rather than local tribalism enters the equation, what happens to the duly celebrated, shape-shifting proclivities of Nollywood stars? Can an Igbo actress traverse a racialized divide as readily and as successfully as she has traversed tribal ones? What does it say about her stardom if she cannot? Moreover, when a Western icon is imitated by a Nigerian film actress—whose rendering hits many of the recognizable notes but remains firmly fixed in the realities of today's Nigeria—can an awareness of the persistent and extreme economic disparities between Nollywood and Hollywood be superseded? A major, sponsor-supported Nollywood star is relatively well paid, but her aggregate annual salary is unlikely to ever touch that of Lady Gaga—a fact that is difficult to discount, and that Ubong Bassey Nya's screenplay makes abundantly clear.

Globalization also plays a major role in *Lady Gaga,* generating heated debates among the film's central characters, some of whom accuse the "real" Gaga of participating in practices of media imperialism, while others view the Nigerian "imitation" as an acceptable substitute, especially since her pirating of Gaga's music represents a mode of resistance to Western economic domination—if not to the apparent *cultural* supremacy of the United States (since Gaga is, after all, everywhere, in one form or another). Significantly, the film itself shares such piracy, making unlicensed use of no fewer than nine of Lady Gaga's songs, which become central components of the film's soundscape as well as explicit, narrativized objects of analysis. Moreover, this illicit employment of Gaga's music makes sense as a kind of auteurist tactic: director Ubong Bassey Nya similarly exploits an unlicensed panoply of BlackBerry products in the trilogy that bears the corporation's name. Linked within a model of cinematic authorship, the bootlegged use of Western products can seem a function not of Nollywood's alleged laziness, poverty of imagination, or essential vice, but instead as a fairly steady source of smart self-reflexivity. Indeed, the Nollywood films in which characters steal imported products are themselves marked by bootleg aesthetics (to borrow a term from Lucas Hilderbrand), creating a complex confluence between subject and style. Viewed in this way, *Lady Gaga* appears to up the ante on the *BlackBerry Babes* trilogy, precisely by transforming loyalty to a smartphone brand into something both broader and more specific—a lasting allegiance to a single American's multidirectional persona. If Austine Erowele's title song for the earlier trilogy indicates that "BlackBerry is a lifestyle," then his original *Lady Gaga* theme suggests that Gaga herself is something more—a many-sided identity that encompasses not just "a life of fame and fortune, a life of bliss," but also "all the stars in the universe." The notion that there is a universal Lady Gaga, however, comes in for some stringent criticism in the film, with several characters decrying efforts to read Gaga as relevant to contemporary southern Nigeria.

The complexities at the center of a Nigerian imitation of Gaga are not simply cross-racial; they also encompass concerns about what Frantz Fanon, in *Black Skin, White Masks,* calls "situational neurosis"—the feelings of inferiority occasioned by the black subject's exposure to a domineering whiteness, as well as the "obsessional" drive of that subject toward the internalizing of white ideals (the wearing of the white masks of Fanon's famous title).[2]

When Oge Okoye's Stefani is first confronted with local critiques of her imitative pretensions, she is forced to respond to allegations that sound distinctly Fanonian: one character in particular says that Stefani feels "inferior" to Gaga—a feeling presumably occasioned by the preponderance in Lagos of Gaga-specific advertising images and commodity tie-ins. Stefani's neurosis is situational, argue certain characters, but so is that of Nigeria itself—a neurosis that in both cases leads, allegedly, to a distinct orientation toward Western media forms. The film *Lady Gaga* resists capitulation to such forms not only by dramatizing local strategies of resistance—in the self-reflexive mode that the film's creators had honed with the *BlackBerry Babes* trilogy—but also by pirating Gaga's music, and using it as the source of a certain kind of juju.

If that very Nigerian juju helps *Lady Gaga* to retain a considerable degree of Nollywood specificity even in the face of wholesale appropriations of Western media, then so, of course, do individual Nollywood stars—especially the Igbo Oge Okoye and the Yorùbá Funke Akindele, who play antagonists with very different, ethnically inflected ideas about both Gaga and Nigeria. It is Akindele's character who describes Stefani's so-called "Gaga act" in Fanonian terms, echoing Fanon's rejection of an allegedly colorless universalism (which for Fanon can only be read as white), and drawing attention to Stefani's embodied visibility as well as to her nationally situated economic status, which leads her to "dress like a *poor* Lady Gaga," and to look like "a bad village copycat."[3] At the same time, Akindele's character acknowledges that Gaga is a globalizing force to be reckoned with, but she confidently deploys her Yorùbá identity as a counterbalance—a bulwark against Western influence. The less secure Stefani, whose Igbo identity is presented as weak (partly because Stefani has witnessed her villainous mother's selfish perversions of Igbo prescriptions), remains powerless in the face of Gaga's global saturation. As Okoye's Stefani inches toward superstardom, the face and voice of the actual Lady Gaga are omnipresent, along with Kentucky Fried Chicken, Coca-Cola, and Mercedes-Benz, painting a portrait of globalization that is impossible to ignore.

With its focus on commodity fetishism and an upward mobility that openly eschews the importance of education, *Lady Gaga* might seem a standard Nollywood film. But worshipping a Mercedes is not the same as worshipping a star.[4] The latter process requires more than just purchase power, combining reverence, awe, desire, close study, and considerable compassion, as well as the acting tools of voice and gesture. For Oge Okoye's Stefani, who worships Lady Gaga so much that she in effect *becomes* the American star (at least in her own mind), imitation is not only the highest form of flattery; it is also the hardest mode of performance—the most complex and, ultimately, the most satisfying style of acting. *Lady Gaga* takes a distinctly Stanislavskian approach to imitation, starting with an abused young woman who must "look inward" in order to find the close emotional connections between herself and the object of her adoration—connections that will enable her to publicly embody that object.

As an actress, Oge Okoye's accomplishment is less to evoke Lady Gaga herself than to create a character who lives and breathes according to Gaga's apparent prescriptions. However, if Stefani's version of Gaga can never be the real thing, then what does that say about the woman who plays this pathetic impostor? Does it mean that Okoye must always be "confined" to her black Nigerian identity? To her Igbo-authorized gender specificity? To her own idiosyncratic "style"? If the line between Lady Gaga and Okoye's Stefani is blurred but still distinct in this film, then the line between essentialism and antiessentialism can seem frustratingly fine in the case of Stefani's crosscultural imitation, even—perhaps especially—given its globalized context. On the one hand, Okoye the Nollywood star continues to be an impressive agent of antiessentialism, portraying a wide range of characters and assuming, in her public appearances, a wide variety of guises—even a Gaga-like willingness to take strange and compelling fashion risks. On the other hand, however, she remains, in *Lady Gaga*, a black African channeling a white American, through a character whose cross-racial identifications are termed pathetic, self-loathing, and even anti-Nigeria by her antagonists in the film.

Whether Okoye's Gaga imitation is successful is hardly at issue, however, since the alleged problem of performance across racial lines represents a major source of controversy among Nollywood fans, despite the efforts of individual films to efface it. While Jane Bryce notes that African popular culture is often "far less squeamish than Western cinema when it comes to non-naturalistic representations of race," it would be difficult to overstate the rancor with which prominent Nigerian bloggers have critiqued the post-racial pretensions of certain Nollywood stars—not to mention the type of "situational neurosis" that seemingly leads to the use of skin-lightening creams.⁵ Tellingly, *Lady Gaga* directly addresses this controversy, suggesting that the nontraditional casting practices that have allowed Yorùbá performers to play Igbo roles (and vice versa) are scarcely different from those that permit Okoye's Stefani to "become" Lady Gaga: when Akindele's character condescendingly tells Stefani that she herself would never imitate another person, Stefani replies that she already has, that she "always does," whether she knows it or not. This implicit reference to Akindele's own self-pluralizing tendencies as a major Nollywood star suggests yet another connection between *Lady Gaga* and the allegorical *BlackBerry Babes* trilogy, which employs competition among smartphone fetishists as a way of satirically skewering Nollywood's star system. Ultimately, the seemingly cheeky *Lady Gaga* offers a resounding endorsement of the antiessentialist project of Nollywood stardom, showing the extent to which that project can embrace cross-racial as well as cross-cultural identifications. If the legacy of Négritude informs those films (such as *Beyoncé and Rihanna*) in which Nollywood stars channel black American icons, "naturalizing" (or at least justifying) the process of cross-cultural imitation, then how might we make sense of films that add a cross-racial dimension to the equation? This chapter addresses that question by looking closely at *Lady Gaga* and by investigating the various critical approaches that have shaped not just the practice of "colorblind" casting but also the southern Nigerian experience of cross-racial identification in the age of globalization. *Lady Gaga* is more directly about stardom than the satirical, allegorical *BlackBerry Babes* trilogy. It traces a relational understanding of the star phenomenon, showing the continuities and discontinuities between black Nigerian and white American personae, as well as, in a far more familiar Nollywood register, those between Igbo and Yorùbá identities. In the process, the film both addresses piracy as a metaphor and actualizes it, depicting the "theft" of Western stardom while at the same time filling its soundtrack with unlicensed American pop songs.

RACING LADY GAGA

One of the most noteworthy aspects of *Lady Gaga* is, in fact, an absence: at no point is race explicitly identified, the "real" Lady Gaga serving to inspire debates about the dichotomy between authenticity and fakery, and not necessarily between black and white. What this suggests is that an idea of race is not central to Stefani's strategies of self-fashioning, and that, in fact, the nonappearance of a neat racial binarism is what facilitates her cross-cultural identification. In its avoidance of racial discourses, *Lady Gaga* not only serves as a reminder of the way that blackness can "go without saying" in a black-majority country like Nigeria; it also opens itself up to a more specific, even Fanonian rejection of Négritude's essentialist division between white European reason and black African emotion. For Stefani, as for her fans, authenticity accrues to those who, like the white Lady Gaga, are capable of using their complex feelings to fuel a dramatic self-fashioning. For Stefani's equally vocal detractors, however, it is precisely the constructedness of Gaga's persona that seems cold and rationalist—a far cry from the allegedly messy emotionalism of Beyoncé, which one character cites as a reason to prefer the latter star, thus suggesting an implicit, almost Senghor-like siding with blackness as an agent of honest "artistry." However, whiteness and blackness represent equally unspoken factors both in the film itself, which does not identify stardom as being in any way "raced," and in the publicity surrounding it, which has tended to foreground the continuity between Okoye's Gaga costumes and her own, equally elaborate personal style.

That no character in the film reads Stefani's Gaga act as a cross-racial imitation would seem to speak to some postmodernist refusal of race's explanatory power, especially when Stefani's fans accept without reservation that she *is* Lady Gaga, referring to her by that name and thereby calling into question the existence of an authentic, "original" star. Even the film's title adopts this strategy, signaling a narrative account not of some phony or faulty approximation of "the real thing" but, instead, of the floating signifier that is "Lady Gaga." However much the film might seem to embrace postmodernism's eschewal of mutually exclusive meanings—particularly with regard to race—it is important to heed Clyde Taylor's caution about the term's limited applicability to African filmic contexts. For Taylor, postmodern theory is guilty of "racism by default," having omitted mention of Africa and Africans in its key iterations. Like the Western-authored postcolonialism that remains problematic in an Africa enmeshed in neocolonial relations of power, postmodernism remains an "alien term."[6]

Like Oyèrónkẹ́ Oyěwùmí, Taylor exposes the false universalism of Western theoretical paradigms; he shares Oyěwùmí's argument that the exporting of feminism, postmodernism, and other Western constructs amounts to a practice of cultural imperialism.[7] Both Taylor and Oyěwùmí, writing about specifically African contexts, provide useful ways of understanding *Lady Gaga*, a film that is itself about local interpretations of Western norms and values. Since *Lady Gaga* addresses the alleged genderlessness of Gaga herself while incorporating the resistant experiences of a Yorùbá-identified character—as played by a Yorùbá-identified star—it suggests the lasting significance of Oyěwùmí's groundbreaking arguments about the relationship between a generalizing Western feminism and a persistent Yorùbá specificity. That Lady Gaga is herself widely seen as an agent of feminism—as well as an active agitator for lesbian, gay, bisexual, and transgender rights—speaks to her sociopolitical as well as academic significance. The title of Jack Halberstam's recent book *Gaga Feminism,* for instance, would seem to suggest a close if ironic kinship between a "genderless" star and a gender-specific social movement, and Halberstam, while noting Gaga's self-engineered appeal to "white gay men in particular," does not address Gaga's whiteness in greater detail.[8] Nor, in fact, does any academic account of the star's alleged feminism, suggesting the lack of currency of race as a framework for making sense of Gaga's iconicity, at least in the West.[9] Given this history, it is possible to view *Lady Gaga*'s refusal to mention race not as a discursive failure but instead as a result of the film's self-conscious adoption—its importation—of the dominant Western reading of Gaga, which the Funke Akindele character openly resists, critiquing it from a specifically Yorùbá standpoint.

If *Lady Gaga* is part of a long Nollywood tradition of "stealing" the names of Western stars—a tradition that includes Ramsey Nouah's Valentino, Genevieve Nnaji's Sharon Stone, Nadia Buari's Beyoncé, and Omotola Jalade-Ekeinde's Rihanna—it is one of the first Nollywood films to make a pirated cross-cultural appropriation a major plot point. In *Lady Gaga*, the illicit use of Gaga's music catalog, which structures the film's soundscape, is also a reason for Stefani's antagonists to condemn her as a "thief" who is not giving Gaga her economic due. But the improper aspects of this acquisition also extend to matters of culture, raising several pressing questions—both for the film's characters as well as for its audiences. For instance, just how "Naija" can *Lady Gaga* be if it relies so heavily on the title character's biography and music? And just how locally relevant can Stefani remain if she continues singing Gaga's songs and adopting her costume choices? Such questions drive the film, giving it a broad resonance that recalls debates about the *BlackBerry Babes* trilogy and its relationship to corporate globalism.

In addressing the films of the Cameroonian Jean-Pierre Bekolo, Jonathan Haynes writes that the "First World is always present as a source of technology, commodities, and styles, and as a place to go, but it is not a controlling force ... the dynamic of colonization is really over. Agency is all with the Africans, mostly involving structures they make themselves."[10] Haynes' reading applies especially well to the depiction of the West in general and of Western technologies in particular in the *BlackBerry Babes* trilogy, which tracks the efforts of its titular vixens to make emphatically personal, mutable meanings of a Western-derived smartphone culture. In *Lady Gaga*, however, the acquisition of a Western product and of Western cultural forms is far more controversial, creating an ongoing rivalry between an Igbo "wannabe" and the Yorùbá woman who torments her, always from the standpoint that to imitate Gaga is to generate concern about the diluting of local customs. It is, however, a measure of the Yorùbá woman's complexity, if not necessarily of her hypocrisy, that she herself supports local appreciation for Beyoncé—a stance that implicitly brings race back into the equation, suggesting that one of the lasting legacies of Négritude, at least in the context of *Lady Gaga*, is the belief that a shared blackness can override concerns about American cultural imperialism.

THE FUNKE FACTOR

When told that a Nigerian woman can never really "be" Lady Gaga, Stefani firmly disagrees, citing the saturation of Gaga's image and music in the media landscape of southern Nigeria—a saturation that has not only normalized Gaga but also, Stefani says, "changed Nigerian ways." For Stefani, the globalization that has turned Africa into a market for American pop music has made Gaga an indispensable daily presence. Stefani has not been able to escape that presence—nor has she wanted to. As Stefani says in defense of Gaga's ubiquity, "It has *made* me"—meaning that it has shaped her identity to such an extent that she starts to see herself as being "like" Lady Gaga. With its reference to the molding power of Western media, Stefani's statement sounds, in fact, suspiciously close to Frantz Fanon's description of the colonized mind, which for Fanon can persist past the point of official colonialism in part because of the acculturating potential of Western products. In *The Wretched of the Earth*, Fanon addresses "the Western culture in which [colonized minds] risk becoming ensnared," concluding that this culture can often make all too clear its own assimilationist agenda, influencing those who are "fully aware [that] they are in the process of losing themselves."[11]

Stefani shares this awareness, but not the willingness to "work with raging heart and furious mind" to resist cultural imperialism.[12] Instead, Stefani *embraces* Gaga's reign over the global media landscape, internalizing the American star's persona in a way that, once again, returns to the teachings of Stanislavsky. When Stefani the aspiring star mentions that she has "looked within" and found evidence of Gaga herself—of the pop singer's "drive" and "personality"—she claims that such introspection has given her license to play a part, to *become* Lady Gaga. This allusion to the Stanislavskian "inner voice"—what James Naremore calls "an imaginative absorption that turns acting into a form of affective thinking"—also suggests a Fanonian dimension: in *Black Skin, White Masks*, Fanon mobilizes the Hegelian notion of "being for the other," through which Hegel suggests that an individual's self-consciousness exists only inasmuch as it recognizably shapes that of another person, in order to further explore the dialectic of colonizer and colonized.[13]

In *Lady Gaga*, Stefani's keen, almost subliminal understanding of her favorite pop star, and her thoroughgoing adoption of that star's complex persona, calls to mind Leigh Raiford's concept of hypericonization, a process of deconstruction through which "viewers [are] presented with the restaging of representations"—with the abstracting of an icon that is already multiply mediated.[14] In addressing Raiford's work, Nicole Fleetwood notes that hypericonization

> suggests a level of familiarity with the icon that goes beyond its decontextualization. With the hypericon meaning has been solidified in such a way that the icon has limitless mobility. It can be transplanted to new arenas that both displace its historicity and abstract certain values, feelings, or ideas associated with its historical context to new audiences and settings. Its specificity is now an abstraction that can circulate throughout public culture, carrying both the weight of historical narrative and a decontextualized vague strain of its pastness.[15]

In the case of *Lady Gaga*, the eponymous icon—already present in the diegesis (mostly via posters and music videos) as a diverse set of representations—

becomes more and more amenable to Nigerian appropriations, in spite of the protestations of those who would resist Gaga's aggressively antiessentialist pretensions. In other words, if Gaga can matter to Nigeria—if her persona can seem at home there—then much of the credit must go to the Stefani who constructs a specific and meaningful relationship between her own experiences and those of the American superstar. If this tactic, too, is traceable to Fanon, then that is due to its dialogism, its willingness to read an Igbo identity in relation not merely to other local ethnicities—a common enough Nigerian practice—but also to complex and idiosyncratic foreign influences. Ella Shohat notes that "a strong feature of Fanon's work" is "his penchant for placing diverse ethnicities and communities in comparative relation to one another," and it is precisely this penchant that is present throughout *Lady Gaga*.[16]

As usual in Nollywood—and certainly in the work of Ubong Bassey Nya—a Yorùbá star is on hand to suggest alternatives to an Igbo-authored view of women and the West. In this instance, the ambassador of Yorùbáland is none other than Funke Akindele, who brings to the film her facility for the kind of rapid-fire comedy familiar from the Yorùbá theater tradition, with its emphasis on broad, often raucous humor; here, that humor is part of a running, caustic commentary on Stefani's pretensions.[17] As Luisa, who works at a Nigerian record label, Akindele has an opportunity to demonstrate her considerable range, playing not only uproariously funny scenes (in which, for instance, she teases several untalented aspirants to music stardom, in a rude, lewd, and liberating way that seems totally foreign to the "nice" judges of, say, *Nigerian Idol*), but also moments that showcase her sensuality as well as her capacity to project self-respect. Luisa's sense of honor is central to *Lady Gaga*, and it helps Funke Akindele walk away with the film.

It is hardly a stretch to say that Luisa is like the Clare Quilty who—in Vladimir Nabokov's 1955 novel *Lolita*, and particularly as played by Peter Sellers in Stanley Kubrick's 1962 film version—hounds protagonist Humbert Humbert as a kind of active conscience, forcing Humbert to face his own transgressions. Like Quilty, Luisa is always showing up when least expected; like Quilty, she causes considerable anguish; and like Quilty—and in keeping with a tradition befitting Nollywood's biggest stars—she can change her appearance at the drop of a hat. After confronting Stefani at a nightclub where the latter has been performing under the name Lady Gaga—and with

Figure 4.1. Funke Akindele on the Abeokuta railroad bridge. *Image courtesy of Bic Leu.*

actual, unlicensed Lady Gaga songs—Luisa laughs triumphantly, having forced Stefani to flee in shame. Confined to a bedroom whose doors are shut and locked, Stefani is like the Humbert who holes up in order to avoid Quilty's "prying eyes," but her Humbert uses Lady Gaga's "Alejandro," instead of an underage sexpot, as a salve.

A central aspect of Funke Akindele's star persona makes Luisa's pursuit of Stefani even more complicated: Akindele's Yorùbá identity. Because Akindele's public image famously encompasses an allegiance to Yorùbá traditions, she is the ideal agent of resistance to an Igbo woman's imitative aspirations.

Luisa's stringent criticisms have nothing to do with Stefani's gendered identity and everything to do with the latter's naïve, uncritical support for Lady Gaga. If Stefani is frequently described as unfeminine—especially when mimicking the allegedly "genderless" American superstar—then it is fitting that a Yorùbá woman should be on hand to address and dismiss as irrelevant Stefani's own gendered identity. That is because, as is typically the case with Akindele's projects, Yorùbá traditions form part of the intertextual fabric of the film, suggesting the lack of significance of a factor that the Igbo characters seize as deeply meaningful: Stefani's decision to straddle the socially sanctioned divisions between masculinity and femininity. That such straddling simply does not matter to the Yorùbá Luisa, who in her occasional bursts of gender-neutral Yorùbá speech cannot even translate the words "he" and "she" (let alone the slurs "tranny" and "dyke"), suggests the depth of her distaste for other aspects of Stefani's cross-cultural, cross-racial identifications.

Unlike a number of gender-essentialist characters in the film, Luisa is not worried about Stefani's gender performance, and so she is free to focus on the separate dimensions of Stefani's "Gaga act"—including the pirating of Gaga's music and the deliberate, almost Marxian mystification of the effects of globalization on local culture. Luisa cannot seem to convince Stefani to accept that, while bootlegging might strike a symbolic blow against the economics of Western media, it still helps that media maintain a stranglehold on Nigerian audiences. Since the Yorùbá Luisa does not exhibit the gender-normative prejudices that are elsewhere on display in the film (especially within its depictions of Igbo culture), we can accept her rejection of Stefani as being based in a broader resistance to Western cultural imperialism. Luisa exhibits not the parochialism of a queerphobic panic but the sting of a principled, pro-Nigeria perspective.

Funke Akindele's capacity to dominate *Lady Gaga* is not just a function of her character's anti-assimilationist stance, which the film itself seems to share (at least at first); nor is it strictly attributable to Luisa's down-to-earth manner, her hard-boiled pragmatism. It is also a product of the sheer force of the star's personality, which has led to her canonization in a range of venues, from fan magazines that tout her as unfailingly brilliant and "always watchable" to novels like Kelechi Emmanuel's *Forever in Love* (in which a central character dons traditional Yorùbá attire—the iro and buba—in order to watch a film featuring Akindele's "spectacular acting skills") to, of course, Globacom ads.[18] In 2012, one such ad asked, "Is there any modern character from any Nigerian movie as popular as [Akindele's] Jénífà?" The question referred to the star's performance in Muhydeen S. Ayinde's 2008 Yorùbá-language film *Jénífà*, which follows the ambitions of a village girl who dreams of moving to the city and "making it big."

The film was so successful that it spawned a sequel, 2012's immensely popular *The Return of Jénífà*, as well as a third film, 2014's *Everybody Loves Jénífà*, in which Akindele's character travels to Jamaica (where she experiments with new languages and accents) and the United States. For several years now, Jénífà has been a franchise unto herself, with Akindele overseeing the manufacture of Jénífà apparel and inspiring young Nigerian women to adopt "the Jénífà look," which combines elegance and comfort. (One of Jénífà's signature styles matches high heels with pajama pants—a dizzying juxtaposition that Akinele sells by projecting sheer self-respecting defiance, whether of Yorùbá, urban, class, or gender norms.) While Jénífà's popularity is of course traceable to Akindele's extreme likability, part of it is surely due to a recurrent theme: in *Jénífà* and its sequels, the title character comes to discover the importance of education, whether in a university classroom that is "better than a brothel" or in a health clinic where crucial information about HIV/AIDS is readily available. In the first film, Jénífà leaves her village for the University of Lagos (Akindele's actual alma mater), where she attempts to resist the temptations of big-city glamour, which include calls to join a profitable prostitution ring.

One of the obstacles that Jénífà faces, beyond the sexually transmitted disease that eventually strikes her, is the preponderance of white Western stars on the walls of university dormitories. In its own way, *Jénífà* shares the investment of the later *Lady Gaga* in understanding the impact of American commodity tie-ins upon young Nigerian women. Faced with a Britney Spears who is always staring down at her—whose posters are a visible part of virtually every interior in the film—Jénífà appears prepared, like her peers, to capitulate to Britney's methods for performing femininity, which the countless posters ably outline (almost as if they were part of an instruction manual on how to seduce). However, when the time comes for the "razz" Jénífà to request a "look"—to submit to a makeover—she names not Britney but the women of Nigerian hip-hop duo P-Square's music video "Do Me," black Nigerian performers who, ironically enough, themselves resemble many an American "video ho" (to borrow Nicole Fleetwood's phrase for describing certain figures familiar from MTV and BET). While by referencing P-Square's "Do Me" girls Jénífà seems to demonstrate her estrangement from the inescapable Spears, she cannot avoid the alarming impact of the American music-video style, which leads her to "look Hollywood," at least to the Igbo man who sells her some sexy clothes. By the end of the film, however, Jénífà has returned to her village, as well as to her Yorùbá roots, her status as HIV-positive having prompted her to renounce the campus prostitution ring of which she once was a part. While HIV may, to many viewers, seem a punishment unto itself, it is important to point out that Jénífà, in the epilogue of the film that bears her name, becomes a proud activist, pushing for enhanced sexual education for young Nigerian women. If, in the film's sequel, Jénífà's virus has miraculously disappeared, the character still spends most of her screen time believing that she is HIV-positive, in the process acquiring considerable knowledge about sexually transmitted diseases, the depredations of social stigmas, and the welcome reality that, with proper treatment, a person can live with HIV. Less sequel than remake, *The Return of Jénífà* dramatically expands the narrative space that its predecessor devotes to HIV/AIDS advocacy—a significant achievement, even if the film's exaggeratedly happy ending seems painfully contradictory, a way of ensuring its commercial success rather than of following through on its claim that HIV need not be a death sentence. Jénífà, it turns out, does not have HIV after all, and she responds with an unseemly ecstasy to the news of her negative test result. What Stefan Sereda, writing about the AIDS-themed Nollywood films *Dark Moment* (Aquila Njamah, 2003) and *Meet You in Hell* (Amayo Uzo-Phillips, 2005), calls "cautionary pedagogy"—an educative gesture that "makes its argument through negative models"—seems, in the case of *The Return of Jénífà*, a form of *contradictory* pedagogy, one predicated on a pair of opposite exhortations.[19] While at first the film urges the spectator to stop fearing HIV/AIDS and to accept that a joyful life is livable whatever one's status, finally it falls back upon pressuring her to "celebrate" Jénífà's negative test result as a "relief" and a kind of moral victory, offering a melodramatic manipulation that is at odds with its erstwhile, analytical approach to consciousness raising. In any case, Akindele, who began her career as the star of *I Need to Know* (1997), a Nigerian television series about sexual health education,

Figure 4.2. In Muhydeen S. Ayinde's *Jénífà* (2008), a young Nigerian woman attempts to transform herself into "a glamorous city girl"; Britney Spears looks on.

has ample opportunities throughout the *Jénífà* series to serve as a complex, multidirectional vessel for HIV/AIDS awareness. What other major movie star can say the same?

Simply put, the iconic *Jénífà* series contributes, via the remarkable Funke Akindele, to the rich intertextuality of *Lady Gaga*, and in a way that exposes the offensive underside of Stefani's star worship. When Akindele enters the film, trailing the glory of what Globacom has called Nollywood's most popular character, the stakes suddenly seem a whole lot higher. At issue is no longer whether Stefani will succeed in "becoming" Gaga, but instead whether such a process can ever be seen as remotely acceptable. It takes several scenes for Luisa to encounter Stefani, but when she does, she begins a campaign to shame the other woman, so distressed is she by the thought of a Nigerian girl "going Gaga." Luisa views Stefani's Gaga fixation as a function of the village girl's African inferiority complex; she calls it "pathetic" and, tellingly, a "slap in the face to Nigeria." That Akindele tends to laugh while delivering these lines is a clear indication of her unique contribution to the film—beyond that provided by the intertextual resonance of her Jénífà. Akindele the Yorùbá superstar makes Luisa less an agent of dramatic exaggeration than an interruption in the film's prevailing mode of address. While the ill-timed encounters between Luisa and Stefani are certainly redolent of the temporal relations of classical melodrama, Akindele's acting style clears away any hint of moralism, replacing high-minded speechifying with suggestive comedy routines that still communicate Luisa's principled stance on Stefani's mimicry.

From its very first shot, *Lady Gaga* highlights the diversity of local practices of media reception and quickly shifts into a comparative presentation of numerous, contested ways of reading—and even of assimilating—Gaga's star persona. Because the film's plot is so complex, and because its formal devices suggest a certain syncretism—a fusion of methods from sources as diverse as Igbo maternal melodramas, Yorùbá theater films, and American music videos—*Lady Gaga* calls out for a close textual analysis. Ultimately, the film's very dialogism suggests that it operates not in a mimetic but in a heteroglossic mode, neither endorsing nor denying Gaga's influence, but always situating it within a diversity of local sociocultural conditions. As Mishra Sudesh points out, "dialogism occurs when incongruous voices and styles press against one another inside a common arena."[20] In the case of *Lady Gaga*, southern Nigeria is used as a site for exploring Igbo, Yorùbá, Christian, "pagan," anti-imperialist, essentialist, and antiessentialist ways of using Gaga's music and persona. While *Lady Gaga*'s protagonist, Stefani, is unashamedly mimetic, the film itself—despite its title—does not share this approach, which is to say that it does not adopt Stefani's perspective only, and that it resists a consistent formal capitulation to the music videos that it displays (via a complicated and ever-shifting screen-within-a-screen aesthetic). Instead, it prefers a heteroglossic tactic of formally relaying a variety of ways of seeing—and even of being—Lady Gaga herself. Mikhail Bakhtin famously defines a heteroglossic approach as one that permits "a multiplicity of social voices and a wide variety of their links and interrelationships."[21] In its remarkable textual diversity, *Lady Gaga* provides opportunities for numerous, dissimilar Nollywood star personae to converge—and for the express narrative purpose of defining Gaga fandom. When the antiessentialist project of Nollywood stardom confronts the imported identity of an American pop performer who, as Anderson Cooper noted in a famous *60 Minutes* interview, "never appears the same way twice," the results are nothing less than electric.

A NAIJA GONE GAGA

Lady Gaga begins with a limo. Long and black, it slithers slowly into a courtyard on an overcast day, its wheels crunching gravel. The camera remains focused on its arrival, in what could be read as a capitulation to Nollywood's car culture—to the obligatory shots of extravagant automobiles that give the industry one of its signature aesthetics—or as a parody of that very same obsession. The fact that the car is in this case a limo, and that it likely contains someone famous, signals the scene's deviation from Nollywood's standard auto shots, which serve, as Lindsey Green-Simms has suggested, to "underscore the ambiguity of cars and the commodity culture of which they are a part," mainly by linking luxury automobile ownership to criminality and the occult. "No longer a part of the discourse of progress, uplift, and rational development," writes Green-Simms, "the automobile becomes a visible sign of the often-invisible duplicity of its owners."[22] It is also, more often than not, an explicit agent of death: in Dickson Iroegbu's 2003 drama *Little Angel*, the Oge Okoye character barely survives a car crash that kills her husband, and in *BlackBerry Babes Reloaded*, Muna Obiekwe's Duke is texting while driving—a decision that leads to his demise, his Mercedes SUV skidding out of control on a street in Lagos. The limo, by contrast, represents a professional obligation, rather than a status-seeking personal choice; it is the standardized vehicle in which a star is simply *supposed* to arrive. It is not an item to be owned—it is a means of transportation to be leased by a management team.

By signifying stardom as well as professionalism, the limo's appearance at the start of *Lady Gaga* generates expectations about the narrative to come —namely, that it will focus not upon corruption (of the kind that so often culminates in the acquisition of a flashy ride) but instead upon hard work (of the sort that can shift someone from the position of mere driver to that of chauffeured star). If the semiotics of the limousine set this sequence apart from more familiar, even formulaic Nollywood shots, then so do the multiplicity of perspectives that, in cinematic terms, structure the automobile's arrival—perspectives that together suggest that several spectators have gathered to watch the wheels turn. The first time the film cuts from the car, it takes us to a trio of children—two girls and one boy—who stand waiting, presumably for the limo's occupant to emerge. Suddenly, a whole crowd gathers, and within seconds it overtakes the automobile, causing the driver to stop before the limo has reached a suitable parking spot.

Especially notable about this crowd is that it contains several adult women who wear wigs of various bright colors—red, pink, purple—and who are even more aggressive than the men who surround them. One of the women is so keyed up that she faints, falling to the gravel at the feet of her fellow revelers. Everyone is chanting, "Gaga! Gaga!" The utterance acquires an incantatory power as the paparazzi ready their flashbulbs. Suddenly a limo door opens, and two men in suits emerge; their crotches almost collide with the camera as it shoots from a low angle. If, given the context with its pushy photographers and frenzied fans, the low angle suggests a certain orientation toward sexual exploitation—toward the possibility that a female star might, in young-Hollywood fashion, emerge from the automobile to reveal that she is not wearing any underwear—it in fact resists this interpretation, or at least complicates it, by offering a good look at a male crotch. This simultaneous satisfaction and subversion of prurient expectations provides a preview of the film's approach to the Nollywood star body—an approach that objectifies men more often than women, and that reveals the shyness, discretion, and humility at the heart of a girl's glamorous and erotic iconicity.

When a female star finally does emerge from the limo, the camera descends to ground level, as first one white leather boot and then another makes contact with the gravel. The boots belong to a beautiful young woman who, like the fan who fainted, wears the kind of purple wig that would befit a punk rocker or drag queen—or, of course, Lady Gaga herself. A shot of the limo's license plate reveals that particular name spelled out in its metal. Along with the chanting masses, the vanity plate lets us know that the bewigged woman *is* Lady Gaga. As she walks, she waves to her fans. Her extremely short black skirt is practically a pair of panties, and her leopard-print blouse is open to show off her cleavage. On her purple wig sits a miniature white top hat—a surrealist touch that would be quite at home in a David Lynch film.

After establishing that this sartorially adventurous star has inspired countless fans to imitate her, the film reveals, through a lap dissolve, that it is all but a dream. The dissolve soon clarifies into a shot of the real Stefani stretched out on a bed and slowly waking from what appears to have been a very long nap. Her purple wig replaced by a cheap brown weave, the leopard-print blouse now a mere monochrome T-shirt, Stefani looks, in a word, ordinary, with faded, relaxed-fit jeans completing the all-too-familiar look. The somnolent Stefani has dreams that take her far away from the quotidian, however, and as soon as she's fully awake, she declares in a voice of unmitigated longing, "I wish this dream could come to pass." In a rather sad visual rhyme with the earlier view of her dream double's glamorously booted feet, the film inserts a ground-level shot of Stefani's unpainted, unmanicured toes as they slide slowly, almost reluctantly into a pair of cheap flip-flops.

Going out to greet the day, the dreamer meets two young women who hiss at her, brandishing their fists and flexing their biceps. To them, Stefani represents nothing short of a whore. Wearing matching black T-shirts and matching dark blue jeans, the two bullies tell Stefani that because she is butch they will beat her up if she so much as looks at them; Stefani, accepting their judgment, meekly turns away, her gaze focused on the ground. The scene establishes two important points: that Stefani is a helpless victim of bullying and that she's surrounded by women who, though they claim that she's unfeminine, are in fact far "butcher" than she could seemingly ever be. By brandishing their impressive arm muscles, the two bullies effectively introduce the twin themes of hateful hypocrisy and of gender inversion that will shape the film's star-centered narrative. When Stefani becomes Lady Gaga, and thus begins to exhibit androgynous qualities, she is accused of deliberately refusing her own femininity—often by women who themselves suggest several shades of masculinity. Among the most odious are the prejudiced aggressors who give Stefani her first post-dream experience, apparently unaware of the fact that they embody the very qualities that they are criticizing.

A subsequent scene takes Stefani to the waterfront where five men are rehearsing a rap number. Wearing a hot-pink miniskirt with matching pink streaks in her weave, as well as a laced (and thus revealing) white T-shirt, Stefani rushes toward the group, apologizing for her tardiness. Eager to begin rehearsal, she's told that the men do not want her. A man named Drake, who appears to be the leader of the group, steps forward to say, "Babe, you're a distraction to us!" Stefani looks perplexed. After a few seconds of silent contemplation, she says—slowly at first, her voice gaining strength as she goes—"Everybody in the neighborhood sees me as a rotten prostitute because I hang out with you guys! And now you say I'm a distraction?" It seems that she has sacrificed a certain moral reputation in exchange for acceptance in an otherwise all-male group. But now, having made that sacrifice—one that has given her a terrible reputation in town—she is no longer wanted.

A flashback clarifies the dynamics among Stefani and the five male rappers. Late for rehearsal—her tardiness appearing to be a pattern—Stefani finds Drake sprawled out on his bed, smoking a blunt and looking lustful. He tries to rape her then and there, throwing her on the bed and tearing off her clothes. Chris (Johnpaul Nwadike), one of the rappers, enters the room just in time to rescue Stefani, pulling her off the bed and berating his colleague. After revealing this last-minute rescue, the film returns to its own present tense—to the waterfront where Drake is now casting Stefani aside, saying, "This was supposed to be an all-guy group. And you," he adds, turning to Chris, "*you* bring this bitch in!" The kindhearted Chris starts to defend Stefani, but it is difficult for him to get a word in when the three other men are all venting their misogynist frustration. One of them says of Stefani, "All she is good for is to whet our erotic desires. If she can't do that, then she has to go!" Since she clearly does not fancy having sex with her fellow aspirants to music-industry stardom, Stefani is banished from the group—and labeled an unfeminine "wench," to boot.

The film cuts from this scene of rejection to a shot of Stefani running through the village, clutching her stomach as if about to vomit, and weeping all the while. She's on her way to meet her mother, whose appearance alone instantly signals her traditional Igbo identity. Her head completely shaved, she sits on the edge of her bed and applies makeup to her face, attempting to furnish the markers of femininity that the *ibo isi* ritual, which marks an Igbo woman as a widow, has removed. (In Igbo, the term *ibo isi* refers to the mandated shaving of the widow's head.) The mother's visible Igbo traditionalism competes, however, with an equally visible modernity, and her style of dress evokes the globalization of fashion: she wears a bright-red Umbro T-shirt on whose front is the Norwegian flag. A so-called "special edition" shirt designed to celebrate Norway's national soccer team, this particular item provides a reminder not just of globalization in general but of Globacom in particular, since the Nigerian telecommunications corporation has been instrumental in promoting local appreciation for soccer. That Ogo Okechi, the film's costume designer, furnished this particular T-shirt is no accident. It reinforces, through the complex semiotics of fashion, the tension between tradition and modernity that the mother represents, but it also signals globalization's capacity to normalize Western styles throughout Nigeria. A symbol of the globalization of fashion, the Umbro T-shirt is also a reminder of the transnational public relations function of soccer itself. As Franklin Foer has noted, soccer both embodies and conceals the operations of globalization.[23] Essentialized as "the world's sport," soccer can deploy its alleged universalism to covertly accomplish some of the aims of cultural imperialism—hence the Umbro T-shirt that an otherwise traditionalist Igbo woman wears in her village in Nigeria, and that celebrates a northern European team.

The contrast between Western dress and Igbo baldness signals more than just a collision between modernity and tradition; it also highlights the mother's disregard for one of the essential terms of Igbo widowhood. While the traditional *uwe uju*, or mourning dress, is meant to be worn merely for a few months—rather than for the rest of the widow's life—certain markers of widowhood, such as an eschewal of facial makeup, are meant to persist. And yet Stefani's mother is first seen applying makeup to her face, further subverting the Igbo-specific semiotics of her shaved head. In her book on Igbo women, Joseph Thérèse-Agbasiere writes that "the denial of all means for beautifying oneself—manicure, cosmetics, coiffure, which are now replaced for a widow with a shaved head—denotes the element of 'sacrifice' as [Igbo] women conceptualize it, generated by loss of a husband, and which all form part of *ijedi*. More specifically, they also symbolize a ritual denial of a woman's usual concern for aesthetics."[24] While the shaved head of Stefani's mother—which in accordance with Igbo tradition would have been

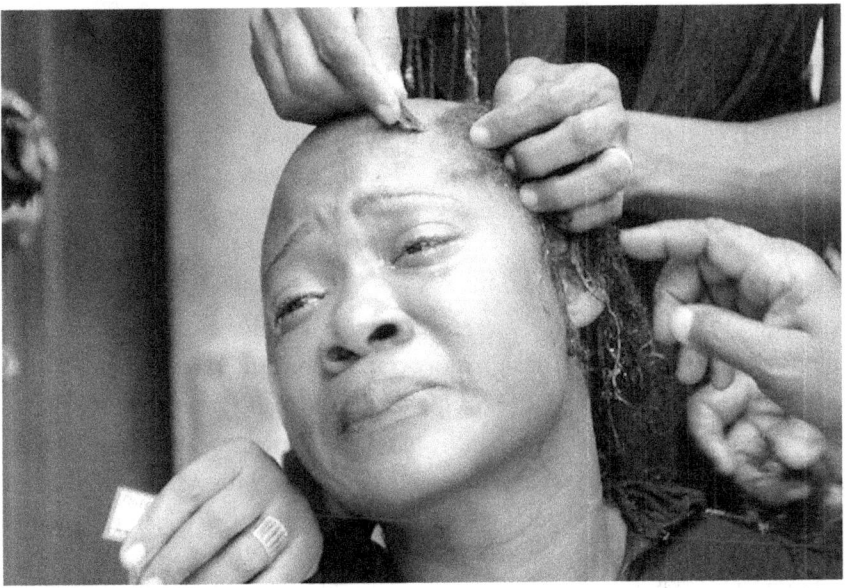

Figure 4.3. All for the (Igbo) role: Mercy Johnson in *Heart of a Widow* (Michael Jaja, 2011).

shaved, at least in part, by Stefani herself—speaks volumes about her Igbo femininity, its semiotic register extends both to gender inversion (and thus to a certain hypocrisy on the part of the mother who denounces her daughter as unfeminine) and to Nollywood's star system, which guarantees extensive publicity for actresses who—like Oge Okoye, Queen Nwokoye, and Rukaya Mashoud in Kalu Anya's 2012 film *The Three Widows*, or like Mercy Johnson in Michael Jaja's 2011 *Heart of a Widow*—shave their heads for their Igbo roles.

In *Lady Gaga*, Igbo tradition provides a compelling subtext, suggesting that the mother's hatred for her daughter is, more specifically, a widow's resentment of the woman who literally helped shave her head. Thus when the mother questions Stefani's performance of femininity, calling it "ugly" and "useless," she seems to be projecting her own self-doubts onto her daughter, displacing anxieties about her own "unfeminine" appearance. As Thérèse-Agbasiere suggests, the rite of *ibo isi* simultaneously eliminates and establishes a marker of femininity, complicating gendered conventions while at the same time preserving them. With *ibo isi*, the woman is "masculinized" strictly in order to signal her heterosexuality, her having had a husband. While *Lady Gaga* does not describe the place of Igbo traditionalism in contemporary Nigeria, the ethnically distinct personae of its stars suggest that the film is part of a complex Nollywood fabric pitting different cultural customs against one another, as in Tunde Kelani's iconic *Thunderbolt*. Strictly with respect to star publicity, however, the depiction of Igbo traditionalism often emerges as a major plus, particularly when *ibo isi* enters the equation: it gives an actress the opportunity to prove that she is willing to dramatically alter her appearance for a role. As a 2013 *Vanguard* article puts it, the renunciation of vanity often signals a certain professionalism among Nollywood stars, as well as an abiding respect for local traditions—for a Nigerian cultural specificity: "It is said that the hair is the crowning glory of a woman, but when movie producers and directors come knocking at the door of star actresses with an offer to portray a mourning traditional African widow, the role requires that they shave off their hair."[25]

"Useless girl!" the bald mother screams at Stefani. "You want to prostitute, eh? It's time for you to take your trade to one of the big cities. Then you can come home to help me. Get out of this ghetto, away from all these good-for-nothing boys." With this endorsement of urbanism, the mother turns triumphantly away, her hands glued to her hips. "I'm in no mood for this, mama. I am not a prostitute," Stefani says in a soft, self-pitying voice. "Of course you're not!" the mother screams, citing once again Stefani's alleged lack of an adequate, appealing femininity. "If you were one, you would be coming home with real money. You're a cheap harlot—an imitation!" "Thank you," Stefani says in response, presumably grateful for this latest, loathsome push. Quietly and without saying goodbye she leaves the room and finds Chris, who sits her down and asks her to "vent" her frustrations. She begins by asking why Chris's male friends have been telling people (including, presumably, Stefani's own mother) that she is bad in bed—a slanderous invention that suggests that Stefani is doubly deviant, a whore who cannot satisfy her "clients" and whose femininity is therefore suspect.

"I know how you feel, Stefani," says the Chris whose sensitivity has marked him as insufficiently masculine among the "thuggish" members of his social group, all of whom have been influenced—significantly—by American hip-hop fashions. However, if Chris is not quite "man enough to hang" with this imitative crowd, he shares with the other men a dream of moving to the United States, as well as a penchant for appropriating American hip-hop. If, as Herman Gray argues, "self-representations of black masculinity in the United States are historically structured by and against dominant (and dominating) discourses of masculinity and race, specifically whiteness," then it is possible to see why the men of *Lady Gaga* respond so negatively to Stefani, a young woman whose open appropriation of a white "female masculinity" offends their own appropriations of an American hip-hop swagger.[26] *Lady Gaga* is alert to multiple forms of American popular culture, and hip-hop serves a central function in the film, both as a marker of a certain brand of black masculinity and as an agent of cross-cultural exchange. Robert Stam and Ella Shohat argue that, "as a global phenomenon," hip-hop "illustrates the transoceanic crossings of diasporic cultures," in the process constituting "an international lingua franca." The authors suggest that the global "imitation" of African American hip-hop artists is more complicated than a complete cross-cultural transposition, however. They detail some of the ways that non-Western performers, in appropriating African American hip-hop techniques, "address partly analogous situations . . . within the constantly mutating Afro-diasporic transtextuality of sampling and cut 'n' mix."[27] Appropriation, in this case, is a profoundly dialogic process, one in which hip-hop form acquires local function.

The notion of the local and of its capacity to infuse imported cultural practices provides Luisa with plenty of ammunition against Stefani's Gaga imitation, since, to Luisa's mind, the imitation does not confront Gaga's persona with "Naija realities." The Luisa who, in accordance with the complex connotations of the term "Naija" itself, experiences both pride and disappointment in twenty-first-century Nigeria—celebrating local cultural expressions but criticizing the state's manifold failures—feels that an unselfconscious appropriation of Lady Gaga's act only evidences Stefani's ignorance and her lack of awareness of the globalizing impulse that allows Western music to dilute local experiences. Viewed from Luisa's own perspective, the film *Lady Gaga* can appear to reclaim the local, simply by being a "traditional" Nollywood film, shot on video and distributed through nontheatrical circuits—a film by, for, and about Nigerians. At the same time, and still following Luisa's line of thinking, the film can seem to actively resist Western economic imperialism, precisely by relying on a series of unlicensed Lady Gaga songs. In the process, the film demonstrates that the illicit use of American pop music is not a product of laziness or of an African artistic bankruptcy: Nigerian musician Austine Erowele in fact wrote a song for the film that, like his title tune for the *BlackBerry Babes* trilogy, provides a running musical and lyrical commentary on the plot that is utterly original, influenced equally by highlife and hip-hop traditions and an audible reminder of the collaborative nature of Nollywood filmmaking.

The illicit use of Gaga's music throughout the film that bears her name is not the product of a criminal impulse, but instead a matter of thematic relevance—and a reflection, moreover, of a specific form of self-reflexivity. In this film about the pirating of an American pop persona—a film in which multiple characters discuss the high costs of an "illegal" cross-cultural appropriation—Gaga's unlicensed music is a reminder of Nollywood agency in relation to Western modes of control. (It is also, of course, part of a new Nollywood tradition, recalling the equally unlicensed use of the title phone in the *BlackBerry Babes* trilogy.) If, through aggressive expansionism and market saturation, economic imperialism helps to produce *cultural* imperialism, then perhaps the latter can be used to subvert the former. Though Luisa sees it as being symbolic at best, perhaps the "stealing" of Gaga's globalized music can undermine, to however minimal a degree, the economic dominance of American popular culture. For the proud Luisa, there is something deeply insidious about Stefani's appropriations, and even though the film does not explicitly identify race, it is obvious that Luisa's protestations are rooted in a rejection of Gaga's specificity, which surely includes the star's whiteness. Perhaps Luisa's beef with Stefani's Gaga imitation is not that it is an imitation per se but instead that it fails to combine Gaga's iconicity with any deliberately fashioned nods to Nigerian cultural forms (what Luisa calls "Naija acts.") While no character in the film seeks to interrogate the privilege that Gaga's whiteness affords the American superstar, Luisa suggests that Lady Gaga—more so than a black American like Beyoncé—represents a powerful neocolonialist force.

Chris, in trying to get Stefani to "drop the Gaga act," takes a somewhat different approach, refraining from criticizing Lady Gaga (because he knows that to do so would be to upset Stefani tremendously) and attempting instead to speak a language of empowerment that sounds not unlike Luisa's "pro-Naija" stance—except that it omits concern for the political economy of Western stardom. Chris comes across like a self-help guru, goading Stefani into accepting her own, "original" star qualities—an approach that ends up reflexively celebrating Oge Okoye's unique iconicity. "Don't allow an unfounded stigma to chase you into your shell," says Chris. "Be tough, Stefani! Come on! Don't give up your dreams!" Like an athletic coach whose star player requires reassurance, Chris continues his pep talk until finally Stefani concedes that she is, in fact, talented. In response, Chris declares, "You have to decide what to do with your talent, then, because it belongs to *you*." No sooner has he uttered this command than Stefani's mother emerges from a back door, stepping out onto the stoop to glare at the pair. Again, she seems to actively renounce her own femininity—or whatever is left after *ibo isi*—by scowling, folding her arms, and grunting derisively, like a triumphant but still disgusted warrior. From her hateful face, the film cuts directly to Stefani dancing in her bedroom to the official music video for Lady Gaga's "Telephone." Wielding a VCD remote as if it were a microphone, Stefani bumps and grinds in a general approximation of Gaga's movements, which remain clearly visible throughout the scene. Indeed, the medium shot makes both women equally visible—Stefani in the "live" space of the cluttered, claustrophobic bedroom and Gaga on a television screen nearby, performing in the studio-manufactured filth of a fake prison.

While the film works to establish and maintain a certain equivalence between Stefani and her onscreen idol—not only in terms of dance but also as a function of their shared contexts of performance (Gaga's prison mirroring the confinement of Stefani's village residence)—the question of whether Stefani can really become Lady Gaga is answered negatively by Stefani's mother, who enters, yet again, at the worst possible moment, just as Stefani, imitating Gaga, is squatting to show off her bottom. "Fool!" the mother screams, interrupting Stefani's performance and spoiling the girl's fantasy of transposition. A sly smile streaks across the older woman's face, suggesting a somewhat nuanced tyrant, one whose ruthlessness is tinged with a certain amusement at the sufferings of others. "Mama, why do you always do this?" asks an embarrassed and exasperated Stefani, as she drops the VCD remote that just seconds before was doubling as a microphone. "Mama, I was trying to rehearse!"

"You're a fool," the mother says in a low register, her eyes shining with contempt. Suddenly, she begins to imitate her daughter imitating Lady Gaga. Significantly, it is a silent imitation, the mother's lips moving as if to synch with a song. But no sound emanates from anywhere in the room—certainly not from the VCD player that the mother has paused in utter disgust, rejecting the "real" Gaga as surely as she has rejected her biggest village fan. There is the distinct suggestion that the mother enjoys lampooning Lady Gaga, since doing so is a way of pointing up her daughter's imitative pretensions. Interrupting her bullying mimicry, the mother suddenly shouts, "Don't touch my food!" and steps in front of the Stefani who has begun to approach a pot of rice, reminding her daughter (as well as the film's spectator) of the extent to which she has abandoned or perverted certain motherly instincts. Shielding her rice from Stefani, who is famished after obsessively rehearsing her Gaga moves, the mother offers some harsh advice: "Hustle if you want to eat! You're not a baby anymore." "But, mama, I'm hungry!" Stefani objects, and, in response, her mother suggests that among the reasons that Stefani will never "be" Lady Gaga are the village girl's lack of self-control; her eagerness to complain; as well as, perhaps most soberingly, the persistent socioeconomic disparity between an urban American and a rural Nigerian. "Does that pussycat girl that you try to imitate say that she's always hungry?" asks the mother—a cruel question to which Stefani does not have a ready answer.

The next scene takes the spectator from the near-silent village to the cacophonies of Lagos, where Funke Akindele's Luisa throws punches at a young journalist who wrote several negative comments about Luisa's employer, the Nigerian hip-hop artist and producer Ray Martins (Yemi Blaq). An earlier scene has suggested that the precise nature of the professional relationship between Ray and Luisa is sadomasochistic, with Ray the brutalizing boss and his assistant, Luisa, a meekly willing victim. This scene, which occurs shortly after the film's opening credits, also suggests that Luisa is an entirely new character type for Akindele, far removed from the boldness of the star's Jénífà. But a more familiar Funke emerges in the fight sequence, in which Luisa lobs insults at the woman who had dared to diss her boss. "You think because you're a journalist you can write anything you want about people?!" screams Luisa—a question she will continue to pose even after a pair of witnesses have dragged her and the journalist to the local police station, where the altercation only intensifies. "Who the freaking hell do you think you are?" asks Luisa, assuming a threatening stance as she crowds the journalist (who is played by the lovely but tough Mary Lazarus, a rising star who can hold her own even with the larger-than-life likes of Funke Akindele). Coming across like a vengeful spouse, Luisa reminds the journalist of her specific transgression: "Today you insulted *Ray Martins* in your stupid and tacky newspaper! Girlfriend, for the very last time, I'm going to tell you to stop."

By this point in the film, Akindele has played only two aspects of Luisa's character: submission (in her first scene with Martins) and brute strength (when she physically threatens Mary Lazarus' journalist). The question of which behavioral register reflects the "real" Luisa is of course impossible to answer—and that is precisely the point. If Nollywood star performances tend to combine multiple acting styles in keeping with a broadly anti-essentialist project, then such performances can sometimes suggest, as in this instance, that a character is putting on airs, assuming a variety of manipulative guises and generating considerable suspicion, forcing the spectator to wonder when the real figure will finally stand up—or whether the character contains an authentic self at all. With a Luisa who begins as meekly deferential but soon becomes tough and vengeful, Funke Akindele draws attention to at least one performance within a performance—to the active self-fashioning of her character. If Luisa's quietly acquiescent behavior with her boss would seem to fly in the face of essentialist assumptions about the power and the pride of contemporary Yorùbá women, it also seems to contradict the very qualities that made Akindele a star, such as a constant iconoclasm as well as a willingness to stand up to male authority.[28] Thus by subverting the spectator's expectations about what an Akindele performance can profitably offer, the film complicates easy, even essentializing assumptions about Yorùbá women.

When Mary Lazarus' journalist tells a cop what Luisa did to her, she paints a portrait of a young woman gone mad: "This girl practically beat me up—tore my clothes into shreds! Injuries all over my body! What did I do? I wrote an article in a newspaper!" Lazarus gives these lines a distinctly comedic flavor, highlighting the irony of the situation and setting up Akindele's amusing response. When dispensing threats, Luisa is like a manic prosecutor—an especially apt simile given that Akindele, quite famously, has a law degree. Rapidly firing off a list of the Lazarus character's offenses, Luisa lets the newspaper writer know that "Ray Martins must not be messed with." In the process, Akindele demonstrates her wit as well as her breath control, rushing her dialogue and adding more than a few vocal curlicues—including her trademark squeals of disgust and purrs of self-approval—in order to suggest that Luisa knows that she is going too far with her condemnation, but that she enjoys the act, perhaps because she is not allowed to perform it at work.

Through parallel editing, *Lady Gaga* continues to track the two storylines—Stefani's and Luisa's—for reasons that remain unclear until the moment when Chris, still trying to improve Stefani's mood, takes her to his fellow rappers in order to prove his moral seriousness. Showboating for Stefani, he tries to take away Drake's marijuana cigarettes, saying, "We don't need to corrupt our brains in order to be creative!"—a statement that certainly does not endear him to the other men, who now have yet another reason to believe Chris to be considerably less than masculine. Turning away from the task of "cleaning up" the group, Chris tells Stefani that Ray Martins is holding auditions for female backup vocalists at his studio, Christian Vibes, which is located on Lagos Island. Stefani recognizes the name immediately, exclaiming, "Ray Martins? He's the biggest rap superstar in this whole world!" She agrees to Chris's suggestion that she audition for Martins, but at that moment, in melodramatic fashion, cops arrive via a pirogue and arrest everyone for pot possession.

Finally, the film's separate plot strands converge, as Stefani, Chris, Drake, and the others are hustled into a jail cell containing Luisa and the journalist. In keeping with her comedic star image, Akindele minimizes the melodrama by making humorous remarks about the situation, offering a running, caustic commentary on a generalized absurdity. Before the six others arrive, Luisa is busy teasing her cellmate, saying, "Journalist by day, prostitute by night!" However, with so many other bodies squeezed into the cell, Luisa has a new reason to complain, and she starts to scream at the prison guard, inveighing against the crowded conditions and declaring herself to be "sick of this inefficiency." While state failure may infuriate her, Luisa is even angrier when faced with the Stefani who fancies herself a twin to Lady Gaga. Turning her attention to this woman whose wig and multicolored costume are clearly designed to evoke the American star, Luisa delivers a lecture on the kind of "Nigerian inferiority complex" that leads to such cross-cultural imitation—a lecture that Akindele punctuates with bouts of delightfully derisive laughter, further leavening the melodrama (as well as downplaying the pedagogy).

Ever the tormentor, Luisa screams, "Finally, Lady Gaga has come home to roost! You know what you look like?" Rolling her eyeballs upward so that only the whites show, gripping the skin beneath her chin to create a flap that she wiggles rapidly, Luisa makes a few comments in Yorùbá—to the effect that Stefani looks like a turkey—and then bristles upon noticing that Stefani cannot comprehend a word. "OK, you don't understand my language," she says to the Gaga clone. "You know what a turkey is? A turkey that's recovering from a high fever—that's what you look like."

Dejected, Stefani turns away—though not before bringing herself to level an insult of her own against Luisa. "You're lucky you're here and not in an insane asylum," she says to the Yorùbá woman, who smiles at the line, apparently considering it a rather pathetic attempt at an insult. Looking at Chris, who has just apologized for making her "miss the big audition," Stefani starts to voice her self-pity, saying, "Nothing ever works out for me, anyway. I might as well get used to it." At this point, a prison employee emerges from the shadows to inform the new arrivals that their bail has been set at 100,000 naira—a figure calculated according to the high price of their pot supply. The scene ends with the characters delivering further criticisms of the inanities of the Lagos prison system, suggesting that Luisa is not the only one who is willing to "diss Nigeria."

By focusing on state failure—and on a figure who expresses disappointment with "today's Nigeria"—*Lady Gaga* suggests that Luisa's resistance to Stefani's imitation is not occasioned by any emphatically nationalist sentiments. That does not mean, however, that Luisa is unconcerned with the potentially negative effects of this imitation on her "home country" of Nigeria, and particularly on the "impressionable" young women who live there. To her, Stefani's act seems only to support and encourage the cultural imperialism of the West: "It's bad for Nigeria," Luisa argues, adding later, "You think I'm a dummy? A mummy? A fool? You think I don't know you're just an imitation?" In denouncing Lady Gaga's cultural imperialism and the mimetic gestures by which Stefani helps to support it, Luisa recalls not only Frantz Fanon but also Kobena Mercer, who famously argues that the mimetic mode can only strengthen a Western-authored commodification of culture. For Mercer, it is "a form of cultural mimicry which demonstrates a neocolonized dependency"—as well as, more specifically, an enacted support for the commodifying codes of cultural imperialism.[29]

If, however, Luisa is anti-Gaga, then she certainly is not anti-Beyoncé, as evidenced in her second scene with Ray Martins, during which the once-meek assistant becomes a force to be reckoned with, telling the young women who audition for Ray that they are terrible. (At one point, she even compares their collective vocal style to "a big ball in a croaky throat.") Ray, as played by Yemi Blaq, is clearly increasingly uncomfortable with Luisa's domineering presence, especially when she expresses her dissatisfaction with a woman who decides to rap rather than sing. "Did we tell you we were looking for Nicki Minaj?" asks the intolerant Luisa, whose revulsion shows in her wrinkled nose and downturned mouth. Seconds later, she is commanding, "Sing! Sing like Beyoncé!"—an instruction that suggests that it is not imitation itself that bothers Luisa, or even a reliance on a Western model, but rather the willingness of someone like Stefani to enact a cross-racial identification. Once again in Nollywood cinema (as in the popular *Beyoncé and Rihanna*), the blackness of the American Beyoncé provides an entrée or alibi for a Nigerian artist who would otherwise reject the West. Indeed, as Luisa's approving comment demonstrates, the trope of Beyoncé as ambassador of blackness—a new form of Négritude?—is so central to recent Nollywood films that it turns up even in this excavation of the dangers of appropriating Western stardom. While the film does not explicitly address race, the topic offers the most readily available reason for Luisa's intense resistance to Stefani's so-called "Gaga act." If Beyoncé's blackness can supersede or at least deflect from her status as Western (and therefore, inevitably, culturally imperialist), the factor that, in Luisa's mind, makes Lady Gaga so abhorrent a source of imitation must be her whiteness.

Luisa's views on Beyoncé do not necessarily contradict her extreme resistance to Stefani's Gaga imitation, however. If, in advocating imitation, Luisa mentions only American stars, she also mentions only black women—precisely, she says, because "Nigerians are auditioning." Blackness, in other words, can indeed "go without saying" in a black-majority country like Nigeria, where it is "normal"—"expected"—and where it need not be constructed for popular consumption. In responding with an uncontainable distaste to the constructedness of Gaga's persona, and in openly preferring the "beauty" of Beyoncé's music, Luisa sounds a lot like the Léopold Sédar Senghor who famously reviled the coldly analytical premeditations of the "white mind" while positing the open, participatory affect of blackness. Luisa even seems to echo Senghor's dichotomizing of Europe and Africa (as, respectively, "reason" and "emotion") by arguing that Gaga "buys and builds" while Beyoncé "simply *sings*." But it is through the identification of specific individuals that Luisa resists Senghor's essentialism, suggesting that for Luisa, Gaga's whiteness is less of a factor than the star's "false" persona, her allegedly stilted self-invention. Furthermore, Luisa's stance on Beyoncé reflects a certain black internationalism, which, as Brent Hayes Edwards makes clear, and as Robert Stam and Ella Shohat have themselves suggested, "is not a 'supplement' to nation-based black thinking; rather, it exists at the very kernel of a struggle for emancipation against racism, colonialism, and imperialism."[30] Beyoncé may be American, but her blackness will not dilute or deface the Nigerian struggle for freedom from the West. Crucially, the pop star has a chance to state her own case in the film, for she is featured in one of several Lady Gaga music videos that Stefani watches—the video for "Telephone," in which Beyoncé joins murderous forces with Gaga, poisons her black boyfriend (played by Tyrese Gibson) before slaying several others, and wears a bikini patterned after the American flag. This mixture of Americana and murderousness makes an interesting counterpoint to the dialogue exchanges that continuously uphold the United States as, in Chris' words, "the promised land for music artists"—a place where "nothing bad can happen to you." Luisa, for her part, knows better, and her support for Beyoncé indeed suggests a new reflection of Négritude.

What is perhaps most fascinating about the rivalry between Stefani the professional Lady Gaga impersonator and Luisa the Yorùbá provocateur is that it does not represent a neat dichotomy between incoherence and authenticity. That is because Luisa, through the complex, ever-changing avenues of Funke Akindele's star persona as well as through the role as written, represents resistance to the numerous social prescriptions of others. Simply put, this iconoclastic character is always *performing* her rejection of prevailing values, always *acting* her subversion of normative expectations. (As she says at one point—and proudly—"I'm good at fooling.") Luisa is always altering her own behavior, whether by becoming a pro-Beyoncé firebrand when auditioning inadequate singers or assuming a submissive stance in some of her "private" moments with Ray Martins. The film furnishes a sexual subtext for these shifts in character—an erotic justification for Luisa's dizzying diversity of personae. Boss and employee, Ray and Luisa are also a role-playing romantic couple—always putting on masks, always trying out new characters. Some work, while many others do not. For instance, when Ray recognizes that Luisa is becoming too domineering for his liking—when he sees that she is eclipsing his authority during the auditions—he attempts to reclaim his power by promptly firing her. "Just like that?" asks a stunned Luisa. "Just like that," replies the newly ruthless Ray. "Go."

As a performing team, Funke Akindele and Yemi Blaq both manage to suggest that this episode is little more than an act—a routine designed to spice up their characters' relationship. In an indication of his lasting lust, Ray watches avidly, his eyes widening, as Luisa walks slowly away. Luisa, for her part, pretends to be pained: she feigns quiet compunction and thus enacts the complete opposite of her erstwhile stance, which had suggested officiousness. Now, instead of coming across like a bullying boss, she seems browbeaten—unable to fight back. However, she proves the falseness of this performance by returning to the studio, mere minutes later, and demanding that Ray make love to her. Suddenly a confident sexpot, she finds Ray sprawled out on the couch, clearly exhausted from the fruitless auditions, and she gets his attention by clucking—a trick that Akindele often employs to telegraph a variety of emotions, from disgust to surprise to a taunting sexual craving. "You want something?" asks Ray, still playing the part of the dismissive boss-*cum*-lover. "Yes: sex," says Luisa in her throatiest voice. Ray's response to this firmly articulated challenge is to tell Luisa that she is crazy, but it is clearly meant as a compliment: his eyes are widening with desire as Luisa walks toward the couch. "Doesn't a little craziness appeal to a big star like you?" she asks, and Akindele's delivery turns the question into a strictly rhetorical one. Luisa does not wait for Ray to get up; she crawls on top of him, maintaining her dominant sexual position for the remainder of the scene.

With its dialectical narrative, *Lady Gaga* provides a telling counterpoint to the conscious, mutually supportive role-playing of Ray and Luisa. Once again, it involves life in the distant village: after her release from prison, Stefani returns home to find her mother in bed with a man. Hastily pulling up his pants to signal the end of a sexual encounter, the man is surprised to discover that his partner has a daughter. "She's not my daughter, sweetheart," the mother lies, "she's my stupid niece. My sister's daughter." Taking her word for it, the man removes a wad of money from his wallet and drops the bills on the bed, making only too clear to Stefani what her mother has been up to.

Doubly hypocritical, this woman whose shaved head signals a grieving widowhood is in fact having sex for money, all while falsely and cruelly claiming that her daughter is a prostitute. Finally—having been caught in the act, as it were—the mother lets the truth come out: "You're the reason for all the misery of my life," she says, explaining that she once cheated on Stefani's dead father, and that Stefani is the product of her illicit tryst. Pumping her chest for emphasis, the mother offers the rather lofty, self-aggrandizing claim that she would "be with an oil tycoon" if only she had not become pregnant with "another man's kid," which makes little sense, considering the actual connubial context. (Does the mother mean to indicate that her late husband would have become a success if she had not strayed? Or simply that the pregnancy, which forced her to remain in the marriage of which it was decidedly not a product, prevented her from pursuing another man?) Pointing up the perplexing melodrama of the situation, she tells Stefani, "You always knew how to barge in on people at the wrong time—from the very beginning!" Softly, almost to herself, a freshly self-pitying Stefani replies by saying, "Mama, you should have gotten rid of the pregnancy." The scene ends with Stefani packing her things and leaving the village "for good."

Her first stop is Ray Martins's studio, where she meets an unceasingly critical Luisa, who insists that she remain confined to the courtyard, as if she were a social undesirable. "I'm here to see Ray Martins, the star," Stefani explains, her tone seemingly innocent enough. Luisa just laughs, pointing at Stefani's gaudy blue eye shadow, ruby-red lipstick, and pink blush. "Sing something!" Luisa commands, presumably looking for another cause to chuckle. With Ray now present in the courtyard, Stefani begins to sing Lady Gaga's "Bad Romance," but her nerves get the better of her, and she flubs the performance, forgetting key lyrics and leaving little doubt about what Luisa calls her delusions. "See that gate there?" asks an enraged Ray, upset at Stefani for having wasted his time. "It's used for coming in and going out. Please go out." Weeping and desperate for a second chance, Stefani begins to sing Gaga's "Paparazzi," but it is a pathetic rendition—so pathetic, in fact, that Ray cannot resist imitating its tone-deaf register. With Luisa giggling beside him, Ray forcibly removes Stefani from the premises.

Her next stop is a bar on the outskirts of Lagos, where she tries to get a job as a singer. "I'm not a prostitute," she says by way of an introduction, attempting to preempt the allegation that has been dogging her for days.

"I'm an entertainer. I can do all the Lady Gaga stuff. Everything about Lady Gaga, *I* can perform." It is, of course, instructive that Stefani mentions not any specific Gaga song but instead the American superstar's entire persona—"the whole package," as she puts it. Stefani's statements suggest that, for her, Gaga is less a series of lyrical selections than a lifestyle—less a compendium of musical choices than a whole state of mind. Turned away by the manager, who is no Gaga fan, Stefani is forced to wait two years for a chance to perform for the bar's patrons. When she finally does perform, it is not as some sort of impersonator but, instead, as Lady Gaga herself—"just Lady Gaga." Calling herself by an American woman's stage name, Stefani lip-synchs to such tracks as "Bad Romance," "Monster," and "Speechless," gaining a loyal following but inciting the ire of her employers. When confronted with what the bar's manager plainly refers to as piracy, Stefani has no way of defending herself, except to maintain the fiction that she *is* Lady Gaga. At no point does she concede that she is stealing, simply plowing confidently ahead and thereby evoking an industry that has remained similarly mum about its own, equally obvious co-optations of Western cultural products.

Indeed, Nollywood films rarely acknowledge, let alone attempt to defend, their own unlicensed use of pop songs. Consider, for instance, *Emotional Crack*, which features Bob Marley's "Turn Your Lights Down Low," Lauryn Hill's "That Thing," Lighthouse Family's "Goodbye, Heartbreak," Puff Johnson's "Some Kind of Miracle," Sade's "Kiss of Love," Yanni's "Renegade," Kool & the Gang's "Ladies' Night," and an instrumental version of Richard Marx's "Right Here Waiting." In the film's closing credits, only four of these eight songs are listed (under the heading "additional music"), but that does not mean that producers actually paid for them. Indeed, the notoriously high cost of music rights and the notoriously slow legal and industrial channels through which those rights necessarily flow—made even slower by movement across cultures and continents—coupled with Nollywood's low budgets and rapid shooting schedules, make it virtually impossible for a Nollywood producer to obtain music licenses. The preponderance of pirated songs in Nollywood films is therefore not a reflection of some stereotyped Nigerian vice but, rather, an indication of the prohibitive difficulty of obtaining (i.e., paying for) official permission. An example of Nollywood's efforts to acknowledge—and, perhaps, defend—the unlicensed use of Western pop music, to redefine piracy as fair use, can be found in *Damage*, which adapts

Pink's hit single "Family Portrait" to suit its narrative. The film's closing credits go so far as to thank Pink for providing inspiration, if not necessarily for granting permission to use the song, in the process suggesting that a definition of fair use can and should extend to considerations of cultural translation that come with clear citations of their sources.

In *Lady Gaga*, Stefani is faced with a choice: confess to "persona stealing" (and thus abandon the illusion that she *is* Lady Gaga) or flee Nigeria in order to "start life anew." When she reunites with her friend Chris, who in the two years since she last saw him has become a major hip-hop star in the United States, he tells her to try to follow his own path by fleeing Lagos. Before leaving, Chris had first shared with Stefani his thoughts on Nigeria: "Trying to make it in music in this country is one hell of a frustration. Accept that you have to have your own money to promote yourself, or you'll go nowhere... I'm done here. I'm going to the States... where I can find the opportunities for my talents."

When Drake, who is now working for Ray Martins, confronts the new Chris, it is to shame the sudden superstar for having "escaped to the States": "Unlike you, I didn't run away to the United States. I stayed back in Nigeria, and weathered the storm. It's what real men do." Drake's masculinist condemnation of Chris is only a warm-up for a more stringent criticism of Stefani, whom Drake says is "Americanized" as well as "a wannabe Lady Gaga." In response, Stefani simply maintains that she *is* Lady Gaga—an assertion that gains some credibility when she performs for a crowd of adoring bar patrons, who not only refer to her as Lady Gaga but who also applaud her lip-synching to Gaga's songs "Speechless" and "Monster." "We love you, Gaga!" they scream, and when Stefani tears off her T-shirt, swings it, and then flings it toward her fans, a grinning young woman catches and caresses it. If Stefani has awakened the woman's lesbian passions, then she seems equally interested in satisfying the men who are present, almost as if she were Marlene Dietrich in *Morocco* (Josef von Sternberg, 1930), making her way from one audience member to another, equally appealing to all. Later, when she practices dancing as well as lip-synching to Lady Gaga's "Bad Romance," she is alone in the bar. Formally, the film begins to evoke a familiar music-video aesthetic by employing rapid editing (including the occasional jump cut) and suggesting a double structure of imitation, whereby the film itself mimics the "Bad Romance" video just as its protagonist is enacting her own, related Gaga routine. Suddenly, a woman wearing a blond wig and a gauzy, diaphanous gown materializes—much to Stefani's surprise. She identifies herself as a muse: "I'm the life and soul that radiates stardom," she says to Stefani, "which is of course something you crave so much. All great entertainers come to me for light, for a new pathway to greatness." Initially too scared to respond, Stefani manages after a few minutes to ask the muse for more information. "I have come," says the spectral woman, "to give you a spirit—to make you Lady Gaga, your idol. I'm offering you stardom beyond your wildest imagination!"

While the appearance of the muse immediately evokes Nollywood's familiar predilection for depicting juju, her specific intentions speak volumes about the film's take on Stefani's Gaga imitation. The implication, of course, is that it requires a kind of juju to "go Gaga," and it is instructive that the muse promises to effectively turn Stefani into her idol, not into some poor approximation thereof. At first dismissed as "just a dream," the muse returns again and again to confer upon Stefani—who accepts that muses "really exist" only after looking them up on Wikipedia—the "complete identity" of Lady Gaga. The muse omits a few key traits, however (including, of course, the "real" Lady Gaga's whiteness), and Luisa continues to recognize Stefani as a "fake" and a "fraud" long after everyone else has accepted her as Lady Gaga. Prior to capitulating to the muse's ministrations, Stefani had asked Chris for some advice, and he had told her to search for her "inner muse," advocating a model of stardom as labor. "Work hard," he advises, "and you will achieve your dreams."

Tellingly, the muse fails to resolve some basic economic conundrums: Stefani remains relatively poor even after "transforming" into Lady Gaga. She cannot command Gaga's ticket prices, nor can she generate the kinds of commodity tie-ins (T-shirts, phone cases, handbags) that first exposed her to the shimmering materiality of the Gaga phenomenon. As Luisa says to the newly refurbished Stefani, "Since I've never been fortunate enough to see Lady Gaga perform live, I thought I'd stay here and see the fake Gaga—the imitation." Luisa explains that she "can't afford the real thing," thereby highlighting the nagging matter of money. Later, Luisa lets Stefani know, in no uncertain terms, that an impoverished Lady Gaga represents a contradiction in terms—a true oxymoron. The film seems to endorse Luisa's perspective, which is, of course, a testament to Funke Akindele's magnetic star power, but also a function of specific formal devices, such as the shots that assume Luisa's literal point of view, her visual perspective on events. One such shot occurs when Luisa is staring critically at Stefani's footwear, arguing that the real Lady Gaga would never wear such cheap shoes. Another comes when she is watching Stefani from behind, laughing at the way the Gaga clone walks (uncomfortably, in an ill-fitting pink jumpsuit—another inspired choice by costumier Ogo Okechi). Try as she might, the muse cannot convince the likes of Luisa that Stefani has transformed into the kind of star who can afford anything she desires.

Tellingly, the muse signals an unexpected confluence of African juju, the aspirational Stefani, and the actual Lady Gaga. At one point, as soon as she has materialized, the muse brings with her the audible sounds of Gaga's "Alejandro," to which she dances exultantly, her diaphanous gown waving to the strains of the song and evoking images of its elaborately costumed singer. While the muse identifies herself (and is identified in the credits) as Terpsichore, one of the nine muses of Greek mythology and the one who rules over dance and the dramatic arts, her clearest link appears to be to juju, since she leads Stefani down a false path and provides her with a fake identity. But Stefani had herself assumed that identity long before the muse's appearance—a fact that does not necessarily detract from Terpsichore's associations with juju, but that definitely places a considerable degree of responsibility on Stefani's shoulders. The muse, in fact, may do more harm than good, serving to make Stefani look bad, particularly vis-à-vis piracy: Terpsichore's closest link to mysticism is her capacity to supersede bootlegging by being a spectral source of Gaga's songs—a semi-corporeal playback device, and one that precludes considerations of legality. At the same time that it presents the muse as a natural Gaga, however, the film itself continues to rely upon unlicensed Gaga songs, including the "Alejandro" that seems to emanate magically from the muse's unearthly being. In a rare, if implicit, endorsement of juju—one that somehow managed to get past the Abuja censors (assuming they vetted the film at all)—Stefani wins in the end, and without renouncing Terpsichore (or, even more tellingly, Terpsichore's evil twin, who tries to orchestrate some sexual shenanigans). Stefani, the "fake Gaga," acquires both fame and, in a dramatic twist, even Luisa's man, Ray Martins. It is Luisa who loses: the last shot of *Lady Gaga* is a fade-out on her suffering face, suggesting the film's rather cynical submission to Western media imperialism. Despite Akindele's dazzling star presence, the principled Luisa is apparently no match for the voracious Lady Gaga, and the film ends in a way that contradicts prevailing assumptions about Nollywood narratives. Matthias Krings and Onookome Okome argue that Nollywood films "tend to reaffirm rather than question viewers' expectations"—that "[n]othing is left open or to ponder, as the narratives require closure."[31] And yet *Lady Gaga* refuses to right the alleged wrongs of Stefani's media piracy and associated identity theft, subverting expectations conditioned both by the typical moralizing of the melodramatic mode and by the sheer triumphalim of Funke Akindele's star image. To gauge the degree of *Lady Gaga*'s subversiveness, particularly vis-à-vis the politics of stardom, one need only recall that Akindele's smash hit *The Return of Jénífà* ends with the title character discovering that she is "miraculously" HIV-negative, despite both her well-founded suspicions and the narrative precedent of its filmic forerunner. At the end of *Lady Gaga*, it is Luisa who is punished, not the deceitful Stefani, raising key questions about the film's ultimate stance on media consumption and morality in the age of globalization.

THE LOSS OF THE LOCAL: *LADY GAGA*'S GLOOMY ENDING

The extent to which *Lady Gaga* is alert to the actual circumstances of Nigerian media stardom is apparent in its depiction of corporate endorsement deals: when Stefani, as the newly popular Lady Gaga, wins a gig with what is described as a "telecommunications giant"—an obvious reference to Globacom—both Ray and Luisa think that she has "stolen" it from them, thus evoking the well-publicized competitions among actual Globacom brand ambassadors (represented allegorically in the *BlackBerry Babes* trilogy). Before the deal has gone through, Ray and Luisa confront Stefani, trying to bully her into turning it down. "You would never *dare* snatch an endorsement deal meant for Ray Martins!" screams an apoplectic Luisa, threatening Stefani as she had earlier threatened the libelous journalist. This time, however, Ray is with her, and he proceeds to defend himself, saying to Stefani, "You're standing in the way of my 20-million-naira endorsement deal!" He warns her, in Yemi Blaq's famously deep voice, "Stay off of my path. Stay away from that deal." She does not, eventually negotiating a contract worth 30 million naira—a victory that only emboldens Luisa to keep pursuing her. Indeed,

Luisa starts to *stalk* Stefani. Interrupting the star's jogging session, which features a pair of beefy bodyguards, Luisa reminds Stefani that, while the muse's trickery may have worked up to a point, it still cannot save Stefani from her economic status—the status that her birth all but guaranteed by (as her own mother puts it) alienating "oil money." "You're trying to be Lady Gaga, but you're a fake, an imitation," Luisa says. "Let me give you some advice, girlfriend: the next time you want to be like someone, do it to the last detail—not like this." She points to Stefani's (relatively) inexpensive and altogether unfashionable SUV, noting that even her own car is "better." Luisa will not let Stefani forget that she is a "poor photocopy of the original"—and that the poverty, in this case, is literal as well as figurative. "Lady Gaga's got countless cars, houses, fancy clothes, shoes," says Luisa. "Grow up, bitch! Get it right!"

Stefani tries to stand up for herself, saying in as condescending a tone as she can muster, "Sweetie, look: I'm not in any form of competition with anyone. I am content with whatever I have been able to achieve for myself." Luisa shoots back by asking, "And what do you have? What have you been able to achieve for yourself, fake girl?" Stefani, tellingly, cannot answer these questions—nor can Oge Okoye quite compete with Funke Akindele, who dominates the scene with her rough-and-tumble antics. Akindele's physical comedy is at its broadest when Luisa is taken aback by Stefani's risible belief that she *is* Lady Gaga. At such moments, Akindele leans rearward in a perilously extreme pose, the top of her head threatening to touch the ground and her eyes turned toward the sky in wicked delight. It is as if Stefani's delusions have literally bent Luisa backwards—but in a most amusing way. Far less entertaining, however, is Stefani's bootlegged use of Gaga's songs, which creates a backlash that goes beyond Luisa's agitation. Drake is also appalled, both because bootlegging only bolsters a certain essentialist stereotype of Nigeria as a hotbed of piracy and because, as Luisa maintains, stealing Gaga's songs can only hurt those local talents who, like Drake himself, hope to make it "legitimately" in the music industry. As Drake says at one point, referring to Stefani, "She's a disgusting imitation. They need to sue this girl for copyright infringement!"

Literally walking away from such criticisms, Stefani repairs to the limo that she hopes will signify her stardom. There is a sudden reprise of the film's opening shot—revealed to have been a foreboding rather than a fantasy. It

Figure 4.4. With her bodyguard nearby, Stefani (Oge Okoye) receives an unexpected call from the "real" Lady Gaga in Ubong Bassey Nya's *Lady Gaga* (2012).

transitions, this time, into a close-up of Stefani emerging from the limo, wearing a replica of Gaga's iconic cigarette glasses (made famous by the music video for "Telephone," which Stefani has studied)—another commodity tie-in available for purchase in Nigeria, along with, as Stefani herself says, "all things Gaga." (In making such a statement, Stefani seems to suggest that she has spent so much money "becoming" Gaga that she cannot afford multiple cars and houses, although Luisa is quick to remind her that buying an identity means "buying all parts of it—everything, down to the last detail.") As she walks away from the limo, Stefani is confronted with a crowd of journalists clamoring for her attention. One of them asks the obvious question: "Why do you do only Lady Gaga songs in your performances? Where is your ingenuity and originality?" When another poses a query commonly addressed to the "real" Lady Gaga (most famously by Barbara Walters on 20/20)—the question of whether to call her by her stage name or by her birth name—the Nigerian star says, "Whether it's Lady Gaga or Stefani, it's all one person—it's all the same!"

Later, Stefani's phone rings. The voice on the other end sounds—well, a lot like Lady Gaga herself, the "real" Gaga with her somewhat raspy register. "Hey, bitch," she says to Stefani, who recognizes the voice at once as belonging to her idol. "Oh, my God—Lady Gaga!" she screams, having been reduced to the giddy dimensions of a genuine fan. "So you're the phony-ass, shitty-ass bitch livin' off my shit, huh?" asks the suddenly angry Gaga, the guttural voice on the other end of the line. After an audible gulp, Stefani claims, "It's not like that! You are my greatest mentor! The only thing I'm doing here is I'm helping to spread your popularity over here." The repetition of the word "here" not only foregrounds the matter of local media reception; it also signals that Stefani is nervous. In response, the voice of Gaga shouts, "Shut the fuck up! I don't need you as a fan. I don't need fake, lying bitches as fans! Go check out my Facebook, my Twitter account—I've got enough fans. Now *you*—you're fake, you're a piece of shit!"

"Please, Lady Gaga, you've got to listen to me. I am your *greatest fan*."

"Fan? You're sick. I don't need you as a fan. I don't like *local* bitches as fans."

"I—I didn't think you would say it that way," says Stefani, crushed, before the film cuts to a close-up of Luisa, revealing her to be the source of the voice on the other end of the line. "Get off my phone, bitch," Luisa sneers, before finally hanging up. That Luisa has managed to sound not unlike Lady Gaga is of course a measure of Funke Akindele's range as an actress, but it also reinforces the fact that Luisa herself can act, as she does with her boss-*cum*-boyfriend, and that she too can become Lady Gaga, even going so far as to change her voice (something that Stefani does not do). The principle difference between Stefani and Luisa is that the latter resists imitation, except when making a prank phone call. In this way, *Lady Gaga* manages to uphold the notion that Nollywood stardom is adaptable and antiessentialist, while also suggesting ways of structuring polysemy. Akindele, as Luisa, can convincingly impersonate even the likes of Lady Gaga (at least vocally), but her Yorùbá cultural identity provides preferable—and multiple—pathways for "authentic" self-expression.

After prank calling Stefani, Luisa considers the elements of her own "false" performance. "How was my accent?" she asks—a crucial question for a native Yorùbá speaker who has just attempted to imitate an American in the English language. She answers with unqualified enthusiasm, screaming,

"Flawless!" Celebrating her own performance—her own successful Gaga act—Luisa begins to laugh uncontrollably. Sobering up eventually, she permits herself another brief soliloquy. This time, it consists of a command that Luisa directs at Stefani: "Stop copying Lady Gaga! Be yourself!" In delivering such a command, Luisa once again raises the possibility that she is more than a bit hypocritical. If her enthusiastic support for Beyoncé would seem to contradict her principled, ethnocentric rejection of Lady Gaga, then her advice for Stefani—that she "be herself"—is advice that Luisa has not quite followed. After all, her relationship with Ray Martins is predicated on role-playing—on the eroticized wearing of multiple masks—and she seems to place great stock in her own chameleonic qualities.

If role-playing keeps Ray and Luisa together, it can also tear them apart: when Luisa at her cheekiest decides to don a Lady Gaga costume, Ray responds with genuine distaste. "What are you doing with this whole Lady Gaga getup?" he asks. "Wow. This Lady Gaga thing is really catching on with everyone—including you." Realizing that her ploy is not working—that Ray really does not enjoy it—Luisa swiftly removes her Gaga wig, saying, "No. Not me. Never." Ray, trying to work up a spark, starts to tease her: "You have to admit that even you have caught the Lady Gaga bug!" Luisa lets him know that her pride remains in place and that she is nothing like Stefani. "You know I don't like imitation," she says. But something has been broken—some bit of desire has died. In the next scene, Luisa shows up in the studio with her hair in Jheri curls, but Ray will have nothing to do with her. He is having an affair with Stefani, whose "caricature of stardom" he finds appealing. (It helps, of course, that the muse's evil twin has used her juju to guarantee the couple's sexual chemistry.) When she finds out, Luisa is heartbroken.

Meanwhile, Stefani still has the moralistic Chris to confront. Now a superstar living in a posh Lagos mansion, Stefani spends her free time watching Lady Gaga music videos (as well as, at one point, the 2003 Richard Linklater film *School of Rock*, starring Jack Black). When Chris walks in on her as she is studying the music video for Gaga's "The Edge of Glory," he sees a woman who narcissistically identifies with the image on her TV screen. "She's quite a phenomenon, isn't she?" Stefani asks, forgoing a conventional greeting for the sake of sheer Gaga love. "Isn't it amazing how completely I melded into her? Or, I should say, *she* into *me*." Chris tries, for the umpteenth time, to talk

Stefani out of her fantasy of fusion, saying, "You've made quite a name for yourself, standing in someone else's shadow. Don't you think it's time you stepped out to carve a niche for yourself?" Stefani groans as if she has heard these comments before—and indeed she has. "This *is* a niche," she explains. "I'm a star already."

Chris is persistent, however, and he tries to remind Stefani of her pre-Gaga dreams. At this point, the film flashes back to her first, seemingly promising meeting with a Lagos-based record executive—an encounter that ends in cruelty and betrayal, as the man steals her demo song and passes it off as the work of a nonexistent performer named Baby Spice (who, spectral though she may be, represents a manufactured imitation of the blonde member of the British pop group The Spice Girls). Stefani hears it on the radio and is devastated. Years later, she uses this one negative experience to justify her piracy—to excuse her theft of Lady Gaga's music and entire star persona. Again, Nigeria's allegedly endemic corruptions are presented as the fuel for new practices of media piracy, but there is an underside to this argument, and it is one that Stefani herself sheds some light upon: with Western media imperialism making original creative expression so difficult in Nigeria, it seems reasonable to fight back through a cynical, wholesale appropriation—a pirating of all aspects of an American superstar's identity. When Chris, still trying to change Stefani's mind, argues that, "for legal reasons," there "never can be two Lady Gagas in the world," Stefani says, "There are not two." And she is right. Stefani is not "her own" Lady Gaga—she is not a "version" of the pop star. She *is* Lady Gaga, down to every lip-synched gesture.

The film ends—rather disappointingly, for fans of Funke Akindele—with Luisa being forced to watch footage of Stefani and Ray making love, which Drake recorded with his BlackBerry phone. When she confronts Ray, saying that she has suspected him for weeks ("I've been around long enough to know when a public rumor is actually an industry truth"), he responds by confessing to his relationship with Lady Gaga. "Don't you mean Stefani?" Luisa asks. Ray shakes his head. Left to writhe in pain, confused and alone, Luisa must face the bitter facts: that the self-respect she has fought for—the pride in an adaptable but still Yorùbá-specific identity—has no place in today's Nigeria, where the only response to Western imperialism is to embrace it, and to assume the personae of its key agents. For those who worship the vibrant Funke Akindele, this ending cannot help but seem intensely upsetting. Akindele is a star who should never have to suffer on screen—not because her acting is not up to the dramatic challenge, but because her persona, especially as established in the role of Jénífà, is exultant, a triumphant amalgamation of sass, self-confidence, and sidesplitting humor. Here, she is a victim of melodrama—the mode's prototypical weeping woman, abused and abandoned. But at least she's antiessentialist.

The sheer mobility of Nollywood star personae does not always settle in pleasing places—on film or in life. This is especially so when kids enter the equation—when child stars grow tired of the limelight, grow into scandalizing figures, or simply grow up. Today, Nollywood stars under the age of twenty-five are pitifully few—a fact that has some fans of the industry calling for the development of Nigerian versions of Hollywood's biggest kid stars. But as *Lady Gaga* makes clear, the cultivation of local imitations can never please everyone, particularly when it follows a process of cross-cultural, cross-racial identification. While Stefani's case is extreme—and increasingly juju-influenced—it still registers as symbolic of what is actually happening in today's Nigeria, as it is throughout a global South that remains enmeshed in Western media. Some Nollywood stars claim that they want to be seen as counterparts to specific Hollywood talents, and numerous Nigerian writers seem happy to position them thus—comparing Genevive Nnaji to Julia Roberts, for instance, or Eniola Badmus to Gabourey Sidibe. Such an analogizing tendency hardly does justice to the unique specificities of Nollywood stardom, however, or to those Nigerian talents who have developed in their own time and on their own terms. As Robert Stam and Ella Shohat suggest, this process of annexing talents from the global South into the evaluative operations of the global North is nothing new: approached through Western power structures, the subaltern cultural producer has long been "legitimated through a comparison to a superaltern predecessor."[32]

What happens, however, when a cross-cultural identification becomes the designated starting point for Nollywood star formation, rather than an imposed eventuality? What happens when the imported abundance of Western youth stars inspires a new form of ageism in Nollywood—one that must confront local modes of resistance to the perceived exploitation of young people? The following two chapters trace the history of child stardom in Nollywood, positing some key reasons for its early emergence, eventual disappearance, and recent resurgence as a talking point among industry practitioners and their fans. With so many prominent adult stars at the center of various child welfare movements, the push to produce new youth talents clashes with a culture of concern for juvenile Nigerians—as well as with the age-defying types who, in their films, would like to continue to play kids.

5

Nollywood's Progeny

Stardom and the Politics of Youth Empowerment

Once Oge Okoye had achieved star status, producers worked to solidify her specific star qualities by casting her in a series of similarly themed films. That, of course, is partly how Nollywood's star system functions—through a process of conscious accretion. Indeed, film roles tend to multiply in ways that recall one another, inviting consumers to see something old in something new—something familiar and comforting in something fresh and untested. Casting the same singular star in even the most divergent of roles offers obvious corporeal and affective similarities, creating a complex creative fabric—an iconic through-line connecting narrative experimentation. "Stars are the product of intertextuality," writes Gaylyn Studlar. "Their reception by audiences is produced by a succession of textual sources as well as by extratextual ones such as advertising and publicity."[1] That is as true for Nollywood as it is for Studlar's subject, the Hollywood studio system. Discourses of craft and authenticity dictate that Okoye could only play Lady Gaga after having first cut her teeth on similarly driven characters, but according to the basic market logic of stardom, such a casting choice was all but inevitable: Okoye had already donned a series of Gaga-style wigs and dresses in public as well as in her previous films about the search for superstardom (such as *Show Girls*), and she had long since demonstrated a willingness to explore her own androgyny on screen. Her past roles and complex public persona thus comprised her audition for *Lady Gaga,* as the film's producers have themselves suggested. Simply "being Oge" was better—more convincing—than any formal screen test.

Since its inception, Nollywood has been hailed as a popular art form, uniquely responsive to Nigerian national conditions and a possible conduit for black African empowerment. Equally entrenched, however, is the notion that Nollywood fosters false consciousness—the kinds of psychic conditions that, in John McCall's words, "reinforce rather than challenge the status quo."² McCall can hardly be said to endorse this interpretation of Nollywood, however. Instead, he views the industry as relevant but not reducible to the precise sociopolitical circumstances of contemporary Nigeria. McCall, in other words, joins forces with Jonathan Haynes and Onookome Okome, who famously argue that Nollywood "give(s) us something like an image of the Nigerian nation—not necessarily in the sense of delivering a full, accurate, and analytical description of social reality, but in the sense of reflecting the productive forces of the nation."³ Since those forces increasingly include Nigerian youth, why is it so difficult to name more than a handful of Nollywood's child performers? Why do so few of them figure into the industry's promotional campaigns? "Children in Nollywood tradition are generally quiet—to be seen and rarely heard," writes Adedayo Ladigbolu Abah. Arguing that this representational system "is in need of a deep critique," Abah notes that it "perhaps fits into Western stereotypes about helpless African children," and that "it is so very far from [the realities] of children's lives in Nigeria." Abah explores this subject through the framework of Yorùbá narratology, suggesting the widespread influence of a Yorùbá belief system that privileges adult experiences over those of children.⁴ It is equally important, however, to attend to the structuring dynamics of Nollywood's star system. Indeed, there is an all-too-obvious disjunction between what Nigerian kids can actually accomplish, in acting terms, and what the Nollywood industry permits them to experience offscreen via the multiple and multidirectional circuits of its star system. If, as McCall notes, Nollywood is an informal industry, why does it seem so formally opposed to publicizing talented youth? If adult stars can help to advance Nollywood's goal of global saturation, and in the process provide positive press for Nigeria and West Africa, then why can kids not help too?

Nollywood's vast output facilitates the intertextual construction of star identities, and Oge Okoye, like her famous counterparts, rose quickly. She did so not simply by making over a dozen films in a year, but also by appearing in projects designed to reunite her with past costars. It is this self-conscious dependence upon the publicity potential of onscreen reunions that both bolsters Nollywood's star system and exposes its shaky relationship to child performers, none of whom have been promoted as part of a reunited onscreen pairing. One could argue that these much-publicized pairings typically bring together amorous leads, thereby sidestepping the question of kid stars. A Genevieve Nnaji-Ramsey Nouah or a Stephanie Okereke-Desmond Elliot onscreen reunion bespeaks sheer romanticism; it sells sex. Surely an underage performer would not suit such a paradigm. It is worth pointing out, however, that this particular promotional scheme often includes non-eroticized, same-sex pairings, as when Omotola Jalade-Ekeinde and Genevieve Nnaji, the stars of Tchidi Chikere's hit film *Blood Sister* (2003), were reunited in 2010 for Chineze Anyaene's *Ijé*, a heavily publicized drama that recalls *The Color Purple*—particularly author Alice Walker's contention that sisters share a unique bond that neither time nor transcontinental travel can break. In *Ijé*, Jalade-Ekeinde and Nnaji play two such sisters, with Nnaji receiving top billing and full glamor treatment on the film's official poster and website, while the second-billed Jalade-Ekeinde appears in tears and without makeup. Fans are thus invited to view the project not simply in terms of a sisterly reunion but also as a source of competition between big stars—more specifically, between two adult women.

In a vivid reminder of Steven Spielberg's 1985 film adaptation of *The Color Purple*, the producers of *Ijé* chose to downplay the contributions of the two remarkable child performers who play younger versions of the Jalade-Ekeinde and Nnaji characters, sacrificing them (in publicity terms) to the shared star power of the older women, but also to *Ijé*'s status as a 35 mm Nollywood "event." With *The Color Purple*, Warner Bros. sought to elevate actress Whoopi Goldberg, who was making her film debut, to star status, furnishing taglines like "Whoopi Goldberg *is* Celie"—in spite of the fact that Celie's screen time is shared between Goldberg and child actress Desreta Jackson, who plays the younger version of the character. In the world of Nollywood, such a youth-phobic approach to publicity is essentially a given. With young performers consistently missing from even the most inclusive promotional campaigns, questions about a generationally specific industry bias are bound to arise. Nollywood's adult stars are made, not born, but the children are rarely even credited.

VIDEO VICTIMS

Given the Nigerian government's relatively desultory record with both local and pan-African youth movements, it is tempting to view Nollywood as just another inheritor of generalized youth allergies. But the government, through military as well as civilian rule, has tried and frequently failed to effect positive change, while Nollywood has long resisted attempts to generate, at the very least, a system for giving due credit to the underage performers who populate the industry. Efforts to achieve or improve a sense of national unity in Nigeria have long involved youth. In 1973, General Yakubu Gowon, then head of Nigeria's military government, instituted the National Youth Service Corps, which required university graduates to perform one year of government service. Designed to combat regionalism and ethnocentrism, the program called upon graduates to work in unfamiliar parts of the country and with people whose customs were far different from their own. As Otwini Marenin makes clear in a remarkable ethnographic analysis, the experience tended to kill rather than cultivate patriotism among the participants, many of whom reported that Gowon's high-minded plan had actually produced the opposite of its intended effect, serving only to reinforce a sense of Nigeria as being irreparably fragmented.[5] With Nollywood still being touted as a possible agent of national unity, then perhaps it is the memory of such youth cynicism that prevents it from fully embracing its youngest stars.

In her seminal essay "African Popular Arts," Karin Barber argues that "the people's arts represent what people do in fact think, believe, and aspire to."[6] If this is true, and if Nollywood is indeed a popular artistic guide, then one might think that the vast majority of Nigerian children look forward only to adulthood; fail to focus on the generationally specific conditions—the joy and the pain—of their own present; and prefer to view themselves as "pre-grownups," rather than as members of a true youth community. Relatively few and far between are the Nollywood films that let kids be kids, instead of vessels for the didactic dissemination of Pentecostal messages or the practically mute "evidence" of successful Lagosian marriages. Strictly within the boundaries of youth representation, Nollywood cannot be said to offer much in the way of realism, but that does not mean that the industry's films refuse to use children as the building blocks of narrative, or as equally abstract objects in the development of a diversity of themes. In fact, at times, Nollywood can seem to lean a little too heavily upon the thematic significance of Nigeria's underage population, though usually when the themes in question are limited to religious ones, or filtered through and "explained" by adult actions. For Abah, this amounts to "a representational strategy where the child functions less as a human being with active roles in cultural production and more as an abstract construct circulating in the adult world."[7] As employed by Barber and applied to this instance, then, the term "people" is hardly youth-inclusive, and it provides a reminder that Nollywood, to the extent that it is a "popular art," privileges what *adults* "think, believe, and aspire to," even as it uses children at seemingly every opportunity. Vis-à-vis the diverse daily experiences of Nigerian youth, Nollywood is hardly a popular art in the sense of assimilating vast, intergenerational swaths of the social fabric, since it often uses children simply as "background," or reduces their roles to rather unconvincing dimensions.

In focusing on Nollywood's development of a range of genres, as well as on its cultivation of sophisticated themes, numerous scholars have helped to position the industry as an ongoing political project, in contrast to the apolitical dimensions implied by the term "popular." However, the sociopolitical import of kids, which can be seen in a smattering of Nollywood film narratives, is not perceptible in the industry's promotional campaigns or in its star system. Nollywood has evolved by embracing new modes of publicity, but child performers do not appear in Nollywood Love commercials on YouTube, and they are also missing from iROKOtv's interstitials. Furthermore, Globacom, whose relationship with Nollywood has represented the fusion of two Nigerian commercial forces, has not contracted a single child actor to appear in any of its countless advertising campaigns, even as the company comes to rely upon more and more adult stars to sell its products and services. John Idriss Lahai argues, "Adult skepticism about the younger members of African society has not only placed young people at the margins of ... political and economic processes, but it has also limited the focus of [academic] analyses."[8] Several scholars have sought to correct this imbalance, tackling the topic of African children as political actors, but none have considered the political economy of child stardom in Nollywood. Lahai suggests a compelling reason for the critical resistance to the study of African youth experiences, arguing that since children are "social beings in the process of social becoming," they are often sublimated to more seemingly solidified political actors—to adults whose public identities can appear (relatively) fixed. However, it is precisely the lack of fixity of child stardom that has made it so salable—so promotable—a part of star systems around the world, including those belonging to Hollywood and even, back in the early 1990s, what is now known as Nollywood.

While Nollywood currently seems blind to the publicity potential of children, it once, at an earlier stage of its evolution, embraced their inchoate charms, making stars of such underage performers as Omotola Jalade-Ekeinde, Sharon Ezeamaka, William Uchemba, and Teju Babyface. Since its inception, the industry has relied upon underage talents, but it has not always allowed them one of the perks of stardom—the opportunity to appear in promotional campaigns and to serve as the faces of a complex, increasingly transnational and transmedial commercial enterprise. At times, Nollywood has seemed simultaneously to canonize and pathologize children—a contradiction that is at the heart of several of the industry's earliest hit films. Consider, for instance, Andy Amenechi's *Mortal Inheritance* (1995), which stars Omotola Jalade-Ekeinde, who was just sixteen years old when the film was shot, as a young woman suffering from sickle cell anemia and "hoping against hope" to have a baby. The disconnect between the character's physical condition and her goal of motherhood is compounded by the age of the performer who plays her, raising key questions about the appropriate contours of child stardom in Nollywood. To her considerable credit, the sixteen-year-old Omotola Jalade-Ekeinde approaches the role with a ravaged intensity well beyond her years, believably communicating extreme physical pain and distinguishing the now-classic film with her precocious power as a performer. That said, the actress's inescapably visible youth compels the spectator to worry as much about her as about her character. Not having seen her before, audiences in 1995 must have marveled at Omotola's gifts as the protagonist of *Mortal Inheritance*, while also brooding over the toll the role likely took on her. Amenechi's film ultimately offers a familiar account of interethnic romance—of the redemptive love of a Yorùbá girl for an Igbo boy—but other films of the mid- to late-1990s relied upon children strictly as vulnerable, corruptible figures. A key example is Tade Ogidan's *The Diamond Ring* (1998), in which child actor Teju Babyface plays a boy whose overbearing parents send him to university prematurely, resulting in his joining a dangerous campus gang. Emphasizing this conflation of youth and risk, the film's tagline asked, "Can you vouch for the company your children keep?"—an alarmist question that seemed to signal the social conditions of child acting as much as the plot of *The Diamond Ring*.

With Nollywood now over twenty years old—with the industry a veritable adult, as it were—it is possible to perceive a certain trajectory of child acting, an arc from Ezeamaka and Uchemba, two young talents who helped to publicize an equally young industry, to today's focus on venerable, senior stars and their connections to new circuits of distribution and new arenas of reception. Nollywood's emergence in the early 1990s was coterminous with a growing government focus on the deleterious effects of entertainment media on Nigerian children. In 1989, the Federal Ministry of Information and Culture began conducting a series of investigations into underage boys' exposure to pornographic videos. Published in book form as *Youth and Pornography*, the ministry's findings helped to position video culture as uniquely damaging to the "ethical development" of Nigerian children. Using language relevant to Nollywood's medium-specific credentials, the book expresses alarm at researchers' observation that Nigerian youth appeared to be "proud owners" of video recording and playback devices, "in an environment where almost all the video cassettes . . . are imported from other countries. The consequence of this situation is that Nigeria has become a dumping ground for movies and video cassettes that are banned in Europe and North America." An aversion to Western cultural imperialism is here conflated with anxieties surrounding the erotic experiences of Nigerian boys; Westernization's sexualizing potential is both improper and pronounced. *Youth and Pornography* thus offers what might be called a moral nationalism, a sense that Western-derived video technologies are bad for the boys who, as the book argues, "represent Nigeria's future." For the Federal Ministry of Information and Culture, videos are detrimental not simply because of what they show but because of where they come from. In an even more alarmist mode, the book reveals that 33 percent of boys surveyed "indicated that they watch [pornographic videos] . . . on their father's

[sic] video recorders," while 67 percent of respondents viewed pornography "either in their friends' houses or in cinema houses." *Youth and Pornography* reserves its most stringent criticism, however, for boys' participation in the production of pornographic videos, and it calls for a strict, federally enforced separation between what it terms "video culture" and "the labor of young Nigerians."[9]

Five years later, the psychologist Chinenye Clare Ochiagha published *The Future of the Nigerian Youth: A Counseling Perspective*, in which Ochiagha argued that "the most deadly organs for exposing youths to . . . negative sexual stimuli" were videocassettes.[10] By that time, the still-expanding Nigerian video industry was already widely believed to represent a major source of "destructive" imagery—an industry uniquely able to "spoil [Nigerian] youth and denigrate [Nigerian] culture."[11] A later study in the *Journal of Instructional Psychology* would show, in Stefan Sereda's words, "Nigerian youth becoming increasingly deficient in social values, to the point where they lack a sense of civic responsibility."[12] Clearly, video culture provided a convenient culprit, and it was into this rather unwelcoming political atmosphere that what is now known as Nollywood was born. Relying upon intense cultural pressures to explain the industry's failure to cultivate a series of child stars can only go so far, however. After all, Nollywood is not always beholden to convention. To say that the industry, by failing to develop underage stars, has simply buckled to a culture of concern for children is to suggest only part of the story. The rest involves the narratives of so-called children's films, as well as the fact that Nollywood has on rare occasions managed to generate actual kid stars. But the industry's ongoing failure to engineer a discrete system for nurturing and publicizing youth performers is worthy of investigation, especially considering its increasingly sophisticated mechanisms for making grown stars glitter.

For many, Nollywood still occupies a dangerous place; it still offers an uncertain social environment, particularly for kids. That is perhaps why the industry's attempts to dramatize the tragedies of youth have so often been marked by an exclusive reliance upon adult performers. When *The Diamond Ring* was released in 1998, a youth vigilante group by the name of the Bakassi Boys was rising to prominence in southeastern Nigeria, offering to protect humble traders from criminal exploitation. Nollywood's first major depiction of the Bakassi Boys—a group that, as Paul Ugor points out, is metonymic of the extreme insecurities of youth in Nigeria—in fact features no youth performers. Lancelot Oduwa Imasuen's *Issakaba* (2001) is a fictionalized account of the exploits of the Bakassi Boys, and one of Nollywood's most luridly violent films, famous for its torture scenes, (simulated) beheadings, and general bloodiness. While his exact age is unclear, lead actor Sam Dede, who plays Ebube, the leader of the boys, was at least twenty-nine years old when the film was shot (his father, a Biafran War veteran, died in 1972), and his costars appear even older. Ugor argues that *Issakaba* represents "how the youth in most places in sub-Saharan Africa react to the pervasive cultural economy of state insecurity," effectively transforming themselves into radical and alarming figures.[13] However, it is important to point out that *Issakaba* achieves this not through the performances of perceptibly youthful actors—through the hiring of boys to play boys—but instead through dialogue. Indeed, the youthfulness of the film's youth vigilante group is solely constructed through spoken exchanges, as well as through scenes in which the "boys" consult with a council of elders. Conceivably, given the brutality of their representation of paramilitary aggression, the filmmakers did not want to burden mere children with embodying violent actions, and yet the realist, muckraking aspirations of *Issakaba* are severely limited by its reliance on adults; if, as several scenes suggest, the film was intended as a critique of the role of children in violent conflicts, then such a critique can only go so far in the face of adulthood's iconographic dominance. Only once, in a terrifying scene in which a criminal wields a gun on a public bus, snatching a baby from the arms of her mother and holding her up for all to see, does the film suggest the unseemly aspects of involving underage performers in a difficult project; indeed, one cannot help but fear for the safety of that baby girl being tossed around as if she were a lifeless prop. Perhaps, then, Imasuen was right to rely on adult actors when casting his Bakassi Boys. In other filmic instances, however, the absence of children is inexcusable—even, to a certain extent, offensive. If Nollywood's development of a well-defined star system has helped it to shed its stereotyped popular rendering as an informal, indiscriminate, and amateurish operation, then its own logics of youth exclusion have, to a certain extent, undermined this progress, precisely by suggesting that something is amiss—or at least inadequate—in the realm of intergenerational relations.

CONTROVERSIAL KIDS

Clearly, the controversies that Oge Okoye's Gaga have generated cannot hold a candle to those surrounding the experiences of child performers in Nollywood. Since the early 1990s—in other words, since the industry's birth—Nollywood has witnessed the waxing and waning of youth stardom. For every Sharon Ezeamaka (the celebrated child star of several early Nollywood dramas), there is a nameless youngster who appears in a string of films, sans billing, and disappears without comment. Contemporary fans, in looking back upon a series of groundbreaking movies, often ask the key question "Who were the kids?" Even today, Nollywood is widely known for its contradictory relationship to child performers. On the one hand, innumerable films rely heavily upon kids, both as extras and as prominent characters. On the other hand, there are very few instances in which child performers are asked to appear at red carpet premieres or to pose for magazine covers. When asked to name some of their favorite youth talents, even Nollywood's die-hard followers draw blanks.

Given the dramatic potential of familial conflicts—but considering as well the evangelical narrative mandates of many films—children are seemingly everywhere in Nollywood, at least on screen. They represent the babies born out of wedlock to wicked, promiscuous parents; they are the vulnerable, victimized little ones whose demonic teachers are in league with Beelzebub; increasingly, however, they are also the sources of inspiration—of hope for the future—both for individual families and for Nigeria itself. If that is the case—if children's narratives are indeed being positioned as uplifting and regenerative—then it seems odd, to say the least, that Nollywood is not doing more to promote the elevation of individual child performers to the highest echelons of industry stardom.

The topic of child stardom is one of the most discussed—and one of the most divisive—in Nollywood fandom. It galvanizes the industry's directors and performers alike, not to mention the millions who watch their films. In West Africa and the diaspora, everyone seems to have an opinion about the debate's components, questioning whether child stardom is possible or even palatable, and wondering why an industry so vast and prolific has refused to make a range of realist youth movies—the kinds that would require the casting of actual kids, not adult icons who can "look young." Just what, precisely, a realist youth movie might entail in *narrative* terms is of course open to discussion. Nevertheless, a range of Nigerian publications have proffered a series of determinants for this mode of cinema, chief among them the ages of the performers involved. According to this particular model, a film's producers need to cast "a genuine youth" in the role of a child if their film is to deserve the label of realism.

The bond between Nollywood and youth culture has always been a contentious one, but it has often benefitted from the interventions of activist adult stars. Stephanie Okereke, for instance, frequently times her film-specific promotional activities to coincide with events related to Nigerian politician Prince Tonye Princewill's Orphans Awareness Campaign, which works to inspire welfare reform for orphans in Rivers State. When Okereke walks a red carpet with orphaned children, as she did at the 2009 premiere of *Nnenda* in Port Harcourt, or publicly performs with the youth choir from Life Time Caring Orphanage Home, she promotes her own star identity—as well as Nollywood itself—as being consciously responsive to the plight of Nigerian kids. Globally, though, one oft-cited lacuna in these admirable efforts is the absence of a bona fide child star to embody generationally specific struggles, which leaves an adult actress like Okereke to assume the responsibility, both onscreen and off, of advocating on behalf of Nigerian orphans.

Press accounts of Okereke tend to focus not simply upon her private life and lasting sex appeal, but also upon her charity work with children. What happens, however, when Nollywood kids actually reach the pages of popular magazines? What does a Nigerian newspaper account of youth stardom actually look like? Popular interest in the aftermath of a child's acting career can often galvanize fan cultures, even in southern Nigeria. In early 2012, *The Punch*, which bills itself as "Nigeria's most widely read newspaper," created a column entitled "Once Upon a Kid Actor."[14] At roughly the same time, Nigeria's *Vanguard* newspaper inaugurated a column that it called "Keeping up with the Kid Stars."[15] Both columns have reconsidered the role that child performers played in shaping the Nollywood industry during the early 1990s, and both are dependent upon heavy doses of nostalgia. *The Punch* looks back upon the child performers who acted onscreen during a period when, as columnist Maureen Azuh puts it, "Nollywood was still at its teething stage." The *Vanguard* invites readers to "take a walk down memory lane" and "remember the stars who seized the Nigerian entertainment scene when they were just pitter-patters of little feet" and at a time when "Nollywood [itself] was just springing up." Instructively, both newspapers have resisted considering the conditions for kids who *currently* work in Nollywood, preferring instead to describe how, for instance, former child star Isosiya Dokubo went to college, acquired a British accent, and decided to pursue an advanced business degree at Middlesex University, or how Tosin Jegede, who recorded the hit 1980s song "Parents, Listen to Your Children" while just a preadolescent, later became a major advocate for youth education in Nigeria.

Jegede's particular story condenses several key reasons why Nigeria's relationship to child stardom has long been fraught. While "Parents, Listen to Your Children" was quickly becoming what *The Punch* calls "a primary school marching song," Jegede herself was struggling to receive an adequate education—a struggle compounded by the popular accusation that her song was "distracting" to school kids, in spite of its being a blatantly pro-education anthem (with lyrics like "Try and pay our school fees" and "Give us a sound education"). When she left Nigeria in 1996, while still in her mid-teens, Jegede said that it was to pursue to her education abroad. In a 2012 interview with the *Vanguard*, however, she claimed that it was also to avoid being kidnapped at a time when "security in Nigeria was not all that tight"—and when child stars were attractive targets.[16] Nigeria, in this scenario, comes across as doubly dangerous to children—doubly detrimental to their development. Not only is it alleged to be a place where educational opportunities are scarce (thus compelling Jegede to return in her early thirties to start the Tosin Jegede Foundation, with its famous "One Child, One Book" initiative); it is also painted in accordance with global popular stereotype, as a veritable wellspring of corruption where a kid might easily be kidnapped.

Exiled from their native Nigeria for want of what Jegede calls "a better life," former child stars can so often seem to embody the high costs of employment in Nollywood, advancing an image of the industry that places it at odds with the youngest generation of Nigerian citizens. Of the former child stars who stayed in Nigeria, many have become youth rights activists (like the Jegede who eventually returned to Lagos). The late, legendary Christy Essien-Igbokwe, who got her start as a teen singing sensation, recording songs in English, Yorùbá, Igbo, and her native Ibibio, made the transition to Nollywood while well into her adult years, but she managed to bring to the industry's then-new table all of the wisdom that she had acquired as a child star. While shooting especially dramatic or risqué scenes, she made sure that no children were around to witness them, thereby helping to publicize the nascent industry as, in a certain sense, kid-friendly. Within the boundaries of Nigeria's music industry, Essien-Igbokwe was instrumental in casting children in her music videos, most of which aired on Nigerian television and tended to show her performing amid a sea of appreciative kids.[17] Shortly before her death in 2011, Essien-Igbokwe appeared as a guest mentor on *Nigerian Idol*, where she taught two young performers to sing (in Yorùbá) her international hit song "Seun Rere," from her remarkable 1981 highlife album *Ever Liked My Person?* Standing on the *Idol* stage, flanked by two teen girls, Christy Essien-Igbokwe provided a reminder not merely of her extraordinary talent but also of her significant impact upon Nigerian popular culture. Her multilingual music had always cut across ethnic lines, consistently embracing kids in the process. ("Seun Rere" is itself about a child asking for the blessings of a parent.) When the *Idol* cameras cut to audience members responding to the group performance of Essien-Igbokwe's most famous song, they lingered on the children who rose to their feet, smiled, and even sang along.

Though perhaps best known for her music, Christy Essien-Igbokwe was one of Nollywood's earliest leading ladies—and one of the first to connect her film work with her offscreen activism. Essien-Igbokwe had a prominent role in *Scars of Womanhood* (Reginald Ebere, 1997), an English-language drama about female genital mutilation and the practice's dependence upon what one character calls "bad mothering" for its very survival. (In other words, mothers who are on principle opposed to genital cutting nevertheless cannot resist the temptation to force their daughters to "experience what they experienced" and submit to the procedure; in the process, they mark themselves as selfish, childishly competitive parents, eager to ensure a physically painful, cross-generational equivalence.) Close to a decade before Ousmane Sembène's *Moolaadé* would galvanize global cinema spectators with its polemical approach to the tradition of genital cutting, Nollywood was offering a remarkable and altogether activist depiction of the very same subject.

A key difference between *Scars of Womanhood* and *Moolaadé*, however, lies in the latter's use of actual child performers to portray the victims (and would-be victims) of genital mutilation. Like most Nollywood films before, and like countless since, *Scars of Womanhood* features adult performers in its central youth roles, a fact that does not necessarily detract from or dilute its politicizing potential—particularly if one considers that director Reginald Ebere may have had in mind a Brechtian style of creating distance, one that would draw the spectator's attention to blatant artifice in order to arouse her to action. However, within both broadly commercial and strictly realist rubrics, the absence of children from a film partly devoted to youth experience can seem inadvisable—a breach that sees obvious adults performing as if they were kids and that plainly subverts audience expectations.

Scars of Womanhood features then-twenty-six-year-old Kate Henshaw (now a Nollywood superstar) in the role of Tamuno, a girl whose circumcision is scheduled as a precondition for her marriage to a prince. Tamuno is meant to be slightly older than the typical victim of genital mutilation, having once witnessed what she calls "this barbaric act" and pledged thereafter to resist it, but she is still, as the film's plot and dialogue make clear, "a mere girl." Henshaw, however, is obviously not; while she gives a remarkable performance in *Scars of Womanhood* (indeed, one of the most skillful and moving film performances that I have ever seen), she cannot, with her great height, possibly convey the impression that she is a child, and a key scene shatters the illusion that she belongs to a group of underage girls. Pressured by her mother (played by Essien-Igbokwe) to "become a woman" through circumcision, Tamuno retreats to the company of "fellow children," all of whom are played by actual kids who throw into stark relief Henshaw's status as an adult. In a remarkable night shot, Tamuno can be seen sitting with these kids around a campfire, her head high above theirs as she recites a beloved fable. Not one of the other kids has a speaking part in the film, however, leaving the obviously adult Henshaw to both embody as well as articulate what one character calls "the youth experience." Even more egregious a breach in generational realism is a later scene in which Tamuno discusses circumcision with yet another figure whom she defines as a "fellow girl," and who is played by an actual child; seated side by side, the two look less like peers than like a mother and her daughter.

In making *Moolaadé*, Sembène did not exactly dispense with his celebrated interest in Soviet social realism—an interest that he famously developed while studying film in Moscow. *Moolaadé* contains sequences clearly designed to rouse oppressed subjects (in this case, girls and women) to collectively resist the systematized powers of their oppressors. Shots of dissenters forming lines through which to protest violently misogynist social policies appear throughout the film, recalling many of the classics of Soviet cinema (from Eisenstein to Dovzhenko). Most significant to the subject at hand is the way Sembène treats children, forcing them to bear witness to adult actions and encouraging them to comment upon those actions, often in a way that directly confronts the spectator. Consider, for instance, the celebrated closing sequence of Sembène's *La noire de . . .* (1966), in which a black Senegalese boy stalks a guilt-ridden white Frenchman while wearing the traditional African mask that the Frenchman once claimed as his own. The sequence famously ends with the boy turning toward the camera and slowly lowering the mask, his gaze firmly fixed upon the lens—and, by extension, upon the spectator, who through this process is further implicated in the complex circuits of art and culture that the film depicts.

African celluloid cinema is full of films about children, from Gaston Kaboré's *Wend Kuuni* (1983) to Souleymane Cissé's *Yeelen* (1987), Idrissa Ouedraogo's *Yaaba* (1989), and beyond. But the one celluloid African art film to have come closest to inciting a bona fide firestorm of kid-centered controversy is Drissa Touré's *Haramuya* (1995). In that film, child performers must bear a variety of burdens, from depicting the victimization of *talibés* (beggars made to masquerade as Islamic apprentices) at the hands of their *marabouts* (Quranic scholars), to acting as agents of exchange and of delivery in the West African drug trade. One underage character is even depicted as pursuing—and enjoying—a sexual relationship with an adult woman. At FESPACO in 1995, *Haramuya* became a hot topic, due in part to its alleged allegiance to a Western style of filmmaking familiar from the multilayered ensemble projects of Robert Altman (especially 1975's *Nashville* and 1993's *Short Cuts*), but also because of the way Touré's film uses children. Questions about who Touré's youth performers actually were—about whether the actors playing *talibés* were actual *talibés*—were asked at FESPACO. Some festival attendees even wanted to know if the young actor who had portrayed the film's pot-smoking kid (one of its most charming and most moving characters) had actually been required to smoke marijuana while shooting—an embarrassingly alarmist question, quickly discounted by Touré and his supporters, but one that helped to position *Haramuya* as controversial from a kid-conscious standpoint.

Far more dramatic controversies, rooted in even more upsetting representations, have long been a part of Nollywood. Even prior to the industry's development, filmmaking in Nigeria was seen as a uniquely dangerous venture for children, with legendary actor-director Hubert Ogunde being accused of abducting and brainwashing underage girls.[18] Later, numerous Pentecostal preachers, in making the transition into filmmaking, and in working on occasion with child performers, would come under fire for allegedly attempting to displace the children's parents, providing on-set tutoring and "conversion" sessions. At a strictly narrative level, the relationship between Pentecostalism and parental responsibility has long stimulated Nollywood. It is, for instance, remarkably well developed—and quite clear—in a Nollywood film like *Miss Queen* (Moses Ebere, 2012), which shows what happens when a Bible-loving little girl uses her Christian wits to outsmart the daughter of Beelzebub, who has been masquerading as her physical education teacher. Since the little girl's mother has been plying her with Bibles, *Miss Queen* can present Pentecostal success as a function of family unity—of the responsiveness of a "good mother" to her child's religious convictions. But the film, operating within a rubric of Afro-optimism, omits mention of one of the more disturbing, real-life expressions of the connection between Pentecostalism and parenting, and one that has attracted the attention of human rights organizations from around the world: the use of Pentecostalism as an alibi for the violent arrogation of parental duties and the disturbing, increasingly elaborate abuse of children by church leaders. Prominent among these leaders is the controversial Helen Ukpabio, head of the African evangelical franchise Liberty Foundation Gospel Ministries, which she runs from Calabar, in Nigeria's southeastern Cross River State. Perhaps unsurprisingly, Helen Ukpabio turned to Nollywood in the 1990s, viewing it as a far-reaching vehicle for the dissemination of her Pentecostal messages, but her film work quickly became the target of local debates about the welfare of child performers. Allegedly accustomed to tossing acid in the faces of unruly children whom she deems "possessed by demons," Ukpabio was instrumental in casting actual kids in Teco Benson's 1999 film *End of the Wicked*, which she wrote and which quickly became enmeshed in controversies that obviously, given the woman's reputation for child-centered brutality, far surpassed those of *Haramuya*.[19]

Controversies with less disturbing sources still pivot around kids and performance. The ever-questionable Lady Gaga, for instance, remains a major source of inspiration for Nollywood stars, particularly those whose risky fashion choices threaten to generate negative publicity, but her persona does not necessarily have much to do with Nigeria's child performers. (The opening sequence of Ubong Bassey Nya's *Lady Gaga* would seem, at least initially, to suggest otherwise, since the first figures we see are three small children who eagerly await the arrival of Oge Okoye's title character. Tellingly, however, this trio is not present at any other point in the film, having disappeared after only a few seconds of screen time.) Despite her obvious popularity among young people, Gaga, generationally speaking, is not a teen, and while her stardom has inspired a range of American "Baby Gagas" (toddlers whose actions are said to evoke her music videos and whose own videos have gone viral), it would be difficult to argue that her image has ever been kid-friendly. Gaga emerged as a star when she was already well into her twenties, and, even setting aside the matter of her brazen eroticism, many of her self-representations—as a heavy smoker in the video for "Telephone," as a gambler in the video for "Poker Face"—preclude legal imitation by children, at least in the United States. In Nigeria, the closest that popular culture has come to uniting Gaga's aesthetics with the actions of local children was in early 2010, when footage of two shirtless Nigerian boys dancing in front of the Keystone Bank in Lagos became the inspiration for a variety of viral mash-ups, most of them intercutting Gaga's "Bad Romance" dance with the children's equally elaborate moves, which seemed to reflect a certain familiarity with American music videos.[20] So far, however, Gaga's popularity among Nigerian youth has been dramatically eclipsed by that of onetime child stars like Miley Cyrus, Justin Bieber, and Selena Gomez—at least as evidenced on the blogosphere and in the Nollywood films that repeatedly show Cyrus, Bieber, and Gomez commodity tie-ins. If the confident imitation of international superstars is one avenue through which Nollywood performers can simultaneously raise their profiles, challenge their talents, and combat essentialist stereotypes, then it is worth investigating why Nigerian children have not been asked to take stabs at mimicking Miley and Justin, and why an industry whose films so often depict kids is so seemingly resistant to child stardom.

The reasons for this resistance clearly have a lot to do with local definitions of child welfare, a key question being whether the performing child is being abused or otherwise exploited while in performance mode. The problem is that public perceptions of child stardom, in West Africa and the diaspora, are often contradictory. What some see as educational and inspirational, others view as intensely corrupting. However, as Jane O'Connor suggests, this interpretive dialectic represents less an irreconcilable obstacle than an ongoing condition of possibility for child stardom, at least in the United States and Western Europe. Controversy, of course, creates publicity, cultural tensions providing constant inspirations from both negative and positive poles, placing child stardom in a privileged commercial location. As O'Connor points out, child stars "inhabit a unique category due to their association with precocious sexuality and eroticized innocence—controversial elements that are often evident in their onscreen representations" and that often constitute significant selling points, in spite of the ire they may raise.[21]

Though O'Connor is primarily concerned with Western contexts, many of her remarks about child stardom are relevant to the media cultures of southern Nigeria. O'Connor argues that a high-minded resistance to the very idea of the performing child does not necessarily preclude the purchasing of tickets to children's films, partly because the act of bearing witness can seem the first step in child welfare promotion, and partly because of plain old human curiosity. In Nigeria, the star-centered culture of gossip to which Nollywood has given rise is not immune to tales either of children's filmic victories or of their victimization at the hands of allegedly corrupt producers, directors, and fellow performers. *Nollywood Magazine* and *Gossip Nigeria*, two Nigerian print publications that both maintain websites as well as Twitter accounts, often report on star scandals. Instructively, such scandals often involve children, as when, in late 2012, *Nollywood Magazine* and Nigeria's *National Mirror* both raised questions about the guardianship of then-five-year-old singer-actor OzzyBosco, asking whether the child (whose birth name is Oziomachukwu Mojekwu) was being properly cared for, and properly compensated, as he performed for the likes of Ike Ekweremadu, Nigeria's Deputy Senate President, and Adeyemi Ikuforiji, the Speaker of the Lagos State House of Assembly.[22] While such high-profile public appearances might appear to confer a degree of cultural legitimacy upon OzzyBosco's precocious stardom, it is important to point out that, not long after meeting the young performer, Adeyemi Ikuforiji was arraigned on charges of money laundering filed by Nigeria's Economic and Financial Crimes Commission.[23] OzzyBosco's most prominent performances have since been recast in terms of their proximity to scandal, suggesting that one of the dangers of child stardom in Nigeria is not what the underage performer actually does, but in whose presence he or she does it.

The trope of scandalous contagion that this example centralizes is typically compounded when Nollywood enters the equation. It is one thing for an OzzyBosco to perform for prominent and possibly corrupt Nigerian politicians; it is quite another for such a young star to actively enter the arena of film production, in which filmmaking's uniquely collaborative nature is bound to furnish a diversity of personality types—some perhaps far less wholesome than others. It is this possibility—that performing in a Nollywood film might mean exposure to unsavory characters—that seemingly prevents many Nigerian cultural critics from fully endorsing child stardom, though many acknowledge the importance of diversifying the industry along generational lines. Concerns about Nollywood's relationship to child welfare are traceable to the first film appearances of actress Sharon Ezeamaka, who was famously just five years old when she was cast in a leading role in the Nollywood drama *Narrow Escape* (Tony Muonagor, 1997). Now an adult, she looks back on her path-breaking early work in terms of its rootedness in what she calls "the old Nollywood." During that pre-digital period, she points out, "people thought Nigerian movies were jokes and nothing to write home about," and it was that popular prejudice—rather than some noble commitment to child welfare—that prevented cultural commentators from taking her work seriously, she says. Now, "people are beginning to see Nollywood movies and know that we are not here to play, that we are here to provide Africa with this amazing movie industry. There's still so much we have to do ... but we're getting there."[24]

More than any other former child star, Sharon Ezeamaka strives to reclaim Nollywood as conducive to the work of kids—and as neither silly nor remotely scandalous. In a 2012 interview with Laju Arenyeka, Ezeamaka points out that she was able to continue her education while working on films as a little girl, the impact of Nollywood on schooling being a major concern for those who do not believe that the industry should develop child stars. Addressing the popular suspicion that Nollywood's male power players—its producers, directors, and distributors—are sexually aggressive or otherwise inappropriate when faced with female performers (particularly child performers), Arenyeka asks Ezeamaka if the young actress has ever felt uncomfortable around her Nollywood bosses or if she believes that a man who works in the industry could possibly constitute marriage material. Ezeamaka responds by saying that she has never encountered objectionable behavior on a film set. "I would love to marry someone who does what I do, who is somehow involved in the media," she says, giving the lie to the notion that Nollywood is no place for "a good girl." In the course of defending Nollywood to Arenyeka, Ezeamaka manages to mention the one bone she has to pick with the industry, the one thing she does not like about it and that makes her intensely uncomfortable: its paucity of young stars. For Ezeamaka, this is not just an academic concern, although she does point out that a lack of new blood is bad for any business, and even worse for Nollywood's global image. It also represents a very practical matter, particularly when it comes to romantic films—the kinds of films in which Ezeamaka, who still acts, might be called upon to kiss a costar. "Most of the guys [who] do all the romantic scenes are older than [me]," she complains. "We don't have a lot of young actors in Nollywood, and I can't say that I want to play a romantic scene with [the much-older] Ramsey Nouah—that would just be weird."[25]

Ezeamaka provides a vital reminder of the race-blind casting practices that embolden Nollywood stars to take on parts like Lady Gaga and Sharon Stone when she says that her dream role would be the lead in a film adaptation of *Fifty Shades of Grey*. While she acknowledges that the "official" adaptation of the bestselling novel is "all the way in Hollywood" and that "the [lead] character is white," she also concedes that Nollywood is an industry in which "anything can happen." If Oge Okoye can play Lady Gaga, then perhaps Sharon Ezeamaka can play Anastasia Steele. While she recognizes—and openly praises—the unique acting opportunities that Nollywood often provides, Ezeamaka continues to struggle with the industry's specific casting practices. Though no longer a child, she nevertheless suspects that she is widely believed to be one, particularly when approached about film projects. "At twenty, people still treat me like a little girl," she says, recognizing that such a condescending response has as much to do with her relatively diminutive stature and self-described baby face as with Nollywood's apparent resistance to cultivating the kind of child star she once was.[26] Now an adult, Ezeamaka faces pronounced pressure to re-embody that image—to play exclusively "kiddie" roles, even against her professional wishes.

If Nollywood screenwriters are coming up with countless child roles, then it would seem only logical to have those roles played by performers who are age-appropriate—who are actual, calendrical kids. In reality, Ezeamaka and other, older Nollywood stars continue to bear the burden of embodying underage youth. For her part, Ezeamaka cites Nollywood's apparent allergy to child stars, but she does not offer any explanations for this resistance—a reluctance that recalls an argument that Lindsey Green-Simms and Unoma Azuah make, in which they note that there is rarely any single reason for the kinds of consistent Nollywood decisions that coalesce into industry convention.[27] Ezeamaka does, however, combat at every opportunity the apparent industrial ideology that helps to make Nollywood an emphatically, even exclusively, adult enterprise—one that seems invested in producing youth empowerment at the narrative level only, through proud and powerful child characters rather than through casting practices that would provide revenue and renown for underage Nigerians.

Of course, the empowerment potential of Nollywood's fictional juvenile characters is severely restricted if they are played by adults, or by actual children who are hardly stars and who are often inadequately credited both on screen and in publicity materials. These, increasingly, appear to be the two options open to Nollywood producers working within a rubric of youth representation. But the situation was not always thus. Ezeamaka describes how empowered she herself felt while performing in her first Nollywood projects—films in which she consistently received top billing, and for which she claims she was properly paid. It is worth pointing out, however, that Ezeamaka's costars in those films (Oge Okoye, Keppy Ekpenyong-Bassey, and Bukky Ajayi) were not yet household names at the time, which suggests that Ezeamaka's top billing was less a conscious, accurate reflection of her majority share of each film's screen time than a response to the praise—and notoriety—that she had previously inspired as the five-year-old star of the rather demanding action film *Narrow Escape*. Ironically, the salable controversy that Ezeamaka had generated while just five years old, which helped to catapult her into the ranks of Nollywood's top-billed performers, would dissuade the industry from cultivating child stars by the time of Ezeamaka's entry into adulthood.

AN EMERGING ALLERGY: CHILD STARDOM AND NIGERIA'S NATIONAL YOUTH POLICY

The period of Ezeamaka's onscreen maturation—roughly 1997 to 2012— witnessed a dramatic spike in Nigerian child poverty rates, as well as Nigeria's widely publicized and ongoing failure to meet the United Nations Millennium Development Goals, many of which, as launched in the year 2000, focused directly upon child welfare. In 2007, however, the Federal Republic of Nigeria managed to pass a national youth policy "promoting employment, social protection schemes and youth funds." Tellingly, however, policy documents mention Nollywood not as a potential source of youth empowerment but instead as a definite threat to child welfare—a threat located solely in the arena of film reception, as if kids could not possibly be cultural producers. The policy's implementation strategies, as finalized the following year, include provisions for the "control of inappropriate films, home videos, and sexually offensive internet sites"—including YouTube, which at the time was a major online source of Nollywood films, through the official Nollywood Love channel. Reflecting a shifting but still inadequate emphasis on Nollywood's role among Nigerian youth cultures, the Second National Youth Policy Document, which was completed in 2009, avoided the earlier emphasis on censorship in favor of promoting a "balance between the traditional-based [sic] leisure activities and the 'individualized leisure time' created by modern technology through the use of mobile phones, computer games, and home videos so as to avoid the negative consequences of the latter." In other words, even in the absence of direct censorship measures, Nollywood is still cited as a source of the kinds of "negative consequences" that can only be counteracted by tradition, although, instructively, that last term is not defined for such an obviously diverse citizenry. Even at the level of ever-shifting national policy, Nollywood has remained a problem whose sexualized dimensions are said to corrupt Nigerian children.[28]

Of course, to see Nollywood as a strictly "sexy" industry—as a factory for titillation—is to ignore altogether its commitment to a rather wide range of genres, many of which do not require depictions of human sexuality. These genres include, of course, the children's film (or, as it is more often called in southern Nigeria, the family film). As Cary Bazalgette and Terry Staples argue, the children's film "deal[s] with the interests, fears, misapprehensions, and concerns of children in their own terms"—that is, without recourse to representations of the kinds of adult dramas that typically include erotic encounters. However, instead of seeing the children's film and the family film as strictly synonymous genres, Bazalgete and Staples suggest that the latter category represents a stab at broader commercial acceptance, and one that depends upon the market value of adult stars: "In a family movie, there normally have to be well-known adult stars to help bring in the audience... Naturally, the producer wants to get full value out of an expensive star, so the part has to be a meaty one, with commensurate production values."[29]

Such an argument finds considerable support in the Nollywood context as it is currently constituted. Since the industry's demonstrably profit-making star system is by now so well advanced, and since it depends exclusively upon adult performers, any attempt to craft a children's film is going to depend upon the participation of an adult star. Consider, for instance, the case of Moses Ebere's 2012 family drama *Miss Queen,* whose standardized VCD case heralds the film as a "children's story." *Miss Queen* focuses heavily upon the experiences of a group of Lagosian schoolchildren who go on a camping trip with their new physical education teacher, a beautiful young woman who gradually reveals herself to be a child-eating demon. While this plot would surely be dramatically sufficient on its own, *Miss Queen* consistently intercuts scenes involving two sets of dissatisfied married couples, slightly diluting the impact of the kid-specific sections.

While the narrative alibi for the couples' inclusion is believable enough (they are the parents of four of the camping kids, and completely oblivious to the dangers that these kids face), it is difficult not to think that the film is relying upon them for strictly commercial reasons, since they are played by four of Nollywood's top stars (Oge Okoye, Halima Abubakar, Muna Obiekwe, and Frederick Leonard). The crosscutting between camping kids and quarreling adults does not even build suspense in a fashion familiar to anyone who has seen a D. W. Griffith film, since at no point in *Miss Queen* is it clear that the adults are capable of saving their children. In fact, one of the themes of the film is the importance and efficacy of youth spirituality, that is, a child's devotion to Christianity. In *Miss Queen* a devout kid can and does save the day.

So why return, every few minutes, to the petty dramas of the children's wealthy parents if not to lean upon the collective star power of the performers who play those parents? The commercial as well as generational biases of *Miss Queen* can be clarified by taking a look at its opening and closing credit sequences, which bill the four adult stars before listing only two of the child performers (leaving the others to go completely uncredited). By this point in Nollywood's development—at the start of its third decade—Oge Okoye and Halima Abubakar are no longer struggling young performers but powerful stars whose presence, even if minimal in terms of screen time, trumps that of talented child performers, none of whom are really permitted to become stars (at least according to the generative potential of a credit sequence). Within the parameters simply of a film's billing practices, such "permission" would of course involve prominent crediting—an invitation to the spectator to put a name to a face. After all, in order for a film star to be born, he or she must first be named. But *Miss Queen* is the kind of Nollywood film whose producers are content to make copious use of child performers without bothering to advance their careers at the textual level of a simple credit sequence—a state of affairs that rather ironically suggests precisely the kind of exploitation that the industrial refusal of child stardom is presumably designed to sidestep.

When Sharon Ezeamaka got started, things were different. Her 2003 drama *Little Angel* (Dickson Iroegbu) featured Oge Okoye, who at the time was not yet a major star, and who was, as a consequence of her relative obscurity, relegated to a supporting role as the Ezeamaka character's mother. *Little Angel* is really Ezeamaka's show, and its willingness to let her take center stage—and occupy a sizable, almost exclusive share of screen time—has obvious practical consequences, including those related to the matter of duration. By so strategically including, as commercial crutches, four adult stars in what is otherwise a genuine children's film, the four-part *Miss Queen* stretches its total running time to over five hours. *Little Angel*, by contrast, comes in at a (relatively) short two hours and fifty-three minutes. Moreover, it grants Ezeamaka top billing; in acting terms, it is *her* movie, and it serves as a reminder of a time, not too long ago, when Nollywood seemed amenable to the development—to the narrative privileging and extra-textual publicizing—of a bona fide child star.

Today, the adult Ezeamaka is working to maintain an acting career while resisting the pressure to perform in a role that should go to an actual kid. One forum through which Ezeamaka manages to present herself as an adult with ideas is Twitter. It is precisely by tweeting her meditations on the state of Nollywood, as well as her gut reactions to Nigeria's global image, that Ezeamaka presents herself as a thoughtful adult woman, in contrast to whatever kiddie roles she may still be offered. Tellingly, her tweets often take on a powerfully politicized dimension, denouncing the totalizing xenophobia that leads many Westerners (including, allegedly, Kim Kardashian) to "dis Nigeria." At every opportunity, it seems, Ezeamaka is willing to tweet about the type of knee-jerk prejudice that feeds global stereotypes of her beloved country. Moreover, in April 2013, she managed to contextualize the kinds of then-popular, "meme-worthy" Instagram images aligning Nigerian women with apes, reminding her Twitter followers that they reflect one of the most insidious stereotypes of black Africans—a deeply disturbing mixture of equal parts racism, ethnocentrism, and misogyny.[30]

Elsewhere on Twitter, and in a far lighter but no less politicized mode, Ezeamaka explains what makes an Igbo accent—and by extension southeastern Nigeria—so distinct (which in itself suggests that she is tweeting at least in part to users outside of the country, who might not be aware of Nigeria's ethnolinguistic diversity). She also proclaims her devotion to pop stars Beyoncé, Rihanna, and Justin Timberlake, as well as to the "sexy" American television star Timothy Olyphant (of *Justified*, a series that Ezeamaka enjoys). Twice, she declares, "I'm proud of the woman I'm becoming."[31] All of these tweets showcase a former child star who, in the age of social media, maintains a growing interest in global popular culture as well as a grounded sense of her own identity as a Nigerian adult. In one of her earliest films, 2003's *Little Angel*, Ezeamaka portrays a schoolgirl who brings together similar qualities, combining a keen appreciation for Western pop with a political commitment to Nigeria's future. Dreaming of one day effecting positive change, the character is a self-inspired dynamo, but her story raises distinct representational challenges. In 2003, it posed its own, painful problems for the publicizing of child stardom in Nollywood.

BIG TROUBLE: THE CASE OF *LITTLE ANGEL*

Ironically, the commitment to Nigeria and the general progressivism that Ezeamaka expresses on Twitter, which help to define her adult image as a proudly politicized one, can be found throughout her early film work, particularly in *Little Angel*. Shot when she was just ten years old, the film follows the travails of a little Lagosian girl whose goal is to be Nigeria's first female president, but who is forced by circumstance to search for money to pay for her injured mother's hospital treatments. The film begins with a curious sequence involving a group of angered elders, including the father of a young man (played by Keppy Ekpenyong Bassey) who wants to marry a woman from outside of his ethnic circle. A fairly familiar Nollywood subject, interethnic conflict provides the prologue with a heavy dose of Nigerian social realism, suggesting that the narrative to come will be similarly devoted to furnishing a degree of authenticity.

The following scene takes place ten years later, and it is set, significantly, in a classroom full of kids. At first, the connection between the prologue's combative family members and the more contemporary setting of a Lagosian classroom seems indistinct, although it is easy to assume that at least one of the schoolchildren represents the product of that controversial interethnic marriage, since all of the kids are ten. When Jessica, Sharon Ezeamaka's character, first speaks, it is to teach her friend and fellow student, Ego (played by Princess Orji), the order of operations in mathematics, furnishing the familiar acronym PEMDAS—for "Please Excuse My Dear Aunt Sally"—in order to clarify that parentheses and exponents require attention before addition and subtraction. Demonstrating her precocious conversance with this mnemonic device, Jessica also shows what a patient and supportive friend she can be, and Ego, who has been struggling with math, smiles in appreciation.

When the instructor finally enters the classroom, it is to return the students' graded exams. Before distributing them, he makes an announcement: Jessica, whom he calls "our own in-class genius," has scored a 98 percent—the highest grade in the class. Proving that they adore Jessica and that they are not tempted by the littlest hint of jealousy, the other students give her a round of raucous applause. At this point, the humble Jessica hides her face behind folded arms, peeking through every few seconds to see if the ovation has subsided. It is an altogether charming moment, and Ezeamaka makes it work. She has enough poise and confidence to project scholastic prodigiousness, but she also suggests a believable child, using her body in awkward ways bespeaking both pleasurable embarrassment and restrained pride.

Jessica earns some ice cream as a reward, but her joy is tempered by the bullying that she receives in the schoolyard after class. One of the boys, who had previously applauded her performance on the exam, finally decides to express his true feelings, shouting, "No one wants to marry you! Boys think you're scary!" to which the self-respecting Jessica calmly replies, "I want to become the first female president of Nigeria. I'll be too busy to marry." Her friend Ego, rather surprisingly, smiles at this exchange, as if it were lightly amusing rather than alternately disturbing and inspiring. When Jessica asks why Ego is grinning, the other girl explains that, in her view, the boy likes Jessica and is lying as a form of flirtation—although he's clearly taking the approach a bit too far, becoming quite cruel in the process. "You always hurt the ones you love" is the aphorism that Ego offers. Jessica will have none of it, however, and Ezeamaka suggests the character's remarkable complexity by letting her grow intensely angry. Suddenly, and in a remarkably powerful voice, she shouts, "Stop it! I don't like it! I *don't* like it!"

Jessica feels that Ego is also teasing her, and, after severely chastising the other girl, Jessica swiftly changes the subject by asking Ego how she feels about family life. When Ego, believably, simply shrugs and makes a few confused faces, indicating her aversion to the odd formality of the question, Jessica returns to her calmest state to say, slowly and with apparent sincerity, "My parents may not buy me everything, but I see them every day, and I love them very much." While that line seems to stand out at first, suggesting the infiltration of an especially telegraphic, Nollywood-style didacticism, it is slowly transformed into yet another component of Jessica's peculiar, precocious pedagogy. Even in the schoolyard, waiting for her ride home, Jessica is in instructive mode, and on this occasion she teaches Ego to better appreciate her own parents. Still grateful to the magnanimous Jessica, Ego hugs her and heads home.

Unsurprisingly, given that this is a Nollywood film, a BMW SUV takes Jessica to a gated Lagosian mansion where, still performing the role of teacher, she tells her mother, Sussy (played by Oge Okoye), that the woman's new perfume is too oppressive, and that her previous scent, which Jessica prefers, better suits the performance of adult femininity. At this point, lest the precocious Jessica seem all but intolerable (and all but unbelievable), the film injects some kid-specific realism, such as Jessica's leaving her filthy socks and shoes in several different parts of the house, as if she has undressed in preposterous piecemeal, and against the express wishes of her neat-freak mother. Sussy confronts Jessica about the socks and the shoes. Jessica apologizes, picks them up, and returns them to their proper place in the mansion's mudroom. When she returns to the kitchen where her mother is making dinner, she describes her disappointment at having earned "only a 98" on the math exam. "I wish I'd scored 100 out of 100," she says. "The president must be clever. Don't you think so, mama?" The camera cuts to a close-up of Okoye's Sussy, whose expression manages to mix exasperation (it is clear that she has heard this self-aggrandizing, semi-rhetorical question before) and a slow-growing willingness to humor her daughter. "Well, let's see," Sussy says, letting her voice trail off in mock contemplation. "For the first female president of Nigeria, I think 98 percent is okay as a start."

Alone in her bedroom, Jessica writes diary entries that reflect her ambitions. As she scribbles slowly and precisely with a pencil, she reads her words in voice-over: "And when I become president, I will help poor people, old people, and children," she begins. "And I will buy everybody a car so they won't have to walk about in the sun. And all the children will have free ice cream and chocolate and bicycles." While her comment about automobiles is an obvious nod to Nigeria's car culture, it also indicates Jessica's interest in specifically adult possessions. Within seconds, however, she is back to offering a very childish appreciation for sweets, demonstrating her truly intergenerational allegiances.

Meeting Ego in the schoolyard the next day, Jessica asks her friend for an update. Ego, it seems, has become quite the Nollywood fan, and she is eager to discuss her favorite films. "My brother rented a new home video," she says breathlessly, "and it's titled *Days of Glory*. I think you should come with me and watch it." Jessica, being Jessica, must one-up her friend, dampening Ego's enthusiasm not only by revealing that she has already heard of *Days of Glory*, but also by dispensing instructions on how best to "evaluate" Nollywood products. "I've seen the promo on TV. The director does a very good job, you know. He is key." While this endorsement of auteurism seems in keeping with Jessica's often-pretentious character, it still stands out as a breach of realism, since the director in question—the man who made *Days of Glory*—is the same man who made *Little Angel:* Dickson Iroegbu. This built-in advertisement is not simply for Iroegbu's sake, however. It also touts Nollywood as conducive to youth culture—as an industry whose films are discussed appreciatively in schoolyards, by kids who know what auteurism is all about.

Clearly, the hyper-intelligent Jessica is both adult and child—both brilliantly self-possessed and churlishly self-pitying. This duality—rare for any adult character, let alone for a child one—is underscored in a sequence in which Jessica watches old *Tom and Jerry* cartoons on television while ironing her own clothes as well as her mother's. The sequence is intercut with moments unfolding in the car that is taking Sussy and her husband back to Nigeria from a visit to the husband's mother (the only member of his Yorùbá family to have accepted his marriage to an Igbo woman) in Benin. In a manner befitting melodrama, the car crashes while Jessica, back in the safety of the Lagosian mansion, irons clothes and watches cartoons. Just as *The Flintstones* is coming on, however, she has a premonition and drops her glass of Fanta, which shatters on the marble floor. Jessica knows that something is wrong, and at one point she is actually able to picture her parents' car as it crashes. Both adult and child, both wise and callow, Jessica is also a soothsayer. Her capacity to predict that her parents will be badly injured makes her more than just a math wiz. While *Little Angel* flirts with realism, offering some convincing depictions of children's schoolyard interactions, it also elevates Jessica—and by extension Sharon Ezeamaka—to a special plane, suggesting that (for writer-director Dickson Iroegbu, at the very least) authenticity alone is no foundation for child stardom. *Little Angel* thus forges, at the narrative level, a discourse of youth exceptionalism, shifting attention from Ezeamaka as an actress (and Jessica as a character) to Ezeamaka as a *star*. The film's first official VHS and VCD cases, as designed and marketed in 2003, showed only Sharon Ezeamaka as Jessica, with her bright smile signaling happy times, her name spelled out in ornate white letters above the title, and "is" added for emphasis: "Sharon Ezeamaka *is* 'Little Angel.'" Indicating just how much had changed in the subsequent decade, the 2013 premiere of *Little Angel* on iROKOtv featured the face of Oge Okoye as the film's sole advertising image; on the website, Okoye, not Ezeamaka, remains *Little Angel*'s only icon, both in the star-specific sense as well as in the parlance of computer graphics; it is Okoye who serves as the shorthand representation of the *Little Angel* data file, the precise point of access to the film; to click on her face is to press "play."

After learning that her visions were accurate—that her parents were, in fact, involved in a car accident—Jessica is rushed to the hospital to visit her ailing mother. There, she finds out that her father has died after having been airlifted to a special treatment center. Sussy, meanwhile, has been in a coma, and even the semi-magical Jessica cannot awaken her. The handsome and humble attending physician (played by the great Richard Mofe Damijo, better known by his initials, RMD) carefully explains to Jessica that the hospital has been covering the costs of Sussy's care, but that she requires an expensive operation. The scene gives Ezeamaka the opportunity to convey Jessica's charmingly realistic inability to pronounce the word "surgery," as well as, simultaneously, the character's sheer, transcendent drive. She sets out to sell her toys, but when a merchant offers her a mere 500 naira for all of them, Jessica balks, then starts bargaining. "I was expecting something like 1,000 naira," she says, pointing to the toys, "so let's try for something closer to that." The merchant offers 759, to which Jessica squints in disgust. He then offers 775, and still she turns him down. Finally, she rounds up all of the toys and takes them back to her house, where she sits, defeated, on the cold marble floor.

She does not try again. The toys remain in a pile about as high as her mother's hospital bills, and the film, in furnishing this subplot, suggests both Jessica's initiative as well as her self-defeating petulance. Had she accepted the merchant's highest offer, she would have been able to make a dent in her mother's debt. Instead, she decides to pursue her uncle—her late father's brother—who is a successful businessman and might be willing to help out. What Jessica does not fully understand is that the uncle, whose name is Josiah (Bruno Iwuoha), never recognized his brother's marriage, joining the rest of his family in condemning—and remaining estranged from—Jessica's father. Josiah is practically a stranger.

But Jessica persists, even walking the dozens of miles to his mansion, where she is met by a guard—a Pidgin-speaking young man who wears a white tank-top and openly ogles the little girl. (It is through this character that the film rather cannily manages to address the matter of pedophiliac aggression, pointing to a lowly gatekeeper, not a Nollywood auteur, as posing a problem for young girls.) When this lecherous mess lets her in, Jessica immediately encounters Josiah's imperious wife, who paces the mansion's balcony while sipping red wine from a huge glass. Surveying the grounds of her compound, clearly aware that the guard in her employ is inadequate to say the least, she suddenly sees Jessica. Recognizing at once who she is (unlikely as this may seem, given Jessica's age and the two families' patterns of estrangement), the woman shouts, "Tell your parents to leave my husband alone! He's one of the richest men in Lagos. Maybe you think my husband is a money-making machine—a bank—for you. But he made this money for us—for *us,* and for our children!" Finally, she screams, "Get out of this compound!" Jessica complies, fearfully running away, clad only in a pair of ill-fitting flip-flops. More than any other physical factor in the film, it is this pair of flip-flops that will prove responsible for the tragedy to come.

On her way back home, having walked for miles without food or water, Jessica wobbles along an unpaved road, trips on a rock, and eventually steps on a rusty nail, her thin sandal offering no protection. The nail pierces Jessica's flesh and she screams in pain. But she is back on her feet in mere minutes, ready to walk again, albeit with a limp. In the nearly ten-minute sequence that follows, Jessica slogs toward home, sometimes stepping into puddles, very rarely keeping her balance, but somehow making it back to that cold marble floor with its mountain of toys. Iroegbu keeps the camera close to Jessica's face as she attempts to dress her wound. This also proves to be a startlingly lengthy sequence, as Jessica slowly, laboriously wraps her foot with whatever bandages she can find, leaving behind a trail of blood. As she makes her way to the hospital, limping along in obvious pain, *Little Angel* begins to resemble a Lars von Trier film, so constantly does it challenge its lead performer with strenuous physical and psychological setups. The key difference, of course, apart from national context, is that Trier's infamous psychodramas are largely about adult women; Iroegbu's film is about a little girl. If Trier is so often said to torture his female performers, satisfying his own deep-seated misogyny in the process, then Iroegbu can be said to take such intensity one step further by forcing a ten-year-old girl to scream in pain, weep with grief, and shake with fear as she hobbles along a highway.[32] As an actress, Sharon Ezeamaka rises to the occasion, but her success as a performer is inseparable, in this instance, from the fear that Nollywood film production may well be "too much" for a mere child.

With its peripatetic young protagonist, and with its long takes letting her slowly weave her way through a bustling urban landscape, *Little Angel* can be said to be a fitting heir to Italian neorealism. When critic André Bazin first championed the films of Roberto Rossellini, Vittorio De Sica, and Luchino Visconti in the 1940s, he defined Italian neorealism in terms of its respect for spatial as well as temporal relations—for the authenticity afforded by loca-

Figure 5.1. Jessica (Sharon Ezeamaka) screams in pain after stepping on a rusty nail in Dickson Iroegbu's *Little Angel* (2003).

tion shooting, depth of field, and the long take. It is through these devices that the spectator is able to "see the whole operation; it will not be reduced to its dramatic or symbolic meaning, as is usual with montage." What this means in the case of *Little Angel* is that the film, in following Jessica down those hazardous roads and in refusing to cut, creates an intensely uncomfortable, almost hallucinatory viewing experience. It recalls Bazin's famous comment about the cinematography of *Citizen Kane* (Orson Welles, 1941) having "restored to reality its visible continuity." Jessica does not simply step on a nail and, seconds later in film time, end up back in her parents' mansion. She walks all the way home, and the viewer walks all the way with her, sharing her experience of the passage of time and perhaps empathizing more extensively with her plight. Precedents for this filmmaking strategy can be found throughout Nollywood—most notably in Chico Ejiro's *Shame* (1996), where characters pound the pavement in search of employment—but *Little Angel* differs in its use of a child protagonist who must, for an unconscionable duration, suffer the slings and arrows of the street. The time-intensive trauma—for Jessica as well as for the spectator—brings to mind more than just Trier's Danish psychodramas. It also recalls Bazin's famous remarks about *Los Olvidados*, Luis Buñuel's 1950 take on juvenile delinquency in Mexico City—a film whose approach, for Bazin, "transcends morality and sociology," offering "a metaphysical reality, the cruelty of the human condition."[33]

It is of course no accident that Buñuel's film, like most of the major works of Italian neorealism, focuses upon the experiences of children. In the case of *Little Angel*, these experiences prove fatal, as Jessica, alone in her parents' house, does up her imported doll to resemble her ailing mother, wrapping a bandage around the doll's head and putting its arm in a sling so that it will evoke Sussy—all the while oblivious to her own deteriorating health. "Don't worry, mommy," Jessica says to the reconfigured doll, Sussy's makeshift stand-in. "You won't die. You won't die." Repeating the phrase again and again, Jessica turns it into an incantation. The scene, one of several in which Jessica is all by herself for an extended period of time, offers a striking commentary on child acting—a meta-commentary, really, in which Ezeamaka enacts a child-centered process of pretending. Make-believe may be Jessica's comfort, but it is Ezeamaka's career.

Jessica's perspective dominates *Little Angel*, making it a true children's film. After the little girl dies of tetanus, her mother Sussy suddenly recovers, and lays Jessica to rest with the help of some grieving Lagosian kids. Even following the child protagonist's demise, then, *Little Angel* does not relinquish the youth perspective. Iroegbu lets a large group of schoolchildren walk, while weeping, through the streets of the city, all the way to the graveyard—another grueling long take and a further nod to neorealism that compels the spectator to reconsider events through two dozen young eyes. "Using children's narrative viewpoint enables the director to turn a critical eye on crucial aspects of social reality," writes Natalia Sui-Hung Chan in an essay on cinematic neorealism. "[T]he innocent eyes of the child make a value judgment on the adult world."[34] This is never truer in *Little Angel* than when Jessica's eyes stare accusingly from beyond the grave, through the school portrait that her mother so lovingly clutches during the girl's funeral. As a mystical elder stops by the gravesite to weep and offer condemnatory remarks about tribalism, he is joined by the many schoolchildren who've come to pay their respects to Jessica. Standing next to Sussy, he starts to speak, offering a lengthy, lacerating sermon that seems indistinguishable from a direct address to the spectator:

> This particular day indicts all of us. Especially those who could have changed Jessica's story. Of course, there are many Jessicas out there. But I ask, shall we because of our petty desires for privacy, continue to allow them to die young? To die unfulfilled? And unsung? Furthermore, I ask what do we stand to gain by keeping to a stupid and unprogressive tradition that forbids cross-boundary marriages? Believe me, all these are our losses. In life, Jessica encouraged all of us. Even in death, she has continued to inspire us.

While he speaks, the children weep—some far more convincingly than others. But the best among them—those who, like Ezeamaka, are remarkably skilled performers—provide primal screams. In mimicking both the crying elder and the equally weepy Sussy, they recall Brecht's suggestion that a child's psychosocial development "proceeds along theatrical lines." When a child "joins in shedding tears," she is "not only weeping because the grown-ups do so," but also because she feels "genuine sorrow." Such an affective response, Brecht argues, "can be seen at funerals, whose meaning escapes children entirely. These are theatrical events [that] form the character. The human being copies gesture, miming, tones of voice. And weeping arises from sorrow, but sorrow also arises from weeping." Here, the most convincing of the child weepers provide *Little Angel* with a kid-specific stamp of authenticity, even in the absence of the remarkable Ezeamaka, recalling Peter Bondanella's contention that "superior child acting has always been a hallmark of [cinematic] neorealism."[35]

There is, of course, the matter of commercialism to consider—as always. In this context, it is important to keep in mind a point that Lucia Nagib makes about Ouedrago's *Yaaba*, which she defines as a moral tale. For Nagib, Ouedrago's focus on the experiences of children, one of whom opens the film in neorealist fashion, running across a vast, arid West African landscape in a stunning long take, provides the key to comprehending the film's remarkable international success. In short, according to Nagib, the kids "facilitated [*Yaaba's*] worldwide distribution and exhibition," helping by their very narrative presence to turn this "moral tale" into a widely salable property.[36] Youth-inclusive, global commercial circuits therefore helped to bring *Yaaba* further in line with Italian neorealism's legacy of making children ideological as well as commercial selling points. As evidenced by the early promotional materials surrounding *Little Angel*, Nollywood once followed a similar path, placing Sharon Ezeamaka at the center of publicity and selling the film by referencing one of Italian neorealism's signal devices, what Colin McCarthur describes as "a recurrent image ... of children moving through the ruins."[37]

In his account of another child-centered African film, Nabil Ayouch's *Ali Zaoua* (1999), Roy Armes argues that Ayouch self-consciously combines "Italian neorealism and the Luis Buñuel of *Los Olvidados*," primarily by relying on child performers. For Armes, *Ali Zaoua* "has a carefully devised dramatic structure built around the efforts of ... three kids," all played by orphaned young performers whose "naturalness" is "counterbalanced by the experienced actors playing the adult roles."[38] Iroegbu's *Little Angel* offers no such divisions, and in fact relies upon the fluidity among the polished, professional talents of both its child performers (especially Ezeamaka) and its adult stars. Another distinction that marks *Little Angel*'s particular relationship to Italian neorealism involves the gender identity of its child protagonist; indeed, the significance of Jessica's femininity cannot be overstated. *Little Angel*, in bringing a girl's experiences into the foreground, calls to mind Inga Pierson's point that, "while the use of children in neorealism is often noted, the fact that they are all *male* children has been ignored."[39] In other words, even vis-à-vis the legacy of Italian neorealism, *Little Angel* can be said to offer something fresh that Nollywood can proudly claim as its own.

PLACING EZEAMAKA

Little Angel provides an empowered young protagonist, but it also kills her. While such an eleventh-hour tragedy clearly bespeaks melodrama, it can also be read as a way of guarding against too much youth agency, turning what could have been purely inspirational into a kind of cautionary tale. The elements of *Little Angel* are no more rooted in melodrama than when Jessica is finally diagnosed with tetanus. RMD's doctor tells a nurse the bad news, saying, "Ironically, the mother that [Jessica] was running around for is getting better now, while [Jessica is] dying." Later, after the little girl's death, the doctor confronts her uncle, who has come to the hospital as a penitent. "It's the walls," the doctor says to the wealthy businessman. "The walls that you built around yourself. They were a little bit too effective." When the uncle asks if there's anything he can do, the doctor says, "It's too late."

A classic melodrama, *Little Angel* is also a film about a female child's ambitions. Its penultimate sequence, which takes place among the aged, rigid traditionalists who had opposed the marriage of Jessica's parents, suggests a confirmation and even a celebration, both of Jessica's drive and of her gender-specific accomplishments. Sussy's mother-in-law softly says, "Try not to cry. She was my president, too." Sussy, in response, employs the moniker that Jessica would have used in addressing the older woman, calling her "Grandma"—another indication of the lasting power and infectiousness of a youth perspective. "Grandma, she was my *hero*," Sussy says, emphasizing the last word with its suggestion of a progressive gender neutrality: "hero," not "heroine." The concept of social progress is, in fact, one that the mystical elder will deploy in the next scene, suggesting that it is possible (in spite of the seemingly punitive death of Jessica) to see the film as a tract on the reformist political potential of a little girl, and one that ends up *confirming* that potential, against considerable odds.

The initial advertising for *Little Angel* represents a kind of parallel text —one that both reflects and resists the film's specific narrative. On the one hand, images of Ezeamaka's smiling face seem to sell the idea of child stardom as profoundly pleasurable in the Nollywood context, upholding Ezeamaka as just as special, just as politically progressive, and just as powerfully confident as her character. However, on the other hand, these publicity materials can be seen to constitute erroneous advertising, offering the false promise of a purely happy story. They do not, for instance, hint at the neorealist presentation of Jessica's victimhood or even at the "mere" fact that *Little Angel* is a melodrama.

Today, such advertising dispenses with Ezeamaka altogether, offering Oge Okoye instead. The possible reasons for this shift include, of course, Okoye's current stardom, but they also, perhaps, include a certain aversion to the subject of child stardom itself and to the thorny, even contradictory, issues that it inevitably raises. Director Dickson Ireogbu has, instructively, shied away from child performers in the years since making *Little Angel*. In 2009 he announced plans to make a film entitled *Child Soldier*—a project that he described at the time as "an intervention." He continued, "I consider the project [a] bold attempt at discouraging the prevalent trafficking in persons, which includes the recruitment of children through force means to the army." Iroegbu's intention, however, was not simply to address one of the globe's most profound child welfare crises. It was also to do something "far removed from the normal Nollywood film production concept":

> The vision is to use *Child Soldier* to redefine and reposition Nollywood. To achieve this we have decided to shoot on 35 mm with other state of the arts [sic] equipment. We are also going to use [an] international crew to ensure international standard practice, and the adoption of global exhibition and marketing strategies. The issue is a topic that attracts global concern. The movie would be exhibited worldwide with its attendant media hype.

While such a description mobilizes many of the familiar terms associated with the so-called New Nollywood Cinema, such as 35 mm film and "global exhibition and marketing strategies," it also furnishes terms that are less clear but still telling. "International standard practice" could conceivably include casting protocol, for example. The question, however, is whether Iroegbu, who has been struggling for years to find financing for the project, would like "media hype" to include positive publicity for child performers and not simply activist attention to the subject of child soldiering. Iroegbu's own take on the project's "ideal cast" is an interesting one, and it suggests the director's current position vis-à-vis child stardom: Iroegbu wants the film to focus on *former* child soldiers, and has stated that his central question is, "What kind of mindset would a child soldier possess as an adult?" For the director of the groundbreaking, youth-inclusive *Little Angel*, then, a film on the subject of child soldiering should emphasize adult experiences—and perhaps preclude child performers altogether.[40]

Demonstrating the significance of child stardom, numerous Nollywood fans have been inclined to highlight Ezeamaka's precocious accomplishments in *Little Angel*. Appreciative responses to her performance span the blogosphere, persisting among those who demand that Nollywood develop a system for generating child stars. In 2008, one Nigerian fan, in characterizing *Little Angel* as a youth-driven film, explained its dependence upon star performance: "Sharon Ezeamaka plays the leading role convincingly from start to finish. Her performance inflicts a great deal of emotion. Intense moments are brought to the surface through the effective portrayal of painful circumstances, delivered through good acting."[41] When all is said and done, Ezeamaka's profound talent appears to matter more to fans than the possibly traumatizing conditions of a shooting style inspired, in part, by Italian neorealism. In any case, the actress has emerged from the experience seemingly unscathed, maturing into a dazzling adult star. Her inspired work on the third season of the MTV series *Shuga* has made her an obvious fan favorite—the object of countless laudatory hashtags on Twitter. As Princess, a young woman who moves from village to city, learning to sidestep dangerous temptations along the way, Ezeamaka enacts a character arc that has helped so many Nollywood performers achieve star status. The irony here, of course, is that Ezeamaka was already a star when she signed on to do *Shuga*, a series that pays tribute to *Little Angel* in multiple ways—not least of all by letting Princess walk for miles down the crowded streets of a busy city, her bold gaze recalling Jessica's. Years after its release, *Little Angel* remains a major advertisement for child stardom, and an influential triumph for Sharon Ezeamaka.

Given his professional history—his much-publicized role in coaxing a major dramatic performance out of a ten-year-old girl—it is hardly surprising that Dickson Iroegbu would want to avoid the challenges associated with certain modes of youth performance. For if Ezeamaka's empowering success in *Little Angel* was inextricable from her character's traumatic journey, then a child performer, in "authentically" impersonating a child soldier, would surely be the source of as much angst as appreciation, and would likely be seen as both victor and victim, both professional and pitiable. Perhaps "international standard practice," as Iroegbu understands it, also entails a resistance to placing too much representational pressure upon children—even at the expense of cinematic realism.

6

Professionalizing Childhood

Nollywood and the New Youth Transnationalism

It would be difficult to overstate the paradoxical dilemmas facing African child performers, who tend to inspire hope while evoking fear. Over the past several years, I have encountered numerous Nollywood fans who criticize the industry for, in their eyes, failing to facilitate child stardom, and for forcing them to accept adult icons Ramsey Nouah, Mercy Johnson, Genevieve Nnaji, and Omotola Jalade-Ekeinde (among many others) in youth roles. While acknowledging that it would be impossible to uncover any one reason for this contentious industrial trend, I nevertheless set out to better understand it. I found, almost at once, that fans' overwhelmingly negative reactions to age-inappropriate casting—to, specifically, the casting of obvious adults in the roles of children—had much to do with these fans' aspirations for Nollywood itself, with their collective hope that the industry might one day achieve a level of aesthetic realism commensurate with perceived global standards. While an orientation toward iconographic realism has fueled the so-called New Nollywood Cinema, with its focus on the ontology of the photographic image, it is clear that it extends as well to age, generating fan demand for the development of child stars to tackle child roles.

Nouah, Johnson, Nnaji, and Jalade-Ekeinde are hardly the only adult culprits, however—nor are they the most egregious offenders. Even those who are only casually acquainted with Nollywood are likely aware of the complexities of Aki and Pawpaw, the wildly popular, fictional youth duo portrayed by the adult actors Chinedu Ikedieze and Osita Iheme. Typically discussed in relation to one another (and often under the names of their filmic alter egos), the two actors starred in the hit 2003 film *Aki na Ukwa* (directed by Amayo Uzo Phillips), an Igbo-language comedy in which they play mischievous pre-teen brothers, in spite of the fact that, at the time of shooting, Iheme was twenty-one and Ikedieze was twenty-six. (In an indication of how firmly each actor is identified with the other, Iheme and Ikedieze are often assumed to be the same age—a false assumption that has managed to make its way into various documentaries about Nollywood, such as Ben Addelman and Samir Mallal's 2008 *Nollywood Babylon*.) Like the American actors Emmanuel Lewis, star of the child-centered 1980s television program *Webster*, and Gary Coleman, star of the roughly contemporaneous, equally youth-driven sitcom *Diff'rent Strokes*, Iheme and Ikedieze are extremely short. As with Lewis and Coleman, this has led them to be typecast in child roles, in spite of widespread public awareness of the actors' actual ages. Indeed, even in the absence of accurate information regarding their dates of birth, the actors' persistent presence in Nollywood has spanned several years, thus making it impossible, at this point, to naively assume that they are as young as the roles that they routinely play.

Ikedieze and Iheme—Aki and Pawpaw—are figures of extreme significance to the subject of child stardom in Nollywood. If, within industry convention, the actors' diminutive stature allows them to be cast as children, then it also appears to underwrite their freedom to play female characters (much as, perhaps, the actress Linda Hunt's diminutiveness "permitted" her to play a male character in Peter Weir's 1982 drama *The Year of Living Dangerously*). It is the stars' transgenerational mobility that most interests me here, although that mobility is inextricable from a particular transgender performance in one of their most popular films, Tchidi Chikere's anarchic 2003 comedy, *Show Bobo* (subtitled *The American Boys*). In this film, Ikedieze and Iheme play two twelve-year-old boys who, born in America to Nigerian parents, fly to Lagos for a one-month "vacation" (the suggestion being that their poor behavior has precipitated this "holiday" away from their put-upon mom and dad). Staying with their proudly Igbo-identified aunt, Chikaodili (played by Eucharia Anunobi), the boys grow bored almost immediately upon arriving in Nigeria; their sense of cultural estrangement is inseparable from a general disgust with the activities of daily life, which here include eating a soup whose name (*egusi*) they cannot pronounce and whose taste they reject as "shitty"—"meant for goats, and not for human beings." Close-ups highlight the boys' allegiance to American brands, from Converse to Kellogg's, and the boys themselves consistently call attention to the American style that they far prefer to whatever Nigerian cultural traditions they witness. "Throw ya hands in the muthafuckin' air!" advises Iheme's character, donning an American-flag bandana and demeaning Chikaodili's traditional dress ("You're wearing the wrong-ass gear, man! This is wack!"). Eventually, the two boys encounter several young Nigerians who want to learn "how to act American," so they set up a "street school" and dispense the following advice: "Use 'nigga,' and always talk about women with big asses—that's how you can lose your African style."

None of *Show Bobo*'s references to an alleged black American "act" are especially surprising, given that the film is an exceedingly satirical depiction of a collection of cultural stereotypes (both African and diasporic). However, what *is* surprising—and, potentially, disturbing—is the manner in which the titular American boys, as played by emphatically adult men, pursue the object of their erotic dreams, a ten-year-old girl who is played by a child actress who appears to be about that age (but who is not billed in the film). Catcalling, drooling, openly articulating the intensity of their sexual desire, Chinedu Ikedieze and Osita Iheme, both playing children, follow a "fellow" child, hoping to fuck her. Within this schema, *Show Bobo* appears to test the limits of its stars' generational mobility, even as it shows them to be impressively adaptable: in pursuit of their paramour, the American boys dress in drag in order to impersonate her friends and thereby gain access to her bedroom. The scheme works, but only up to a point: successfully passing as girls, the boys nevertheless face obstacles that include their inamorata herself, who manages to evade their famished advances. By explicitly depicting the child-centered sexual appetites of two boys who happen to be played by adult men, *Show Bobo* suggests some of the conflicts, outright contradictions, and explosive controversies at the heart of Nollywood's relationship to youth representation. In promoting the stardom of Ikedieze and Ihime, *Show Bobo* declines to similarly uphold the child actress who plays a key role in the film, either by giving her much screen time or simply by clearly crediting her. These issues—the solidification or extension of adult stardom through the impersonation of children and the refusal to cultivate the stardom of actual kids through adequate billing practices—are central to this chapter. Like the broadly defined entertainment industry in general, Nollywood has not been known to endear itself to "traditional" Nigerian parents, whatever their ethnic backgrounds. Indeed, according to a popular saying, one of the "thousand Nigerian ways to die" is for a child to inform a parent of his or her artistic ambitions. The former child star Sharon Ezeamaka, now an adult actress, has addressed this stereotype through recourse to her own experiences. Asked in 2012 if there is anything she would like to change about Nigeria, Ezeamaka responded, "I'd love to change the way a lot of parents think." Then, addressing a hypothetical parent in the second person, she added, "I understand that you want to protect your child, but you can't do that forever, you need to let your child make mistakes and learn; it's a process."[66] Numerous Nigerian online commentators appear to agree, linking education-centered parenting styles to the absence of child stars in one of the world's leading media hubs. At the same time, these commentators acknowledge the Nigerian familiarity with Hollywood's child stars and with American youth movies, suggesting that a Nigerian popular appreciation for Zac Efron, Selena Gomez, Miley Cyrus, and Justin Bieber signals a certain contradiction in local conceptions of youth culture. If film stardom is an acceptable path for Western kids, then why can Nigerian ones not share the glory?

The short answer for many is that they *can*, and that they *will*, but only when Nigerian political and industrial contexts prove more conducive to child welfare—to programs designed to ensure all manner of educational opportunities for youth performers. Efforts to establish a productive, pedagogical intersection between Nollywood and African youth are currently underway among industry professionals and NGOs alike; they have steadily expanded beyond Lagos to encompass cultural practices in multiple West African countries as well as in Britain and the United States. Viewed from this perspective, Nollywood's transnationalism occasions a wide range of responses to the presence of African children in and around film projects. In a post-conflict society like Liberia, could Nollywood possibly be positioned as a key means of facilitating local interest in film and media? Could children who have been traumatized by years of unrest turn to Nollywood as a sort of restorative agent, positioning film reception as a therapeutic practice? In their work on creative arts therapy for war-affected youth in northern

Uganda, Julia Hanebrink and Alayna Smith note that nontraditional forms of treatment and rehabilitation can be especially effective within a rubric of post-conflict reconstruction. As the authors point out, the practice of art-as-therapy—in which children produce their own artistic works using instruments with which they are already familiar and that are at their immediate disposal, such as dyes and clay—is typically envisioned as a low-cost alternative to traditional forms of psychotherapy, as well as an accessible avenue for children who have been robbed of formal education.[1]

Nollywood, by contrast, might seem prohibitive, both from an economic standpoint as well as from the perspective of professionalism. For all its "amateur" associations, Nollywood is still a bona fide business—still a commercialized set of precise filmmaking practices. Only those who continue to view Nollywood as sloppy, lazy, or as immune to standardization—who see it as a preconscious kids' game—are likely to attempt to reorient the industry toward the youth-inclusive practice of art-as-therapy. In other words, only those for whom Nollywood seems "easy" are apt to encourage post-conflict societies to adopt the industry's perceived production methods for the rehabilitation of traumatized young people. On the one hand, promoting Nollywood as conducive to kids can serve as a useful corrective to the notion that the industry is shady or salacious—that its on-screen depictions of eroticism are rooted in off-screen sexual exchanges or that the vicious duplicity that so often acts as narrative fuel can be found as well in the interactions of performers, producers, writers, and directors. On the other hand, however, aligning Nollywood with youth can go too far in the opposite, deeply reactionary direction, conflating the industry's home-video aesthetic with "unskilled" image production. One would do well to recall that the Kenneth Nnebue who so famously transitioned from importing blank VHS cassettes to shooting *Living in Bondage* was, within the former practice, operating in a salaried, professional capacity. Capturing the technically "low-quality" images examined in chapter 2 is hardly an amateur venture.

If Nollywood, in spite of its stereotyped popular rendering, requires considerable skill in the use of mere camcorders, then it also, of course, requires the camcorders themselves, as well as the electrical and battery power essential to operate them. If video production is allegedly far more accessible than celluloid techniques, it still centralizes technology, and necessitates a certain skill set. As FESPACO has made abundantly clear, an ideological preference for one format over another—for, say, 35 mm film over VHS tape—often entails practical considerations. For FESPACO, the longstanding focus on African celluloid cinema is both an art-conscious ethos and the result of a (literal and ongoing) investment in 16 and 35 mm projection. After years of regional dispute, these circumstances were finally, officially tweaked at the 2013 iteration of the festival, when it was decided that DVD projection (and thus wide Nollywood inclusion) would be possible at future FESPACO gatherings, albeit with the contribution of considerable capital for the restructuring of exhibition spaces as well as for the sorting and judging of the hundreds, perhaps even thousands of discs that will be submitted for festival consideration. As FESPACO indicates, even DVD distribution and exhibition can be prohibitive—an important point, and one that often limits efforts to promote Nollywood's minor transnationalism.

With format compatibility a major problem for a Nollywood that increasingly combines VHS, VCD, DVD, and 35 mm film, the industry's biggest stars have taken it upon themselves to provide "in-the-flesh" representations of children's rights in those parts of West Africa where, for example, Nollywood films do not or cannot travel, given a lack of equipment or electricity. The need for such live, embodied actions does not simply reflect the difficulty of guaranteeing exhibition for Nollywood's differently formatted films; it also speaks to the rarity in Nollywood of products that both narrativize youth empowerment and generate offscreen success for child stars. Even a film like *Little Angel*, which relies heavily upon the remarkable talents of ten-year-old Sharon Ezeamaka, ends with the death of its child protagonist; it is hardly the kind of film that one would want to screen for disadvantaged kids. And even Ezeamaka, though a stunningly gifted screen presence, could not inspire wide support for a child-inclusive Nollywood star system.

Aware of Africa's global reputation as a continent where human rights violations are common, and aware as well of the way that images of starving, orphaned, or otherwise victimized kids circulate as metonyms for Africanity, Nollywood's adult stars are engaged in ongoing efforts to simultaneously obliterate stereotypes and suggest some of the minor transnational conditions for cultivating child welfare. Traveling from country to country within West Africa, Nollywood stars become walking commercials for a series of stances: the approving view of Nollywood that positions the industry as amenable to philanthropy; the notion that Nigeria, whatever its myriad state failings, must not and indeed *cannot* be viewed as metonymic of poverty and suffering; and the sense that West Africa's regional diversity does not obscure the essential connections among kids. The last of these three stances threatens, of course, to undermine the antiessentialist project that this book has traced, suggesting what can happen in the absence of direct or immediate experience—when, for instance, adults substitute for children.

If, in fact, there were actual Nollywood child stars tasked with traveling throughout West Africa on a philanthropic crusade to combat youth abuse, then it is likely that their own, inevitably varied performance techniques, inevitably discrepant points of view, and inevitably diverse ethnic, cultural, religious, and linguistic identities would prevent (or at least militate against) the production of a narrow or essentialized view of West African youth. It is in the absence of actual, activist kids that Nollywood's adult stars have come together to agitate for a unifying childhood education reform. Whatever their backgrounds, these established stars have agreed upon one thing: children matter. While their activist inflections have occasionally differed— Oge Okoye's youth-centered NGO, for instance, whose name is Positive Life Children (PLC), focuses on those with special needs, while Genevieve Nnaji, with her charitable fashion label St. Genevieve, promotes female youth empowerment through style—they all highlight the importance of fulfilling the child-related Millennium Development Goals, implicitly endorsing the United Nations' rather universalist view of youth. If so many of these stars tell touching stories about their own difficult childhoods, they are in most cases too far removed from those childhoods to suggest any ongoing, nuanced personal responses to specific processes of educational provision. Most of the stars whose activism centers on children are, in fact, mothers, suggesting a philanthropic dimension that, while undoubtedly "personal," is nevertheless filtered through the experiences of a second party—the child who comes home from school in order to share her own stories.

Only Omotola Jalade-Ekeinde has consistently articulated the connections between her personal, hyper-specific youth experiences and the child-focused work that she makes so central a component of her adult stardom and associated global activism. Born and raised in Lagos and the eldest of three children, Omotola was informed of her father's untimely death while preparing for school exams. "I had to become the mom in the house because of the two younger ones," she recalls. "So my priorities and responsibilities changed." As a powerful star—one of the 100 most influential people in the world, according to *Time* magazine—Omotola has worked to ensure that what she calls "the defining experience" of her youth has thoroughly informed her activism. In practical terms, this means that Omotola makes a point of rejecting the binarism that so often leads, in Africa, to the construction of two separate and equally rigid categories for children: orphans and non-orphans. Having lost her father but not her mother, Omotola was "semi-orphaned"—but nonetheless grief-stricken and robbed of a variety of youth experiences. "I couldn't do so many of the things that people my age were doing," she points out, "not because my mom was stopping me from doing them, but because I didn't have the time. I had two kids to take care of."

Having found it so difficult, two decades ago, to be both child and adult, Omotola has recently worked with Amnesty International to promote recognition of the liminal or hybrid spaces that children so often occupy, but that rarely receive mention in official child welfare programs. "When my father was alive, we were living well," Omotola remembers. "But when he died, so many things went wrong. And we practically went to a point where we had almost nothing, except the house we were living in." Those school officials who cited the survival of Omotola's mother, as well as the evident maintenance of stable living quarters, could not perceive the nuances of Omotola's harsh experiences; they could not see the emotionally violent hybridity inside her superficially "typical" and unified youth persona or the pain behind her productivity. Says the star, "I knew what it felt like to not know where [the] next meal was going to come from ... At age fourteen or fifteen, you'd think I was nineteen or twenty."[2]

OMOTOLA'S LESSONS: DIFFERENTIATING CHILD-FOCUSED PHILANTHROPY

Stored as they are within specific material formats that require electricity for playback, Nollywood's films might not be able to trace a truly minor transnationalism in West Africa; they might find themselves limited to urban locations where VCRs as well as VCD and DVD players are plentiful, along with generators. Nollywood stars, on the other hand, suggest a dramatically different story. Simply put, their bodies travel, engaging in a far-flung philanthropy that preempts the relative costliness as well as the persistent technical requirements of material media. Circulating through a multiplicity of philanthropic venues, Nollywood stardom, as a partly corporeal phenomenon, can prove considerably cheaper than Nollywood films, particularly when activist stars agree to appear for free in a range of locations. Embodied by individual performers who carry it with them into a variety of physical spaces, Nollywood stardom can thus remain widely accessible, especially when tied to charity work. When Oge Okoye travels to Sierra Leone in order to empower children there; when Stephanie Okereke follows Prince Tonye Princewill's Orphans Awareness Campaign into various rural pockets of West Africa; or when Omotola Jalade-Ekeinde's work for Amnesty International takes her into the heart of Liberia, Nollywood star images become tangible, itinerant, and costless. Okoye does not charge a fee to meet with convalescent Sierra Leonean kids; the pan-African Orphans Awareness Campaign does not position Okereke as a salaried adjunct; and Omotola is not paid to appear in post-conflict zones.

Such star-centered charity crusades are hardly pedagogical in the traditional sense, suggesting that when Nollywood, via its adult stars, penetrates post-conflict societies in order to mingle with kids, it does so strictly in a therapeutic, productively distracting capacity, not necessarily as a source of statistical information about societal reconstruction or individual rehabilitation. Nollywood stars enter suffering spheres as saintly agents of change, but Nollywood itself, in spite of the transnationalism of these very same stars, enters as a specifically southern Nigerian media form, one that (literally) might not speak to certain peoples—as Omotola Jalade-Ekeinde discovers during an episode of her reality television series, in which questions of language and translation emerge to throw a wrench in Nollywood's transnational aspirations. (Omotola finds, for instance, that even a Ghallywood-Nollywood collaboration can require considerable work.) Marisa Ensor notes that, in studying African childhoods, it is especially important to remain "cautious about situating the whole African continent in one single descriptive trajectory," and Nollywood stars are certainly aware of the fact that the multiculturalism of Nigeria points to an even broader—and perhaps impenetrable—diversity across West Africa's sixteen countries.[3] This awareness becomes the subject of a memorable episode of *Omotola: The Real Me*, in which the star spends a significant period of time in Ghana, confronting anew the fact that even official uses of the English language leave little room for cultural equivalences—a topic taken up in Nollywood films as otherwise dissimilar as *Liberian Girl* (Mykel C. Ajaere, 2010), in which the title character's Kreyol is incomprehensible to Nigerians; the classic *Domitilla: The Story of a Prostitute* (Zeb Ejiro, 1997), in which thick Sapele Pidgin provides the dirty words and phrases befitting the film's risqué narrative; and *Everybody Loves Jénífà*, in which Funke Akindele's iconic creation travels to Jamaica in order to perfect her Patois.

Minor transnationalism, as enacted by Nollywood stars, thus entails a constant process of translation and exchange—an active challenge rather than an effortless outcome. That said, as Ensor herself suggests, the notion that "children's issues" are universal remains persistent—upheld not merely by the United Nations Millennium Development Goals and by the African Child Policy Forum but also by the Nollywood stars whose performances of transnationalism increasingly entail the promotion of region-wide welfare measures for vulnerable (especially orphaned) children. If Omotola knows better than to suggest that all orphans are alike—or that there is a clear and inviolate difference between orphan and non-orphan—then that is because she brings the hard-won wisdom of her own youth to bear upon her adult activism. The tenacity that has informed her star image—that has, in fact, all but ensured her itinerant iconicity—is not necessarily open to everyone. That is why Omotola works to promote not some shapeless sense of what it takes to succeed—not some broadly defined moral "backbone"—but rather a more nuanced approach to youth welfare development, one that would accept the nonexistence of an "essential" or "universal" child and would search instead for even the subtlest distinctions among seemingly similar kids, precisely as a way to better comprehend and respect their emergent identities.

Dramatic differences between the kinds of post-conflict West African societies that are typically lumped together within the framework of trauma theory tend to reveal the nagging truth that geopolitically distanced children require a variety of remedial measures in the realm of education. As Hannah Hoechner notes in her work on northern Nigeria, "'education' is not an autonomous force operating in isolation from wider political, economic, and cultural power dynamics."[4] Nevertheless, the transnationalism of Nollywood stardom, which tends to contribute to the polysemy of individual star images—making them seem more global and better informed by a wide range of experiences, and by major as much as by minor transnationalism—

Figure 6.1. Child performers convene in a schoolhouse to shoot a violent scene in Newton Aduaka's *Ezra* (2007). Image courtesy of California Newsreel.

runs the risk of glossing over the many experiential discrepancies among West African children, precisely because such stardom remains very much an adult phenomenon. As Omotola Jalade-Ekeinde suggests, it is necessary for adult stars to remember their younger selves to better combat the universalist view of youth. It is perhaps a measure of Omotola's influence—as well as of the survival of Nollywood's general antiessentialist ethos—that so many star-driven NGOs promote a boundless conception of kids (with Oge Okoye's Positive Life Children offering the tagline "Children Learn Differently . . . and Every Child Deserves a Chance"). A few contemporary Nigerian films have attempted to counter the notion that any one philosophy of child welfare is applicable across West Africa's heterogeneous terrain. Newton Aduaka's remarkable 2007 drama *Ezra*, for instance, suggests that the invocation of a shared, anglophone educational ethos can conceal striking experiential differences, and that the adoption of a southern Nigerian model of therapeutic instruction is inadvisable in those post-conflict societies that lie just to the west.

Ezra opens with shots of a schoolhouse in Sierra Leone: the children are seated peacefully inside, awaiting instruction; some gaze listlessly out the open windows, while others fix their eyes upon the chalkboard in front of them. Within minutes, however, all hell breaks loose. Shots are fired, and the children are compelled to leave the schoolhouse, some of them eventually joining up with the forces that have effectively divested them of their education. The eponymous Ezra, who becomes a brutalizing member of a rebel army—a mass-murderer as well as a thief and a drug addict—is on his way to school at the start of the film, skipping down a dirt path, providing an image of innocence blissfully oriented toward traditional pedagogy. Ezra's violent removal from that purview is among the film's most lacerating images, and it lingers as a reminder of the high cost of child-inclusive conflicts. Years later, the adult Ezra is brought before the Truth and Reconciliation Commission, where his inability to adequately recollect his actions as a child soldier is tied not simply to his memory's having suffered the deleterious effects of drug abuse but also to his loss of schoolhouse instruction.

Ezra brilliantly portrays the catch-22 associated with West African conflict and post-conflict societies—a catch-22 that centers on children and education. For those who wish to resist the cultures of violence that surround them, escaping a schoolhouse in order to find refuge in remote locations can prove effective—though only up to a point, since the loss of formal instruction can itself force kids to fall into the so-called "conflict trap."[5] Fittingly, *Ezra* lingers upon the loss of education for children in Sierra Leone, as well as upon the efforts of a few youth groups to locate a promised land of levity and pedagogy elsewhere in West Africa—as when cadres of kids cry out for Lagos. "We've got to get to Lagos," they say, forgetting that they are not Nigerian, and that the social construction of Lagos-as-dreamland is just that— an Afro-optimist invention designed to further diffract West Africa by upholding an imagined, essentialized heaven.

The sobering reality that southern Nigeria cannot possibly furnish a cure-all for post-conflict West African societies is one that Nollywood's activist stars must contend with when traveling throughout the region. In any case, nationalism lives, as Omotola Jalade-Ekeinde discovers on her reality show, encountering in Takoradi a certain cultural chauvinism that leads a

Ghanaian real estate developer to cheekily prescribe the remedy for an allegedly ailing Nigeria. (Unification is key, he says, but what might that mean? What could it possibly entail?) Omotola, in response, loses her cool, but she quickly regains it—possibly because she's sufficiently self-aware to recognize that her own "Naija pride" reflects an obvious bias. Returning to her children in Lagos, she reaffirms her philosophy about "kids' differences"—about the importance of recognizing and reacting to those differences, of personalizing and individualizing young people, of rejecting the temptations of a generation-specific essentialism even amid a cautious support for a certain brand of nationalism. On *Omotola: The Real Me*, the star is alert to the possibility that her children might one day "enter the Nollywood arena." They already exhibit varying degrees of interest in the industry—and certainly in their mother's protean stardom—but the series seems, through Omotola herself, to take for granted that they will not act professionally until they've reached adulthood. Which may, of course, be for the best. Nevertheless, even during the second decade of the twenty-first century, and even when engagingly gifted little ones are on display in the realm of reality television, Nollywood's resistance to child stardom continues to seem axiomatic.

Some of the old, local social problems (such as youth tribalism) persist, but they are now met with an influx of challenges from the West—from the Hollywood whose global revenues depend upon the factory production of teen talent. Already—in a real-life variation on *Lady Gaga*—Nigerian child performers are working to embody, critique, and recast the personae of young Western pop stars, particularly Miley Cyrus and Justin Bieber, and in the process they have inspired both acclaim and denunciation (and have employed both piracy and plagiarism, along with some decidedly more licit strategies). On the one hand, with Boko Haram upping the ante on its efforts to co-opt disaffected youth, Nollywood stars, in apparent ideological agreement with their fans, are working to ensure employment and lifestyle alternatives for Nigerian children, largely by promoting the kinds of educational measures that can effectively guard against political extremism. But if such alternatives are to include media stardom, then certain problems need to be addressed, such as the sheer difficulty of developing and maintaining a star image and, more importantly, the lack of likelihood that every aspiring child performer will become famous. In their charity work with children, Nollywood's adult stars must contend with kids who pin their hopes upon impossible achievements, as Oge Okoye herself discovered in taking PLC to Cameroon, where some of the least disillusioned kids appeared to expect stardom in sports or on screen—to become instantly famous following their brief contact with a Nollywood star.

The industry's adult icons cannot be expected to sell stardom as a skill set. That is partly why Okoye works to promote assistance for students with special needs, while Omotola Jalade-Ekeinde, rather than offering pep talks designed to inculcate a craving for fame, focuses on raising awareness about the different forms that hardship can assume for young people. Considered in the context of such principled, practical activism, Nollywood's apparent, ongoing aversion to developing child stardom might not represent an operative ethos or a working prejudice. It might, in fact, reflect the rarity of stardom itself—the fact that not everyone gets to be famous. This book has consistently invoked only a relative handful of stars—Omotola Jalade-Ekeinde, Oge Okoye, Funke Akindele, Eniola Badmus, Desmond Elliot, Stephanie Okereke, Ramsey Nouah, Genevieve Nnaji, Van Vicker—partly because these stars have been around for a long time, and they show no signs of going away any time soon. Remaining committed to their profound star talents, Nollywood has demonstrated considerable respect for what it has, rather than an interest in acquiring what it does not. In contrast to the Hollywood that continues to flood West Africa with the sounds and images of cookie-cutter kids—a constantly rotating crop of young, transmedia stars who, when they cease to be relevant, are often painted as insane or simply pitiable in global publicity—Nollywood has seemingly been immune to a commercialized dissatisfaction with "old" stars, even amid the cacophonous voices of filmmakers who keep touting 35 mm and new star discoveries as representing the future of an industry whose origins are on fading cassette tapes.

That said, there remain problems inherent in the industry's on- and off-screen uses of children—problems made visible by examining inadequate or misleading casting, crediting, and promotional protocols, whereby youth performers are both everywhere and nowhere at once, both essential and seemingly unnecessary. Nollywood's adult stars—whatever their activist persuasions, whether they like it or not, and whether they even know it or not—are complicit in this process. If their philanthropic activities centralize children offscreen, their considerable, indispensable star power tends to downplay the contributions of child performers to their films, forcing the latter's names to be buried in credit sequences or banished altogether. Operating against the backdrop of increasing star activism in the arena of child welfare development, Nollywood's efforts to obscure youth participation continue to suggest a fear of negative publicity—of the false assumption of exploitation or of a lack of on-set support for education (assumptions that Sharon Ezeamaka, through the frameworks of personal memory and testimony, has attempted to debunk). With more and more stars serving as transnational agents of youth protection, more and more films are limiting audience awareness of child performers, suggesting either a lack of ideological continuity between stars and their industry or a certain consensus about protection entailing suppression—a need to keep kids out of the limelight altogether. Ironically, however, the limelight is what vulnerable children find when confronted with the philanthropy of Nollywood's biggest stars, raising the ever-challenging question of whether the publicizing of a child's plight can counteract efforts to provide much-needed remediation.

ECLIPSING KIDS

The heavily charged concept of child employment, coupled with the popular assumption that the terms "child stardom" and "exploitation" are necessarily synonymous, has seemingly prevented the Nollywood industry from nurturing a cadre of kid performers, but Sharon Ezeamaka demonstrates that such negative stereotypes are largely unfounded. The former child star's comments, both in interviews as well as on Twitter, confirm the importance of respecting young performers' own social experiences as they themselves describe them. Marisa Ensor addresses this issue when she notes that a "lack of attention to children's realities" has prevented African development efforts from creating "the conditions under which children's work may advance their social and physiological development."[6] If the study of stardom is to make better sense of the experiences of child performers in Nollywood, then it needs to take into account the voices that consistently and from a self-proclaimed youth perspective draw attention to the specific circumstances of employment in Nigeria. Ezeamaka, for instance, claims that her welfare was never in question during the time she spent as an underage actress on Nollywood film sets. She also points out that she was properly compensated (with the funds being channeled through her parents), and that no filmmaker ever prevented her from furthering her education. She describes the mandated sessions in which she would complete schoolwork on set, the presence of tutors in various shooting locations, and a constant regard for a healthy balance between work and play, all of which helped Ezeamaka to feel like "a normal girl."[7]

Ezeamaka serves as a crucial example of a Nollywood star whose very public pronouncements (and social media skills) work to systematically destigmatize the Nollywood industry. As a former child star, Ezeamaka uses personal experience to separate Nollywood from its stereotyped association with scandal. At the same time, she works to advance the cause of child performers, advocating the creation of the kinds of (largely ideological) industrial conditions that will, in her estimation, prove conducive to the development of child stars. In so doing, Ezeamaka offers a reminder that stars are constructed not simply through film roles and public appearances but also by the specific industrial circumstances governing employment. For a new child star to begin the process of image construction in Nollywood, she must first be hired—and, specifically, hired over the less generationally qualified Ezeamaka, Omotola Jalade-Ekeinde, Genevieve Nnaji, and Oge Okoye, who may well represent the industry's top choices, albeit for reasons having to do not with any rubric of realism but instead with the pressures of public relations. Ezeamaka suggests that for Nollywood to continue to advance its global image, it needs to cogently divorce itself from the stereotypes that still surround it, including and especially those that mix a fear of movies and movie culture with timeworn, essentialist suspicions about the licentiousness of Nigerian men. As Marisa Ensor argues, omitting children from equations of employment is, in sub-Saharan Africa, often the means through which the formal sector seeks to distance itself from the prying eyes of local and international human rights watchdog groups, even as it covertly co-opts youth workers. The denial of legitimate employment opportunities to children thus marks itself not as a morally sound gesture but instead as a smokescreen designed to conceal corrupt practices, further contributing to Afro-pessimist stereotypes about the continent's lack of potential for "development."[8]

Nollywood is not necessarily in the business of resisting children's work altogether, as evidenced by the industry's continued use of little-known child performers as well as youth extras; but its lack of a well-defined system for generating child stars might suggest an anti-youth measure, particularly when set against its well-entrenched mechanisms for developing adult talents. While a film like Moses Ebere's *Miss Queen* features at least nineteen child extras and two child leads, its publicity materials still pivot around the presence in the film of five of Nollywood's biggest adult stars: Tonto Dikeh, Oge Okoye, Halima Abubakar, Muna Obiekwe, and Frederick Leonard. Of those five names, only the first, third, and fourth have significant roles in the film; in terms of screen time, all are eclipsed by child performers, whose names are far from familiar and whose images figure in none of the film's publicity intertexts (from posters to VCD covers to ads on YouTube and iROKOtv).

As the case of *Miss Queen* suggests, Nollywood can seem to occupy a murky middle ground between a realist appreciation for children's stories and a marked resistance to developing underage stars. If the industry does indeed reflect, as well as shape, Nigerian social realities, positioning itself as a national cinema of sorts, then it is important to point out that Nigerian children, especially as defined by local and global child welfare groups, as well as by state policy, are seen as both uniquely vulnerable and uniquely useful to discourses of progress, particularly those that centralize industry. That means that if Nigeria is to develop as a nation-state by both empowering and protecting its children (as per the Second National Youth Policy Document), then Nollywood must similarly showcase economic, moral, and practical support for the kids with whom it comes into contact (as per the youth policy's official implementation strategies). Discussing West African contexts, Cati Coe argues that "because of their age-related link to time and the future, children function as indicators of a nation's potential and progress in popular discourse." But given their age-specific vulnerabilities and capacity to create negative publicity for a developing nation (by appearing to be the victims of exploitation, for example, and by sounding specific alarm bells for UNICEF and other aid organizations), children (who represent a growing, majority percentage of Africa's population) have forced West African countries—especially media-rich ones like Ghana and Nigeria—to confront what Coe calls a "crisis of youth."[9]

There are many ways of potentially assuaging, if not eliminating, this crisis. In the Nollywood context, one method appears to be to blatantly honor the family focus of Nigeria's official youth policies, casting child performers but also, for the same film project, their parents, grandparents, and/

or older siblings. Sharon Ezeamaka describes this relatively new, seemingly expanding casting practice as redundant, recalling that when she was a child star, producers would contact her primarily through her parents, whose appearance on Nollywood's radar did not require their participation in Nollywood films. Added to Ezeamaka's response is the distinct possibility that this casting practice, which seeks to include, as performers, adult members of a child's immediate family, represents little more than a public relations scheme designed to telegraph Nollywood's commitment to child welfare. When the credits roll and four of the performers' surnames are the same, the spectator can perhaps be assured of Nollywood's family-friendly credentials—if not at the level of narrative then at least at the extra-textual level of casting. Consider, for instance, Kunle Afolayan's 2009 film *The Figurine*, in which the actress Omoni Oboli appears with her real-life son, Tobe Oboli, who plays her son in the film. Fittingly, Tobe is billed prominently alongside his mother, who describes the process of making *The Figurine* as "stressful," since she was forced to combine performance and parenting duties: "I had to shoot with my son, which made it even more difficult for me as an actress, because I had to be an actress [and] I had to be a mother on set. I had to shield him away from the likes of [director] Kunle and [costar] Ramsey [Nouah], who wanted to talk about adult stuff!" Describing acting-*cum*-childcare as "challenging but, ultimately, fun," Oboli notes that it is quite common in today's Nollywood.[10] It is important to point out, however, that the practice is not exactly conducive to child stardom—quite the opposite, in fact, as the case of *Miss Queen* makes abundantly clear.

CASTING *MISS QUEEN*

There is a moment in Moses Ebere's *Miss Queen* in which Oge Okoye, playing a passionate, wealthy mother of two who wants to revive her moribund marriage with an elaborate second honeymoon, hears her kids bickering. At one point, her eight-year-old daughter calls her nine-year-old son a Nazi, and Okoye, as Evelyn, asks why the little girl has seized upon so loaded a word. It seems that the daughter, Carol (Uchenna Ogbuefi), has grown tired of her brother's sexism. The boy, Bob (played by an uncredited child actor), has been shouting insults at Carol, calling her "stupid, like all girls." Worse, he has even gone so far as to defame the children's new physical education teacher, the titular Miss Queen (Tonto Dikeh). It seems that Miss Queen, in Bob's sexist conception, is unqualified to teach physical education for no more elaborate reason than that she is a woman.

When she realizes that her brother's misogyny has extended well past the boilerplate, I-hate-my-sister stage to encompass an impassioned refusal to respect a grown and apparently professional woman, Carol calls Bob a Nazi—an utterance that elicits considerable confusion from her mother. Evelyn, the film makes clear, has already been forced to contend with Carol's capacity to correct her brother's sexist assessments of women—a capacity that Evelyn admires, except when it interferes with mealtime. At the breakfast table, Carol reads books when she should be eating, and she holds each volume close to her face, not simply to shield that face from the prying eyes of her prickly brother but also to prove to him that little girls can be delightedly literate.

In the same, wealthy section of Lagos lives a woman named Vivian who, like Evelyn, is a mother of two, and who, unlike her counterpart, has cast aside the husband who has been cheating on her with his seductive secretary. As played by Halima Abubakar, Vivian is a modern Lagosian whose emotions often get the better of her—a successful businesswoman whose temper prevents her from giving her husband the second chance that he so desperately desires. In familiar Nollywood fashion, *Miss Queen* lingers on the pricey automobiles parked in Vivian's driveway—on the cars that belong to her as well as to her best friend, Amber (Ejine Okoroafor), who comes to Vivian's big house in order to provide comfort and companionship.

After catching him cheating, Vivian quarrels with her shunned husband, Michael (Muna Obiekwe), not merely about matters of the heart but also about parental responsibilities. It seems that the headstrong Vivian has decided to fight for sole custody of the kids, despite Michael's frequently affirming that he in fact loves and is fit to care for them—despite, in other words, his caution against equating husbandly failure with fatherly failure. When finally the film identifies the estranged couple's kids, it reveals that they are the classmates of Carol and Bob. Vivian's youngest, a daughter, is also named Carol, and she is played, in a confusing bit of casting, by Uchenna Ogbuefi's twin sister, Tochukwu. While Evelyn's children are two of the most significant characters in *Miss Queen*, only Uchenna Ogbuefi's Carol receives billing in the film, as well as on every poster, DVD, and VCD cover that I have seen. The same is true of Vivian's kids: Tochukwu Ogbuefi's Carol, who has almost no lines, is credited, but her garrulous brother is not, and thus the young actor who plays him remains completely anonymous to the spectator.

How to explain this generationally specific gender gap? Why is it that the girls are credited while the boys remain unnamed? These questions become especially difficult to address when one considers that the complicated, gendered politics of billing extend to the film's other performers, as well—most notably to Muna Obiekwe, who receives top billing despite his relatively small share of screen time, and to Frederick Leonard, who plays Evelyn's sexy (and often shirtless) husband Richard, and who receives billing above Oge Okoye despite his minor role in the film. The seemingly contradictory strategies of billing girls (but not boys) and privileging men (but not women) become even more confusing when read through the lens of the film's focus on a particular brand of feminism, which mixes imported Western models with a local, Pentecostal sense of gender equality. In *Miss Queen*, the book-reading Carol quickly becomes the Bible-thumping Carol; her brother's sexist suspicions are redeemed and reconfigured when it is revealed that Miss Queen, the physical education teacher, is in fact a demon—the daughter of Beelzebub—who has come to destroy all Nigerian children. Bob's reflexive sexism is thus recast as prescience (especially after he describes a dream of his, in which Miss Queen eats him), but it is up to the hyper-literate Carol, who has begged her mother for "a real, adult Bible" to replace her old, picture-book Bible, to save the day. She does, and the film ends with a celebration both of Carol's devoutness and her mother Evelyn's decision to finally buy her daughter that "proper, adult Bible"—a decision that has led, ultimately, to the vanquishing of Dikeh's Miss Queen.

But the Bible-loving Carol and her mother Evelyn represent just one aspect of the story. Another involves the combustible Vivian and her more docile daughter—the *other* Carol, who happens to look just like Evelyn's kid. Vivian shares with her daughter an appreciation for American media, and in particular for tween-oriented American pop music. *Miss Queen*, which unfolds in four hour-long parts, lingers on the significance of what Vivian's daughter calls "girl power," providing, in addition to the proud and politicized comments of Evelyn's precocious kid Carol, the iconography of several white, Western agents of feminism—all of them, tellingly, teen girls. Most visible among these markers of an American brand of girl power is Miley

Cyrus, whose face adorns several commodity tie-ins that appear in Vivian's house, including a collectible plastic cup that rests atop her entertainment center. It is this cup—impossible to ignore in a shot of a defeated Vivian slumped on the floor and slowly describing her emotional pain to a patient and compassionate Amber—that serves as the strongest of the film's many reminders of global girl culture. But it is also this cup, on which Cyrus appears as her alter ego, multimedia superstar Hannah Montana, that raises several challenging questions, not just about Cyrus' specific popularity in southern Nigeria, but also about her persona's relevance to a Nollywood-style child stardom.

It is important to look at Nollywood's star system through the lenses both of global and local youth movements, addressing the questions that surround the industry's inability to generate a roster of child stars in spite of its devotion both to stardom itself and to a diversity of films about kids. *Miss Queen* relies heavily upon the language of youth empowerment, portraying young, southern Nigerian children as media literate, devoutly religious, and buoyantly energetic. The film's billing, however, suggests major contradictions that cannot be dismissed, and that matter both practically and semiotically. While the issue of star billing is often difficult to address, partly because it can appear to be underwritten both by individual egos and the professional minders (from agents to publicists) who manage those egos, a film like *Miss Queen* demonstrates its potential to suggest several key questions about casting protocol.

Lest the perplexing credit sequences of *Miss Queen* be dismissed as further evidence of Nollywood's "sloppiness," it is important to point out that Hollywood cinema also has a long and hardly coherent history of crediting performers for their work. Within the Hollywood context, there are five basic, recurrent instances in which a thespian will not receive billing: the performer is hired as a last-minute addition to the cast and is asked to ad lib (Bill Murray in *Tootsie* [Sydney Pollack, 1982], David Bowie in *Yellowbeard* [Mel Damski, 1983]); the performer is functioning in little more than a cameo role and as an unpaid or barely paid favor to a writer, director, producer, or fellow performer (Jack Nicholson in *Broadcast News* [James L. Brooks, 1987], Walter Matthau in *Earthquake* [Mark Robson, 1974], Bruce Willis in the Quentin Tarantino segment of *Four Rooms* [1995]); the performer is profoundly self-critical or simply unhappy with the finished film (Ron Liebman in *Up the Academy* [Robert Downey Sr., 1980], Darren McGavin in *The Natural* [Barry Levinson, 1984]); the performer appears under makeup so heavy that billing is deemed too confusing or distracting (Gary Oldman in *Hannibal* [Ridley Scott, 2001], Boris Karloff in the first prints of *Frankenstein* [James Whale, 1931]); or the performer plays a pivotal role requiring, within a familiar formula for suspense, a complete lack of audience foreknowledge (Kevin Spacey in *Se7en* [David Fincher, 1995]). What these general, often overlapping categories share—apart from gender—is, of course, a certain degree of recognizability on the parts of the uncredited male performers. While Jack Nicholson is inarguably a far bigger star than Ron Liebman, the latter nevertheless enjoyed, in 1980, considerable public acclaim—a fact that led him to request that his name be removed from a film that he considered unfit for his fans as well as damaging to his reputation.[11]

The above examples have something else in common: age. In none of these cases is the performer in question a child, which does not necessarily suggest that recognizable young talents have been guaranteed billing in Hollywood cinema. Since the development of commercial feature films in the United States, children have been central to plots as well as to publicity, but they have often been denied the productive career consequences of onscreen billing, which can serve not only to advertise individual talents but also to establish an aura of professionalism. As Gaylyn Studlar points out, the politics of billing often precluded the crediting of child performers in early cinema, precisely because prevailing assumptions equated youth performance with sheer amateurishness, making a credited child thespian almost a contradiction in terms. "A significant number of children appeared in films during the first decade of features," Studlar writes, "but few of these child screen performers ever achieved star billing."[12] The extent to which these prejudicial practices continued into Hollywood's classical period can be deduced through reference to any one of a range of child stars on whom the industry depended but who rarely received adequate billing.

If, as Richard deCordova argues in his groundbreaking book *Picture Personalities: The Emergence of the Star System in America,* performers never received billing in the early feature films produced at Biograph studios, then that was because the Biograph ethos was, by the 1910s, almost embarrassingly outdated—beholden to the condescending assumption that anonymity would sell, or (more absurd still) that performers *were* their characters. De-

Cordova famously outlines the extent to which the transition to billing was bound up with new ideals of professionalism and publicity, arguing that the development of a recognizable star system was essential to the development of a commercial film industry itself. But does the history that deCordova so beautifully elucidates hold any direct relevance to Nollywood? Can it help explain the fact that Nollywood often seems simultaneously dependent upon stars and resistant to publicizing—or even crediting—young ones? If Richard Dyer's frameworks for studying media stardom are productive only up to a point in African contexts, then surely there are limitations to the similar application of deCordova's approach, wherein technological and narrative developments are coterminous with the solidification of a star system.

I have resorted to citing historical Hollywood examples not simply because they are widely known and reliably controversial, but also because Hollywood's billing protocols are all too familiar in southern Nigeria, where they often elicit confusion and consternation, and where a concerted effort on the part of an individual film exhibitor can effectively rewrite an unpalatable, above-the-title billing block. For instance, in the spring of 2013, Silverbird Cinemas reframed the official poster for the American film *Gangster Squad* (Ruben Fleischer, 2013) so that Ryan Gosling, and not Josh Brolin, would receive top billing. The decision was undoubtedly spurred by the local popularity of Gosling's romantic melodrama *The Notebook* (Nick Cassavetes, 2004), which inspired its own series of Nollywood remakes and tributes; clearly, in Nigeria, Gosling is far bigger than Brolin. Silverbird has thus offered frequent, stark reminders that the politics of star billing matter in Nigeria, where, in September 2009, the local premiere of Izu Ojukwu's Nollywood melodrama *Nnenda* raised concerns about the potential sexism underlying the organization of the film's credit sequences.

A remarkable dramatization of the plight of orphans in Nigeria, *Nnenda* takes its name from a character played by Stephanie Okereke, who fights for the rights of the abandoned children of prostitutes, junkies, and rape victims, and who lobbies for government support for more adequate orphanages—the kinds of facilities that would feature more advanced medical services and more compassionate male physicians and administrators. As this description suggests, *Nnenda* is as much about a professional woman's encounters with male chauvinism (and sheer incompetence) as it is about child welfare. Stephanie Okereke plays the title role without ever hinting that her character is at all surprised by the misogyny that she discovers, and Okereke's trademark capacity to deliver rapid-fire dialogue, uttering (or, as is so often the case, shouting) dozens of words in mere seconds, suggests a woman who is strong and smart enough to take on "the system." Nnenda the trailblazing activist is not unlike Sally Field's Norma Rae or Julia Roberts' Erin Brockovich, but she is played by a woman who—in contrast to her Hollywood counterparts—does not receive top billing in the film's original opening and closing credit sequences. While such on-screen sequences are often immune to alteration, particularly in Nollywood's low-cost context (where tinkering with motion graphics would almost certainly represent a prohibitive and allegedly unnecessary expenditure), posters and other publicity materials are a different matter entirely. For the Port Harcourt premiere of *Nnenda*, Okereke's fans (and some of her colleagues) succeeded in persuading Silverbird managers to print new posters on which she would receive top billing, the better to reflect her lead performance in the film's title role—a matter more of accuracy (and of loving fandom) than of ego. (On previous posters, Okereke had received fourth billing, after the male stars Francis Duru, Ramsey Nouah, and Uti Nwachukwu.) Revising the *Nnenda* posters did not necessarily represent a stab at stroking a star's self-regard: Okereke's newly prominent name—her above-the-title-billing—helped, in this instance, to publicize her off-screen, philanthropic connection to the Orphans Awareness Campaign. If, as the revised posters revealed, "Stephanie Okereke is *Nnenda*," then Okereke is also, in her own life, a child-rights activist like her character.

While the Port Harcourt premiere may have represented a victory of sorts for Okereke's expansive star image, and a blow against the sexism implicit in certain baffling billing practices, it did nothing to advance the cause of child stardom in Nollywood. Actual Nigerian orphans may have famously walked the red carpet for *Nnenda* events, but where were the dozens of children who perform as orphans in the film? How did public gatherings designed to publicize both a muckraking melodrama and its associated Orphans Awareness Campaign manage to ignore the significance of child stardom? *Nnenda*'s revised posters offer a reminder that film reception is never a fixed experience; it is mutable, almost by definition, and responsive to ongoing events. With Princewill's Orphans Awareness Campaign gaining widespread recognition by late 2009, along with his Rivers State Rural

Women Empowerment Program, the intersection between child welfare and women's rights campaigns contributed to the decision to "correct" *Nnenda's* publicity materials by making them better reflect this intersection.

If *Nnenda's* original posters were almost preposterously misleading, then an equally inadequate, but as yet uncorrected, set of billing practices characterize Moses Ebere's *Miss Queen*, which fails to credit its prominent underage male performer in either its official on-screen credit sequences or in its publicity intertexts. Within the latter category, the standard cover for the DVD of parts 1 and 2 of *Miss Queen* is instructive. As designed by Sanga Films, the cover suggests that *Miss Queen* is about a love triangle among adults—two women (Tonto Dikeh and Oge Okoye) and one man (Muna Obiekwe). A double distortion, this DVD cover not only conceals the fact that the film is very much about the efforts of a diversity of kids to combat Dikeh's eponymous demon; it also unites three characters who never appear together in the film, and in the process suggests that Okoye's Evelyn is romantically, even jealously involved with Obiekwe's Michael. While the image certainly serves as a testament to star power, suggesting the extent to which that power can be appreciated even in the absence of respect for a film's actual plot, it still bespeaks an exclusively *adult* stardom—a high irony for a film that not only makes extensive use of children but that also, in narrative terms, presents one little girl as a star in her own right.

A FAMILY AFFAIR

In *Miss Queen*, Uchenna Ogbuefi's Carol, the devout daughter of Oge Okoye's Evelyn, does not simply save the day by brandishing her Bible in the face of Tonto Dikeh's demon. She also emerges, by the end of the film, as a celebrated juvenile ballerina. Always willing to stand up to her sexist brother Bob—a little girl who gives as good as she gets—Carol is also an aspiring performer who hopes to translate the precociousness that she privately shares with her family into something that she can impart to the wider world. Since dance is one of her passions, she practices often. Fittingly for the heroine of this religiously inflected film, Carol refuses to see dancing as being in any way at odds with her devotion to God; in fact, like the reverent track athletes of the iconic British film *Chariots of Fire* (Hugh Hudson, 1981),

Carol can see God's pleasure in her strenuous bodily movements, as well as in her grace under pressure. The film ends with her dressed (symbolically) in a white tutu, with an elaborate white tiara atop her head, as she dances to a crowd of hundreds, all gathered to see her solo recital. As soon as she confidently, smilingly ends her performance, audience members rush to their feet to give her a lengthy standing ovation—to stamp her as a star.

Uchenna Ogbuefi, however, is not a star, and no one in the Nollywood industry seems intent on turning her into one. Unlike *Miss Queen*'s adult performers, she does not appear in any YouTube ads for the film, nor does her character figure in the official trailer. On *Miss Queen*'s iROKOtv page, only Tonto Dikeh's image is employed to advertise the film, and only the names of the four adult stars are listed. In the film's opening and closing credit sequences, however, there appears the name of Uchenna Ogbuefi's grandmother, Beak Ogbuefi, who plays the school principal responsible for having hired Dikeh's villainous character. Her prominent inclusion in the credits helps to mark *Miss Queen* as a family affair—the product of a casting practice designed, according to a 2012 Africa Magic promotional campaign, to confirm for audiences that Nollywood is in fact a "family-focused" industry. Undoubtedly, this casting practice is motivated partly by convenience: hiring all members of an immediate family, including the children, obviates the need for professional childcare, freeing adult cast members from the difficulty of leaving their little ones behind. It may also, of course, relieve a performer of the need to fake affection for a stranger. As Omoni Oboli points out, working with her son—and playing his screen substitute's mother—was a way of honoring her love for him, even if it created some unrelated and unforeseen challenges. Oboli offers the crucial reminder that, whatever its difficulties and rewards, there is more to this transparently family-friendly casting convention than practicality alone: it is also rooted in the rigors of public relations, suggesting that Nollywood's awareness of its audiences extends to their assumed solicitude toward children.

In working to guarantee the welfare of child performers, it may be insufficient simply to cast an adult who can serve simultaneously as a performer and, through a presumed familial obligation, a minder. Moreover, opening and closing credit sequences may not do enough to telegraph to audience members that Nollywood is invested in protecting its youth talents. In the case of *Miss Queen*, for instance, the name "Ogbuefi" seemingly functions to confer a sense of comfort and intrafamilial security upon the film's conditions of production. In the past, the surname "Uchemba" served a similar purpose in Nollywood films featuring child actor William Uchemba, his sister Sandra Uchemba, and several other members of the Uchemba family, all usually billed as "relatives."[13] It is tempting, in approaching *Miss Queen*, to read the credits' prominent inclusion of the name "Ogbuefi," which is shared by three people—all members of the same immediate family—as a disclaimer of sorts, a statement asserting the filmmakers' interest in providing, via an ostensibly family-friendly casting practice, a built-in child welfare service. This is, in fact, how Omoni Oboli views the inclusion of her son's name in the credits of *The Figurine*, and how, in Nollywood's northern counterpart, Kannywood, stars like Sani Danja and Ali Nuhu promote their children's costarring roles in their films.[14]

Such an interpretation cannot, however, quite explain the erasure of the child actor who plays Bob in *Miss Queen*, although it is possible to read that erasure as a way of further highlighting the girls and their on-set proximity to their presumably watchful and loving grandmother. Like numerous films produced after 2007 (an industrial turning point that witnessed the attempts of the National Film and Video Censors Board to formalize Nollywood), *Miss Queen* suggests a systematic orientation toward child welfare, as well as a rebuke to some of Nollywood's least seemly representations of family life. The irony is that such development strategies, as Santorri Chamley points out, are very much dependent upon ideals of realism—on making Nollywood less a fount of the fantastical and more a source of images of the "actual" Nigeria.[15] Given that the majority of Nigeria's population now belongs to what UNICEF has called "the youth category," Nollywood's growing focus on authenticity has come to mean an embrace of child performers—but not, significantly, of child stars.[16] For many proponents of Nollywood realism, the casting of adult performers in child roles represents a blight on the face of a still-growing industry—an embarrassment that becomes even more pronounced when Nollywood films reach the kinds of Western countries that have their own, well-developed systems for generating child stars. An even bigger problem, however, is what happens when Western youth superstars arrive in Nigeria, their saturated images serving as near-constant reminders of a major Nollywood lacuna.

NOLLYWOOD, YOUTH CULTURE, AND "THE NEW EXPLOITATION"

In attempting to publicize Nollywood as a family-friendly industry, Oge Okoye has consistently echoed a conventional hierarchical view of Western and African child stars, suggesting that the latter, while fewer than the former, are also far less apt to experience meltdowns. Approached from this perspective, Nollywood's "youth allergy" loses its negative associations, transforming into a purely constructive, even ethical stance. For Okoye, Nollywood's resistance to actively cultivating Western-style child stardom can and does coexist with local support for Justin Bieber, Miley Cyrus, and other "teen" imports. Refusing to generate a Nigerian Justin Bieber becomes, in other words, indistinguishable from systematically guarding against youth neuroses, but it also speaks to what Okoye sees as the familial atmosphere of a typical Nollywood film set. Describing her first experience with what she calls an "international project"—Afam Okereke's 2003 film *Sister Mary*, in which Okoye portays the eponymous nun—the star indicates that a minor transnationalism, one that traces a movement among West African countries and that involves a range of West African performers, provides a space for "protecting" the youngest and thus most vulnerable members of a film project, not necessarily limiting their participation but certainly preventing their maltreatment.[17] By bringing their multiculturalism to bear upon the down time between shots, a diversity of West African performers can also effectively ensure that no single conception of child welfare will win out. For Okoye, the pluralism of the *Sister Mary* set helped make families feel at home there, whatever their West African backgrounds.

However much its circumstances of production might have suggested an intergenerational multiculturalism, *Sister Mary* is hardly a kids' film. It does not, in fact, depict children at all, and so it did not require the participation of youth performers. Shot in Enugu with Nigerian, Beninese, Togolese, and Ghanaian talents, *Sister Mary* was cast according to a distinctly transnational ethos, with diverse performers who could confer upon the film a sense of a cooperative West Africa, one unified through the glue not simply of a common interest in Nollywood but also through a certain respect for the mobility of stardom. Because Oge Okoye is now one of numerous Nollywood icons who oversee far-reaching, youth-centered NGOs, her prominent, star-making presence in *Sister Mary* seems to anticipate her particular brand of itinerant philanthropy. The film would appear, in other words, to have offered a literal and figurative roadmap for Okoye, an especially philanthropic star. Her titular Sister Mary moves freely, at least at first, always modulating her saintly activism in accordance with her shifting geographical and cultural surroundings. Eventually, however, she settles upon southern Nigeria as the most important physical and affective site for her saintly operations. If that location similarly represents a nerve center for Nollywood's activist stars, it is because it remains very much the hub of the Nollywood industry itself—for better *and* for worse.

Child-focused philanthropy may indeed be transnational, but a Lagos meeting point will continue to be practical, as long as Nollywood production remains entrenched in that metropolis. Despite its much-publicized excursions into Sierra Leone, Benin, and Cameroon, Okoye's NGO, for instance, does most of its work in southern Nigeria, while—in a considerably more complicated reflection of transnationalism—Okoye herself divides her time among Lagos, where she shoots most of her films; London, where she and her children were born; and Belguim, where her husband is based. That this peripatetic actress became a star on the basis of *Sister Mary* is somewhat ironic, since the film's title character comes to embrace localism, proclaiming her profound commitment to an Enugu that "needs her," as well as vowing to combat the kind of travel bug that can lead to bad parenting. This rather striking tension between the itinerant Okoye and the ultimately immobile Sister Mary provides a powerful reminder of Nollywood stars' offscreen deviations from some of their most cherished and well-known characters. Though the role made her famous, Oge Okoye has not lived her life according to Sister Mary's mandates.

While it might seem obvious to point out that an actress is not a nun, Nollywood offers numerous examples of performers who have quit the industry in order to explore their religious roles. *Sister Mary* is no exception, providing a stunning, emotionally ravaged performance by an actress, Eucharia Anunobi, who would go on to become an evangelist minister. Fittingly, given Nollywood films' frequently Christian inflections, an individual's transition from perfomer to religious figure is typically presented (at least in Nigerian press accounts) as a natural or inevitable offscreen continuation of an on-screen saintliness, especially in the case of an actress like

Anunobi, who once portrayed good Christian women (in addition to villains or vamps). But even Anunobi's story expresses the contentious aspects of acting transnationalism—of performing an activist orientation toward Europe and the United States as well as to the sixteen countries of West Africa and beyond. When Anunobi accepted an award from an American Pentecostal organization in 2013, her local commitments were suddenly called into question; despite the globally circulating publicity that positions Pentecostalism as a truly transnational movement, local concerns about Westernization persist in southern Nigeria, recalling many of the debates that *Lady Gaga* embraces, and that center on the matter of cultural imperialism. In what direction does Anunobi's Christian philanthropy "flow"— toward the Philadelphia-based Jesus Embassy Network, which named her an Ambassador of Religious Peace and International Unity, or toward a more local, needier circuit of churches? Memories of *Sister Mary*, which so strongly suggests that Christian charity should be focused exclusively upon local concerns, were brought to bear upon the Anunobi whose evangelism attracts global attention. As always, the transnational appeal of a Nollywood star—even in her post-Nollywood, evangelical iteration—creates tensions that play out in complicated ways. And as references to the "old" *Sister Mary* suggest, these tensions can serve a retrospective function, helping keep Nollywood's earlier triumphs alive. Popular Nigerian press accounts tend to stress the similarities between Anunobi's offscreen evangelism and the unrestrained emotionality of her Nollywood performances. In the process, however, they threaten to essentialize her as naturally impassioned; they run the risk of suggesting that she was never a remotely conscious actress, but rather an unquestioning vessel for affective expression. Nevertheless, they emphatically point to the Nollywood past, drawing attention to skillful performances that should be studied as such.[18]

The contested relationship between a star's screen performances and her personal activities only intensifies when children enter the equation. Marrying in 2004 and becoming a mother shortly thereafter, Oge Okoye has been a one-woman advertisement for long-distance marriage and transnational parenting: with her husband in Belgium, she works primarily in Lagos (but also, on occasion, in Accra, New York, and Los Angeles), while her children follow her across continents (and enjoy dual citizenship, to boot). Honoring the contrasts between a Nollywood star's stated approach to child-rearing and the dedicatedly local, conservative commitments of one of her most beloved characters—in other words, separating Okoye from Sister Mary—can shed considerable light upon Nollywood stardom's defiance of primitivist conceptions. Contrary to Western essentialist assumption, Nollywood stars are not reducible to their roles—or even to the localism of some of their characters. Nevertheless, I frequently hear fellow academics referring to Nollywood star Nkem Owoh not by his own name but by that of his most famous film character, Osuofia, of Kingsley Ogoro's 2003 hit *Osuofia in London*.[19] Conflating this remarkably skilled star with Osuofia means not only denying Owoh's agency as an actor—his professional separation from a fictional character—but also avoiding an awareness of his other, diverse triumphs, such as his powerful work as a desperate apologist for 419 scams in Andy Amenechi's *The Master* (2005), or his award-winning performance in Tchidi Chikere's 2007 film *Stronger Than Pain*, in which he plays a passionate man unashamedly in love with his wife (played by Kate Henshaw). While referring to Owoh as Osuofia might well suggest an affectionate attachment to the role itself among scholars—akin to referring to Chinedu Ikedieze and Osita Iheme as Aki and Pawpaw—those same scholars are not apt to refer to a Hollywood star by the name of his most famous film character; "Leonardo DiCaprio" or "Tom Hanks" would surely suffice. If, as Jonathan Haynes has argued, those of us committed to the study of Nollywood should "decide collectively not to accept any critical work that does not cite films adequately, in accordance with normal professional protocols," then we should also be allergic to any attempt, however well-meaning, to erase the line between performer and role.[20]

Oge Okoye's many deviations from Sister Mary suggest not simply her agency and adaptability but also her nuanced, *embodied* philosophies of parenting and transnationalism. Added to her much-publicized experiences with her own kids is Okoye's work with the NGO that she herself developed, Positive Life Children, which gives her a further opportunity to complicate Sister Mary's localism. PLC is largely limited to Lagos for practical rather than ideological reasons; Okoye, who is heavily involved in the NGO's activities, shoots most of her films there. Ironically, when PLC made the trek into Sierra Leone in 2013, local newspapers identified its film-star administrator as "Oge Okoye of *Sister Mary*."[21] Contrary to the popular presumption that West African audiences are hungry only for new Nollywood films, "old

Nollywood" matters: it adds to the intertextuality of stardom, enriching an individual star image with an array of associations.

If stars' complicated public images, considered in conjunction with their long filmographies, suggest a constant give and take—a certain "structured polysemy," to adopt Richard Dyer's famous phrase—then maybe Nollywood will one day be able to balance an apparent popular appetite for child performers with its own, ever-shifting and always contentious entanglements with kids. Perhaps a remake of *Little Angel* will make use of a new youth performer, and perhaps producers will permit her to become a star by affording her the opportunity to walk the red carpet (at the Africa Magic Viewers' Choice Awards, say, or at a Silverbird event combining film fandom with child-focused philanthropy); perhaps she will be allowed to appear in a promotional capacity on Nigerian television, "selling" her films on programs as varied as *The Juice, The Glo G-Bam Show, VHS,* and *A.M. Express.* Perhaps a recontextualized *Miss Queen* will give its kid performers the top billing that they deserve, not necessarily denying the presence of adult stars but giving those older icons proper placement based upon screen time. Given the vagaries of stardom, the politics of screen credits will always be complicated. But as Stephanie Okereke discovered at the Port Harcourt premiere of her film *Nnenda,* a logical, justifiable alteration of an unaccountable credit sequence—one that corrects the suppression of a film's true star—can create positive publicity for Nollywood.

A credit sequence alone cannot reveal the nature of Nollywood's relationship to youth, however, no more than an individual plot can provide an entrée into debates that are ongoing and multidirectional. If one were to attempt to extrapolate a notion of Nollywood from the narrative of one of its most popular films—thereby skipping over the complex semiotics of stardom and ignoring the polemical aspects of reception and fandom—one would be left with a dramatized set of biases and also with the temptation to view them as reflective of the "real" Nigeria. From a consideration of the mutually contesting examples of Oge Okoye's stardom and of *Sister Mary*'s narrative, however, it is clear that the latter's localism is, if not exactly a joke, then certainly far from compulsary for Nollywood stars—even for those who, like Eucharia Anunobi, have become Nigerian evangelical icons. While it does not entail a direct representation of the dramas of youth, the narrative of *Sister Mary* suggests some of the negative effects of minor transnationalism upon children—effects that the film's star has worked to disprove both through her regional NGO as well as with her own style of itinerant parenting.

Specifically, *Sister Mary* shows what can happen when a desire to remain mobile within West Africa becomes synonymous with an abdication of parental responsibilities—when a mother who wants to travel from the Bight of Benin all the way to Niger decides to drop off her child in Enugu. Letting this sin propel the plot, *Sister Mary* displays anxieties not about Westernization or about tribalism within Nigeria (two more typical sources of child-centered narrative tensions), but about a wanderlust that restricts itself to West Africa. While such measures as the development of the Trans-West African Coastal Highway and the creation of INTELCOM (an Economic Community of West African States [ECOWAS] project designed to connect West African capitals through standardized media technologies) have famously embraced a utopian view of travel and connectivity, *Sister Mary* suggests that movement among ECOWAS countries is a risky proposition, one that the film communicates through a rather conservative, even misogynist injunction against mobile motherhood. As Okoye's case makes clear, however, Nollywood stars' child-focused offscreen actions can powerfully contest this localist approach, providing a series of productive semiotic collisions that together suggest the limitations of taking a strictly narratological view of Nollywood. Stars' transnational operations offer important alternatives both to individual films as well as to standard ways of critically positioning them.

Sister Mary begins with a young woman arriving by car in southern Nigeria, an infant girl in tow. Nervously and hurriedly, she hands the child over to the first person she sees, having tucked a note into the baby's blanket. Without so much as a rote goodbye, the woman swiftly escapes "to the north"—never to return. Left with an abandoned infant, Eucharia Anunobi's Nene asks, in voice-over, "Who is she? And where is she from?" Nene never finds out. Stuck with a stranger's baby, she begins to cry uncontrollably—not simply because she's suddenly burdened with a new and extreme responsibility, but also because she fears what her husband will say about the situation. Upon discovering that his wife is taking care of someone else's child, Clement (played by the deep-voiced Justus Esiri) begins berating her rather brutally, until she comes perilously close to a nervous breakdown. Significantly, however, the husband's "sin" is not simply that he is so mean to his Jesus-quoting wife. It is that he wants to travel, having, as he says, "earned vacation time." Knowing that Nene's sudden motherhood would make a trans-West African journey quite difficult—that a baby would weigh them down—Clement tries to drive his wife out of the house. Accusing her of having stolen the baby, he shouts insults into Nene's ear, until finally she must leave him, taking the baby with her. Significantly, this is one of the few instances in which the film endorses travel; here, it is positioned as a last resort—the only way of saving a baby.

Jumping ahead by nearly two decades, the film next portrays the consequences of Nene's decision to "follow fate"—the adult result of her unplanned mothering: the beautiful nun Sister Mary, who happens to be a miracle worker, curing diseases as easily as she breathes. Fittingly for a film that seems so resistant to even minor transnationalism, Sister Mary, following a kind of pilgrimage throughout West Africa, commits herself exclusively to local cases, arguing that "there is so much need" in her own backyard. A later, pivotal scene suggests that the situation is not so simple, however—that the film is in fact ambivalent about travel within West Africa. When Nene decides that it is time to tell Mary the story of her adoption, she reveals that her own child-toting itinerary was wide-ranging, "and for good reason," since it kept Nene and the infant Mary away from "the forces of evil." Even if a last resort, then, constant travel can keep demons at bay and can save a victimized child.

In *Sister Mary*, an appetite for travel leads to many things: for one woman, an orientation toward the north leads to an abdication of parental responsibility; for a selfish man, the desire to enjoy middle age by exploring West Africa compels him to abuse his wife; and for a woman who takes to the road in order to raise an abandoned baby, the journey leads to romantic fulfilment as well as to "real," biological motherhood. Nene, as is her dream, eventually finds Mary's father; much to her surprise, she falls in love with him, and the two give Mary a "miraculous" half-brother. Travel, then, is not in itself strictly good or bad, recalling Suzanne Gearhart's argument that transnationality "is not a panacea but rather a dilemma and a challenge."[22] Nollywood stars tend to meet that challenge in ways that do not necessarily correspond to the philosophies of their films, suggesting a multiplicity of potential approaches to youth empowerment.

Ironically, Oge Okoye's star-making performance in *Sister Mary* necessitated the exclusion of a child actress: the narrative purpose of the film is to reveal how an adult woman copes with the knowledge that she was abandoned as a baby. The film shifts from showing that baby, for all of a few opening scenes, to revealing the grown woman that the baby becomes. No middle developmental stage is represented, and so no child actress was required. In this way, *Sister Mary* both reflects a concern for child welfare—a concern that would inform but not restrict its star's eventual activism—and indicates a lack of interest in directly depicting kids. Childhood is both everywhere and nowhere in *Sister Mary*—both a steady discursive construction and a representational lacuna; it is both much-discussed and never seen. Perhaps that is why Okoye, in a further indication of how a Nollywood star image can contribute to the construction of a film's multiple meanings, has insisted in interviews that the set of *Sister Mary* offered a "family-friendly" atmosphere. At the level of personal recollection (retrospective magazine interviews clearly offering another means of keeping "old Nollywood" alive), she seems to be critiquing and counterbalancing *Sister Mary*'s concerns about the effects of transnationalism on children, claiming that, in fact, this "international production" was good for kids—even if it did not end up using them onscreen.[23]

If she has rarely been surrounded by children in her films, Okoye still embodies a star image that is distinctly open to the influence of young Africans. Unlike Genevieve Nnaji, Okoye has not played child roles while in her thirties, but she has, like Nnaji, posed for countless photographs with her youngest fans, as well as with the kids who come to her NGO for various forms of remedial education. Charity work continues to contribute to the construction of Nollywood stardom—not just discursively, giving a humanitarian spin to a star image, but also *visibly*, through photographs that suggest an intergenerational connection. Okoye's philanthropy, for instance, consistently places her among crowds of kids. More importantly, images of the star's work with PLC suggest an active suppression of her adult iconicity—an admirable willingness to assume a subsidiary position within a visual field: Okoye is always in the background of such shots, always a bit off center—sometimes buried or barely recognizable. Semiotically, these publicity images suggest that the kids matter the most—which is, of course, precisely as it should be. A star who seems to practice what she preaches, Oge Okoye does not need to dominate the arenas of philanthropy that her stardom has helped to establish.

If Tonto Dikeh's star image has sometimes centralized Hillary Clinton, leading to Nigerian magazine covers that position Dikeh's face next to Clinton's name and next to the American politician's words, then Oge Okoye's notion of a family-friendly transnationalism suggests one of Clinton's most famous catchphrases, allegedly borrowed from an unspecified African proverb—namely, that "it takes a village" to raise a child.[24] In Okoye's case, as implicitly in Clinton's, the village must be so expansive as to exceed the limitations of the local, creating a truly transnational space in which to develop healthy world citizens. As Hannah Hoechner notes, "the hope that imparting the requisite skills will turn [Nigerian children] into a productive labor force and responsible citizenry has been paired with fears of growing social tensions in case of a failure to do so"—fears that are arguably most pronounced when kids encounter Nollywood stardom, either as a discursive construction that combines glamour, erotic appeal, and "big money," or as a practically impossible professional path, one limited to a few "lucky" individuals.[25] Such fears are equally apparent when the publicizing of adult stars' charity work—a requisite part of raising awareness for their philanthropic campaigns—shines too bright or too distorting a light upon victimized kids, who in the process become accidental stars.

Increasingly, however, some of Nigeria's most vulnerable children are at the center of glitzy television productions, suggesting that Nollywood stardom represents the next logical step, especially given the historical synergy between the Nigerian film and TV industries. Consider, for instance, *The Melody Shelters TV Show*, a reality program that premiered on Nigeria's Silverbird Television in the spring of 2012. Billed as "the *Nigerian Idol* of orphanages," the series is a competition program involving musically gifted orphans from all around Nigeria (and even from Benin and Cameroon). Like the wildly successful *Glo Soccer Academy*, a Globacom-produced reality competition series that brings together Nigerian, Ghanaian, and Beninese boys between the ages of fourteen and seventeen, *Melody Shelters* embraces a relatively broad youth category while remaining open to the participation of kids from outside of Nigeria. So far, however, publicity has centered upon Nigerian orphanages only, suggesting that *Melody Shelters* is part of a conscious effort to improve the country's image vis-à-vis its parentless children. Not surprisingly, Nollywood stars have figured prominently in this publicity, as well as throughout the series itself. *Melody Shelters*' first episode features, among several other icons, Rita Dominic, Nse Ikpe-Etim, and Stephanie Okereke, the latter providing a powerful reminder of her activist *Nnenda* character, who struggles to reform orphanages throughout Nigeria.

Melody Shelters consistently uses Nollywood's adult icons to endorse the program's capacity to uncover "the stars of tomorrow." That such future stars can, according to the series, be found in African orphanages suggests a distinctly egalitarian view of entertainment-industry success, one dependent not upon money or connections but instead upon talent and hard work. In her talking-head testimonial, Nse Ikpe-Etim offers another determinant: diversity, whether of ethnicity, culture, religion, or language. For her part, Nigerian singer Keffi, one of the series' judges, offers a familiar conception of stardom-as-labor, announcing that *Melody Shelters* provides "proper training" for emerging talents, while Rita Dominic and Stephanie Okereke are both on hand to deliver the series' tagline, "Leaving No One Behind," which in the context of a reality competition program suggests less a charitable munificence than a commitment to finding the proverbial needle in a haystack.

Articulated alongside this search-for-a-star framework is a certain investment in discourses of realism—in the notion that *Melody Shelters* simply "reveals" the untutored talents of countless orphans through a process of ongoing, observational, *vérité*-style recording rather than of conscious and commercialized selection (a cherry-picking of the "best" or most photogenic kids). As Adonijah Owiriwa, one of the program's producers, declares during the first episode, "I embarked on a tour of orphanages . . . and I noticed that all of these orphanages have organized singing groups. When you visit an orphanage, you make any donations or any presentations to them. Before you leave, you see all the kids come around you, gather around you, and *sing*. This actually runs across all oprhanages." In this way, Owiriwa positions *Melody Shelters* as less a well-planned competition program than a "hands-off" documentary—less a product of commercialized picking and choosing than a reflection of "what orphanages actually are and actually do." As Owiriwa's statements suggest, *Melody Shelters* expresses a series of tensions: between essentialism (the notion that "all orphanages," and therefore all orphans, are alike) and antiessentialism (the "reality" that some orphans are more talented than others, and that their "dramatic differences" require "proper training"); between localism (a stated commitment to orphanages in southern Nigeria) and pan-Africanism (a frequently articulated interest in "the continent's future leaders," as well as an openness to orphans from Benin and Cameroon); and between star quality as something that "someone is simply born with" and stardom itself as the product of a conscious, laborious construction of meanings.

Throughout *Melody Shelters*, Nollywood stars dispense advice to the program's child contestants, but they also endorse the broadly egalitarian view of stardom that sees orphanages as potential sources of "tomorrow's talents." For Rita Dominic, the *Melody Shelters* contestants together constitute an underrepresented majority in Nigeria—a group that is both conspicuous and invisible, both expanding "on the ground" and disappearing from the purview of media representations. "These orphans deserve an opportunity that will maximize their full potential, just like any other kid out there," says Dominic on *Melody Shelters*, directly addressing the series' viewer and suggesting a certain defense of its content—a defense designed, perhaps, to preempt public criticism. It is, of course, precisely as an "*Idol* for orphanages" that *Melody Shelters* raises numerous nagging questions: Is it seemly to place orphans in competition with one another? Is it remotely appropriate to judge them, in *Idol* fashion, based upon standards of performance and professionalism? Or does *Melody Shelters* offer a means of de-essentializing Nigerian orphans, presenting them apart from an Afro-pessimist conception of disease and mistreatment? The line between empowerment and exploitation has rarely been as fine as it appears on *Melody Shelters*, where vulnerable children confront the complex determinants of stardom.

Whatever its contradictions, the series suggests that when Nollywood stardom intersects with youth subjects, the matter of transnationalism is never far behind. In 2010, official events commemorating of the fiftieth anniversary of Nigerian independence relied heavily upon children, bringing Nollywood's biggest stars together with the nameless young ones said to represent "the future of Nigeria"—the girls and the boys who will one day, presumably, participate in centennial celebrations. However, in a sobering indication of the persistence of Afro-pessimism, a preponderance of Nigerian newspapers and magazines have adopted a less-than-celebratory approach to these events, suggesting several untenable aspects. As the policy analyst and writer Ike Okonta noted, "Nigerians do not quite know how best to mark the fiftieth anniversary of their country's independence"—a confusion stemming not simply from a widespread awareness of the realities of neocolonialism (realities so memorably confronted in the star-driven *BlackBerry Babes* trilogy as well as in *Lady Gaga*), but also from a lack of consensus about how to position Nigeria's multiculturalism in relation to transnational circuits of cultural exchange.[26]

If Nollywood stars, by so famously expressing a number of complex identities, help to publicize Nigerian multiculturalism for broad African as well as diasporic audiences, then children, essentialized along generational lines, may continue to seem strictly metonymic of vulnerability and suffering, precisely because they lack the antiessentialist media platforms of Nnaji, Okoye, Okereke, and others. Western media outlets, for their part, tended to condemn Nigeria's golden jubilee celebrations for using youth performers at a time when, according to *The Guardian* (UK), "26 percent of Nigerian children [were] malnourished." Since "Nigeria would need until at least 2025 to meet the [Millennium Development Goals] target to halve child hunger," numerous Western publications suggested that the golden jubilee's "celebratory tone [was] misplaced."[27] No one questioned the participation of Nollywood's well-known adult stars in the fiftieth anniversary celebrations, however. No prominent publication accused these stars of misrepresenting their compatriots—arguably because it is nearly axiomatic that Nollywood stars reflect Nigeria's vast diversity, offering a variety of well-defined, iconic identities. When kids, by contrast, are mobilized in nameless, undifferentiated ways, they embolden commentators to collapse them into Afro-pessimist pronouncements. Couched as the products of statistical certainties, such pronouncements read Nigeria's underage masses as metonymic of tragedy—an approach that could perhaps be counterbalanced by the development of a diversity of well-differentiated youth stars.

Some familiar players have recently attempted to do just that, using children to neutralize the prevailing Western view of Nigeria as a fount of underage pain and bringing their own notions of transnationalism to bear upon the subject of African youth. Globacom, for example, has employed more and more children in its ad campaigns, but, like Nollywood, the corporation has neglected to credit, if not to compensate, the children whose images it uses. Whereas Van Vicker's name is both visible and audible throughout his commercials for Globacom, the names of youth participants are conspicuously missing from the corporation's similar ads, strengthening the sense that children lack distinct identities and are thus interchangeable. However, in other, crucial ways, Globacom has attempted to correct an essentialist conception of Nigerian kids, deploying youth performers who, while they remain nameless, nevertheless reflect a remarkable ethnic, cultural, religious, and linguistic diversity. Like the stars who speak Standard English, Pidgin, Igbo, Ibibio, Bini, and Yorùbá in their ads, thereby demonstrating both their own differences and adaptability as well as the cultural pluralism of southern Nigeria, the several dozen children who appear in Globacom's 2013 commercial "One Nigeria" are distinguished through dress (from the *iborun* and *gele* veils of Yorùbá girls to the *hijab* of a Hausa Muslim), language, as well as through the substance of their respective speeches (with one little boy acclaiming Nigeria's status as "the fifth biggest oil producer in the world," and another focusing proudly upon art and culture). As in *Melody Shelters*, the lines between empowerment and exploitation, and between realism and fantasy, can seem perilously fine in this particular commercial. As one user commented on Globacom's YouTube channel, drawing attention to the commercial's contradictory aspects, "What da f*k! This same oil keeping us Nigerians corrupt is mentioned by a kid as one of the things that make Nigeria great? I remember being fed this same line as a child, & based solely on this I thought Nigeria was the best country. Then I grew up."[28]

Though enmeshed in an obvious Afro-pessimism, the YouTube comment powerfully signals the less-than-seemly aspects of any promotional co-optation of children. Indeed, it is more than a bit distressing to hear a small child tout the importance of politically vexed and environmentally devastating oil extraction. In highlighting the alleged lack of agency of children—their susceptibility to false statements and adult manipulation—the YouTube comment dismisses some of the Globacom commercial's specifically antiessentialist tactics. However effective these tactics may be on their own terms, the commercial's title ("One Nigeria") would seem to contradict or at least complicate its commitment to diversity, as would the presence of President Goodluck Jonathan, who materializes toward the end to announce his intentions to "unify Nigeria": "My government is committed to the true transformation of Nigeria," he says, "for the benefit of the present and future generations. My mission is to consolidate the unity of our nation." Suggesting some of the lasting tensions between Négritude and nationalism, the commercial's address swings between endorsing pan-Africanism and affirming the need for all Nigerians "to work as one . . . for the strength of the nation." Still more complicated is the commercial's use of the term "centennial celebration"—its open orientation toward the 100-year anniversary (in 2014) of Britain's colonialist amalgamation of northern and southern protectorates. Since such amalgamation was hardly unifying—since it did not preclude the administrative separation of North, South, and Lagos Colony—and since it was, more importantly, a *colonialist* operation, it seems questionable to so celebrate its 100-year anniversary, although Nigeria's Federal Ministry of Information, without so much as a hint of irony, maintains a steady stream of information regarding what it refers to as "Nigeria's Centennial."

If recognizing that dubious marker has given Globacom an opportunity to contribute to the ongoing, contentious use of children as complex avatars of Nigeria's future, then so have events commemorating a certain Nollywood milestone. Throughout 2012, regional celebrations of Nollywood's twentieth anniversary, which ranged from Globacom-sponsored festivities in Lagos to low-key gatherings in Accra and Dakar, used children to represent "Nollywood's tomorrow" as well as to enact a new transnationalism, one dependent upon West African and diasporic media flows to carry Nollywood's complex messages to potentially resistant consumers. In early 2012, in an obvious attempt to supersede satellite television as a youth-driven agent of pan-Africanism, Globacom hired talented teen rollerbladers from multiple African countries, bringing them together for a series of ads touting the corporation's "unsurpassed, lighting-fast" delivery and "limitless" mobile data service—as well as its clear connections to Nollywood's "legacy." Later that same year, the young South African skaters Chris van der Merwe, Earl Abrahams, and Pontsho Sekiti joined the equally young Nigerian skaters J Swagz da Sugarboy and Skate Crash for Glo's big-budget television commercial "Wheelz 4 Mealz," which imagines the prodigiously gifted rollerbladers as a team of fast-food delivery boys whose speed—revealed in elaborate shots of their street moves—is said to mirror that of Globacom itself.

Metaphors for mobile data delivery, the "Wheelz 4 Mealz" boys are also symbolic of the next generation of Nollywood stars. Shot on 35 mm, the commercial not only assumes a cinematic style suggestive of Globacom's recent forays into Nollywood film production (such as 2012's *Phone Swap*); it also mobilizes established stars in a torch-passing capacity: in a brief, almost subliminal shot, Globacom brand ambassador Rita Dominic can be seen from the back seat of her chauffeured car marveling at the talents of the teen boys who 'blade by. Even beyond their spectacular skating skills, these kids seem suitable heirs to certain Nollywood traditions—fitting future film stars. With their contrasting costumes and accents, with their common use of Pidgin, but most importantly with their sheer adaptability—which the commercial dramatizes in visual terms as the teens weave their way through busy streets, executing certain classic moves and riskily improvising others—the rollerbladers make a strong case for shared stardom, illustrating some of the most exciting, Nollywood-inspired ways of tracing a glamorous migration.

With its conspicuous and growing presence throughout West Africa, Globacom invests in Nollywood stars both literally and symbolically, regularly generating commercial advertisements that double as sincere celebrations of a number of remarkable talents. If the typical Globacom ad campaign touts the corporation's alleged reliability as a service provider, it also suggests that Nollywood stars are similarly dependable—consistently entertaining, at the very least, and largely because they are so versatile as performers. "You can count on us!" screams a 2012 ad featuring Rita Dominic and Funke Akindele—ostensibly a reference to Globacom's corporate stewardship, but also a statement that speaks to the authority of skilled movie stars. However, as Globacom's marketing directors well know, there is a fine line between extoling a star and ignoring her competition—the up-and-coming talents who stand a good chance of becoming famous, especially with Globacom in their corner. That is partly why the corporation, in working with Nollywood stars, limits its contracts to no more than a few years. While Nigerian gossip columnists like to allege that certain venerable stars have been "sacked," the truth is often less dramatic.

Whatever its shortcomings, and however much it may seem a strictly, irredeemably commercial enterprise, it is clear that Globacom understands something significant about stardom: that making way for the new can easily involve honoring the old. Consider Rita Dominic's role in the "Wheelz 4 Mealz" commercial, which she shot toward the end of her tenure as a Globacom brand ambassador. It is her hallowed presence that seems to anoint the rollerblading boys as beautiful new talents—to consecrate them as stars —and it is she who first notices them after they've carefully donned protective gear. It is almost as if her aura—the poise that she has perfected over the years—has inspired the young skaters not simply to work hard but also to shield themselves. Strapping on helmets and kneepads, the boys become symbolic of the sheer dangers of stardom, but also of the possibility of emerging unscathed from fame's vagaries. Crucially, Dominic is there—an established star who, without necessarily ceding professional ground, can lead by example, doing her part to safeguard the fates of a few newcomers. If their names are not nearly as familiar as Dominic's, then perhaps Globacom, with its ubiquitous ad campaigns, will help to change that.

One of the ironies of contemporary African cinema is that, with Nollywood generating iconic movie stars whose names are known the world over, child performers remain as anonymously prominent as they were in the days of *The Boy Kumasenu* (Sean Graham, 1952), a production of the colonial Gold Coast Film Unit that employs an adult narrator—British actor Russell Napier—who singlehandedly provides the voices of a range of young characters.[29] To its credit, *The Boy Kumasenu* is that rare colonial film whose closing title cards offer the names of all its child performers, including Nortey Engmann, the Cape Coast schoolboy who plays the title role. Engmann does not receive star billing, however; that distinction goes to the invisible Napier, ensconced in his recording suite in London. Given their plainly imperialist intentions, there is no reason to believe that the British filmmakers were eager to elevate Engmann—to present him as a performer in his own right, rather than a simple vessel for their artistry. A fiction film that employs multiple documentary devices, *The Boy Kumasenu* gives the spectator little reason to suspect that Engmann is not the character he plays, and I have found no written reference to the actor's presence in the film—to his precise (if silent) contributions as a nonprofessional performer. Perhaps, then, the appearance of Engmann's name in the closing credits is less an honorable gesture than an accident or afterthought.

Furthermore, as the case of *Miss Queen* makes painfully clear, visible billing cannot ensure stardom for child performers—or even simple respect for their artistic centrality; nor can such minor African Movie Academy Award categories as "Best Child Actor" and "Best Young/Promising Actor," which, apart from reflecting an alarming gender bias, raise important questions about their precise parameters. However, lest this perplexing scenario suggest an essentially anonymous Africanity—a lapse endemic to sub-Saharan cultural conditions—it is worth reemphasizing some of the startling, understudied parallels between African art films and Italian neorealism: if the names of *Yaaba*'s child actors elude memory, it is likely that the names of *Shoeshine*'s young thespians do, too; if no one can name the underage performers who appear prominently in Mahamat-Saleh Haroun's *Abouna* (2002), it is perhaps equally difficult to identify the boy at the center of *Bicycle Thieves* (Vittorio de Sica, 1948). Neither Italian neorealism nor the first wave of African auteur films managed to inspire widespread awareness of child performers, even as both developed vital iconographies of youth in peril. Having established its own, conspicuous star system, Nollywood stands as strong a chance as any global film industry of bucking this trend. It did it once, with the extraordinary William Uchemba and Sharon Ezeamaka; it will surely do it again.

Afterword

Honoring Nollywood Stars

Now that Nollywood has succeeded in supplying a long roster of African movie stars, it is worth reflecting upon those stars' semiotic effects. That the industry's onscreen talents are globally famous is not arguable; Omotola Jalade-Ekeinde's reality series receives approximately 150 million viewers per episode, and the ubiquity of Globacom billboards guarantees a basic familiarity with stars throughout West Africa. For some Nollywood fans, however, there may be a fine line between a glamorous migration and a distracting set of impossible and perhaps appalling privileges. A star's special mobility may well remove her from the harsh realities with which hundreds of millions of Africans must daily live, thus widening the gap between producers and consumers of an African popular art. As I write this, ethnic conflict in South Sudan is culminating in a humanitarian crisis of staggering proportions, while, one thousand miles to the west, terrorist violence continues to wreak havoc in Nigeria. In light of these tragic circumstances, it may seem, at best, painfully naive to suggest that mere movie stars might play a part in combating interethnic prejudice or in repairing the damage done to Nigeria's global image by recent, rather alarming political measures, many of which threaten to turn the country once again into a bona fide pariah state. These of course include President Goodluck Jonathan's decision to sign a law imposing up to fourteen years in prison for, among other alleged offenses, publicly self-identifying as gay, convening a gay-themed meeting, and promoting membership in a gay-rights group. So draconian is this multipronged law—an undeniably Western-derived legitimation of anti-gay violence—that many gay Nigerians are presently scrambling to conceal any evidence that might link them to the so-called "public visibility of homosexuality." The wealthy, well-connected ones have likely expatriated; others must simply improvise, acting out a series of idiosyncratic ways of remaining in the closet, and keeping their keenly defined identities very much under wraps while performing strange and ever-shifting "apolitical" personae for legal public consumption.

Against such an odiously censorious political backdrop, will Nollywood stars not be required to restrict the cultural meanings that they can embody in their films, and that they might promote through various platforms of authorized publicity? I do not think so. Over the past two decades, Nollywood stardom has proven prodigiously impervious to the most monolithic of political injunctions—marvelously immune to paralyzing, pigeonholing proclivities. While some stars have not exactly taken kindly to my own identity as a gay man, furnishing the familiar, essentialist assertion that homosexuality is un-African, others have candidly and cogently described what they have learned through accepting queer-identified roles—what the process of portraying lesbian characters has taught them about eroticism in general, and about sexual prejudice in particular. If a masculinist actor of a certain age once smiled condescendingly at my "misplaced" interest in queer Nollywood, then several scholars have played a similar game, telling me in no uncertain terms that I am imposing a Western and personal interpretation upon a media phenomenon that, rooted in Africa, is by definition straight-identified. However, as is now widely known—thanks in large part to the pioneering work of Lindsey Green-Simms and Unoma Azuah—Nollywood films are *deliberately* rich in representations of queerness, and even the most seemingly conservative concede that gay men and lesbians, far from being "un-African," in fact exist throughout the continent, where they proudly claim the labels of (among many others) Cameroonian, Ghanaian, Ugandan, Senegalese, and, yes, Nigerian. "You know how many people—including married women—are into this?" asks Dakore Egbuson's lesbian-identified Camilla in *Emotional Crack* as she seduces Stephanie Okereke's Crystal. Produced exactly one decade later, the star-driven *Girls on Fire* seems an elaboration and confirmation of that confidently rhetorical question, as it traces the efforts of its title characters to target and sexually satisfy closeted Nigerian housewives. By way of comparison, how many mainstream American films concede the existence of more than one lesbian, let alone of a nationwide cohort of closeted married women? How many approach the persistent politics of the closet at all, let alone with the blunt forcefulness of *Girls on Fire*? At the center of a revolutionary industry, a skilled Nollywood star can play just about any imaginable role and can, more to the point, play *against* any extant cultural trend or political position, even one that threatens by law to collapse queerphobia into a set of strictly defined Nigerian national traits.

Stardom remains a tricky business, however, and there have been minor embarrassments as well as major mishaps. During preproduction on his adaptation of Chimamanda Ngozi Adichie's novel *Half of a Yellow Sun*, Nigerian director Biyi Bandele cast actress Thandie Newton as Olanna—a lead role that many believed ought to have gone to a Nollywood star. Compounding the problem, Bandele hired Genevieve Nnaji to play a relatively minor role—a move that seemed distinctly condescending, as if Bandele and his British backers were throwing Nollywood a bone, even as they were trying to tell a very Nigerian story and, in fact, preparing to shoot in Nigeria. (They were also, perhaps, preparing to borrow a few of Nollywood's own representational tactics, such as the recurrent use of archival footage and radio broadcasts to help dramatize the Biafran War in Izu Ojukwu's 2004 film *Across the Niger*, which Bandele's *Half of a Yellow Sun* resembles.) That said, it is Nnaji who triumphs in the finished film, infusing her five minutes of screen time with a dizzying diversity of performance techniques, from clipped diction to drunkenly slurred speech. Indeed, Nnaji seems the most vivid and most electric presence in *Half of a Yellow Sun*—an impressive advertisement for Nollywood stardom.

Promoting the film on Canadian television, however, Nnaji managed to jokingly suggest that black Africans are, by definition, "extremely dramatic" —a statement that did not exactly endear her to her colleagues, especially since it seemed to constitute a kind of apology for Nollywood's theatrics. One of those colleagues, Stella Damasus, has made her own controversial remarks on television, angrily debating Nigerian senator Ahmad Yerima on the topic of child marriage. On an episode of Al Jazeera's *The Stream*, Damasus upset many viewers by appearing to essentialize Islamic jurists, mischaracterizing Muslim northern Nigeria even as she purported to speak for the region's underage female inhabitants. A prominent exponent of efforts to end child abuse in Nigeria, Damasus has aligned herself with the popular, hashtag-dependent Twitter campaigns "Child Not Bride" and "Bring Back Our Girls," demonstrating a commitment to causes that have galvanized internet users across the globe. For some of Damasus's fans, this a sincere commitment, and nothing less than a noble pursuit; for others, it smacks of opportunism, and Damasus, who was born and raised in southern Nigeria, is no more an expert on northern girls than fellow activist Anne Hathaway. Whatever Damasus's intentions, one thing seems clear: Nollywood stars are willing to co-opt trending topics at least as frequently as any other internet users, and they stand to incite at least as much controversy in the process.

I credit Nollywood stars with, at the very least, serving as positive role models, particularly for young African women who want to escape the oppressive circuits of gender essentialism and sexual discrimination but who otherwise might not know how. My evidence for the empowering effect on teen girls of Omotola, Funke, Uche, and others is almost entirely anecdotal, but it is awe-inspiring: living in Dakar, I ran into a group of young Senegalese women who had just formed a support group for girls newly diagnosed with HIV. Citing the film *Jénífà* as their principle inspiration, these women talked about the title character's commitment to medical reform and social change in ways that, I am ashamed to admit, led me to suspect that they were unaware of the actress-screenwriter behind her. "You mention Jénífà," I said, "but what about Funke Akindele? Are you a fan?" I will never forget the response that arrived like a bolt of humbling lightning: "Listen, I wouldn't talk about a film character as if she were real if she weren't played by someone as good as Funke. Okay?" I must have blushed.

Thus chastened, I steered the conversation into a slightly different direction, by saying a few celebratory words about *I Need to Know*, the mid-1990s Nigerian television program that is an obvious precursor of *Jénífà*, inasmuch as it anticipates the later film's ultimate focus on sexual and reproductive health education, especially for young women. Making her dazzling acting debut in the series' central role, the teenaged Funke Akindele managed to suggest, often simultaneously, her character's sheer intellectual curiosity, budding libidinal interests, and eagerness to escape the stereotypes of girlhood threatening to prevent her from comprehending her sexual impulses—all while flashing her now-iconic smile. Produced over a decade later, the film *Jénífà* comes to a close with quotations from Kofi Annan, but also with Akindele's own impassioned appeals to the spectator, which begin with the star's trademark swagger and end with a moving tribute to people living with HIV/AIDS:

> The movie *Jénífà* obviously has made you laugh, but the reality of HIV/AIDS is the rationale behind it. AIDS is killing us in Africa. The AIDS pandemic is the world's deadliest undeclared war, and Africa has so far borne its brunt... This is not a battle that one person or one part of the society can fight alone. We cannot leave [it] up to the medical community only; it will take the combined efforts of all of us... AIDS is REAL, so show love to people living with HIV/AIDS.

One could hardly ask for a more urgent, apposite entreaty, and Akindele's words resonate both with the film's ultimately activist narrative as well as with her electrifying offscreen projects. In 2011, the star established The Jénífà Foundation, an NGO that aims to inspire "a culture of self-reliance among Nigerian youth," and that works to encourage children to use their "talent and intelligence to achieve their set goals without getting involved in social vices." Later that same year, Akindele opened the Scene One School of Drama, a Lagos vocational program for disadvantaged youth. In December, 2013, Scene One held its first graduation ceremony, at which Akindele was joined by fellow Nollywood icons (and activists) Uche Jombo and Eniola Badmus in celebrating the achievements of twenty-eight newly minted alums. Fittingly, in delivering her valedictory address, Akindele reminded graduates that, whether they had studied acting, screenwriting, directing, or fashion design, their Scene One education had been organized along the lines of the icon's own multidirectional self-development, and according to the equally expansive contours of Nollywood's remarkable star system. Indebted as much to her experiences at Moshood Abiola Polytechnic and the University of Lagos (where she took degrees in mass communications and law, respectively) as to her wide-ranging involvement in Nollywood's industrial development, Funke Akindele's youth-centered school is structured to provide innumerable strategies of self-empowerment and to promote a courageously iconoclastic adaptability—the emancipating pursuit of ever more glamorous, self-respecting, boundary-shattering migrations.

Nollywood, then known as "Nigerian video," first entered my life through its stars: living at the intersection of major Liberian and Somali diasporas, I found myself borrowing a VHS copy of *Glamour Girls* from a friend who had recently emigrated from Monrovia. I was twelve years old. I remember well the waxen cardboard sheath that protected the cassette inside, and that displayed the names and faces of some remarkable women: Liz Benson, Barbara Udoh, Gloria Anozie, and Jennifer Okere. These four stars, among many others, were identified as such before the industry itself had a name—before the term "Nollywood" had even been coined. Today, as during its inaugural stages, the industry might seem to lack certain professional standards—might appear to cannibalize and to plagiarize, generating a succession of purely commercialized, ephemeral messes from which no artistic or pedagogical value might be extracted. However, as I hope to have made reasonably clear with this book, one would have to be a rigid, Eurocentric film snob to see Nollywood as valueless.

Actors—even Western ones—know better. In my circles of close friends and casual acquaintances, there isn't a single professional performer who doesn't marvel, often enviously, at the manifold opportunities that the Nollywood industry extends to its star thespians, for whom the concept of a dry spell—of a dearth of scripts—is seemingly so foreign as to appear absurd. Nollywood's extreme productivity—renowned or notorious, depending upon one's point of view—is such that its stars are always working, always testing, always tweaking. If dissatisfaction should ever strike, the transnationalism that the industry promotes and relies upon and that often obliges stars to travel, can also inspire them to pursue new opportunities—as when Stephanie Okereke repaired to New York City to study filmmaking, and then, degree in hand, moved to southern California to shoot her own feature. Boundary-defying stars like Okereke have something to teach performers of all stripes. Hollywood's female film stars continue (quite rightly) to complain: where are the plum roles for women? What might a self-respecting actress *do* with yet another stock role? The African stars to whom this book is dedicated and who gave it life are not likely to ask those questions. They have always embodied the answers. What they stand to accomplish in the years to come will undoubtedly demand attention.

NOTES

INTRODUCTION

1. Quoted in Ahluwalia, *Politics and Postcolonial Theory*, 23.
2. For more on this initiative, see Connor Ryan, "Nollywood and the Limits of Informality," 181–83.
3. Stam and Shohat, *Unthinking Eurocentrism*, 17.
4. Diawara, *African Cinema*, viii.
5. Larkin, *Signal and Noise*, 222.
6. Quoted in Ukadike, *Black African Cinema*, 144–145.
7. Ibid., 144–145.
8. Ibid., 145.
9. Ebony, "'Countdown at Kusini,'" 94.
10. Barber, "Popular Arts in Africa," 23.
11. Jedlowski, "From Nollywood to Nollyworld," 31.
12. Haynes, "The Nollywood Diaspora," 88.
13. Mbembe, *On the Postcolony*, 102.
14. In posing this question, I am obviously indebted to Brian Larkin, who, in *Signal and Noise*, asks "what a theory of media would look like if it began from Nigeria rather than Europe or the United States," 253.
15. In *Multiculturalism, Postcoloniality, and Transnational Media*, 7.
16. Adesokan, "Nollywood: Outline of a Trans-ethnic Practice," 116–117.
17. Ibid., 121–22.
18. Soyinka-Airewele, "Insurgent Transnational Conversations in Nigeria's 'Nollywood' Cinema," 117.
19. Ibid., 113–14.
20. Fuss, *Essentially Speaking*, 1.
21. Bryce, "*Elmina*: Obroni Art or Popular Melodrama," 139.
22. Tariq Modood, "Anti-Essentialism, Multiculturalism, and the 'Recognition' of Religious Groups," 179. Hall quoted on 179.
23. Corliss, "Omotola Jalade-Ekeinde."

24. Gearhart, "Inclusions," 38–39.
25. As Carmen McCain rightly reminds me, "[Nollywood] films don't always resist tribalism; sometimes, they enact it." McCain notes that Nollywood's "epic" films (such as those about ancient Igbo royalty) tend to be "a bit essentializing in [their] vision of pristine kingdoms." She also adds that she has "seen Hausa films that essentialize Tuaregs and other ethnic groups, and often the Hausa 'maigadi' in English-language films is essentialized as an ignorant buffon." Personal correspondence, December 4, 2013.
26. For more on this particular component of postcolonial theory, see Shohat, "Notes on the 'Post-Colonial.'"
27. Adesokan, "Nollywood," 117.
28. Fanon, *The Wretched of the Earth*, 11.
29. Corliss, "Omotola Jalade-Ekeinde."
30. Larkin, *Signal and Noise*; McCain, "Kannywood, the Growth of a Nigerian-language Industry" and "Nollywood, Kannywood, and a Decade of Hausa Film Censorship"; See also Adamu, "Transgressing Boundaries."
31. For more, see the edited collection *Global Nollywood*.
32. Lawrence, *The Passion of Montgomery Clift*, 142.
33. Naremore, *Acting in the Cinema*, 263.
34. iROKtv interview with Dikeh, conducted in October 2012. See http://www.youtube.com/watch?v=eCgZ8QrWWBc
35. Haynes, "Nollywood in Lagos, Lagos in Nollywood Films," 139.
36. Okome, *Onome*, 149.
37. Dyer, *Stars*, 1.
38. Mojúbàolú Olufúnké Okome and Olufemi Vaughan, "West African Migrations and Globalization: Introduction," 2.
39. Jedlowski, "From Nollywood to Nollyworld," 32.
40. Diawara, "Toward a Regional Imaginary in Africa," 124.
41. In Jedlowski, "From Nollywood to Nollyworld," 32.

1. FROM YORÙBÁ TO YOUTUBE

1. Sereda, "Curses, Nightmares, and Realities," 200.
2. Kernan, *Coming Attractions*, 126.
3. Gray, *Show Sold Separately*, 74.
4. A good example of a film whose opening-credit sequence is lengthy, elaborate, and revealing of the politics of star billing is Moses Ebere's *Miss Queen* (2012).
5. Wilson, "Reality Television Celebrity," 421, 427.
6. Soyinka, "A Name is More Than the Tyranny of Taste."
7. See Burr, *Gods Like Us*.
8. For an overview of the discipline, see Marsha Orgeron, "Media Celebrity in the Age of the Image."
9. See Green-Simms and Azuah, "The Video Closet."
10. Jones Magazine, "Brains & Beauty."
11. Haynes, "Nollywood in Lagos, Lagos in Nollywood Films"; Haynes, "What Is to Be Done?"; Onookome Okome, "Nollywood and Its Critics"; Barber, "Popular Arts in Africa."
12. Orgeron, "Media Celebrity in the Age of the Image," 214.
13. Haynes, "Nollywood in Lagos, Lagos in Nollywood Films," 138, 140.

14. Funke Akindele, for instance, has used both her screenwriting and acting skills to tweak her most iconic role (that of Jénífà), occasioning considerable press coverage throughout anglophone West Africa. See Okiche, "Funke Kan! Nigeria Kan!"
15. See Samuel Olatunji, "The New Nollywood."
16. See Golden Icons, "Uche Jombo: Exclusive Interview."
17. For more on literacy (and, for that matter, the English language) in relation to Nollywood production and reception, see Adejunmobi, "English and the Audience of an African Popular Culture."
18. Golden Icons, "Uche Jombo: Exclusive Interview," 18.
19. See Ouellette and Murray, "Introduction."
20. Ogundele, "From Folk Opera to Soap Opera," 110.
21. Tell Communications Limited, *Tell*, 14.
22. Babson Ajibade notes that "some actors [as distinct from stars] get as little as 10,000 naira, or 83 US dollars," per movie. Ajibade, "Nigerian Videos and Their Imagined Western Audiences," 269.
23. See Olatunji, "*Kajola* Sparks Trouble at Silverbird, Ozone."
24. Genevieve, "Meet the Elliots," 7.
25. Ibid.
26. Given the ascendancy of the Nollywood star system, it is surprising that few scholars have addressed it in detail. Carmen McCain's article "Video Exposé" represents a rare attempt to address Nollywood's awareness of its own, celebrity-centered culture of upward mobility—an awareness that McCain finds reflected in a series of self-referential films about Nigerian media. Lindsey Green-Simms, in her essay "Hustlers, Home-Wreckers, and Homoeroticism," focuses on those films (most of which belong to Nollywood's popular "campus" genre) that use the glamor and sex appeal of female stars to craft a cautionary—and ultimately misogynist—pedagogy. Finally, "The Video Closet," which Green-Simms co-wrote with Unoma Azuah, considers the role of deliberate repetition in Nollywood's star system. For instance, the authors argue that Nollywood producers frequently seek to develop a star by solidifying his or her image through a series of similar roles, as when the actress Stephanie Okereke became one of the industry's top choices for lesbian roles following her success in the gay-themed films *Emotional Crack* and *Beautiful Faces*. The authors also point out that Mercy Johnson's stardom has been essential to the development of the lesbian comedy genre, and vice versa—suggesting, in other words, that genrefication and star-shaping are mutually supportive processes in Nollywood.
27. deCordova, *Picture Personalities*; Martin Shingler, *Star Studies*.
28. See Purefoy, "'Nollywood Love.'"
29. See, for example, Gray, "Nigeria On-Screen."
30. Purefoy, "'Nollywood Love.'"
31. Larkin, *Signal and Noise*, 114.
32. Burchette, "World's 12 Sexiest Accents."
33. For more on the complex connections between Nollywood and Ghanaian films, see Carmela Garritano, *African Video Movies and Global Desires*, 154–94.
34. "Cynthia Ihebie's Project Fame Wild Card Entry . . . ," http://www.youtube.com/watch?v=HHY7_of1oBA
35. Nigeria Films, "Stephanie Okereke."
36. Niba, "Stephanie Okereke," 58.
37. McCain, "Video Exposé," 29.

38. The film's public screening represented the first time that the accident entered Okereke's own self-presentation, rather than "junk journalism" or a vaguely biographical film narrative. "I've always wanted to share my story with people," Okereke said on the red carpet. "A lot of people knew that I'd had an accident, but they didn't really see me, to see how my face was, at the time." Viewing her essay film as an inspirational account of "bouncing back," Okereke said, "I wanted to give people hope."

39. Barber, *The Generation of Plays*, 15.

2. GLITTERING VIDEO

1. See Nigeria News, "Omotola Jalade-Ekeinde at Grammy Awards."

2. For more on these discourses of empowerment, see Fleetwood, *Troubling Vision*, 105–46.

3. See Africa Magic's principal promo for *Omotola: The Real Me:* http://africamagic.dstv.com/category/shows/omotola-the-real-me/.

4. For more on reality television as a global platform, see Kavka, "Industry Convergence Shows," and Oren and Shahaf, *Global Television Formats*.

5. See Africa Magic, http://africamagic.dstv.com/category/shows/omotola-the-real-me/.

6. Haynes, "Nigerian Cinema: Structural Adjustments."

7. Larkin, *Signal and Noise*, 62.

8. See Wang, *Framing Piracy*, 50.

9. For more on VCD's precise historical moment of emergence, see ibid. For more on *Living in Bondage* and the political economy of videotape, see Haynes, "Nigerian Cinema."

10. Harrow, *Trash*, x.

11. Garritano, *African Video Movies and Global Desires*, 23.

12. Larkin, *Signal and Noise*, 20.

13. For more on the so-called "home-video aesthetic" of VHS, see Moran, *There's No Place Like Home Video*. For more on the "folk" associations of VCD in the global South, see Rajagopal, "Fast-Forward into the Future, Haunted by the Past: Bollywood Today."

14. See, for example, An, "Hanoi Jane Française: Transnational in Time."

15. For a comprehensive account of the production and circulation of these associations in an American, strictly VHS-based context, see Hilderbrand, *Inherent Vice* (especially 33–72). For more on the ways that VHS and VCD are metonymic of piracy, see Larkin, *Signal and Noise*.

16. *Across the Niger* is the sequel to Simi Opeoluwa's *The Battle of Love* (2001).

17. Hilderbrand, *Inherent Vice*, 13.

18. See This Day, "Nigeria: Conflicting Signals Over Preparations for 2015 Digital Migration."

19. While the acronym in this instance stands for "Video Hits Show," the use of "VHS" is clearly an homage to the format itself, especially considering the frequency with which the series offers self-conscious "shout-outs" to videotape.

20. Haynes, "Nollywood in Lagos, Lagos in Nollywood Films," 132.

21. Ibid.

22. For more on Afro-pessimism and its relationship to the political economy of media, see Diawara, *In Search of Africa*.

23. Haynes, "Nollywood in Lagos, Lagos in Nollywood Films," 137.
24. Larkin, *Signal and Noise*, 241.
25. Hilderbrand, *Inherent Vice*.
26. The Morin quote comes from King, "Articulating Stardom," 172.
27. Ibid.
28. In Wang, *Framing Piracy*, 50.
29. Ibid., 94.
30. Moran, *No Place Like Home Video*.
31. See footage of Ogunjiofor's 2011 interview with NollywoodDK at http://www.youtube.com/watch?v=z3uxV2IHleg
32. Benson-Allott, *Killer Tapes and Shattered Screens*, 13.
33. Ibid., 132.
34. Naremore, *Acting in the Cinema*, 172.
35. Hilderbrand, *Inherent Vice*, 189.
36. Diamond Celebrities, "Fan Craze."
37. Moran, *No Place Like Home Video*, 106.
38. Naremore, *Acting in the Cinema*, 174.
39. Moran, *No Place Like Home Video*, 107.
40. Haynes, "Nollywood in Lagos, Lagos in Nollywood Films," 137.
41. Naremore, *Acting in the Cinema*, 3.
42. Adejunmobi, "Nigerian Video Film."
43. For an overview of some of these discourses, see Schoonover, *Brutal Vision*.
44. Perez, *The Material Ghost*, 37.
45. Ibid., 37–38.
46. Quoted in Deborah Shapple Spillman, *British Colonial Realism in Africa*, 108.
47. Hilderbrand, *Inherent Vice*, 72.
48. Ibid.
49. Ibid., 65.
50. Larkin, *Signal and Noise*, 218.
51. In Hilderbrand, *Inherent Vice*, 66.
52. Ibid.
53. Larkin, *Signal and Noise*, 241.
54. McCain, "Video Exposé."
55. Azuh, "Reflecting on Ali-Balogun's *Tango with Me*."
56. Njoku, "Old Actors Return in *Tango with Me*."
57. For more on FESPACO's relationship to Nollywood, see McCain, "FESPACO in a Time of Nollywood."
58. Naremore, *Acting in the Cinema*.
59. Lawrence, *The Passion of Montgomery Clift*.
60. For more on Osetura and Baba Sala, see Haynes, "Nigerian Cinema: Structural Adjustments."
61. Kaplan, "Wicked Old Ladies from Europe," 240.
62. Bruzzi, *Undressing Cinema*, xvi.
63. Reich, "Slave to Fashion," 249.
64. Falola and Heaton, *A History of Nigeria*, 194.
65. For a detailed discussion of the film, see Okome, "*Onome*."

66. Barrot, *Nollywood*, 70.
67. The *Naija Parrot* piece is entitled "Nineteen Faded and Outdated Nollywood Stars Who Are No Longer Relevant in the Industry." The *Nigerian Voice* piece, by Azuh Amatus, is entitled "'My First Love is Stronger than Acting.'" See also Oreyeni, "'Men Can't Kill My Dream.'"
68. Amatus, "'My First Love is Stronger than Acting.'"
69. Ibid.
70. Oyĕwùmí, *The Invention of Women*.
71. Barrot, *Nollywood*, 70.
72. Sereda, "Curses, Nightmares, and Realities," 195.
73. Adesokan, *Postcolonial Artists and Global Aesthetics*, 94.
74. Vanguard News, "Fathia Balogun Drags Oge Okoye to the Street."
75. Ibid.
76. See, for instance, *Gist Mania*, "Van Vicker's Bold Fashion Statement."
77. Lawrence, *The Passion of Montgomery Clift*, 211.
78. Fleetwood, *Troubling Vision*, 29.
79. Ibid., 36.
80. Nigeria News, "Yoruba Actress Funke Akindele Opens Up About Pregnancy." In stark contrast to its rather misleading title, this Nigeria News article focuses on Akindele's refusal "to publicly denounce or confirm if she's pregnant or not."
81. Oyĕwùmí, *The Invention of Women*, 36.
82. Ibid., 30, 31.
83. Nigerian Compass, "Tribalism in Nollywood." See also Nigeria Films, "Tribalism is Killing Nollywood."
84. *The Guardian*, "Nicki Minaj: 'I Model My Accent on Scary Spice.'"
85. See Bruzzi, *Undressing Cinema*, 118.
86. For more on the so-called "video ho," see Fleetwood, *Troubling Vision*, 105–46.
87. Ibid., 125.
88. Bruzzi, *Undressing Cinema*, 118.
89. Quoted in Sereda, "Curses, Nightmares, and Realities," 199.
90. Ibid.

3. A MOBILE GLOW

1. Larkin, *Signal and Noise*, 241.
2. Ibid., 219.
3. Powell, "Knowledge, Culture, and the Internet in Africa."
4. Larkin, *Signal and Noise*, 11.
5. Ibid., 255.
6. Obadare, "Playing Politics with the Mobile Phone in Nigeria," 94, 98.
7. Ibid., 98.
8. Ibid., 101.
9. Ibid.
10. Nworah, "Glo," 100.
11. See, for instance, Glo Story: http://www.youtube.com/watch?v=SeN6yE0MsH0.
12. Obadare, "Playing Politics with the Mobile Phone in Nigeria," 105.
13. Nworah, "The Rise and Rise of Nigeria's First Multinational Conglomerate."

14. Obadare, "Playing Politics with the Mobile Phone in Nigeria," 94.
15. "Van Vicker Talks About Being a Glo Ambassador," posted by Ameyaw Debrah, 1 September 2009, http://www.youtube.com/watch?v=Mm879DDOCTw.
16. Bryce, "Signs of Femininity, Symptoms of Malaise," 79, 78.
17. Green-Simms, "The Return of the Mercedes," 222.
18. Debrah, "Van Vicker Talks About Being a Glo Ambassador."
19. Nusselder, *Interface Fantasy*, 121.
20. The comment appears in the comment box for the second installment of *BlackBerry Babes*. Nobathembu Mcinga (user), November 2012, http://irokotv.com/video/253/blackberry-babes-2#comment-733089640.
21. Bella Naija, "'BlackBerry Babes': What Does This Movie Say About Us?"
22. Bryce, "Signs of Femininity, Symptoms of Malaise," 84.
23. Quoted in King, *Film Comedy*, 94.
24. Naremore, *Acting in the Cinema*, 295.
25. Latham, *The Art of Scandal*, 9.
26. King, *Film Comedy*, 94.
27. See the user comments on the iROKOtv page for the first film, *BlackBerry Babes*, in particular: irokotv.com/video/484/blackberry-babes.
28. For more on the presence of Stanislavsky in Nollywood, see Lani Akande's blog *Nollywood Staple*: http://nollywoodstaple.wordpress.com/author/josephaniyi/
29. Oghuma, "Nse Ikpe-Etim Exclusive: 'I Wasn't Born to Get Married.'"
30. Haynes, "'New Nollywood,'" 68.
31. Okon, "*Phone Swap*: Movie Review."
32. Akande, "Movie Review: *Phone Swap*."
33. See @karenigho (Karen_Igho), https://twitter.com/Karen_Igho.
34. Ibid., tweet on April 23, 2013.
35. "*BlackBerry Babes*: The Future of Capitalism?"
36. From Dikeh's 2011 iROKtv interview: http://www.youtube.com/watch?v=QH1MIp9PMfE.
37. Bryce, "Signs of Femininity, Symptoms of Malaise," 79.
38. Haynes, "Nollywood in Lagos, Lagos in Nollywood Films," 139.
39. Examples span the Hollywood landscape but are particularly pronounced in the cases of Christian-identified figures as well as Scientologists. See Burr, *Gods Like Us*.
40. In Dovey, *African Film and Literature*, 202.
41. King, *Film Comedy*.
42. Naija Gists, "Globacom Manager Tayo Smith Commits Suicide Due to Frustration from Boss."
43. Ogbonge Blog, "Glo Ramadan Offer."
44. See Johnson, "Boko Haram: Mobile Operators Lose N8 Billion Daily."
45. Gist Mania, "The List of Glo Ambassador [*sic*]. Where is Tribalism Here?"
46. African Movies News, "Rita Dominic, Funke Akindele, and BasketMouth Sizzle in New Promo."

4. WHEN STARS COLLIDE

1. As I noted at the beginning of this book, I will be referring to this film with the title that appears on screen during the opening credit sequence (as well as on the covers of the li-

censed VHS, VCD, and DVD copies that I have purchased in West Africa and New York)—not with the stylized "Lady GagaA" or "Queen GagaA" that appear on iROKOtv.com. For more on the complex and often contradictory industrial pressures that promote the retitling of Nollywood films across platforms, see Tsika, "A Lagosian Lady Gaga: Cross-Cultural Identification in Nollywood's Anti-Biopic Cycle."

2. Fanon, *Black Skin, White Masks*, 42.
3. For more on Fanon's response to "colorless universalism," see Ella Shohat, "Post-Fanon and the Colonial," in Shohat, *Taboo Memories, Diasporic Voices*, 254.
4. Green-Simms, "The Return of the Mercedes."
5. Bryce, "Elmina," 146.
6. Quoted in Dovey, *African Film and Literature*, 214. For more on postcolonialism's limited applicability, see Shohat, "Notes on the 'Post-Colonial,'" in Shohat, *Taboo Memories*, 233–249.
7. Oyěwùmí, *The Invention of Women*.
8. Halberstam, *Gaga Feminism*, 103.
9. See, for example, Fogel and Quinlan, "Lady Gaga and Feminism: A Critical Debate," 184–88.
10. Quoted in Dovey, *African Film and Literature*, 215.
11. Fanon, *The Wretched of the Earth*, 148.
12. Ibid.
13. Fanon, *Black Skin, White Masks*, 43–5. Naremore, *Acting in the Cinema*, 71.
14. Quoted in Fleetwood, *Troubling Vision*, 37.
15. Ibid., 37.
16. Shohat, "Post-Fanon and the Colonial," 258.
17. For more on Yorùbá comedy, see Haynes, "Structural Adjustments," and Barber, *The Generation of Plays*.
18. Emmanuel, *Forever in Love*, 43.
19. Sereda, "Curses, Nightmares, and Realities," 195.
20. Mishra Sudesh, *Diaspora Criticism*, 58.
21. Quoted in Ibid.
22. Green-Simms, "The Return of the Mercedes," 221.
23. Foer, *How Soccer Explains the World: An Unlikely Theory of Globalization*.
24. Thérèse Agbasiere, *Women in Igbo Life and Thought*, 152.
25. Njoku, "Actresses Who Dare to Go Bald in Movies."
26. Halberstam, *Female Masculinity*. Gray quoted in Fleetwood, *Troubling Vision*, 172.
27. Shohat and Stam, *Race in Translation*, 146.
28. See, for instance, Marjorie Keniston McIntosh, *Yoruba Women, Work, and Social Change*.
29. Quoted in Young, *Fear of the Dark*, 159.
30. Shohat and Stam, *Race in Translation*, 47.
31. Krings and Okome, "Nollywood and Its Diaspora," 17.
32. Shohat and Stam, *Unthinking Eurocentrism*, 396.

5. NOLLYWOOD'S PROGENY

1. Studlar, "Marlene Dietrich and the Erotics of Code-Bound Hollywood," 213.
2. Quoted in *Viewing African Cinema in the 21st Century*, 20.

3. Haynes and Okome, "Evolving Popular Media: Nigerian Video Films," 51.
4. Abah, "Representing Children and Childhood in Yoruba Nollywood," 295, 299.
5. Marenin, "National Service and National Consciousness in Nigeria," 629–54.
6. Barber, "Popular Arts in Africa," 8.
7. Abah, "Representing Children and Childhood in Yoruba Nollywood," 298.
8. Idriss Lahai, "Youth Agency and Survival Strategies in Sierra Leone's Postwar Informal Economy," 47.
9. *Youth and Pornography*, 21, 147.
10. Ochiagha, *The Future of the Nigerian Youth*, 44.
11. Quoted in Okome, "Nollywood and its Critics," 36.
12. Sereda, "Curses, Nightmares, and Realities," 203.
13. Paul Ugor, "Failed States and the Militarization of Youth in Sub-Saharan Africa," 100.
14. The column was written by Maureen Azuh. See, for instance, Azuh's profile of "former Nollywood child actor" Isosiya Dokubo in Azuh, "Once Upon a Kid Actor."
15. Vanguard News, "Keeping up with the Kid Stars."
16. See Njoku, "'I Left the Country to Escape from Being Kidnapped.'"
17. Nigeria's Channels TV broadcast a tribute to Essien-Igbokwe in September, 2011, highlighting her child-centered music videos. A portion of the broadcast can be viewed on YouTube: http://www.youtube.com/watch?v=AtyymOnb1W8
18. See Nigeria Films, "My Life with Hubert Ogunde, His Regrets." For more on Ogunde, see Haynes, "Structural Adjustments," and Bryce, *The Generation of Plays*.
19. For more on Ukpabio, see Oppenheimer, "On a Visit to the U.S., a Nigerian Witch-Hunter Defends Herself."
20. See, for instance, "Lady Gaga Meets Nigerian Kids" (2010), http://www.youtube.com/watch?v=SfAoARwf-WE. The footage of the two Nigerian boys appears in the first episode of the controversial BBC documentary series *Welcome to Lagos* (2010).
21. O'Connor, *The Cultural Significance of the Child Star*, 9.
22. See gossipnigeria, December 16, 2012, https://twitter.com/gossipnigeria
23. Alamutu, "Nigeria: Lagos Speaker, Adeyemi Ikuforiji, Arrested Over Alleged N7 Billion Fraud."
24. Arenyeka, "'At 20, People Still Treat Me Like a Little Girl.'"
25. Ibid.
26. Ibid.
27. Green-Simms and Azuah, "The Video Closet," 48.
28. Second National Youth Policy Document of the Federal Republic of Nigeria, 2009, 61.
29. Quoted in Addison, "Children's Films in the 1990s," 177.
30. https://twitter.com/SharonEzeamaka.
31. Ibid.
32. See Badley, *Lars von Trier*.
33. Bazin, *The Cinema of Cruelty*, 54.
34. Sui-Hung Chan, "Cinematic Neorealism," 224.
35. Bondanella, *Italian Cinema*, 451.
36. Nagib, *World Cinema and the Ethics of Realism*, 43.
37. Quoted in Landy, *Italian Film*, 248.
38. Armes, *African Filmmaking*, 151.

39. Pierson, *Toward a Poetics of Neorealism*, 23.
40. Husseini, "'With Child Soldier... I'll Get the Oscars.'"
41. Nigeria Films, "Who Is Sharon Ezeamaka?"

6. PROFESSIONALIZING CHILDHOOD

1. Hanebrink and Smith, "Painting a Picture of Creative Arts Therapy for War-Affected Youth in Northern Uganda."
2. These Omotola quotes come from the star's appearance on an episode of *Talk Time Africa* (Atlanta), which was broadcast in March 2011.
3. Ensor, "Conclusion: The Next Generation of African Children," 236.
4. Hoechner, "Striving for Knowledge and Dignity: Young Qur'anic Students in Kano, Nigeria," 157.
5. This phrase, which comes from a 2003 World Bank publication entitled "Breaking the Conflict Trap: Civil War and Development Policy," has received a much-needed reconsideration in the work of Julia Paulson, especially "Education, Conflict, and Development," 7–14.
6. Ensor, "Introduction," 6.
7. Arenyeka, "'At 20, People Still Treat Me Like a Little Girl'—Sharon Ezeamaka." See also Ezeamaka's website: http://www.sharonezeamaka.com/
8. Ensor, "Introduction," 7. In 2003, the International Labor Organization estimated that eight million Nigerian children between the ages of five and fourteen were working while enrolled in school. See Abah, "Representing Children and Childhood in Yoruba Nollywood," 299.
9. Coe, "Representing Youth: School Dramas and Youth Authority in Ghana," 129.
10. These Oboli quotes come from the documentary *The Making of 'The Figurine'* (2010).
11. For more on these and other examples, see Marc Weinberg, "The Battle Over Billing," 168–69.
12. Studlar, *Precocious Charms*, 5.
13. See, for instance, the credits for Chikere's *Dorathy, My Love* (2005), costarring Sharon Ezeamaka (who plays William Uchemba's teenage love interest).
14. My thanks to Carmen McCain for sharing her research on Kannywood with me, and for alerting me to Danja's star persona and to the film appearances of Nuhu's children.
15. Chamley, "New Nollywood Cinema."
16. UNICEF, "The State of African Children 2008: Child Survival."
17. Boulor, "'I Am Not an Accomplished Actress'—Oge Okoye."
18. Naija Gists, "'Being an Evangelist Doesn't Stop My Acting Career'—Actress Ucharia Anunobi"; Ogunbunmi, "Evangelist Eucharia Anunobi Receives Christian Leadership Award."
19. In published scholarship, an important exception to this trend can be found in Okome's essay "Reversing the Filmic Gaze," which literally gives Owoh the last word on his character.
20. Haynes, "What Is to Be Done?," 14.
21. See, for instance, "Oge Okoye (Sister Mary) Will Be Coming to Sierra Leone."
22. Gearhart, "Inclusions," 39.
23. Boulor, "'I Am Not an Accomplished Actress.'"
24. Clinton, *It Takes a Village*.

25. Hoechner, 157.

26. Quoted in Provost, "Nigeria's Golden Jubilee: Cause for Celebration of Pause for Evaluation?"

27. Ibid.

28. See user comment, "meinghost," http://www.youtube.com/watch?v=DvaV_Q2jL18, April, 2013. For Globacom's corporate self-defense, see Glo World, "Glo Celebrates Nigerian Children, Affirms Faith in Nigeria's Bright Future."

29. For a detailed analysis of this film, see Garritano, *African Video Movies and Global Desires*, 26–46.

BIBLIOGRAPHY

Abah, Adedayo Ladigbolu. "Representing Children and Childhood in Yoruba Nollywood." *Interactions: Studies in Communication & Culture* 4, no. 3 (December 2013): 289–303.

Adamu, Abdalla Uba. "Transgressing Boundaries: Reinterpretation of Nollywood Films in Muslim Northern Nigeria." In *Global Nollywood: The Transnational Dimensions of an African Video Industry*, edited by Matthias Krings and Onookome Okome, 287–305. Bloomington: Indiana University Press, 2013.

Addison, Heather. "Children's Films in the 1990s." In *Film Genre 2000: New Critical Essays*, edited by Wheeler W. Dixon, 177–92. Albany: SUNY Press, 2000.

Adejunmobi, Moradewun. "English and the Audience of an African Popular Culture: The Case of Nigerian Video Film." *Cultural Critique* 50 (Winter 2002): 74–103.

———. "Evolving Nollywood Templates for Minor Transnational Film." *Black Camera* 5, no. 2 (Spring 2014): 74–94.

———. "Nigerian Video Film as Minor Transnational Practice." *Postcolonial Text* 3, no. 2 (2007): 1–16.

———. *Vernacular Palaver: Imaginations of the Local and Non-Native Languages in West Africa*. Ontario, Canada: Multilingual Matters, 2004.

Adeleye-Fayemi, Bisi. "Images of Women in Nigerian Television." In *Readings in African Popular Culture*, edited by Karin Barber, 125–31. Bloomington: Indiana University Press, 1997.

Adesokan, Akin. *Postcolonial Artists and Global Aesthetics*. Bloomington: Indiana University Press, 2011.

———. "Nollywood and the Idea of the Nigerian Cinema," *Journal of African Cinemas*, 4, no. 1 (2012): 81–98.

———. "Nollywood: Outline of a Trans-ethnic Practice." *Black Camera* 5, no. 2 (Spring 2014): 116–33.

Adorno, Theodor W. and Max Horkheimer, *Dialectics of Enlightenment*. London: Verso, 1979.

African Movies News. "Rita Dominic, Funke Akindele, and BasketMouth Sizzle in New Promo." AfricanMoviesNews.com, February 15, 2012. Accessed January 2, 2014. http://www.africanmoviesnews.com/2013/02/rita-dominic-funke-akindele-and-basketmouth-sizzle-in-new-promo-photos/

Agbasiere, Joseph Thérèse. *Women in Igbo Life and Thought*. London: Routledge, 2000.

Aglanu, Ernest Dela. "Actress Omotola Jalade-Ekeinde Bags N5M Per Movie." *Joy News,* July 21, 2012. Accessed December 29, 2013. http://entertainment.myjoyonline.com/pages/news/201206/88193.php

Ahlan, Shariff. *SuperStars Video Magazine,* Nigeria: Video Villa, 2008.

Ahluwalia, Pal. *Politics and Postcolonial Theory: African Inflections.* London: Routledge, 2011.

Ajibade, Babson. "Nigerian Videos and Their Imagined Western Audiences: The Limits of Nollywood's Transnationality." In *Global Nollywood: The Transnational Dimensions of an African Video Industry,* edited by Matthias Krings and Onookome Okome, 264–86. Bloomington: Indiana University Press, 2013.

Akande, Peju. "Movie Review: *Phone Swap,*" DStv Network, May 7, 2012. http://www.dstv.com/News/Movie-Review-Phone-Swap/92671

Akande, Victor. *Hazy Pictures: The Arts, Business and Politics of the Nigerian Motion Picture Industry.* Ibadan, Nigeria: Kraft Books, 2010.

Alamutu, Sulaimon. "Nigeria: Lagos Speaker, Adeyemi Ikuforiji, Arrested Over Alleged N7 Billion Fraud." *The Moment,* September 3, 2011, via AllAfrica.com. Accessed June 5, 2013. http://allafrica.com/stories/201109050459.html

Allen, Robert C. "Film and History: Theory and Practice." In *Film Theory and Criticism,* edited by Leo Braudy and Marshall Cohen, 606–19. New York: Oxford University Press, 2004.

Amatus, Azuh. "'My First Love is Stronger than Acting'—Star Actress, Uche Mac-Auley." *The Nigerian Voice,* October 10, 2012, via Nigeria Films.com. Accessed May 14, 2013. http://www.nigeriafilms.com/news/9280/27/my-first-love-is-stronger-than-acting-star-actress.html

An, Grace. "Hanoi Jane Française: Transnational in Time." In *Transnational Stardom: International Celebrity in Film and Popular Culture,* edited by Russell Meeuf and Raphael Raphael, 53–76. London: Palgrave MacMillan, 2013.

Appadurai, Arjun. *Modernity at Large: Cultural Dimensions of Globalization.* Minneapolis: University of Minnesota Press, 1996.

Arenyeka, Laju. "'At 20, People Still Treat Me Like a Little Girl'—Sharon Ezeamaka." *The Vanguard,* December 22, 2012. Accessed October 4, 2013. http://www.vanguardngr.com/2012/12/at-20-people-still-treat-me-like-a-little-girl-sharon-ezeamaka/

Armes, Roy. *African Filmmaking: North and South of the Sahara.* Bloomington: Indiana University Press, 2006.

Azuh, Maureen. "Once Upon a Kid Actor." *The Punch,* February 10, 2012. Accessed on September 17 2013. http://www.punchng.com/entertainment/arts-life/once-upon-a-kid-actor/

———. "Reflecting on Ali-Balogun's *Tango with Me.*" *The Punch.* June 8, 2011. Accessed on August 21, 2013. http://odili.net/news/source/2011/jun/8/803.html

Bhabha, Homi K. "DissemiNation: Time, Narrative, and the Margins of the Modern Nation." In *Nation and Narration,* edited by Homi K. Bhabha, 291–322. London: Routledge, 1990.

———. *The Location of Culture.* London: Routledge, 1994.

———. "Postcolonial Authority and Postmodern Guilt." In *Cultural Studies,* edited by Lawrence Grossberg, Cary Nelson, and Paula Treichler, 56–68. London: Routledge, 1992.

Badley, Linda. *Lars von Trier.* Urbana: University of Illinois Press, 2011.

———. R. Barton Palmer, and Steven Jay Schneider, eds. *Traditions in World Cinema.* New Brunswick, NJ: Rutgers University Press, 2006.

Bakare, Bukola and Yinka Quadri. "Nnebue Produced 27 Yoruba Films Before 'Living in Bondage.'" *Nigeria Daily News,* February 15, 2011.

Balogun, Françoise. "Booming Videoeconomy: The Case of Nigeria." In *Focus on African Films*, edited by Françoise Pfaff, 173–84. Bloomington: Indiana University Press, 2004.

Bamgbose, Ayo. "English in the Nigerian Environment." In *New Englishes: A West African Perspective*, edited by Ayo Bamgbose, Ayo Banjo, and Andrew Thomas, 9–26. Ibadan, Nigeria: British Council, 1995.

Barber, Karin. "Concluding Remarks." *Passages: A Chronicle of the African Humanities* 8 (1994): 23–24.

———. *The Generation of Plays: Yoruba Popular Life in Theater*. Bloomington: Indiana University Press, 2000.

———. "Popular Arts in Africa." *African Studies Review* 30.3 (1987): 1–78.

———. "Popular Reactions to the Petro-Naira." *Journal of Modern African Studies* 20, no. 3 (1982): 431–50.

———. "Preliminary Notes on Audiences in Africa." *Africa* 67.3 (1997): 347–62.

———, ed. *Readings in African Popular Culture*. Bloomington: Indiana University Press, 1997.

———. and Christopher Waterman. "Traversing the Global and the Local: Fuji Music and Praise Poetry in the Production of Contemporary Yoruba Popular Culture." In *Worlds Apart: Modernity Through the Prism of the Local*, edited by Daniel Miller, 240–62. London: Routledge, 1995.

Barlet, Olivier. *African Cinemas: Decolonizing the Gaze*. New York: Zed, 2000.

Barrot, Pierre, ed. *Nollywood: Le phénomène video au Nigeria*. Paris: L'Harmattan, 2005.

Bayart, Jean-François. *The State in Africa: The Politics of the Belly*. London: Longman, 1993.

Bazin, André. *The Cinema of Cruelty: From Bunuel to Hitchcock*. New York: Arcade, 1982.

Bella Naija. "'BlackBerry Babes': What Does This Movie Say About Us?" BellaNaija.com, March 18, 2011. Accessed September 23, 2013. http://www.bellanaija.com/2011/03/18/blackberry-babes-what-does-this-movie-say-about-us/

Ben-Amos, Paula. "Pidgin Languages and Tourist Art." *Studies in the Anthropology of Visual Communication* 4 (1977): 128–39.

Benson-Allott, Caetlin. *Killer Tapes and Shattered Screens: Video Spectatorship from VHS to File Sharing*. Berkeley: University of California Press, 2013.

Boateng, Boatema. *The Copyright Thing Doesn't Work Here: Adinkra and Kente Cloth and Intellectual Property in Ghana*. Minneapolis: University of Minnesota Press, 2011.

Böhme, Claudia. "Bloody Bricolages: Traces of Nollywood in Tanzanian Video Films." In *Global Nollywood: The Transnational Dimensions of an African Video Industry*, edited by Matthias Krings and Onookome Okome, 327–46. Bloomington: Indiana University Press, 2013.

Bokamba, Eyamba. "The Africanization of English." In *The Other Tongue: English across Cultures*, edited by Braj Kachru, 77–98. Urbana-Champaign: University of Illinois Press, 1982.

Bondanella, Peter. *Italian Cinema: From Neorealism to the Present*. London: Continuum, 2007.

Bordwell, David, Janet Staiger, and Kristin Thompson. *The Classical Hollywood Cinema: Film Style and Mode of Production to 1960*. New York: Columbia University Press, 1985.

Boulor, Ahmed. "'I Am Not an Accomplished Actress'—Oge Okoye." NaijaGists.com, April 14, 2013. Accessed on December 23, 2013. http://naijagists.com/oge-okoye-talks-about-children-life-history-im-not-an-accomplished-actress/

Bourdieu, Pierre. *Language and Symbolic Power*. Cambridge: Harvard University Press, 1991.

Boyce-Davis, Carol. "Motherhood in the Works of Male and Female Igbo Writers: Achebe, Emecheta, Nwapa, and Nzekwu." In *Ngambika: Studies of Women in African Literature,* edited by Carole Boyce-Davies and Anne Adams Graves, 241–56. Trenton, NJ: Africa World Press, 1986.

Bryce, Jane. "Donor Values and the Case of Film in Tanzania." In *Viewing African Cinema in the 21st Century: Art Films and the Nollywood Video Revolution*, edited by Mahir Saul and Ralph A. Austen, 160–77. Athens, OH: Ohio University Press, 2010.

———. "*Elmina*: Obroni Art or Popular Melodrama?" *Black Camera* 5, no. 2 (Spring 2014): 134–50.

———. "Signs of Femininity, Symptoms of Malaise: Contextualizing Figurations of 'Woman' in Nollywood." *Research in African Literatures* 43, No. 4 (Winter 2012): 71–87.

Bruzzi, Stella. *Undressing Cinema: Clothing and Identity in the Movies*. London: Routledge, 1997.

Burchette, Jordan. "World's 12 Sexiest Accents." CNN International, November 30, 2012. Accessed October 12, 2013. http://travel.cnn.com/explorations/life/worlds-sexiest-accents-130333

Burns, James. "'The West is Cold': Experiences of Ghanaian Performers in England and the United States." In *The New African Diaspora*, edited by Isidore Okpewho and Nkiru Nzegwu, 127–45. Bloomington: Indiana University Press, 2009.

Burr, Ty. *Gods Like Us: On Movie Stardom and Modern Fame*. New York: Anchor Books, 2013.

Chamley, Santorri. "New Nollywood Cinema: From Home-Video Productions Back to the Big Screen." *Cineaste* 37.3 (Summer 2012): 21–23.

Chan, Natalia Sui-Hung. "Cinematic Neorealism: Hong Kong Cinema and Fruit Chan's 1997 Trilogy." In *Italian Neorealism and Global Cinema*, edited by Laura E. Ruberto and Kristi M. Vilson, 207–25. Detroit: Wayne State University Press, 2007.

Clinton, Hillary Rodham. *It Takes a Village*. New York: Simon & Schuster, 1996.

CNN International. "Genevieve Nnaji in Conversation with Pedro Pinto." CNN International: African Voices, March 25, 2011. Accessed 14 January 2014. http://articles.cnn.com/2011-03-29/world/nigeria.genevieve.nnaji_1_nigerians-gn-exceptional-talent?_s=PM:WORLD

CNN World. "Genevieve Nnaji: Nollywood's Julia Roberts." CNN World, March 29, 2011. Accessed September 17, 2013. http://articles.cnn.com/2011-03-29/world/nigeria.genevieve.nnaji_1_nigerians-gn-exceptional-talent?_s=PM:WORLD

Coe, Cati. "Representing Youth: School Dramas and Youth Authority in Ghana." In *African Childhoods: Education, Development, Peacebuilding, and the Youngest Continent*, edited by Marisa O. Ensor, 127–40. London: Palgrave MacMillan, 2012.

Comaroff, Jean, and John L. Comaroff. "Occult Economies and the Violence of Abstraction: Notes from the South African Postcolony." *American Ethnologist* 26.2 (1999): 279–303.

———. "Millennial Capitalism: First Thoughts on a Second Coming." *Public Culture* 12.2 (2000): 291–343.

———. *Modernity and Its Malcontents: Ritual and Power in Postcolonial Africa*. Chicago: University of Chicago Press, 1993.

Corliss, Richard. "Omotola Jalade-Ekeinde." *Time*, April 18, 2013. Accessed June 19, 2013. http://time100.time.com/2013/04/18/time-100/slide/omotola-jalade-ekeinde/

Crofts, Stephen. "Reconceptualizing National Cinema/s." In *Film and Nationalism*, edited by Alan Williams, 25–51. New Brunswick, NJ: Rutgers University Press, 2002.

Debrah, Ameyaw. "Van Vicker Talks about Being a Glo Ambassador." *Modern Ghana*, September 6, 2009. Accessed December 29, 2013. http://www.modernghana.com/music/9947/3/van-vicker-talks-about-being-a-glo-ambassador-and-.html de Certeau, Michael. *The Practice of Everyday Life*, translated by Steven Rendall. Berkeley: University of California Press, 1984.

deCordova, Richard. *Picture Personalities: The Emergence of the Star System in America*. Urbana: University of Illinois Press, 1990.

de Saussure, Ferdinand. *Course in General Linguistics*. Trans. Roy Harris. Chicago: Open Court, 1972.

Diamond Celebrities, "Fan Craze: Nollywood Actor Johnpaul Nwadike Gets Warm Welcome in USA." DiamondCelebrities.com, March 18, 2013. Accessed September 8, 2013. http://diamondcelebrities.com/2013/03/18/fan-craze-nollywood-actor-johnpaul-nwadike-gets-warm-welcome-in-usa/

Diawara, Manthia. *African Cinema: Politics & Culture*. Bloomington: Indiana University Press, 1992.

———. *African Film: New Forms of Aesthetics and Politics*. Berlin: Prestel, 2009.

———. "Dial Ouaga for African Cinema." *Nka: Journal of Contemporary African Art* 3, no. 1 (1995): 46–49.

———. *In Search of Africa*. Cambridge: Harvard University Press, 1998.

———. "Popular Culture and Oral Traditions in African Film." *Film Quarterly* 41, no. 3 (Spring 1988): 6–14.

———. "Toward a Regional Imaginary in Africa." In *The Cultures of Globalization*, edited by Frederic Jameson and Masao Miyoshi, 103–24. Durham, NC: Duke University Press, 1998.

Dixon, Wheeler Winston and Gwendolyn Audrey Foster. *21st-Century Hollywood: Movies in the Era of Transformation*. New Brunswick, NJ: Rutgers University Press, 2011.

Dolby, Nadine. "Popular Culture and Public Space in Africa: The Possibilities of Cultural Citizenship." *African Studies Review* 49.3 (2006): 31–47.

Dovey, Lindiwe. *African Film and Literature: Adapting Violence to the Screen*. New York: Columbia University Press, 2009.

Dyer, Richard. *Heavenly Bodies: Film Stars and Society*. London: Routledge, 2004.

———. *Stars* (Second Edition). London: British Film Institute, 2008.

———. *White: Essays on Race and Culture*. London: Routledge, 1997.

Ebony. "'Countdown at Kusini,'" *Ebony* (April, 1976): 90–94.

Eckert, Charles. "Shirley Temple and the House of Rockefeller." *Jump Cut*, no. 2 (July–August 1974): 17–20.

Ejiro, Zeb. "We Are the Leaders." *Nigerian Videos* 4, no. 3 (1998): 18–19.

Ekwuazi, Hyginus Ozo. "The Igbo Video Film: A Glimpse into the Cult of the Individual." In *Nigerian Video Films: Revised and Expanded Edition*, edited by Jonathan Haynes, 131–47. Athens, OH: Ohio University Center for International Studies, 2000.

Ellerson, Betti. "Africa through a Woman's Eyes: Safi Faye's Cinema." In *Focus on African Films*, edited by Françoise Pfaff, 185–202. Bloomington: Indiana University Press, 2004.

Emmanuel, Kelechi. *Forever in Love*. Bloomington, IN: WestBow Press, 2012.

Ensor, Maria O. "Conclusion: The Next Generation of African Children." In *African Childhoods: Education, Development, Peacebuilding, and the Youngest Continent*, edited by Marisa O. Ensor, 235–48. London: Palgrave MacMillan, 2012.

———. "Introduction." In *African Childhoods: Education, Development, Peacebuilding, and the Youngest Continent*, edited by Marisa O. Ensor, 1–18. London: Palgrave MacMillan, 2012.

Erlmann, Veit. *African Stars: Studies in Black South African Performance*. Chicago: University of Chicago Press, 1991.

Espinosa, Julio Garcia. "For an Imperfect Cinema." *Jump Cut* 20 (1979), 24–26.
FAB Magazine 2, no. 4, 2012.
Falola, Toyin and Ann Genova, *The Politics of the Global Oil Industry: An Introduction*. Westport, CT and London: Praeger, 2005.
Falola, Toyin and Matthew M. Heaton. *A History of Nigeria*. Cambridge: Cambridge University Press, 2008.
Fanon, Frantz. *Black Skin, White Masks*. Translated by Richard Philcox. New York: Grove, 2008 [1967].
———. *The Wretched of the Earth*. Translated by Richard Philcox. New York: Grove, 2004. [1968].
Faustinus, Nwaorgu. "The Alluring Narrative of Tonye Princewill." *Diaspora Scope*, April 24, 2013. Accessed on January 4, 2014. http://www.diasporascope.com/the-alluring-narrative-of-tonye-princewill-part2-by-nwaorgu-faustinus/
Federal Ministry of Information and Culture. *Youth and Pornography: A Publication of the National Orientation Movement*. Abuja, Nigeria: Federal Ministry of Information and Culture, 1989.
Fiske, John. *Understanding Popular Culture*. London: Routledge, 1989.
Fleetwood, Nicole R. *Troubling Vision: Performance, Visuality, and Blackness*. Chicago: University of Chicago Press, 2011.
Foer, Franklin. *How Soccer Explains the World: An Unlikely Theory of Globalization*. New York: HarperCollins, 2004.
Fogel, Curtis and Andrea Quinlan. "Lady Gaga and Feminism: A Critical Debate." *Cultural Communication* 7.3 (2011): 184–88.
Foucault, Michel. *The Archaeology of Knowledge*. London: Tavistock, 1972.
Fuss, Diana. *Essentially Speaking: Feminism, Nature, and Difference*. Princeton, NJ: Princeton University Press, 1989.
Gabriel, Teshome. *Third Cinema in the Third World: The Aesthetics of Liberation*. Ann Arbor, MI: UMI Research Press, 1982.
———. "Towards a Critical Theory of Third World Films." In *Questions of Third Cinema*, edited by Jim Pines and Paul Willemen, 30–52. London: BFI.
Garritano, Carmela. *African Video Movies and Global Desires: A Ghanaian History*. Athens, OH: Ohio University Press, 2013.
———. "Introduction: Nollywood—an Archive of African Worldliness." *Black Camera* 5, no. 2 (Spring 2014): 44–52.
———. "Women, Melodrama, and Political Critique: A Feminist Reading of *Hostages, Dust to Dust,* and *True Confessions*." In *Nigerian Video Films: Revised and Expanded Edition*, edited by Jonathan Haynes, 165–91. Athens, OH: Ohio University Center for International Studies, 2000.
Gates, Henry Louis. *The Signifying Monkey: A Theory of African-American Literary Criticism*. Oxford: Oxford University Press, 1988.
———. *Tradition and the Black Atlantic: Critical Theory in the African Diaspora*. New York: Basic Books, 2010.
Gearhart, Suzanne. "Inclusions: Psychoanalysis, Transnationalism, and Minor Cultures." In *Minor Transnationalism*, edited by Francoise Lionnet and Shu-mei Shih, 27–40. Durham, NC: Duke University Press, 2005.
Genevieve. "Meet the Elliots," *Genevieve* 88, June 2012.

Geschiere, Peter. *The Modernity of Witchcraft: Politics and the Occult in Postcolonial Africa.* Charlottesville: University Press of Virginia, 1997.

Gist Express. "'My Teenage Pregnancy Experience'—Genevieve Nnaji." GistExpress.com, May 8, 2011. Accessed December 29, 2013. http://www.gistexpress.com/2011/05/08/my-teenage-pregnancy-experience—-genevieve-nnaji/

Gist Mania. "The List of Glo Ambassador [sic]. Where is Tribalism Here?" GistMania.com, December 29, 2011. Accessed September 29, 2013. http://www.gistmania.com/talk/topic,75946.0.html

Glo World. "Glo Celebrates Nigerian Children, Affirms Faith in Nigeria's Bright Future." GloWorld.com, May 27, 2013. Accessed September 19, 2013. http://www.gloworld.com/nigeria/news/glo-celebrates-nigerian-children-affirms-faith-in-nigerias-bright-future/

———. "Van Vicker's Bold Fashion Statement." GistMania.com, December 16, 2012. Accessed December 26, 2013. http://www.gistmania.com/talk/topic,138907.0.html

Golden Icons. "Uche Jombo: Exclusive Interview." *Golden Icons*, December 2011. Accessed December 29, 2013. http://www.goldenicons.com/uche-jombo-excl-interview/

Green-Simms, Lindsey. "Hustlers, Home-Wreckers, and Homoeroticism: Nollywood's *Beautiful Faces*." *Journal of African Cinemas* 4, no. 1 (July 2012): 59–79.

———. "The Return of the Mercedes." In *Viewing African Cinema in the Twenty-First Century: Art Films and the Nollywood Video Revolution*, edited by Mahir Saul and Ralph A. Austen, 209–24. Athens, OH: Ohio University Press, 2010.

Green-Simms, Lindsey and Unoma Azuah. "The Video Closet: Nollywood's Gay-Themed Movies." *Transition* 107 (2012): 32–49.

Gray, Jonathan. *Show Sold Separately: Promos, Spoilers, and Other Media Paratexts.* New York: New York University Press, 2010.

Gray, Steven. "Nigeria On-Screen: 'Nollywood' Films' Popularity Rising Among Émigrés." *Washington Post*, November 8, 2003: E01.

Guardian. "Nicki Minaj: 'I Model My Accent on Scary Spice.'" November 1, 2012. Accessed April 3, 2013. http://www.theguardian.com/music/audio/2012/nov/01/nicki-minaj-english-accent-scary-spice

Gugler, Josef. *African Film: Re-Imagining a Continent.* Bloomington: Indiana University Press, 2003.

Halberstam, J. Jack. *Female Masculinity.* Durham, NC: Duke University Press, 1998.

———. *Gaga Feminism: Sex, Gender, and the End of Normal.* Boston: Beacon Press, 2012.

Hamblin, Sarah. "Towards a Transnational African Cinema: Image and Authenticity in *La Vie sur terre*." *Black Camera* 3, no. 2 (Spring 2012): 8–30.

Hanebrink, Julia R. and Alayna J. Smith, "Painting a Picture of Creative Arts Therapy for War-Affected Youth in Northern Uganda." In *African Childhoods: Education, Development, Peacebuilding, and the Youngest Continent*, edited by Marisa O. Ensor, 219–34. London: Palgrave MacMillan, 2012.

Harrow, Kenneth. *Postcolonial African Cinema: From Political Engagement to Postmodernism.* Bloomington: Indiana University Press, 2007.

———. *Trash: African Cinema from Below.* Bloomington: Indiana University Press, 2013.

———. "Women with Open Eyes, Women of Stone and Hammers: Western Feminism and African Feminist Filmmaking Practice." In *African Cinema: Postcolonial and Feminist Readings*, edited by Kenneth W. Harrow, 225–40. Lawrenceville, NJ: Africa World Press, 1999.

———. "World Cinema versus Subjectivity: How to Read Tunde Kelani's *Abeni*." *Black Camera* 5, no. 2 (Spring 2014): 151–67.

Haruna, Iddrisu. "Glo Mobile to Start Operations in Ghana." Ghana News Link, November 5, 2010. Accessed December 29, 2013. http://www.ghananewslink.com/lyrics/index.php?id=10152

Haynes, Jonathan. "African Cinema and Nollywood: Contradictions." *Situations: Project of the Radical Imagination* 4.1 (2011): 67–90.

———. "African Filmmaking and the Postcolonial Predicament: *Quartier Mozart* and *Aristotle's Plot*." In *African Cinema: Postcolonial and Feminist Readings*, edited by Kenneth W. Harrow, 23–48. Lawrenceville, NJ: Africa World Press, 1999.

———. "Evolving Popular Media: Nigerian Video Films." In *Nigerian Video Films: Revised and Expanded Edition*, edited by Jonathan Haynes, 51–88. Athens, OH: Ohio University Center for International Studies, 2000.

———. "Introduction." In *Nigerian Video Films: Revised and Expanded Edition*, edited by Jonathan Haynes, 1–36. Athens, OH: Ohio University Center for International Studies, 2000.

———. "New Nollywood: Kunle Afolayan." *Black Camera* 5, no. 2 (Spring 2014): 53–73.

———, ed. *Nigerian Video Films: Revised and Expanded Edition*. Athens, OH: Ohio University Center for International Studies, 2000.

———. "Nigerian Cinema: Structural Adjustments." *Research in African Literatures* 26, no. 3 (1995): 97–119.

———. "Nnebue: The Anatomy of Power." *Film International* 28 (2007): 30–40.

———. "The Nollywood Diaspora: A Nigerian Video Genre." In *Global Nollywood: The Transnational Dimensions of an African Video Industry*, edited by Matthias Krings and Onookome Okome, 73–99. Bloomington: Indiana University Press, 2013.

———. "Nollywood in Lagos, Lagos in Nollywood Films." *Africa Today* 54.2 (2007): 131–150.

———. "Nollywood: What's in a Name?" *The Guardian*, July 3, 2005, 56. Rpt. *Film International* 28 (2007): 106–08.

———. "Political Critique in Nigerian Video Films." *African Affairs* 104.421 (2006): 511–33.

———. "What Is to Be Done? Film Studies and Nigerian and Ghanaian Videos." In *Viewing African Cinema in the Twenty-First Century: Art Films and the Nollywood Video Revolution*, edited by Mahir Saul and Ralph A. Austen, 11–25. Athens, OH: Ohio University Press, 2010.

Hilderbrand, Lucas. *Inherent Vice: Bootleg Histories of Videotape and Copyright*. Durham, NC: Duke University Press, 2009.

Hoechner, Hannah. "Striving for Knowledge and Dignity: Young Qur'anic Students in Kano, Nigeria." In *African Childhoods: Education, Development, Peacebuilding, and the Youngest Continent*, edited by Marisa O. Ensor, 157–72. London: Palgrave MacMillan, 2012.

hooks, bell. *Black Looks: Race and Representation*. South End Press, 1992.

Husseini, Shaibu. "'With Child Soldier . . . I'll Get the Oscars.'" *Guardian Life Magazine*, March 23, 2009. Accessed on March 19, 2013. http://theguardianlifemagazine.blogspot.com/2009/03/with-child-soldier-ill-get-oscars.html

Inusah, Mustapha Ayinde. "Silverbird Bans 'Boko Haram' Movie." NigeriaFilms.com, March 23, 2013. Accessed December 23, 2013. http://www.nigeriafilms.com/news/20931/37/

Jameson, Fredric. *The Geopolitical Aesthetic: Cinema and Space in the World System*. Bloomington: Indiana University Press, 1992.

Jedlowski, Alessandro. "From Nollywood to Nollyworld: Processes of Transnationalization in the Nigerian Video Film Industry." In *Global Nollywood: The Transnational Dimensions of an African Video Industry*, edited by Matthias Krings and Onookome Okome, 25–45. Bloomington: Indiana University Press, 2013.

———. "Small Screen Cinema: Informality and Remediation in Nollywood." *Television and New Media* 13, no. 5 (Fall 2012): 431–46.

Jenkins, Henry. *Convergence Culture: Where Old and New Media Collide*. New York: New York University Press, 2006.

Johnson, Alaba. "Boko Haram: Mobile Operators Lose N8 Billion Daily." *Naija Pundit*, September 10, 2012. Accessed September 16, 2013. http://www.naijapundit.com/news/boko-haram-mobile-operators-lose-n8bn-daily

Jones Magazine. "Brains & Beauty: Stephanie Okereke Shares Arts & Activism." *Jones Magazine*, February, 2013. Accessed September 3, 2013. http://jonesmagazine.com/content/lifestyle/1238/brains.beauty.stephanie.okereke.shares.arts

Kafewo, Samuel, ed. *Nollywood and Theatre for Development (TFD): Exploring the Bridges of Interaction, Proceedings of SONTA 2011 Conference*. Ahmadu Bello University, Zaria, 2011.

Kaplan, E. Ann. "Wicked Old Ladies from Europe: Jeanne Moreau and Marlene Dietrich on the Screen and Live." In *Bas: Infamy, Darkness, Evil, and Slime on Screen*, edited by Murray Pomerance, 239–54. Albany: State University of New York Press, 2004.

Kavka, Misha. "Industry Convergence Shows: Reality TV and the Leisure Franchise." In *Flow TV: Television in the Age of Media Convergence*, edited by Michael Kackman, Marnie Binfield, Matthew Thomas Payne, Allison Perlman, and Bryan Sebok, 75–92. London: Routledge, 2011.

Kernan, Lisa. *Coming Attractions: Reading American Movie Trailers*. Austin: University of Texas Press, 2004.

Kerrigan, Finola. *Film Marketing*. London: Routledge, 2009.

King, Barry. "Articulating Stardom." *Screen* 26, no. 5 (1985): 27–51.

King, Geoff. *Film Comedy*. London: Wallflower Press, 2002.

Koshy, Susan. "The Postmodern Subaltern: Globalization Theory and the Subject of Ethnic, Area, and Postcolonial Studies." In *Minor Transnationalism*, edited by Francoise Lionnet and Shu-mei Shih, 109–34. Durham, NC: Duke University Press, 2005.

Kraidy, Marwan M. *Hybridity, or the Cultural Logic of Globalization*. Philadelphia: Temple University Press, 2005.

Krings, Matthias. "Nollywood Goes East: The Localization of Nigerian Video Films in Tanzania." In *Viewing African Cinema in the Twenty-First Century: Art Films and the Nollywood Video Revolution*, edited by Mahir Saul and Ralph A. Austen, 74–91. Athens, OH: Ohio University Press, 2010.

———. and Onookome Okome, eds. *Global Nollywood: The Transnational Dimensions of an African Video Industry*. Bloomington: Indiana University Press, 2013.

Lahai, John Idriss. "Youth Agency and Survival Strategies in Sierra Leone's Postwar Informal Economy." In *African Childhoods: Education, Development, Peacebuilding, and the Youngest Continent*, edited by Marisa O. Ensor, 47–60. London: Palgrave MacMillan, 2012.

Landy, Marcia. *Italian Film*. Cambridge: Cambridge University Press, 2000.

Larkin, Brian. "Degraded Images, Distorted Sounds: Nigerian Video and the Infrastructure of Piracy." *Public Culture* 16, no. 2 (2004): 289–314.

———. "The 'Nollywood Rising' Conference." *Film International* 128, no. 4 (2007): 109–11.

---. *Signal and Noise: Media, Infrastructure, and Urban Culture in Nigeria.* Durham, NC: Duke University Press, 2008.
Latham, Sean. *The Art of Scandal: Modernism, Libel Law, and the Roman à Clef.* New York: Oxford University Press, 2009.
Lawrence, Amy. *The Passion of Montgomery Clift.* Berkeley: University of California Press, 2010.
Lawuyi, Olatunde. "The Political Economy of Video Marketing in Ogbomoso, Nigeria." *Africa* 67, no. 3 (1997): 476–90.
Leu, Bic. "iREP 2011 Wrap-Up." *Finding Nollywood,* January 24, 2011. Accessed September 19, 2013. http://findingnollywood.com/2011/01/24/irep-2011-wrap-up/
---. "The Rise of Nollywood: The Social Impact of the Nigerian Movie Industry." *Finding Nollywood,* no date. Accessed December 20, 2013. http://findingnollywood.com/about/
Lionnet, Francoise and Shuh-mei Shih. "Introduction." In *Minor Transnationalism,* edited by Francoise Lionnet and Shu-mei Shih, 1–26. Durham, NC: Duke University Press, 2005.
Maher, George Ciccariello. "Brechtian Hip-Hop: Didactics and Self-Production in Post-Gangsta Political Mixtapes." *Journal of Black Studies* 36, no. 1 (2005): 129–60.
Marenin, Otwini. "National Service and National Consciousness in Nigeria." *Journal of Modern African Studies* 17, no. 4 (1979): 629–54.
Marshall-Fratani, Ruth. "Mediating the Global and Local in Nigerian Pentecostalism." *Journal of Religion in Africa* 28, no. 3 (1998): 278–315.
Marx, Karl. "From Capital, Volume I." In *The Portable Karl Marx,* edited by Eugene Kamenka, 432–503. New York: Penguin, 1983.
Mbembe, Achille. "African Modes of Self-Writing." *Public Culture* 14.1 (2002): 239–73.
---. *On the Postcolony.* Berkeley: University of California Press, 2001.
McCain, Carmen. "FESPACO in a Time of Nollywood: The Politics of the 'Video' Film at Africa's Oldest Festival." *Journal of African Media Studies* 3, no. 2 (May 2011): 241–61.
---. "Kannywood, the Growth of a Nigerian-language Industry." *Nigerians Talk,* October 9, 2012. Accessed September 17, 2013. http://nigerianstalk.org/2012/10/09/kannywood-the-growth-of-a-nigerian-language-industry-carmen-mccain-2/
---. "Nollywood Greats Emem Isong and Lancelot Oduwa Imasuen on Nigerian Language Films." *Weekly Trust.* July 21, 2012. Accessed January 23, 2014. http://www.weeklytrust.com.ng/index.php/my-thoughts-exactly/6429-nollywood-greats-emem-isong-and-lancelot-oduwa-imasuen-on-nigerian-language-films
---. "Nollywood, Kannywood, and a Decade of Hausa Film Censorship." In *Silencing Cinema: Film Censorship around the World,* edited by Daniel Biltereyst and Roel Vande Winkel, 223–40. New York: Palgrave MacMillan, 2013.
---. "Politics of Hollywood's *Half of a Yellow Sun.*" *Weekly Trust.* February 4, 2012. Accessed September 12, 2013. http://weeklytrust.com.ng/index.php/my-thoughts-exactly/6436-politics-of-hollywoods-half-of-a-yellow-sun
---. "The 'Second Coming' of Kannywood." *Weekly Trust,* May 21, 2011: 18–19, 24.
---. "Video Exposé: Metafiction and Message in Nigerian Films." *Journal of African Cinemas* 4, no. 1 (2012): 25–57.
McCall, John C. "The Capital Gap: Nollywood and the Limits of Informal Trade." *Journal of African Cinemas* 4, no. 1 (2012): 9–23.
---. "Juju and Justice at the Movies: Vigilantes in Nigerian Popular Videos." *African Studies Review* 47.3 (2004): 51–67.

McDonald, Paul. "Reconceptualizing Stardom." In *Stars*, edited by Richard Dyer, 175–211. New Ed. London: British Film Institute, 1998.

McIntosh, Marjorie Keniston. *Yoruba Women, Work, and Social Change*. Bloomington: Indiana University Press, 2009.

Mediolana. "BlackBerry Babes: The Future of Capitalism?" Mediolana.wordpress.com, August 31, 2011. Accessed on October 7, 2013. http://mediolana.wordpress.com/2011/08/31/blackberry-babes-the-future-of-capitalism/

Meeuf, Russell and Raphael Raphael, eds. *Transnational Stardom: International Celebrity in Film and Popular Culture*. London: Palgrave MacMillan, 2013.

Mercer, Kobena. "'1968'": Periodizing Politics and Identity." In *Cultural Studies*, edited by Lawrence Grossberg, Cary Nelson, and Paula Treichler, 424–49. London: Routledge, 1992.

———. "Ethnicity and Internationality: New British Art and Diaspora-Based Blackness." *Third Text* 49 (Winter 1999–2000): 51–62.

———. *Popular Art and Vernacular Cultures*. Cambridge, MA: MIT Press, 2007.

———. *Welcome to the Jungle: New Positions in Black Cultural Studies*. London: Routledge, 1994.

Meyer, Birgit. "Popular Ghanaian Cinema and 'African Heritage.'" *Africa Today* 46, no. 2 (1999): 93–114.

———. "The Power of Money: Politics, Occult Forces, and Pentecostalism in Ghana." *AfricanStudies Review* 41, no. 3 (1998): 15–37.

Meze, Ifeoma. "'My Kids Will All Have British Citizenship'—Oge Okoye." NigeriaFilms.com, March 22, 2011. Accessed October 14, 2013. http://www.nigeriafilms.com/news/11027/1/my-kids-will-all-have-british-citizenship-oge-okoy.html.

Michael, Alonge. "Nollywood Actress Oge Okoye Goes PLC." NigeriaFilms.com, May 5, 2013. Accessed September 17, 2013. http://www.nigeriafilms.com/news/21503/10/nollywood-actress-oge-okoye-goes-plcshoots-first-m.html

Modood, Tariq. "Anti-Essentialism, Multiculturalism, and the 'Recognition' of Religious Groups." In *Citizenship in Diverse Societies*, edited by Will Kymlicka and Wayne Norman, 175–98. Oxford: Oxford University Press, 2000.

Moran, James M. *There's No Place Like Home Video*. Minneapolis: University of Minnesota Press, 2002.

Mosco, Vincent, and Lewis Kaye. "Questioning the Concept of the Audience." In *Consuming Audiences? Production and Reception in Media Research*, edited by Ingunn Hagen and Janet Wasco, 31–46. Creskill, NJ: Hampton Press, 2000.

Naficy, Hamid. *An Accented Cinema: Exilic and Diasporic Filmmaking*. Princeton, NJ: Princeton University Press, 2001.

Nagib, Lúcia. *World Cinema and the Ethics of Realism*. London: Continuum, 2011.

Naija Gists. "'Being an Evangelist Doesn't Stop My Acting Career'—Actress Ucharia Anunobi." NaijaGists.com. April 23, 2013. Accessed on December 29, 2013. http://news.naij.com/31968.html

———. "Globacom Manager Tayo Smith Commits Suicide Due to Frustration from Boss." NaijaGists.com, September 11, 2012. http://naijagists.com/globacom-manager-commits-suicide-in-ibadan-tayo-smith/

Naija Parrot. "Nineteen Faded and Outdated Nollywood Stars Who Are No Longer Relevant in the Industry." NaijaParrot.com, July 17, 2012. Accessed November 1, 2013. http://naijaparrot.com/19-fading-and-outdated-nollywood-stars-who-are-no-longer-relevant-in-the-industry/

Naremore, James. *Acting in the Cinema*. Berkeley: University of California Press, 1990.
National Film and Video Censors Board (NFVCB). *The Classifier: The Official Newsletter of the National Film & Video Censors Board* 4, no. 1 (2011): 1–50.
Niba, Belle. "Stephanie Okereke: Bouncing Back After a Painful Divorce and a Near-Death Experience." *African Vibes* 17 (October 2011): 55–59.
Nigeria. "Nigeria." *Nigeria* no. 71, (October, 1961): 324.
Nigerian Compass. "Tribalism in Nollywood." November 20, 2008. Accessed November 2, 2013. http://www.naijarules.com/xf/index.php?threads/tribalism-in-nollywood-producers-asked-me-to-adopt-igbo-name.30890/
Nigeria Films. "'Everything is Oversize in the Birthplace of Nollywood'—Wole Soyinka Speaks on African Film." NigeriaFilms.com, March 1, 2013. Accessed December 3, 2013. http://www.nigeriafilms.com/news/20655/20/everything-is-oversize-in-the-birthplace-of-nollyw.html
———. "My Life with Hubert Ogunde, His Regrets." NigeriaFilms.com, no date, but ca. 2005. Accessed September 17, 2013. http://www.nigeriafilms.com/star_profile_details.asp?yes_id=10
———. "Stephanie Okereke: 'The Accident I Had Changed My Life.'" NigeriaFilms.com, December 22, 2009. Accessed January 5, 2013. http://www.nigeriafilms.com/news/6405/5/actress-stephanie-okereke-tells-usthe-accident-i-h.html
———. "'Tribalism is Killing Nollywood'—Halima Abubakar." NigeriaFilms.com, May 29, 2013. Accessed January 1, 2014. http://nigeriafilms.com/news/21859/1/tribalism-is-killing-nollywood-halima-abubakar.html
———. "Who is Sharon Ezeamaka?" NigeriaFilms.com, April 17, 2008. Accessed December 29, 2013. http://www.nigeriafilms.com/content.asp?contentid=2426&ContentTypeID=2
Nigeria News. "Nollywood Star Halima Abubakar, Dumped by Edo Oil Baron Lover." NigeriaNews.com, July 2, 2012. Accessed November 18, 2013. http://news2.onlinenigeria.com/entertainment/138687-nollywood-star-halima-abubakar-dumped-by-edo-oil-baron-lover.html
———. "Omotola Jalade-Ekeinde at Grammy Awards: Fans Rip Omosexy!" NigeriaNews.com. February 18, 2011. Accessed November 1, 2013. http://news2.onlinenigeria.com/main-news/74476-omotola-jalade-ekeinde-at-grammy-awards-fans-rip-omosexy.html
———. "Yoruba Actress Funke Akindele Opens Up About Pregnancy." NigeriaNews.com. September 11, 2012. Accessed December 20, 2013. http://news2.onlinenigeria.com/entertainment/212772-yoruba-actress-funke-akindele-opens-up-about-pregnancy.html
Njoku, Benjamin. "Actresses Who Dare to Go Bald in Movies." *The Vanguard*, February 9, 2013. Accessed September 19, 2013. http://www.vanguardngr.com/2013/02/actresses-who-dare-to-go-bald-in-movies/
———. "'I Left the Country to Escape from Being Kidnapped': Tosin Jegede, Former Child Star." *The Vanguard*, September 8, 2012. Accessed on January 3, 2014. http://www.vanguardngr.com/2012/09/i-left-the-country-to-escape-from-being-kidnapped/
———. "Old Actors Return in *Tango with Me*." *The Vanguard*. December 18, 2009. http://www.vanguardngr.com/2009/12/old-actors-return-in-tango-with-me/
Nwelue, Onyeka. "In Conversations: Onyeka Nwelue Talks to Sharon Ezeamaka." *We Run Things*, September 8, 2012. Accessed January 14, 2013. http://www.werunthings.net/in-conversations-onyeka-nwelue-talks-to-sharon-ezeamaka/

Nworah, Uche. "Glo: As India Beckons Adenuga and Globacom." Gamji.com, May 2006. Accessed May 17, 2013. http://www.gamji.com/article5000/NEWS5931.htm

Nusselder, André. *Interface Fantasy: A Lacanian Cyborg Ontology*. Cambridge, MA: MIT Press, 2009.

Obadare, Ebenezer. "Playing Politics with the Mobile Phone in Nigeria: Civil Society, Big Business, and the State." *Review of African Political Economy* 33, no. 107 (March 2006): 93–111.

Obaseki, Don Pedro. "La vidéo nigériane est née de la television, pas du cinema." In *Nollywood: Le phénomène video au Nigeria*, edited by, Pierre Barrot, 72. Paris: L'Harmattan, 2005.

Obiaya, Ikechukwu. "Nollywood on the Internet: A Preliminary Analysis of an Online Nigerian Video-Film Audience." *Journal of African Media Studies* 2, no. 3 (2010): 321–38.

Ochiagha, Chinenye Clare. *The Future of the Nigerian Youth: A Counseling Perspective*. Enugu, Nigeria: Snaap Press, 1994.

O'Connor, Jane. *The Cultural Significance of the Child Star*. London: Routledge, 2008.

Ogbonge Blog. "Glo Ramadan Offer: Get Daily SMS Alerts and Listen to Quranic Citations, Duas." ObangeBlog.com, July 20, 2012. Accessed on September 9, 2013. http://www.ogbongeblog.com/2012/07/glo-ramadan-offer-get-daily-sms-alert.html

Oghuma, Hilda. "Nse Ikpe-Etim Exclusive: 'I Wasn't Born to Get Married.'" *Nigerian Entertainment Today*, March 26, 2012. Accessed on September 1, 2013. http://thenet.ng/2012/03/i-wasnt-born-to-get-married-nse-ikpe-etim/

Ogunbunmi, Babajide. "Evangelist Eucharia Anunobi Receives Christian Leadership Award." NigeriaFilms.com, May 14, 2013. Accessed November 22, 2013. http://www.nigeriafilms.com/news/21611/2/evangelist-eucharia-anunobi-receives-christian-lea.html

Ogundele, Wole. "From Folk Opera to Soap Opera: Improvisations and Transformations in Yoruba Popular Theatre." *Nigerian Video Films: Revised and Expanded Edition*, edited by Jonathan Haynes, 89–130. Athens, OH: Ohio University Center for International Studies, 2000.

Ojajune, Ayo. "Nigerian Languages and Culture Project: A Diaspora Initiative." *African Examiner*, March 24, 2011. Accessed December 7, 2013. http://africanexaminer.com/ojajune0324

Okiche, Wilfred. "Film Review: 'Weekend Getaway' Gathers All the Stars, Has No Idea What to Do With Them." YNaija.com, May 5, 2013. Accessed September 23, 2013. http://www.ynaija.com/film-review-weekend-getaway-gathers-all-the-stars-but-has-no-idea-what-to-do-with-them/

———. "Funke Kan! Nigeria Kan!" *Y! Magazine* 7 (2012): 40–45.

Okome, Mojúbàolú Olufúnké and Olufemi Vaughan. "West African Migrations and Globalization: Introduction." In *Transnational Africa and Globalization*, edited by Mojúbàolú Olufúnké Okome and Olufemi Vaughan, 1–16. New York: Palgrave Macmillan, 2011.

Okome, Onookome. "Nollywood and Its Critics." In *Viewing African Cinema in the Twenty-First Century: Art Films and the Nollywood Video Revolution*, edited by Mahir Saul and Ralph A. Austen, 26–40. Athens, OH: Ohio University Press, 2010.

———. "Nollywood, Lagos, and the *Good Time* Woman." *Research in African Literatures* 43, no. 4 (2012): 166–86.

———. "Nollywood: Spectatorship, Audience, and the Sites of Consumption." *Postcolonial Text* 3.2 (2007): 1–21.

———. "*Onome*: Ethnicity, Class, Gender." In *Nigerian Video Films: Revised and Expanded Edition*, edited by Jonathan Haynes, 148–64. Athens, OH: Ohio University Center for International Studies, 2000.

———. "Reversing the Filmic Gaze: Comedy and the Critique of the Postcolony in *Osuofia in London*." In *Global Nollywood: The Transnational Dimensions of an African Video Industry*, edited by Matthias Krings and Onookome Okome, 139–57. Bloomington: Indiana University Press, 2013.

———. "Women, Religion, and the Video Film in Nigeria." *Film International* 7.1 (2004): 4–13.

———. "Writing the Anxious City: Images of Lagos in Home Video Films." *Under Siege: Four African Cities: Freetown, Johannesburg, Kinshasa, Lagos. Documenta 11, Platform 4*, edited by Okwui Enwezor, et al. 315–35. Ostfildern-Ruit, Germany: Hatje Cantz, 2002.

Okon, Augusta. "*Phone Swap*: Movie Review," 9ija Books and Movies, April 25, 2012. Accessed December 29, 2013. http://9aijabooksandmovies.wordpress.com/2012/04/25/phone-swap-movie-review/

Okoye, Chukwuma. "Looking at Ourselves in Our Mirror: Agency, Counter-discourse, and the Nigerian Video Film." *Film International* 5, no. 4 (2007): 10–19.

Olatunji, Samuel. "*Kajola* Sparks Trouble at Silverbird, Ozone." NigeriaFilms.com, August 8, 2008. Accessed July 10, 2013. http://www.nigeriafilms.com/news/8579/34/kajola-sparks-trouble-at-silverbird-ozone.html

———. "The New Nollywood: Factors and Faces Driving It." NigerianFilms.com, August 15, 2010. Accessed October 12, 2013. http://www.modernghana.com/ movie/8468/3/the-new-nollywood-factors-and-faces-driving-it.html

Onishi, Norimitsu. "Step Aside, L. A. and Bombay, for Nollywood." *New York Times*, September 16, 2002. Accessed November 16, 2013. http://www.nytimes.com/2002/09/16/world/step-aside-la-and-bombay-for-nollywood.html

Oppenheimer, Mark. "On a Visit to the U.S., a Nigerian Witch-Hunter Defends Herself." *New York Times*. May 21, 2010. Accessed November 17, 2013.

Opubor, Alfred E. and Onuora E. Nwuneli, eds. *The Development and Growth of the Film Industry in Nigeria*. Lagos and New York: Third Press International, 1979.

Oren, Tasha and Sharon Shahaf, eds. *Global Television Formats: Understanding Television Across Borders*. London: Routledge, 2011.

Oreyeni, Odunayo. "'Men Can't Kill My Dream'—Uche Mac-Auley." *Modern Ghana*, January 8, 2011. Accessed November 12, 2013. http://www.modernghana.com/moviethread2/10133/67/141421

Orgeron, Marsha. "Media Celebrity in the Age of the Image." In *The Oxford Handbook of Film and Media Studies*, edited by Robert Kolker, 187–223. New York: Oxford University Press, 2008.

Ouellette, Laurie and Susan Murray, "Introduction." In *Reality TV: Remaking Television Culture*, edited by Laurie Ouellette and Susan Murray, 1–22. New York: New York University Press, 2009.

Oyěwùmí, Oyèrónkẹ́. *The Invention of Women: Making an African Sense of Western Gender Discourses*. Minneapolis: University of Minnesota Press, 1997.

Paulson, Julia. "Education, Conflict, and Development." In *Researching Conflict in Africa: Insights and Experiences*, edited by Julia Colson, 7–14. Oxford: Symposium Books, Ltd.

Perez, Gilberto. *The Material Ghost: Films and Their Medium*. Baltimore, MD: The Johns Hopkins University Press, 1998.

Pfaff, Françoise. "African Cities as Cinematic Texts." In *Focus on African Films,* edited by Françoise Pfaff, 89–106. Bloomington: Indiana University Press, 2004.

Pierson, Inga M. "Toward a Poetics of Neorealism: Tragedy in the Italian Cinema, 1942–48." PhD diss., New York University, 2009.

Powell, Mike. "Knowledge, Culture, and the Internet in Africa: A Challenge for Political Economists." *Review of African Political Economy* 28, no. 88 (2001): 241–60.

Provost, Claire. "Nigeria's Golden Jubilee: Cause for Celebration of Pause for Evaluation?" *The Guardian,* October 1, 2010. Accessed October 5, 2013. http://www.guardian.co.uk/global-development/poverty-matters/2010/oct/01/nigeria-50th-anniversary-development-progress

Purefoy, Christian. "'Nollywood Love': Nigerian Blockbusters for the Internet Generation." CNN International: "African Voices," August 2, 2011. Accessed September 17, 2013. http://edition.cnn.com/2011/BUSINESS/08/02/jason.njoku.nollywood.love/index.html

Rajagopal, Arvind. "Fast-Forward into the Future, Haunted by the Past: Bollywood Today." In *Global Bollywood,* edited by Anandam P. Kavoori and Aswin Punathambekar. New York: New York University Press, 2008.

Reclaiming Popular Culture to Promote Gender Equality and Women's Empowerment. Accra: African Women's Development Fund (AWDF), 2010.

Reich, Jacqueline. "Slave to Fashion: Masculinity, Suits, and the *Maciste* Films of Italian Silent Cinema." In *Fashion in Film,* edited by Adrienne Munich. Bloomington: Indiana University Press, 2011.

Rice, Andrew. "A Scorsese in Lagos." *New York Times,* February 23, 2012. Accessed November 3, 2013. www.nytimes.com/2012/02/26/magazine/nollywood-movies.html

Ryan, Connor. "Diversity Within Yoruba-Language Video Films." *African Studies Review* 55, no. 2 (September, 2012): 180–85.

———. "Nollywood and the Limits of Informality: A Conversation with Tunde Kelani, Bond Emeruwa, and Emem Isong." *Black Camera* 5, no. 2 (Spring 2014): 168–85.

———. "Yoruba Video Comedies: You Don't Know Lagos." *African Studies Review* 56, no. 1 (April 2013): 215–19.

Saleh-Hanna, Viviane. *Colonial Systems of Control: Criminal Justice in Nigeria.* Ottowa: University of Ottowa Press, 2008.

Salone Films. "Oge Okoye (Sister Mary) Will Be Coming to Sierra Leone." SaloneFilms.com, May 19, 2013. http://www.salonefilms.com/oge-okoye-sister-mary-will-be-coming-to-sierra-leone/

Saro-Wiwa, Noo. *Looking for Transwonderland: Travels in Nigeria.* Berkeley, CA: Soft Skull Press, 2012.

Saul, Mahir, and Ralph A. Austen, eds. *Viewing African Cinema in the Twenty-First Century: Art Films and the Nollywood Video Revolution.* Athens, OH: Ohio University Press, 2010.

———. "Introduction." In *Viewing African Cinema in the Twenty-First Century: Art Films and the Nollywood Video Revolution,* edited Mahir Saul and Ralph A. Austen, 1–8. Athens, OH: Ohio University Press, 2010.

Schoonover, Karl. *Brutal Vision: The Neorealist Body in Postwar Italian Cinema.* Minneapolis: University of Minnesota Press, 2012.

Second National Youth Policy Document of the Federal Republic of Nigeria, 2009. Abuja, Nigeria: Government of the Federal Republic of Nigeria, 2009.

———. "Draft Action Plan and Implementation Strategy for the National Youth Policy 2009–2014." Nigeria: Government of the Federal Republic of Nigeria, 2009: 1–38.

Semple, Kirk. "Seeking a Hollywood Audience for *Doctor Bello*, a Nollywood Film." *New York Times*, February 21, 2013. Accessed May 15, 2013. http://cityroom.blogs.nytimes.com/2013/02/21/seeking-a-hollywood-audience-for-a-nollywood-film/

Sereda, Stefan. "Curses, Nightmares, and Realities: Cautionary Pedagogy in FESPACO Films and Igbo Videos." In *Viewing African Cinema in the Twenty-First Century: Art Films and the Nollywood Video Revolution*, edited Mahir Saul and Ralph A. Austen, 194–208. Athens, OH: Ohio University Press, 2010.

Sharpe, Jenny. "Cartographies of Globalization, Technologies of Gendered Subjectivities: The Dub Poetry of Jean 'Binta' Breeze." In *Minor Transnationalism*, edited by Francoise Lionnet and Shu-mei Shih, 261–82. Durham, NC: Duke University Press, 2005.

Shingler, Martin. *Star Studies: A Critical Guide*. London: BFI, 2012.

Shohat, Ella. "Notes on the 'Post-Colonial.'" *Social Text* 31/32 (1992): 99–113.

———. "Post-Fanon and the Colonial: A Situational Diagnosis." In *Taboo Memories, Diasporic Voices*. Durham, NC: Duke University Press, 2006. 250–89.

———. and Robert Stam. *Multiculturalism, Postcoloniality, and Transnational Media*. New Brunswick, NJ: Rutgers University Press, 2003.

———, and Robert Stam. *Race in Translation: Culture Wars Around the Postcolonial Atlantic*. New York: New York University Press, 2012.

———. and Robert Stam. *Unthinking Eurocentrism: Multiculturalism and the Media*. London: Routledge, 2014 [1994].

Soyinka, Wole. "A Name is More Than the Tyranny of Taste." Keynote Address, CODESRIA-Guild of African Filmmakers, FESPACO workshop on Pan-Africanism: Adapting African Stories/Histories from Text to Screen. February 26, 2013, Ouagadougou, Burkina Faso.

Soyinka-Airewele, Peyi. "Insurgent Transnational Conversations in Nigeria's 'Nollywood' Cinema." In *West African Migrations: Transnational and Global Pathways in a New Century*, edited by Mojubaolu Olufunke Okome and Olufemi Vaughan, 101–44. London: Palgrave MacMillan, 2013.

Spillman, Deborah Shapple. *British Colonial Realism in Africa: Inalienable Objects, Contested Domains*. London: Palgrave MacMillan, 2012.

Spivak, Gayatri. *The Spivak Reader: Selected Works of Gayatri Chakravotry Spivak*. London: Routledge, 1995.

Stacey, Jackie. *Star Gazing: Hollywood Cinema and Female Spectatorship*. London: Routledge, 1994.

Staiger, Janet. *Interpreting Films: Studies in the Historical Reception of American Cinema*. Princeton, NJ: Princeton University Press, 1992.

Stam, Robert. "Beyond Third Cinema: The Aesthetics of Hybridity." In *Rethinking Third Cinema*, edited by Anthony R. Guneratne and Wimal Dissanayake, 31–50. New York: Routledge, 2003.

Straubhaar, Joseph D. "Beyond Media Imperialism: Assymetrical Interdependence and Cultural Proximity." *Critical Studies in Mass Communication* 8.1 (1991): 39–59.

Studlar, Gaylyn. "Marlene Dietrich and the Erotics of Code-Bound Hollywood." In *Dietrich Icon*, edited by Mary R. Desjardins and Gerd Gemunden, 211–38. Durham, NC: Duke University Press, 2007.

———. *Precocious Charms: Stars Performing Girlhood in Classical Hollywood Cinema*. Berkeley: University of California Press, 2013.

Sudesh, Mishra. *Diaspora Criticism*. Edinburgh: Edinburgh University Press, 2006.

TED. "Fellows Friday with Peace Anyiam-Osigwe." TED Blog, October 22, 2010. Accessed December 4, 2013. http://blog.ted.com/2010/10/22/fellows-friday-with-peace-anyiam-osigwe.

Telecompaper. "Ghanaians Protest Against Noisy Mobile Phone Mast Generators." Telecompaper.com, September 3, 2013. Accessed January 14, 2013. www.telecompaper.com/news/ghanaians-protest-against-noisy-mobile-phone-mast-generators—964474.

Tell Communications Limited. *Tell* (Nigeria). April 20–25 (2008).

Thackway, Melissa. *Africa Shoots Back: Alternative Perspectives in Sub-Saharan Francophone Film*. Bloomington: Indiana University Press, 2003.

This Day. "Nigeria: Conflicting Signals Over Preparations for 2015 Digital Migration." *This Day* (Lagos), January 20, 2013, via AllAfrica.com. Accessed December 26, 2013. http://allafrica.com/stories/201301210946.html

Tsika, Noah. "From Yorùbá to YouTube: Studying Nollywood's Star System." *Black Camera* 5, no. 2 (Spring 2014): 95–115.

———. "A Lagosian Lady Gaga: Cross-Cultural Identification in Nollywood's Anti-Biopic Cycle." In *Multiplicities: Cycles, Sequels, Remakes and Reboots in Film & Television*, edited by Amanda Ann Klein and R. Barton Palmer. Austin: University of Texas Press, forthcoming.

———. "Projected Nigerias: *Kajola* and its Contexts." *Paradoxa* 25 (2013): 89–111.

———. "Soft Power Cinema: Corporate Sponsorship, Visual Pedagogy, and the Cultural Cold War in West Africa." *The Velvet Light Trap* 73, no. 1 (Spring 2014): 51–65.

Ugor, Paul. "Failed States and the Militarization of Youth in Sub-Saharan Africa." In *Narratives of Citizenship: Indigenous and Diasporic Peoples Unsettle the Nation-State*, edited by Aloys N.M. Fleischmann, Nancy van Styvendale, and Cody McCarroll, 81–106. Edmonton: The University of Alberta Press, 2011.

———. "Nollywood and Postcolonial Predicaments: Transnationalism, Gender, and the Commoditization of Desire in *Glamour Girls*." In *Global Nollywood: The Transnational Dimensions of an African Video Industry*, edited by Matthias Krings and Onookome Okome, 158–78. Bloomington: Indiana University Press, 2013.

Ukadike, Nwachukwe Frank. *Black African Cinema*. Berkeley: University of California Press, 1994.

———. *Questioning African Cinema: Conversations with Filmmakers*. Minneapolis: The University of Minnesota Press, 2002.

UNESCO Institute for Statistics (UIS). "INFORMATION SHEET No. 1. Analysis of the UIS International Survey on Feature Film Statistics." April 2009. Accessed May 26, 2013. http://www.uis.unesco.org/template/pdf/cscl/Infosheet_No1_cinema_

UNICEF. "The State of African Children 2008: Child Survival." Accessed October 3, 2013. www.unicef.org.

Vanguard News. "Fathia Balogun Drags Oge Okoye to the Street." VanguardNGR.com, March 2, 2012. Accessed on October 1, 2013. http://www.vanguardngr.com/2012/03/fathia-balogun-drags-oge-okoye-to-the-street/

———. "Keeping up with the Kid Stars." VanguardNGR.com, December 7, 2012. Accessed on October 13, 2013. http://www.vanguardngr.com/2012/12/keeping-up-with-the-kid-stars/

Violence Against Children in Africa: The Challenges and Priorities for Action. Document prepared for the fifteenth session of the African Committee of Experts on the Rights and Welfare of the Child, for the African Child Policy Forum, Addis Ababa, Ethiopia, March 15–19, 2010.

Walters, Ronald W. *Pan-Africanism in the African Diaspora: An Analysis of Modern Afrocentric Political Movements*. Detroit, MI: Wayne State University Press, 1993.

Wang, Shujen. *Framing Piracy: Globalization and Film Distribution in Greater China.* New York: Rowman & Littlefield, 2003.
Weinberg, Marc. "The Battle Over Billing." *Orange Coast Magazine,* February, 1989.
Wilson, Julie. "Reality Television Celebrity: Star Consumption and Self-Production in Media Culture." In *A Companion to Reality Television,* edited by Laurie Ouellette, 421–36. Oxford: Wiley Blackwell, 2014.
Wong, Cindy Hing-Yuk. *Film Festivals: Culture, People, and Power on the Global Screen.* New Brunswick, NJ: Rutgers University Press, 2011.
Young, Lola. *Fear of the Dark: "Race," Gender, and Sexuality in the Cinema.* London: Routledge, 1996.
Zelizer, Viviana. *Pricing the Priceless Child: The Changing Social Value of Children.* Princeton, NJ: Princeton University Press, 1985.
Zion Felix. "Majid Michel Turns Boko Haram Member." March 9, 2013. Accessed on August 30, 2013. http://zionfelix.com/majid-michel-turns-boko-haram-member/

FILMOGRAPHY

Abulu, Tony. *Doctor Bello.* 2012. Black Ivory Communications. Nigeria/United States. 95 min.
Addelman, Ben, and Samir Mallal. *Nollywood Babylon.* 2008. AM Pictures/National Film Board of Canada. Canada. 75 min.
Adebayo, Femi. *Jelili.* 2012. Epsalum Productions. Nigeria. 272 min.
Adejumo, Yomi. *Internet Love.* 2012. Jessica Concept Productions. Nigeria. 150 min.
Ademinokan, Daniel, and Desmond Elliot. *Bursting Out.* 2010. Emem Isong Productions/Royal Arts Academy. Nigeria. 135 min.
Aduaka, Newton. *Ezra.* 2007. Amour Fou Filmproduktion/CINEFACTO/Centre National de la Cinématographie (CNC)/California Newsreel. France/Nigeria/United States/United Kingdom/Austria. 110 min.
Afolayan, Kunle. *The Figurine.* 2009. Golden Effects. Nigeria. 122 min.
———. *Phone Swap.* 2012. Golden Effects. Nigeria. 110 min.
Ajaere, Mykel C. *Liberian Girl.* 2010. Bold Steps Pictures. Nigeria. 93 min.
Akinmolayan, Niyi. *Kajola.* 2010. Adonis Productions. Nigeria. 110 min.
Ali-Balogun, Mahmood. *Tango with Me.* 2010. Talking Drum Entertainment. Nigeria. 110 min.
Altman, Robert. *Nashville.* 1975. ABC Entertainment/Paramount Pictures. United States. 159 min.
———. *Short Cuts.* 1993. Fine Line Features/Spelling Films International/Avenue Pictures Productions. United States. 187 min.
Amata, Fred. *Letters to a Stranger.* 2007. Amata Movies. Nigeria. 95 min.
Amata, Jeta. *Black Gold: Struggle for the Niger Delta.* 2011. Jeta Amata Concepts/Rock City Entertainment/Starkid/Wheels Entertainment. Nigeria/United States. 110 min.
Amenechi, Andy. *The Master.* 2005. Kas-Vid Productions. Nigeria. 150 min.
———. *Mortal Inheritance.* 1995. Silverscreen Studios. Nigeria. 104 min.
Amilo, Jerry. *Another World.* 2009. Global Concept Production/New Movies Inc. Nigeria. 188 min.
Anya, Kalu. *The Three Widows.* 2012. Sanga Entertainment. Nigeria. 121 min.
Anyaene, Chineze. *Ijé: The Journey.* 2010. Xandria Productions. United States and Nigeria. 101 min.

Anyiam-Osigwe, Peace. *La Viva*. 2007. Peace Fiberesima Productions. Nigeria. 118 min.
Fiberesima, Greg. *Fear of the Unknown*. 2003. Peace Fiberesima Productions. Nigeria. 129 min.
Arase, Frank Rajah. *Sisters at War*. 2014. Venus Films Productions. Ghana. 187 min.
Ayinde, Muhydeen S. *Jénífà*. 2008. Olasco Films Ltd. Nigeria. 233 min.
———. *O o M'Eko* [You Don't Know Lagos]. 2012. Headmaster Films. Nigeria. 197 min.
———. *The Return of Jénífà*. 2011. Olasco Films Ltd./Scene One Productions. Nigeria. 172 min.
Ayouch, Nabil. *Ali Zaoua: Prince of the Streets*. 1999. 2M/Ace Editing/Alexis Films. Morocco/Tunisia/France/Belgium/United States. 99 min.
Balogun, Fathia. *Street Girls*. 2012. Zentury Pictures/Fathia Balogun Powerhouse Productions. Nigeria. 168 min.
Balogun, Ola. *Ajani Ogun*. 1976. Ola Balogun Productions. Nigeria. 120 min.
———. *Black Goddess*. 1978. Magnus Films. Nigeria/Brazil. 95 min.
———. *Ija Ominira/The Fight for Freedom*. 1978. Friendship Motion Picture Company. Nigeria. Running times vary from print to print.
———. *The Magic of Nigeria*. 1993. Polystar Productions/Delka Productions. 29 min.
———. *River Niger, Black Mother*. 1998. Polystar Productions/Delka Productions. Nigeria. 43 min.
Bekolo, Jean-Pierre. *Aristotle's Plot*. 1996. JBA Production, BFI. France/Zimbabwe. 72 min.
Benson, Teco. *End of the Wicked*. 1999. RJP/Liberty Films. Nigeria. 93 min.
———. *Formidable Force*. 2002. RJP. Nigeria. 108 min.
———. *Terror*. 2005. RJP. Nigeria. 122 min.
Beresford, Bruce. *Mister Johnson*. 1990. Avenue Pictures. United States. 97 min.
Borbor, Courage. *Hatred*. 2012. GG Film. Ghana/Liberia/Nigeria. 137 min.
Buñuel, Luis. *Los Olvidados*. 1950. Ultramar Films. Mexico. 81 min.
Chikere, Tchidi. *Blood Sister*. 2003. Great Movies Industries/Great Future Production. Nigeria. 120 min.
———. *Dorathy, My Love*. 2005. P. Collins Productions. Nigeria. 151 min.
———. *Efficacy*. 2006. Annex Merchandise Ltd. Nigeria. 71 min.
———. *Show Bobo: The American Boys*. 2003. Outstrip Movies Investment Ltd. Nigeria. 70 min.
———. *Stronger Than Pain*. 2007. O. Gabby Innovations, Ltd. Nigeria. 135 min.
Chukwu, Andy. *Powerful Civilian*. 2007. Get Rich Productions Ltd. Nigeria. 149 min.
Cissé, Souleymane. *Yeelen*. 1987. Atriascop Paris/Burkina Faso Ministry of Life and Culture/Centre National de la Cinématographie (CNC). Mali/Burkina Faso/France/Germany/Japan. 105 min.
Davis, Ossie. *Black Girl*. 1972. Cinerama Releasing Corporation. United States. 97 min.
———. *Cotton Comes to Harlem*. 1970. Formosa Productions. United States. 97 min.
———. *Countdown at Kusini* [Cool Red]. 1976. DST Telecommunications/Nigeria Glipp Productions/Tam International Ltd./Columbia Pictures. Nigeria/United States. 101 min.
———. *Gordon's War*. 1973. Palomar Pictures. United States. 90 min.
———. *Kongi's Harvest*. 1970. Calpenny Nigeria/Herald. Nigeria/Sweden/United States. 85 min.
De Sica, Vittorio. *Bicycle Thieves*. 1948. Produzioni De Sica. Italy. 93 min.
———. *Shoeshine*. 1947. Societa Cooperativa Alfa Cinematografica. Italy. 93 min.
———. *Umberto D*. 1952. Rizzoli/De Sica/Amato. Italy. 89 min.

Diawara, Manthia. *Bamako Sigi-Kan*. 2003. K'a Yéléma Productions. Mali/France/United States. 76 min.
———. *Conakry Kas*. 2004. K'a Yéléma Productions/Nova Prod. Guinea/France. 82 min.
———. *Rouch in Reverse*. Formation Films/California Newsreel. Germany/United States. 52 min.
Djansi, Leila. *Ties That Bind*. Turning Point Media Productions. Ghana/Nigeria/United States. 111 min.
Ebere, Moses. *Miss Queen*. 2012. Divine Touch Productions. Nigeria. 249 min.
Ebere, Reginald. *Scars of Womanhood*. 1997. Standard Vision/Sanga Entertainment. Nigeria. 90 min.
Egbon, Kabat Esosa. *Beautiful Faces*. 2003. Kas-Vid Productions. Nigeria. 129 min.
Ejiro, Chico. *Blood Money*. 1997. OJ Productions. Nigeria. 180 min.
———.*Onome*. 1996. Consolidated Fortunes Limited. Nigeria. 94 min.
———.*Shame*. 1996. OJ Productions. Nigeria. 197 min.
Ejiro, Zeb. *Domitilla: The Story of a Prostitute*. 1997. Zeb Ejiro Productions. Nigeria. 109 min.
Elliot, Desmond. *Weekend Getaway*. 2013. Emem Isong Productions/Royal Arts Academy. Nigeria. 120 min.
Emelonye, Obi. *Last Flight to Abuja*. 2012. Nollywood Film Factory. Nigeria/United Kingdom. 81 min.
———. *The Mirror Boy*. 2011. OH Films. Nigeria/United Kingdom. 120 min.
Faye, Safi. *La passante*. 1972. Senegal. 10 min.
Furie, Sidney J. *Lady Sings the Blues*. 1972. Jobete Productions/Motown Productions/Paramount Pictures. United States. 144 min.
Ganda, Oumarou. *Cabascabo*. 1968. Argos Films. Niger/France. 45 min.
Graham, Sean. *The Boy Kumasenu*. 1952. The Gold Coast Film Unit. Ghana/United Kingdom. 63 min.
Griffith, D. W. *Broken Blossoms or The Yellow Man and the Girl*. 1919. D.W. Griffith Productions. United States. 90 min.
———. *True Heart Susie*. 1919. D. W. Griffith Productions. United States. 61 min.
Halilu, Adamu. *Shehu Umar*. 1976. Federal Film Unit. Nigeria. 140 min.
Haroun, Mahamat-Saleh. *Abouna*. 2002. Duo Films/Goi-Goi Productions/Tele-Chad. Chad/France/Netherlands. 84 min.
———. *Bye Bye Africa*. 1999. California Newsreel. Chad/France. 86 min.
Hudson, Hugh. *Chariots of Fire*. 1981. Twentieth Century Fox Film Corporation/Allied Stars Ltd./Enigma Productions. United Kingdom. 124 min.
Imasuen, Lancelot Oduwa. *The Celebrity*. 2008. Simony Productions. Nigeria. 111 min.
———. *Emotional Crack*. 2003. RJP. Nigeria. 122 min.
———. *Enslaved*. 2004. RJP. Nigeria. 70 min.
———. *Games Men Play*. 2006. RJP. Nigeria. 298 min.
———. *Games Women Play*. 2005. RJP. Nigeria. 357 min.
———. *Issakaba*. 2001. Kas-Vid/Mosco. Nigeria. 431 min.
———. *Last Celebrity*. 2008. Simony Productions. Nigeria. 106 min.
———. *Rosy the Troublemaker*. 2013. Effixzzy International. Nigeria. 235 min.
Inojie, Charles. *The Price of Fame*. 2006. Great Future Productions. Nigeria. 127 min.
———. *Spirit of Love*. 2006. Simony Productions. Nigeria. 237 min.
Inwang, Moses. *Damage*. 2011. Uche Jombo Studios. Nigeria. 91 min.
———. *My Life, My Damage*. 2013. Uche Jombo Studios. Nigeria. 96 min.

———. *Nollywood Hustlers*. 2009. Royal Arts Academy. Nigeria. 151 min.
Iroegbu, Dickson. *Little Angel*. 2003. Great Movies Ind. Ltd. Nigeria. 180 min.
Jaja, Michael. *Heart of a Widow*. 2011. Magic Movies Productions. Nigeria. 61 min.
Kaboré, Gaston. *Wend Kuuni*. 1983. Direction du Cinema de Haute Volta/California Newsreel. Burkina Faso. 75 min.
Kelani, Tunde. *The Campus Queen*. 2003. Mainframe Film and Television Productions. Nigeria. 104 min.
———. *Thunderbolt: Magun*. 2001. Mainframe Film and Television Productions/California Newsreel. Nigeria. 110 min.
Kubrick, Stanley. *Lolita*. 1962. MGM/Seven Arts Productions/A.A. Productions Ltd. United Kingdom/United States. 152 min.
Linklater, Richard. *School of Rock*. 2003. Paramount Pictures. United States. 109 min.
Mac-Auley, Solomon. *In a Lifetime*. 2010. QNX Ltd. Nigeria. 121 min.
———. *Violence against Women: A Widow's Plight*. 2009. AWC Inc. Nigeria. 5 min.
Magnoli, Albert. *Purple Rain*. 1984. Warner Bros./Purple Films/Water. United States. 111 min.
Mambéty, Djibril Diop. *Touki Bouki*. 1973. Cinegrit/Studio Kankourama. 89 min.
M'Bala, Roger Gnoan. *Andanggaman*. 2000. Abyssa Film/Amka Films Productions/Canal+ Horizons/New Yorker Video. France/Burkina Faso/Switzerland/Italian. 90 min.
Neilan, Marshall. *Rebecca of Sunnybrook Farm*. 1917. Mary Pickford Company. United States. 78 min.
Njamah, Aquila. *A Time to Kill*. 1998. Zulu Films. Nigeria. 116 min.
Nya, Ubong Bassey. *BlackBerry Babes*. 2011. Simony Productions. Nigeria. 147 min.
———. *Lady Gaga*. 2011. Simony Productions. Nigeria. 241 min.
———. *Return of BlackBerry Babes*. 2011. Simony Productions. Nigeria. 151 min.
———. *BlackBerry Babes Reloaded*. 2012. Simony Productions. Nigeria. 262 min.
Nzekwe, Lonzo. *Anchor Baby*. 2010. Alpha Galore Films. Nigeria. 95 min.
Ogidan, Tade. *The Diamond Ring*. 1998. OJ Productions/OGD Pictures Ltd. Nigeria. 94 min.
———. *Hostages*. 1997. OGD Pictures Ltd. Nigeria. 116 min.
Ogbonna, Ifeanyi. *Fazebook Babes*. 2012. Bold Steps Pictures. Nigeria. 121 min.
———. *Fazebook Lovers*. 2012. Bold Steps Pictures. Nigeria. 118 min.
Ogoro, Kingsley. *Osuofia in London*. 2003. Ulzee Nig. Ltd. Nigeria. 156 min.
Ogunyemi, Sunday. *Ojó Ketàlá: The 13th Day*. 2005. Olasco Films Ltd. Nigeria. 231 min.
Ojukwu, Izu. *Across the Niger*. 2004. Kingsley Ogoro Productions. Nigeria. 76 min.
———. *Nnenda*. 2009. Adonis Productions. Nigeria. 122 min.
Okereke, Afam. *Beyoncé & Rihanna*. 2008. Simony Productions. Nigeria. 273 min.
———. *Sister Mary*. 2003. Great Movies Ind. Ltd. Nigeria. 124 min.
Okereke, Stephanie. *Through the Glass*. 2008. Next Page Productions. Nigeria/United States. 93 min.
Okoh, Okey Zubelu. *Girls on Fire*. 2013. Magic Movies Ind. Ltd./Playback Movie Productions/Uche Nancy Productions. Nigeria. 190 min.
Olanrewaju, Abiodun. *Agbefo*. 2006. Olasco Films Ltd. Nigeria. 242 min.
Olumowe, Afe. *Show Girls*. 2011. Global Update Pictures Ltd. Nigeria. 150 min.
Onukwufor, Chika. *Glamour Girls*. 1994. NEK Video Links. Nigeria. 125 min.
———. *True Confession*. 1995. NEK Video Links. Nigeria. 101 min.
Onyeka, Ikechukwu. *Baby Oku in America*. 2013. Amaco Investments Ltd/i.com International Ltd. Nigeria. 117 min.
Opeoluwa, Simi. *The Battle of Love*. 2001. Kingsley Ogoro Productions. Nigeria. 96 min.

Ouedraogo, Idrissa. *Yaaba*. 1989. Arcadia Films/Les Films de l'Avenir/Thelma Film AG. Burkina Faso/Switzerland/France. 90 min.

Philips, Amayo Uzo. *Aki na Ukwa*. 2003. Soft Touch Movies. Nigeria. 245 min.

———. *Baby Police*. 2003. Dubem Holdings Nigeria Ltd./Onye-Eze Productions Ltd. Nigeria. 143 min.

Ramaka, Joseph Gaï. *Karmen Geï*. 2001. Canal+ Horizons/Crédit d'Impôt Cinéma et Télévision/Euripide Productions/Film Tonic/Les Ateliers de l'Arche/Sofica Sofinergie 5 /Téléfilm Canada/UGC International/Zagarianka Productions/arte France Cinéma /California Newsreel. Senegal/France/Canada. 86 min.

Rapu, Chris Obi. *Living in Bondage*. 1992. NEK Video Links. Nigeria. 260 min.

Rogosin, Lionel. *Come Back, Africa*. 1959. Lionel Rogosin Films. United States/South Africa. 83 min.

Rossellini, Roberto. *Paisan*. 1946. OFI/Foreign Film Productions. Italy. 134 min.

Rouch, Jean. *Moi, un noir*. 1958. Les Films de la Pléiade. France/Niger. 70 min.

———. *Petit à petit*. 1968. Les Films de la Pléiade. France. 92 min.

Sacchi, Franco. *This is Nollywood*. 2007. Center for Digital Imaging Arts/Eureka Film Productions/California Newsreel. United States. 56 min.

Sembène, Ousmane. *Faat Kiné*. 2001. Doomireew Films/California Newsreel. Senegal. 90 min.

———. *Mandabi*. 1968. Comptoir/Doomireew Films. Senegal. 90 min.

———. *Moolaadé*. 2004. Ciné-Sud Promotion/Centre Cinématographique Marocain /Cinétéléfilms/California Newsreel. Senegal/France/Burkina Faso/Cameroon/Morocco /Tunisia. 124 min.

———. *La noire de . . .* 1966. Doomireew Films/Les Actualités Françaises. France/Senegal. 65 min.

Sissako, Abderrahmane. *Bamako*. 2006. New Yorker Video. Mali/France/USA. 115 min.

———. *Life on Earth*. 1998. CNC/Haute et court/La Sept Arte. Mauritania/Mali/France. 62 min.

———. *Waiting for Happiness*. 2002. Duo Films/Arte France. Mauritania. 92 min.

Spielberg, Steven. *The Color Purple*. 1985. Amblin Entertainment. United States. 154 min.

Tillman, George. *Soul Food*. 1997. Fox 2000 Pictures/Edmonds Entertainment Group. United States. 115 min.

Touré, Drissa. *Haramuya*. 1995. 3B Productions. Burkina Faso/France. 87 min.

Ukaegbu, Morgan. *Barren Women*. 2013. Sylvester Obadigie Productions. Nigeria. 149 min.

Verhoeven, Paul. *Basic Instinct*. 1992. Carolco Pictures/Canal+. United States and France. 128 min.

Vicker, Van. *Joni Waka*. 2012. Sky + Orange Productions. Ghana. 134 min.

Visconti, Luchino. *La Terra Trema*. 1948. Universalia Film. Italy. 165 min.

Von Sternberg, Josef. *Morocco*. 1930. Paramount Pictures. United States. 91 min.

Weir, Peter. *The Year of Living Dangerously*. 1982. MGM. Australia. 117 min.

Welles, Orson. *Citizen Kane*. 1941. RKO Radio Pictures/Mercury Productions. 119 min.

Wenner, Dorothee. *Peace Mission*. 2008. Pong. Germany. 80 min.

Wexler, Haskell. *Medium Cool*. 1969. H & J. United States. 111 min.

Whitaker, Forest. *Waiting to Exhale*. 1995. Twentieth Century Fox. United States. 124 min.

Williams, Adim. *Sharon Stone*. 2003. Louis Merchandise Ltd. Nigeria. 304 min.

———. *Valentino*. 2002. Classic Productions/OJ Productions. Nigeria. 301 min.

Wyler, William. *Roman Holiday*. 1953. Paramount Pictures. United States. 118 min.

INDEX

Page locators in *italic* indicate photographs.

1900 (1976), 1
Abacha, Sani, 123, 126
Abah, Adedayo Ladigbolu, 213, 216
Abouna (2002), 293
Abrahams, Earl, 290
Abubakar, Halima, 91; acting styles of, 22–23, 113; as household name, 20; in *Miss Queen*, 234–235, 266, 268
Abulu, Tony, 2, 6–7
Accra, Ghana, 279, 290
Across the Niger (2004), 75–76, 296, 304n16
acting, 49, 65, 95, 101, 103; in African cinema, xii–xvi, xxi–xxii; and antiessentialism, 10, 17; and brand ambassadorships, 53–54, *55*, 140–141, *145*, 161–163, 290–292; and ethnic traditions, 11–12, 112, 177–178, 181; and media technologies, 70, 82–83, 85–86, 88–90; and "The Method," 29, 142–143; on Nigerian television, 32–33; Nollywood as "acting school," 22–23, 41; and performance of transnationalism, 8, 13–14, 19, 21, 29–30, 52, 166–169, 279; and postcolonial theory, 87; and reality television, 32–35, 147; stage vs. screen, xxii, 80; and Western theories/techniques, 142–143, 174; and youth roles, 213, 218, 222, 226, 231–235, 244–253
Adejumo, Moses, 3, 93–94
Adejumo, Muyiwa, 94

Adejumo, Yomi, 11, 128
Adejunmobi, Moradewun, 85, 114–115
Adenuga, Michael, 124–126, 160
Adesokan, Akin, 10, 16–17, 105–106
Adichie, Chimamanda Ngozi, 296
Aduaka, Newton, 260
advertising, 153, 178, 288–289; and pairings of Nollywood stars, 53–54, 161–162, 291; and Pidgin, 62; and telecommunications, 116–117, *119*, 126, 130, *131*, 291–292; on television, 68–69, *71*
Afolayan, Kunle, 3, 143–144, 267
Africa Magic (television channel), xv, xxvi, 51, 70, 75, 144, 275
Africa Magic Viewers' Choice Awards, 98–99, 281
African cinema, xv, 9, 18, 24, 246, 292; and acting/stardom, xi–xiv; and celluloid, 16, 132, 226, 255; and intersections with Nollywood, xvi, 224–226
African Movie Academy Awards, 63, 99, 292
African urbanism: and Lagos, xxvi, 3, 242; and new technologies, 158, 257; and Nollywood stardom, 84; performance of, 56; as relational, 192; women and, 23, 110, 112, 137–138, 145, 178, 188
Afromodernity, 7
Agbasiere, Joseph Thérèse, 186–187

337

Agu, Francis, 30, 33
AIDS. *See* HIV/AIDS
Ajani Ogun (1976), 3
Ajayi, Bukky, 143, 232
Akande, Peju, 144
Aki and Pawpaw. *See* Iheme, Osita; Ikedieze, Chinedu
Aki na Ukwa (2003), 251
Akindele, Funke, *206*, 263; acting styles of, xxii, 197–198, 205, 207, 209–210, 297, 303n14; appearances in ad campaigns, 55, 115, 161–162, 178, 291; and dialect, 23, 91, 259; fans of, xxii, 297; and fashion, xxii, xxv, 98–99, 178–179; and HIV/AIDS activism, 178–180, 297–298; and *Jénífà* series, xxii, 34, 178, 259, 297, 303n14; in *Lady Gaga*, 168, 170, 172, 175–194, 202–205, 207, 209–210; on *Screen Divas*, 115; screenplays of, xxii, 38, 47, 303n14; and social media, xxii; star power of, 202–204, 209–210; Yorùbá identity of, 16–17, 108, 110–112, 177, 306n80
Akinmolayan, Niyi, 49–50
Al Jazeera, 296–297
Alausa, Toyin, xxiii, 22, 36
Algiers Charter of the Pan-African Federation of Filmmakers, xiii
Ali-Balogun, Mahmood, 92–93, 99
Altman, Robert, 226
Amenechi, Andy, 217, 280
Amnesty International, 257–258
Aniston, Jennifer, 22
Anozie, Gloria, 299
antiessentialism, 11, 16, 85, 114, 118; and ethnicity, 12, 110, 169; and nationalism, 14–15, 101, 286. *See also* essentialism
Anunobi, Eucharia, 251, 278–279, 281–282
Anya, Kalu, 187
Anyaene, Chineze, 99, 214
Appiah, Jackie, 157
Arenyeka, Laju, 230–231
Armes, Roy, 246
Atlanta, Georgia, 18, 21, 37, 45, 51, 83–84, 310n2
Azuah, Unoma, 232, 298, 303n26

Baba Sala. *See* Adejumo, Moses
Babyface, Teju, 217–218
Badmus, Eniola, 210, 263, 298; acting styles of, 130, 134; appearances in ad campaigns, 130, *131*; in the *BlackBerry Babes* trilogy, 26, 129, 130–136, 145–146, 149, 152, 161, 164; and body image, xxi–xxii, 112, 131, 136; and Gabourey Sidibe, 210; Yorùbá identity of, xxi–xxii, xxv, 111–112, 134, 161
Bae, Doona, 1
Bakassi Boys (militia), 219–220
Bakhtin, Mikhail, 182
Balogun, Fathia, 12
Bamako (2006), 77–78
Barber, Karin: and African popular arts, 6, 28, 36, 215–216; and Nigeria's oil economy, 4; and "realisms," 66; and theories of reception/consumption, 45, 140, 158
Barrot, Pierre, 102–104
Basic Instinct (1992), 88
BasketMouth, 161–162
Bassey, Ebbe, 1
Bassey, Keppy, 232, 237
Bassey, Khing, 157–158, 160
Bazalgette, Cary, 233–234
Bazin, André, 242–244
Bekolo, Jean-Pierre, 173
Benin, West Africa, 16, 63, 240, 277–278, 282, 285, 287
Benjamin, Joseph, 100
Benson, Liz, 10, 35–36, 299
Benson, Teco, 31–32, 227
Benson-Allott, Caetlin, 81–82
Berlin, Germany, 18
Bertolucci, Bernardo, 1
Beyoncé, 165, 172, 190, 208, 236; and Négritude, 170–171, 173, 196–197; Nollywood critiques of, 21, 172
Beyoncé & Rihanna (2008), 27, 60, 170
Biafran War, 3, 75, 220, 296
Bicycle Thieves (1948), xii, 293
Bieber, Justin, 27, 228, 253, 262, 277
Bizo, Télésphore Mba, xii
Black, Yomi, 77
Black Girl (1972), 4
Black Gold: Struggle for the Niger Delta (2011), 1
Black Skin, White Masks (Fanon), 197–198
BlackBerry, 47, 116–119, 127, 129–130; and convergence culture, 147; and ideals of

INDEX

connectivity, 133–134, 136; popularity in Nigeria, 139, 141, 149; and product placement, 143, 167; and "techno-fetishism," 133, 209

BlackBerry Babes (2011): and Globacom, 117–133, 137, 141–154, 158–163; promotional campaigns for, 116–122, 118, *119*, *131*; representations of commodity culture in, 126–168; significance of title, xxvi; and stardom, 21, 26, 47, 116–163

BlackBerry Babes Reloaded (2012), xxvi, 120, 158, 182; and allegory, 130, 134–135, 150–151, 157; and Karen Igho, 146–147, 151–152

Blaq, Yemi, 192, 196, 198, 204

Blige, Mary J., 42

Blood Sister (2003), 214

Blyden, Edward Wilmot, 87

Boko Haram, 15, 160, 262, 294

Bollywood, 17–18, 50, 304n13

Bowie, David, 270

Boy Kumasenu, The (1952), 292

Brando, Marlon, 20

Brecht, Bertolt, 85, 142, 225, 245

"Bring Back Our Girls," 297

Britain (England, United Kingdom), 2, 11, 87, 209, 290; and British accents, 91, 113–114, 223; cinema in, 274, 292; Nollywood films in, 51, 100, 149; Nollywood stardom in, 61–62, 82, 114, 127, 253; representations of Nigeria in, 288, 296

British Broadcasting Corporation (BBC), 18, 309n20

Brolin, Josh, 272

Brown, Melani, 112–113

Bruzzi, Stella, 99, 114

Bryce, Jane, 12, 127, 138–139, 152–153, 169

Buñuel, Luis, 244, 246

Burr, Ty, 84, 307n39

Cabascabo (1968), xi

Cameroon, 16, 173, 263, 278, 285, 287, 295

Campus Queen, The (2003), 148–149

Casilio, Maria Pia, 86–87

Celebrity, The (2008), 56, 63, 67, 139–140, 164; opening credits of, 33; performance of Uche Jombo in, 40–44, 54; screenplay of, 47

celluloid, 70, 75, 78, 89–90; and African cinema, xiv–xvi, 226; and exhibition in Nigeria, 3, 5–6, 50, 82, 272–273; and FESPACO, 132, 254–255; and film theory, 25, 73, 80, 91; and glamor, 70, 73–77, 80–81, 88–89; and "New Nollywood," xxvii, 7, 92, 143, 214, 248, 250, 290; obsolescence of, 92

Césaire, Aimé, 2

Chamley, Santorri, 276

Chan, Natalia Sui-Hung, 244

Chariots of Fire (1981), 274

Chicago, Illinois, 18

Chikere, Tchidi, 55, 95, 96, 214, 251, 280, 310n13

"Child Not Bride," 297

Christianity, 181, 194, 227, 234, 278–279, 307n39

Cissé, Souleymane, 2, 226

Citizen Kane (1941), 243

Clift, Montgomery, 93–94

Clinton, Hillary Rodham, 116, 118, *119*, 285

Cloud Atlas (2012), 1

CNN (Cable News Network), 18, 53, 62

Coe, Cati, 266

Coleman, Gary, 251

colonialism, 2, 4, 11, 16, 197, 290; resistance to, 52, 87; and theories of acting, 87

Color Purple, The (1985), 214

Comaroff, Jean, 7

Comaroff, John L., 7

Come Back, Africa, xii

consumerism, 128, 137, 139, 148

Cooper, Anderson, 182

Corliss, Richard, 18

Countdown at Kusini (1976), 4–8

Cyrus, Miley, 27, 228, 253, 262, 269–270, 277

Dakar, Senegal, xiii, 21, 290, 297

Damage (2011), 43–45, 200

Damasus, Stella, 296–297

Danja, Sani, 276

Dark Moment (2003), 179

Davis, Ossie, 4–9

de Certeau, Michael, 4

de la Vega, Isio, 75

De Sica, Vittorio, 242

deCordova, Richard, 50, 271–272

Dede, Sam, 220
Dee, Ruby, 5, 7, 9
Diamond Ring, The (1998), 218–219
diasporas, African, xviii, 19, 21, 24, 27, 122, 298; in Britain, 2, 11, 87, 209, 290; in the Caribbean, 113; influence on Nollywood, 16, 52, 274, 292; in United States, 1, 5, 18, 82–84
Diawara, Manthia, xvi, 2, 28
Dietrich, Marlene, 201
Diff'rent Strokes, 251
Dikeh, Tonto, *119*, *131*, 164, 285; in *BlackBerry Babes* trilogy, 26, 48, 116–118, 127–135, 140, 144, 146, 150, 155–162; career as reality TV star, 22, 33, 151–152, 154; in *Miss Queen*, 266–267, 269, 274–275
Diop, Mbissine Thérèse, xii–xiii
Doctor Bello (2012), 1–3, 7–8, 15
Dominic, Rita, 91, 113, *115*; appearances in ad campaigns, 162, 290–292; on *Screen Divas*, *115*; television appearances, 74–76, 85, 286–287
Domitilla: The Story of a Prostitute (1997), 12, 23, 259
Dovzhenko, Alexander, 226
Duru, Francis, 32, 273
Dyer, Richard, xiv, 19, 22–24, 272, 281

Ebere, Moses, 227, 234, 266–267, 274, 302n4
Ebere, Reginald, xv, 224–225
Ebeye, Amanda, 57–58, 64
Ebony (magazine), 5
Edo, Ini, 40, 53
Edwards, Brent Hayes, 197
Efficacy (2006), 55–57, 63, 142
Efron, Zac, 253
Egbuson, Dakore, 31, 38, 295
Eisenstein, Sergei, 226
Ejiro, Chico, 102, 243
Ejiro, Zeb, xvi, 12, 259
Elise, Kimberly, 29
Ellerson, Beti, xiv, xvi
Elliot, Desmond, 53, 61, 107, 263; acting range of, 46–47, 49–50; appearances in ad campaigns, 126, 214; in *Efficacy*, 55–56; and pan-Africanism, 14

Elmina (2010), 12
Eluke, Adaeze, 107–109
Emmanuel, Kelechi, 177–178
Emotional Crack (2003), 31, 43–44, 200, 295, 303n26
End of the Wicked (1999), 227
Engmann, Nortey, 292
Ensor, Maria O., 259, 264–265
Entertainment Industries Intervention Fund (Nigeria), 1, 6
Erowele, Austine, 164, 167, 190
Esin, Eve, 107
Esiri, Justus, 282
essentialism, 112, 129, 138, 297; in Nigeria, 11, 13, 262, 286; and race, 169, 197; and Western misrepresentations of Africa, 22–23, 53, 109, 141. *See also* antiessentialism
Essien-Igbokwe, Christy, 223–225, 309n17
ethnicity: and conflict, 294; in Nigeria, xvii, xxi, 4, 6, 9–11, 14, 26, 134, 154, 168, 175, 224, 256, 289; and Nollywood filmmaking "sectors," 12, 111–112; and Nollywood genres, 217, 237; and Nollywood stardom, xxii, 12–13, 16–17, 19, 24, 28, 34, 98, 100–101, 111–114, 125–126, 136, 161, 188, 286; and pan-Africanism, 3, 125, 160
Ezeamaka, Sharon: career as adult, 248–249, 253, 264–267; career as child star, 217–218, 221, 230–233; in *Little Angel*, 235–238, 240–249, 255
Ezra (2007), 260–261
Ezuruonye, Mike, 40

Faat Kiné (2001), xiii
Facebook, 83, 108, 114–115, 207; and the *BlackBerry Babes* trilogy, 122, 127, 134–135, 141–142, 153, 157
Falola, Toyin, 101
Fanon, Frantz, 171, 195; *Black Skin, White Masks*, 197–198; *The Wretched of the Earth*, 17, 173–175
fashion, 183, 298: and consumerism, 117; and ethnicity, 101–102, 177–178, 289; and format specificity, 70, 72; and globalization, 186, 188–189; and narrative, 114; and Nollywood stardom, xvi, xxii, 7–8, 48, 61, 98–100, 155, 169, 228, 256; and the Second

World African Festival of Arts and Culture, 101; and self-empowerment, 131
Faye, Safi, xii, 2
Fazebook Babes (2012), 128
Fazebook Lovers (2012), 128
Federal Ministry of Information and Culture (Nigeria), 218
FESPACO (Festival Panafricain du Cinéma et de la Télévision de Ouagadougou), 33, 99, 226; and format specificity, 92, 132, 254–255
Fifty Shades of Grey (James), 231
Figurine, The (2009), 267, 276
Fleetwood, Nicole R., 109, 113, 174, 179
Foer, Franklin, 186
Fonda, Jane, 73
Fox, Vivica A., 1, 8
Frye, Northrop, 139
Fuss, Diana, 11

Gabara, Rachel, xii
Gabon, 14, 160
Games Men Play (2006), 38–43, 54, 63
Ganda, Oumarou, xi–xii
Garbo, Greta, 86–87
Garritano, Carmela, 72
G-Bam Show, The (NTA, Nigeria), 75–78, 81–82, 85, 281
Gearhart, Suzanne, 15, 283
Getino, Octavio, xii
Ghana, 2, 7, 19, 33, 45, 117, 295; media production in, 12, 14–15, 19, 157, 266, 285; Nollywood films in, xxvi, 51, 277; Nollywood stardom in, 14–15, 21, 53, 69–70, 132–133, 157–158, 258–262; and Twi, 14–15
Gibson, Tyrese, 197
Girls on Fire (2013), 142–143; and fashion, 108–115; and lesbian representation, 107, 127, 295–296
Gish, Lillian, 96–97
Glamour Girls (1994), xxvi, 35, 48, 298–299
Glissant, Édouard, 27
Glo Soccer Academy, The, 150–151, 285
Globacom: and the *BlackBerry Babes* trilogy, 117–163; and brand ambassadors, 53–54, 55, 140–141, 145, 161–163, 290–292; and product placement, 143–144, 151, 290

globalization, 21, 122, 177, 186; and Nollywood stardom, 24, 167, 170, 173; and media piracy, 6, 26, 79–83, 121, 164–170, 200, 204–205, 209, 262
Gold Coast Film Unit, 292
Goldberg, Whoopi, 214
Gomez, Selena, 27, 228, 253
Gordon's War (1973), 4
Gosling, Ryan, 272
Gowon, Yakubu, 215
Grammy Awards, xii, 68–69, 98
Green-Simms, Lindsey, 128, 182, 232, 295
Griffith, D. W., 96, 234

Halberstam, J. Jack, 172
Half of a Yellow Sun (Adichie), 296
Half of a Yellow Sun (2013), 296
Halilu, Adamu, 5
Hall, Stuart, 13
Hanebrink, Julia R., 253–254
Hanks, Tom, 1
Haramuya (1995), 226–227
Harrow, Kenneth, 72
Hausa people/language, xxvii, 5, 10, 14, 18, 289, 302n25
Haynes, Jonathan: on acting, 22–23, 153, 308n17; on the auteur theory, xv; on ethnicity, 6; on location shooting, 45; on materiality, 78, 85, 173; on Nollywood as national cinema, 213; on Nollywood studies, 280; on Nollywood's productivity, 36; on postcolonial theory, 173; on structural adjustment, 5
Heart of a Widow (2011), 187
Heaton, Matthew M., 101
Henshaw, Kate, 38, 145, 225, 280
Hepburn, Audrey, 108
Hewatch, Kiera, 57–58
Hilderbrand, Lucas, 70, 75, 79, 83, 88–90, 167
Hill, Lauryn, 200
HIV/AIDS, 102, 178–180, 204, 297–298
Hoechner, Hannah, 259, 285
Holiday, Billie, 97
Hollywood films: and billing practices, 270–273; and child stardom, 212, 231, 262–263, 271; and cultural imperialism, 166, 179, 263; and fashion, 107, 114, 179, 183;

342   INDEX

influence on Nollywood, 1–4, 8, 15, 17, 61, *101,* 114, 154; Nollywood stars in, 49; reception in Nigeria, 27, 210, 253; and star studies, 10–11, 25, 50–51, 73, 81, 87–89, 212, 280; and theories of acting, 93, 102, 108, 299; in West Africa, xi

Hollywood stardom, 280, 299; and film theory, 81, 87–89; and stage work, 93–94; and the studio system, 212; and youth performers, 27

hooks, bell, 113

Houston, Texas, 18, 37, 51

Hunt, Linda, 251

I Need to Know (1997), xxii, 179–190, 297

Igbo people/language, xxvii, 10, 23, 51, 127, 134, 181; and accents, 62, 113–114, 236; and antiessentialism, 110, 170; and chieftancy titles for Nollywood stars, 106; depictions of interethnic romance, 101–102, 104–106, 217, 240; and English-language "sector" in Nollywood, xvii, xxi, 106, 251; and ethnic conflict, xvii, 101, 111, 173; and fashion, 179; and gender, 166, 175–177; and identity politics, xxi, 166, 168, 175, 302n25; and *Living in Bondage,* 72; and Nollywood stardom, 12, 14, 16, 111–112, 289; and promotional campaigns, 161; and *Tango with Me,* 100–101; and theories of acting, 11–12, 16, 23; and *Thunderbolt,* 101–102, 104–106; and widowhood, 185–188

Ihebie, Cynthia, 57–58

Iheme, Osita, 27, 44, 251–252, 280

Ijé: The Journey (2010), 99, 214

Ikeagwu, Kalu, 44

Ikedieze, Chinedu, 27, 44, 251–252, 280

Ikem, John, xv

Ikpe-Etim, Nse, 143, 286

Illrymz, 75

Imasuen, Lancelot Oduwa, xvi, 27, 31, 33, 38, 139, 220

In a Lifetime (2010), 103–104

Internet Love (2012), 11, 128

Iroegbu, Dickson, 63, 182, 239–240, 242–244, 246–249

iROKOtv, xvi, xxvi, 70, 83, 90; star-centered advertisements for, 52, 54, 61–62, 92, *131, 145,* 146, 216, 240, 266, 275; user comments on, 138, 141

Islam, xxvii, 5, 77, 160, 226, 289, 296

Isong, Emem, 38, 40, 44

Issakaba (2001), 220

Italian neorealism, xii, 86, 242–246, 292–293

Iyke, Jim, 14, 38, 82, 160

J Swagz da Sugarboy, 290

Jackson, Desreta, 214

Jaja, Michael, 187

Jalade-Ekeinde, Omotola, 46, 250, 265; activism of, xxiii, 257–258, 259, 263, 297; and Amnesty International, 257–258; in *Blood Sister,* 214; career as child star, 217–218; in *The Celebrity,* 41–43, 63; in Ghana, 21, 261–262; as household name, 20; in *Ijé,* 214; and media technologies, 74, 76; in *Mortal Inheritance,* 217; Nollywood depictions of, 59, 66; and occult economies, 7; and *Omotola: The Real Me,* 21, 68–69, *71,* 261–262, 294; popularity of, 294, 297; promotional appearances, *71,* 214; on *Hit the Floor,* xxiii, 29–30; as Rihanna, 172; and social media, xxii–xxiii, 29–30; in *Time* magazine, 17; and youth experiences, 256–257, 259–260

Jamaica, 178, 259

Jedlowski, Alessandro, 6, 27

Jegede, Tosin, 223

Jénífà (2008), 112, 178–181, 192, 210, 303n14; and Britney Spears, 34, 179; and fashion, xxii, xxv, 179; HIV/AIDS in, 297–298

Jénífà Foundation, The, 298

Johnson, Mercy, *187,* 250, 303n26

Johnson, Puff, 200

Jombo, Uche; acting styles of, 23, 39; activism of, 298; on ageism, 47; in *The Celebrity,* 40–42, 44, 47; in *Damage,* 43–45; in *Games Men Play,* 38–40; in *Last Celebrity,* 42–44, 47; promotional appearances in US, 45; screenplays of, 38, 40, 43, 47; and Uche Jombo Studios, 43; work for Globacom, 53–54

Jonathan, Goodluck, 2, 289–290, 294–295

Joni Waka (2012), 14

juju, 127, 136, 168, 202–203, 208, 210

INDEX 343

Kaboré, Gaston, 226
Kajola (2010), 49–50
Kanayo, Kanayo O., 30, 76
Kannywood, xvii, xxvii, 90, 276, 310n14
Kaplan, E. Ann, 94
Kardashian, Kim, 40, 236
Karmen Geï (2001), xiii
Karloff, Boris, 271
Kayode, Femi, 101–102
Kelani, Tunde, xvi, 101–106, 110, 148–149, 188
Kernan, Lisa, 30
Ke$ha, 112
King, Barry, 80
King, Geoff, 140, 158
Kool & the Gang, 200
Krings, Matthias, 204

Lady Gaga, 18, 21, 79; significance of title, xxv–xxvi
Lady Gaga (2012), 16, 26–27, 82–83, 164–210; and media piracy, 81, 83; and the "real"
Lady Sings the Blues (1972), 97, 108
Lahai, John Idriss, 216–217
Lagos, Nigeria, xxvii, 34, 43, 56, 58; American products in, 168; and car culture, 182; as epicenter of Nollywood, xxvi, 278–280, 290; FESTAC in, 101; and Idumota market, xvi; links to Atlanta, 84; links to London, 62; links to Los Angeles, 46; as multiethnic, 10; and Nollywood Love, 52; Nollywood representations of, 2, 4, 97, 102, 107, 128, 192, 195; premiere of *Doctor Bello* in, 8; production of *Countdown at Kusini* in, 5; as "promised land," 55, 134, 261; and Scene One School of Drama, 298; women in, 39, 56, 107, 128
Larkin, Brian, 122, 301n14; on colonial media, 52, 121; on Kannywood, 18, 90; on materiality, 72, 90–92, 123; on piracy, 79, 90; on pirate infrastructures, 3; on technological breakdown, 70, 79, 90, 92, 120–121, 123
Last Celebrity (2008), 27, 42, 44, 47, 63, 67, 142
Latham, Sean, 140
Lawal, Moyo, 57–58
Lawrence, Amy, 19, 93, 108
Lazarus, Mary, 57–58, 192–193

Leonard, Frederick, 234, 266, 269
Lewis, Emmanuel, 251
Liberia, West Africa, 14, 87, 253, 258–259, 298–299
Liebman, Ron, 270–271
Lighthouse Family, 200
Little Angel (2003), 63, 182, 235–249, 255, 281
Living in Bondage (1992), 48; and language, 12, 23; and Nollywood's star system, 30, 33; and videotape, 72, 81, 254
Lolita (1962), 175
Lopez, Jennifer, 98
Los Angeles, California, 30–31, 37, 65
Lunt, Alfred, 93–94
Lynch, David, 184

Mac-Auley, Solomon, 103–104
Mac-Auley, Uche, 103–105, 110
MacLaine, Shirley, 73
major transnationalism, 15, 19
Makeba, Miriam, xii
Makinwa, Toke, 77
Mama G. *See* Ozokwor, Patience
Mambéty, Djibril Diop, xxii
Mandabi (1968), xiii
Marks, Laura, 90–91
Marley, Bob, 200
Marx, Richard, 200
Mashoud, Rukaya, 187
Master, The (2005), 280
Matthau, Walter, 270
Mbembe, Achille, 7, 24
McCain, Carmen, on "junk journalism," 65; on Kannywood, 18; on *The Price of Fame*, 66, 303n26; on self-reflexivity, 92; on tribalism, 302n25, 310n14
McCall, John C., 213
McGavin, Darren, 271
Mediolana (website), 149–150
Medium Cool (1969), 86
Meet You in Hell (2005), 179
Michel, Majid, 15
Minaj, Nicki, 196; and accents, 113; and fashion, 109, 112; Nollywood depictions of, 18, 108–110; and pan-Africanism, 113
minor transnationalism, 15–16, 19, 255, 257, 259, 277, 283

Mirror Boy, The (2011), 62, 99
Miss Queen (2012), 266–270, 281, 292, 302n4; adult stars in, 154, 235, 275; child performers in, 235, 266, 274–276; depiction of Christianity in, 227, 234, 269; and genre, 234
Mobile telephony, 53, 120–121, 123, 126–127, 133. *See also* BlackBerry
Modood, Tariq, 13
Mofe-Damijo, Richard, 10, 241
Moi, un noir (1958), xi–xii
Molokwu, Ofunneka, 33
Monroe, Marilyn, 20
Moolaadé (2004), xv, 224–225
Moran, James M., 81, 84, 304n13
Morocco (1930), 201
Mortal Inheritance (1995), 217
Moscow, Russia, 225
Mr. Box Office, 8
MTV Base Africa, 117, 179, 249
Murray, Bill, 270

Nagib, Lúcia, 245
Napier, Russell, 292
Naremore, James, 19–20, 93; on Brecht, 85; on naturalism, 82; on Stanislavsky, 174; on star images, 20, 84–85, 139
Narrow Escape (1997), 230, 232
Nashville (1975), 226
National Communications Commission (NCC, Nigeria), 123–124
National Film and Video Censors Board (Nigeria), 104, 203, 276
National Youth Policy (Nigeria), 233, 266
National Youth Service Corps (Nigeria), 215
N'Diaye, El Hadj, xiii
Négritude, 2, 4–5, 171; and Beyoncé, 173, 196–197; and nationalism, 101; and Nollywood stardom, 170
Nelson, Yvonne, 157
neocolonialism, xiv, 2–3, 52, 139, 190, 287–288
"New Nollywood," 7, 92, 143, 214, 248, 250
New York, New York, 1, 15, 18, 37, 279, 299, 308n1
Niang, Magaye, xiii
Nicholson, Jack, 270–271

Nigeria: anti-gay legislation in, 294–295; award shows in, 99; centennial celebrations in, 290; corporatism in, 120; FESTAC in, 101; filmgoing in, 3, 45; independence celebrations in, 287–288; as information society, 121–133, 139–146, 149, 154; and multiculturalism, 10, 16, 23, 69, 104, 134, 188; National Youth Service Corps in, 215; Nollywood fandom in, 85, 107, 138, 177–178, 248; Ossie Davis in, 4–5, 9; as postcolony, 7; print media in, 46–53, 63, 83, 116–118, *119*, 229, 291; stereotypes of, 11, 128, 141, 205, 209; television in, xi, xxii, xxvi, 32, 48, 76, 145–146, 151–152; terrorist attacks in, 294; video technologies in, 79, 81, 89–90; women in, 113, 138, 164; youth in, 216, 218–224, 227, 233, 287–288
Nigerian Civil War. *See* Biafran War
Nigerian film: as distinguished from Nollywood, 260–261, 296; before Nollywood, 3–6, 93–94
Nigerian Idol, 58, 175, 285
Nigerian Television Authority (NTA), 75
Njoku, Benjamin, 52–53
Nnadi, Ihuoma, 107–109
Nnaji, Genevieve, 20, 46–47, 49, 94, 250, 263; acting styles of, 82, 97–98; and antiessentialism, 288; on Canadian television, 296; in *Doctor Bello*, 1, 7; and fashion, 7, 74, 100, 256; in *Free Giver*, 95–100, 106–107; in *Half of a Yellow Sun*, 296; in *Ijé*, 214; and Julia Roberts, 210; and Nigerian pride, 62; and occult economies, 7; rumors surrounding, xvi, 66–67; as Sharon Stone, 172; in *Tango with Me*, 92, 99–100, 106–107, 111; and youth roles, 95–100, 106–107, 250, 265, 284
Nnebue, Kenneth, xvi, xxvi, 12, 36, 72, 81, 254
Nnenda (2009), 32–35, 222, 272–274, 281, 286
La noire de . . . (1966), xiii, xiv, 226
Nollywood Babylon (2008), 251
Nuhu, Ali, xvii, 53, 276, 310n14
Nwachukwu, Uti, 32–35, 273
Nwadike, Johnpaul, 82–84, 185
Nwoke, Kingsley, 97
Nwokoye, Queen, 187
Nworah, Uche, 125

INDEX

Nya, Ubong Bassey, 175; and *BlackBerry Babes* trilogy, xxvi, 26, 47, 116–118, 120, 139, 148, 162, 164; and *Lady Gaga*, xxv–xxvi, 79, 164, 166–167, 175, 228
Nze, C. O. C., 96

Obadare, Ebenezer, 122–124, 126
Obadigie, Sylvester, 139, 164
Obiekwe, Muna, 153–155, 182, 266–269, 274
Obiora, Uche, 96
Obi-Osotule, Uche, 101–103, 105, 105. *See also* Mac-Auley, Uche
Oboli, Omoni, 267, 275–276
Oboli, Tobe, 267
occult economies, 6–7, 182
O'Connor, Jane, 229
Ogbonna, Ifeanyi, 128
Ogbuefi, Beak, 275
Ogbuefi, Tochukwu, 268–269
Ogbuefi, Uchenna, 267–268, 274–275
Ogidan, Tade, 218
Ogunde, Hubert, 3, 93–94, 227
Ogunjiofor, Okey, 81, 305n31
Ojukwu, Izu, 32, 75–76, 272, 296
Okechi, Ogo, 131, 164, 186, 203
Okere, Jennifer, 299
Okereke, Afam, 27, 277
Okereke, Stephanie, 49, 214, 222, 263, 281; and antiessentialism, 288; and autobiographical essay film, 65; car accident and recovery, 62–63, 65; in *Doctor Bello*, 1, 7; in *Efficacy*, 55–56, 63; in *Emotional Crack*, 31, 43, 295; as household name, 20; and lesbian representation, 35, 295; on *Melody Shelters*, 286; in *Nnenda*, 32, 222, 272–273; Nollywood representations of, 65–66; and Orphans Awareness Campaign, 222, 258; in *Terror*, 32; and *Through the Glass*, 37–38; in the United States, 37–38, 299; versatility of, 21
Okoh, Okey Zubelu, 107, 127
Okome, Mojúbàolú Olufúnké, 24
Okome, Onookome, 23, 36, 204, 213
Okonta, Ike, 287
Okoye, Oge, 26, 46, 48, 113, 212, 214, 231–232, 265; and antiessentialism, 288; appearances in advertising campaigns, 240, 247, 274, 277; in Benin, 278; in the *BlackBerry Babes* trilogy, 144, 152, 154–158, 160, 164; in Cameroon, 263, 278; and fashion, 100, 107, 111; in *Girls on Fire*, 107–111, 114; in *Lady Gaga*, 79, 164–166, 168–171, 191, 205, 206, 221, 228; in *Little Angel*, 182, 238–240, 266; in *Miss Queen*, 234–235, 266–267, 269; philanthropic activities, 256, 258, 260, 263, 278, 282; in *Show Girls*, 63–65, 106; in Sierra Leone, 258, 278; in *Sister Mary*, 277–284; in *Street Girls*, 12; in *The Three Widows*, 187; and transnationalism, 21, 61–62, 284–285; use of Pidgin, 23
Oldman, Gary, 271
Los Olvidados (1950), 246
Onome (1996), 102
Orgeron, Marsha, 36, 302n8
Orji, Zack, 95
Orji, Princess, 95, 237
Osetura. *See* Ogunde, Hubert
Osotule, Obi, 103
Osuofia. *See* Owoh, Nkem
Osuofia in London (2003), 8, 280
Ouedraogo, Idrissa, 226
Owiriwa, Adonijah, 286
Owoh, Nkem, 280, 310n19
Oyěwùmí, Oyèrónkẹ́, 104, 110–111, 138–139, 171–172
Ozokwor, Patience, 31
Ozone Cinemas (West Africa), 5, 50
OzzyBosco (Oziomachukwu Mojekwu), 229–230

Paisan (1946), 86
Paris, France, 15, 18–19, 51
La passante (1972), xii
Peck, Gregory, 108
Pentecostalism, 215–216, 227, 269, 279
Perez, Gilberto, 86
Perry, Tyler, 15, 17–18
Peters, Oliver O., 148
Petit à petit (1968), xii
Phone Swap (2012), 143–144, 151, 290
Pickford, Mary, 96–97
Pink (Alecia Moore), 200–201

piracy, 83, 203–204; and access, 79, 81, 262; as fair use, 164–165; and globalization, 26, 209; infrastructures of, 3, 6; and popular music, 167, 170, 200; and stereotypes of Nigeria, 205; as tool of resistance, 81, 121
PM Express (Multi TV, Ghana), 56
pornography, 90–91, 218–219
postcolonial condition: and cinema, xii–xiii, 32; and "crisis of representation," 138; and media technologies, 122; and Nollywood stardom, 7, 24
postcolonial theory, 16, 171
Powell, Mike, 121
Price of Fame, The (2006), 27, 66–67
primitivism, 11, 280
Princewill, Prince Tonye, 222, 258, 273
Project Fame West Africa (MTN, Nigeria), 58
Pryor, Richard, 108
P-Square, 178–179
Purefoy, Christian, 52

racism, 11, 16, 18, 22, 87, 171, 197, 236
Raiford, Leigh, 174
Ramaka, Joseph Gaï, xiii
reality television, 9–10, 22, 154, 262; *Big Brother Africa*, 32–35, 47, 147, 151–152; *Big Brother Nigeria*, 144–146; corporate sponsorship of, 150–152; *Melody Shelters*, 285–287, 289; *The Next Movie Star*, 151–152; *Omotola: The Real Me*, 68–69, 71, 258–259; and performance theory, 22, 32–35, 152; *Screen Divas*, 115
Reich, Jacqueline, 100
Remmy, Mary, 26, 145–146, 145, 152, 162
Return of BlackBerry Babes (2011), xxvi, 120, 134, 149, 164
Return of Jénífà, The (2011), 178–179, 204
Rihanna, 21, 172, 236
RMD. *See* Mofe-Damijo, Richard
Roberts, Julia, 210
Robinson, Edward G., xi
Rogosin, Lionel, xi
Roman Holiday (1953), 108
Rome, Italy, 18–19
Ross, Diana, 97, 108
Rosselini, Roberto, 86, 242

Rouch, Jean, xi–xii
Ryan, Connor, 301n2

Sade, 200
Same-Sex Marriage Prohibition Act (Nigeria), 294–295
Sanga Films, xxvi, 274
Scars of Womanhood (1997), xv, 224–225
School of Rock (2003), 208
Screen Divas (2013), 115
Sekiti, Pontsho, 290
Sekondi-Takoradi, Ghana, 69, 261–261
Sembène, Ousmane, 2, 15; and auteur theory, xiii–xvi; and *Faat Kiné*, xiii; and *Moolaadé*, 224–225; and *La noire de . . .* , xiii, 226; performances in films of, xiii
Senegal, West Africa, xiii, xviii, 6, 15, 83, 226, 295
Senghor, Léopold Sédar, 171, 196–197
Sereda, Stefan, 30, 104, 179, 219
Seye, Venus, xiii
social realism, xii, 225, 237
Société National du Cinéma (Senegal), 6
Soky, Barbara, 92
Solanas, Fernando, xii
Shame (1996), 243
Shehu Umar (1976), 5
Short Cuts (1993), 226
Show Bobo: The American Boys (2003), 23, 251–252
Show Girls (2011), 56–58, 61, 63–65, 67, 212
Shuga (MTV Base Africa), 249
Sierra Leone, West Africa, 15, 51, 258, 261, 278, 280
Sissako, Abderrahmane, 77–78
Shingler, Martin, 50–51
Shoeshine (1947), 86, 293
Shohat, Ella, 2, 9–10, 175, 189, 197, 210
Silva, Joke, 92
Silverbird Cinemas (West Africa), 6, 50, 272–273, 281
Silverbird Television (Nigeria), 117, 285
Sister Mary (2003), 277–284
Sisters at War (2014), 157
Skate Crash, 290
Smith, Alanya J., 253–254
Somalia, 298

INDEX 347

Soyinka, Wole, 4, 33
Soyinka-Airewele, Peyi, 10–11
Spacey, Kevin, 271
Spielberg, Steven, 214
Spivak, Gayatri, 13
Stam, Robert, 2, 9–10, 189, 197, 210
Stanislavsky, Konstantin, 85, 142–143, 174, 307n28
Staples, Terry, 233–234
star studies, 9–10, 35–37, 49, 51, 80; and Eurocentrism, 20, 25, 50
stereotypes, 228: of Africa and Africans, 24–25, 118, 124, 128–129, 200, 205, 213, 236, 252–253; ethnic, 10, 102, 106; gender, 54, 103, 118, 128, 137–138, 297; and media forms, 90, 114–115, 124, 128–129; of Nollywood, 100, 106, 220, 254–255, 264–265
Stone, Sharon, 88
Street Girls (2012), 12, 23, 106
Stronger Than Pain (2007), 280
structural adjustment programs (SAPs), 5, 70, 77, 82, 123–124
Studlar, Gaylyn, 212, 271
Sudesh, Mishra, 181
Switzerland, 37

Talk Time Africa, 18, 310n2
Tango with Me (2010), 92, 99–100, 106–107, 111
Tarantino, Quentin, 270
telenovelas, 88
La Terra Trema (1948), xii
Terror (2005), 31–32
Thackway, Melissa, xii
Third Cinema, xii–xiii
This is Nollywood (2007), xxiii, 22, 36, 61
Three Widows, The (2012), 187
Through the Glass (2008), 37–38
Thunderbolt: Magun (2001), 101–102, 104–106, 110, 188
Time to Kill, A (1998), 75–76
Toronto, Canada, 18
Touki Bouki (1973), xiii
Touré, Drissa, 226
transnationality/transnationalism, 1, 6, 8, 13–21, 250–293. *See also* major transnationalism; minor transnationalism

tribalism, 9, 112, 160–161, 166, 244, 262, 282; effects on Nollywood stardom, xxi–xxii, 16, 134
Trier, Lars von, 242, 244
True Confession (1995), 35–36
Twitter, xv, xxii, 83, 146–147, 246, 249, 264, 297; Nollywood depictions of, 115, 122, 128, 135, 207

Uchemba, Sandra, 276
Uchemba, William, 217–218, 276, 293, 310n13
Udoh, Barbara, 299
Uganda, 33, 254, 295
Ugor, Paul, 220
Ukattah, Barbara, 11
Ukpabio, Helen, 227
Umberto D. (1952), 86
UNICEF, 266, 276
United Nations Millennium Development Goals, 233, 256, 259, 288
United States: and cultural imperialism, 167; Nollywood production in, 1, 5, 37–38, 178; Nollywood reception in, 45; Nollywood representations of, 188–189, 197, 201, 251; Nollywood stars in, 37–38, 45, 83–84, 178, 279, 310n2
Usifo, Alex, 92

van der Merwe, Chris, 290
Vaughan, Olufemi, 24
VCD (video compact disc), 6, 20, 25, 52, 69–92
Versace, Donatella, 98
VHS (*Video Hits Show*, Nigeria), 77, 304n19
VHS (video home system), 6, 20, 25, 52, 69–92; and *Living in Bondage*, 254
Vicker, Van, 14–15, 53–54, 263; and fashion, 107; and Globacom, 127, 132–133, 288; Nollywood representations of, 157–158, 160–161
Violence against Women: A Widow's Plight (2009), 103
Visconti, Luchino, 242

Waiting to Exhale (1995), 114
Walters, Barbara, 206
Wang, Shujen, 81

Washington, D.C., 1, 18
Washington, Isaiah, 1
Weaving, Hugo, 1
Webster, 251
Welles, Orson, 243
Wend Kuuni (1983), 226
Whitaker, Forest, 114
Williams, Wendy, 42
Willis, Bruce, 270
Wilson, Julie, 32
Winfrey, Oprah, 38, 42
WizKid, 58–59, 150
Wretched of the Earth, The (Fanon), 17, 173–175

Yaaba (1989), 226, 245, 293
Yanni, 200
Year of Living Dangerously, The (1982), 251
Yeelen (1987), 226
Yerima, Ahmad, 296

Yorùbá people/language, xxvii, 3, 10, 14, 23, 34, 91, 223, 289; and antiessentialism, 11–13, 16–17, 104, 114, 170, 197; and ethnic conflict, xvii, xxi–xxii, 101, 104–106; depictions of interethnic romance, 101–102, 104–106, 217, 240; and fashion, 100, 105, 110–111; and gender, 16, 100, 110, 177–179, 193; and identity politics, xxi–xxii, xxv, 16, 112, 134, 160–161, 168, 170, 172–173, 176–177, 207, 209; and narratology, 213; and orthography, xxv; "Seun Rere," 224; stereotypes of, 10; and Yorùbá "sector" in Nollywood, 12, 106, 111; and Yorùbá theatrical traditions, xxii, 93, 175, 181, 308n17
YouTube, xv–xvi, 20, 77, 92, 122–123, 266, 275, 289; and Nollywood Love, 52, 54, 61, 216, 233
Zimbabwe, 11, 34
Zuckerberg, Mark, 141–142

NOAH A. TSIKA is Assistant Professor of Media Studies at Queens College, City University of New York, with specializations in African cinema and cybercultures. He is author of the book *Gods and Monsters: A Queer Film Classic,* and his articles have appeared in *Black Camera, Cineaste, Paradoxa, Senses of Cinema, Studies in the Humanities,* and *The Velvet Light Trap.* He has contributed essays to numerous edited collections on such topics as globalism from below, film criticism in the digital age, queer cinema, and African popular arts.

www.ingramcontent.com/pod-product-compliance
Lightning Source LLC
Chambersburg PA
CBHW061929220426
43662CB00012B/1850